The
Liberal
Mind

\\\\\\\\\\\\\\\\\\\\\\\////////////\\\\\\\\\\\\\\\\\\\\///////

The Psychological Causes of Political Madness

LYLE H. ROSSITER, JR., M.D.

ISBN 0-9779563-0-X

Library of Congress Control Number: 2006926407

Printed in the United States
Second Printing: March 2008
Publication Date: October 2006

10 9 8 7 6 5 4 3 2

Cover and title page design by George Foster

Interior book design by Bob Spear

Free World Books, LLC
St. Charles, IL

Table of Contents

Dedication

To Jane and Laura, and the Memory of My Parents.

Acknowledgments

My sincere thanks to the many friends who have taken the time and trouble to read manuscripts of *The Liberal Mind* at various stages of its development. I greatly appreciate inputs from Vern Miller, Shaukat Jamal, Harry Schaffner, Curt Danekas and Arthur Biddle, among others. Darlene Wingard generously proofread an early manuscript. My daughter, Laura Rossiter Spicer, has made especially valuable suggestions in editing the text and in supervising the book's publication. I am most deeply indebted to my wife, Jane Ann Rossiter, for her exceptional editing skills. Her insistence on clarity, logical coherence and economy of language have aided immensely in turning sometimes turgid prose into readable exposition. Of course, ultimate responsibility for the final product with all of its faults and failings remains mine.

LHR Jr.

Preface

This book is about human nature and human freedom, and the relationship between them. Its contents are an outgrowth of my life-long interest in how the mind works. That interest, beginning at about age twelve, eventually led me to careers in clinical and forensic psychiatry and to the particular access these disciplines provide to human psychology. Disorders of personality have been a special focus of this interest. First in clinical practice and then in forensic evaluations, I have had the opportunity to study the nature of personality and the factors which affect its development. The practice of forensic psychiatry has permitted an especially close look at the manner in which all mental illnesses, including personality disorders, interact with society's rules for acceptable conduct. These rules, both civil and criminal, largely define the domains of human freedom and the conditions that ground social order.

Historically, of course, western ideas about freedom and social order have come from fields quite distant from psychiatry: philosophy, ethics, jurisprudence, history, theology, economics, anthropology, sociology, art and literature, among others. But the workings of the human mind as understood by psychiatry and psychology are necessarily relevant to these disciplines and to the social institutions that arise from them. This book is an attempt to connect mechanisms of the mind to certain economic, social and political conditions, those under which freedom and order may flourish. Although I have made strenuous efforts to follow where reason leads, I have not written this book out of intellectual interest alone. My intent has been more "generative" than that, to use one of Erik Erikson's terms. It has, in fact, grown out of a deep concern for the future of ordered liberty. In their efforts "to form a more perfect Union," America's founding fathers intended, as the Preamble tells us, to establish justice, insure peace, provide for the nation's defense, promote its general welfare, and secure the blessings of liberty. But the entire twentieth century, and the dawn of the twenty-first, have witnessed modern liberalism's relentless attacks on all of these goals and on all of the principles on which individual liberty and rational social order rest. Although they are strikingly deficient in political substance, these attacks have nevertheless been successful in exploiting the psychological nature of man for socialist purposes. To counter the destructiveness of these attacks requires a clear understanding of the relationship between human psychology and social process. It is my hope that this book makes at least a small contribution to that purpose.

L.H. Rossiter, Jr. February 2006

PART I

1

The Bipolar Nature of Man

The only way forward is to study human nature as part of the natural sciences, in an attempt to integrate the natural sciences with the social sciences and humanities. I can conceive of no ideological or formalistic shortcut. Neurobiology cannot be learned at the feet of a guru. The consequences of genetic history cannot be chosen by legislatures. Above all, for our own physical well-being if nothing else, ethical philosophy must not be left in the hands of the merely wise. Although human progress can be achieved by intuition and force of will, only hard-won empirical knowledge of our biological nature will allow us to make optimum choices among the competing criteria of progress.

Edward O. Wilson

Overview

This book offers a broad conception of human nature and explores its implications for individual liberty. The exploration begins with the fact of man's bipolar nature: a human being is an autonomous source of action, on the one hand, but thoroughly embedded in relationships with others through economic, social and political processes, on the other hand. His ability to act independently emerges inevitably from his ability to perceive his environment and respond to it by choice. His relatedness to others emerges with equal inevitability from his development as an inherently social animal.

Within this bipolar conception I distinguish the biological, psychological and social elements of human nature. All three elements give rise to independent initiative and joint cooperation. The biological nature of man requires independent and joint action to produce the *material* needs and comforts of life. His psychological and social natures require independent and joint action to satisfy his *personal* and *relational* needs and comforts. To ensure physical safety and promote social order in these efforts, human beings create certain rules to govern their economic, social and political behavior. These rules become the infrastructure of human society.

My purpose in this work is to establish a biological, psychological and social basis for a particular form of human society, that of ordered liberty. I seek a theory of freedom grounded in human nature and the realities of the human condition. From this theory, I attack the dominant socialist paradigm, the modern liberal agenda's welfare statism and moral relativism, as pathological distortions of normal social instincts. In the course of this effort, I note that all healthy developmental influences from infancy to maturity enhance both individual autonomy and mutuality with others. Acquiring occupational and social skills in preparation for adult living in a free society is central to that development. Competence in these areas permits the achievement of individual self-responsibility as a necessary basis for *voluntary* economic and social cooperation. I observe, by contrast, that the liberal agenda's invasive social policies foster economic irresponsibility, pathological dependency and social conflict. The reasons for these destructive effects are noted throughout the book.

First Terms

A few basic ideas will orient the reader. As the term is used in this book, human *nature* consists of the biological, psychological and social characteristics common to all human beings. Human *freedom* consists largely in the ability to live as one chooses, subject to certain constraints needed to keep peace and order. Taken together, the characteristics of human nature and the constraints needed for social order determine the substance of human freedom. They are the basis for those claims to freedom of action known as natural rights.

Unless human beings are impaired, they naturally seek freedom from others who would interfere in their lives. Because some persons interfere by committing crimes or by acting in dangerous disregard for the safety of others, freedom requires a social order based on the rule of law, an order that protects safety and allows for material security. Freedom cannot survive in the random aggression or callous indifference of anarchy.

The rule of law needed for freedom consists in rules which the people give to themselves. They are written and enforced by a government whose power is authorized by the people it governs. But power vested in government has a price: the people necessarily surrender some of their freedoms in order to secure others. The trade-off is unavoidable; some form of government with at least some power over the people is necessary for ordered liberty.

Freedom and social order impose limits on each other. With no constraints on freedom, order rapidly descends into chaos. Where power is sufficient to ensure order with near certainty, there can be no freedom, only oppression. It is a simple reality of life that the human need for freedom always competes with human needs for safety and security. To create a rational society, a balance must be found between a lawless freedom that permits everything, and a totalitarian order that permits nothing except its own tyranny.

The key to solving this problem, as Henry Hazlitt has argued, is social cooperation: the combined, voluntary efforts of many persons in pursuit of shared goals for mutual benefit. (Hazlitt 1988) It is the essential integrating force in man's simultaneous search for freedom and order. To be effective, social cooperation requires two major virtues in the citizen, autonomy and mutuality. Autonomy is the ability to act freely and independently through responsible self-direction in the pursuit of self-interest. Mutuality is the willingness to consider the effects of one's actions on others and to collaborate with them voluntarily in the pursuit of jointly held goals. The individual who is both autonomous and mutual believes that he is entitled to pursue his own reasonable goals—to have a life of his own—in his self-interested search for personal fulfillment. This belief empowers him to make a good life for himself. Without this belief, he will not fully understand the value of freedom nor appreciate what is required for it. He will not claim the authority—the personal sovereignty—over his own life that is rightfully his.

But the autonomous and mutual individual must also be able to govern himself without a policeman at his elbow. He must be willing to respect the rights of others and live by the rule of law. To create the social fabric on which freedom and order depend, he must be willing to *cooperate* with others by mutual consent to reach shared goals. This fabric is vulnerable. It cannot survive the chaos of anarchy. It unravels under the oppression of collectivism. The virtues of autonomy and mutuality, and the cooperation that grows out of them, depend for their existence on the protection of laws. Those laws must be grounded in the *ideals* of individual liberty and social cooperation. Governments unable to enforce laws based on these ideals will eventually be guilty of two sins: they will disregard the individual's autonomy, and thus override his personal sovereignty; they will preempt his mutuality, and thus undermine social cooperation.

The question then arises: do a given society's rules for the conduct of human affairs support the means and ends of ordered liberty, or do they undermine them? The analysis in this book answers the question for the dominant social paradigm in contemporary western societies. The modern liberal agenda with its policies of welfare statism, moral relativism, and invasive regulation undermines the foundations of freedom, order and cooperation. Essentially socialist/collectivist in its core values, the agenda is founded on fundamental misconceptions of human nature and human freedom. It misconceives the biological, psychological and social nature of man. It misconceives the development of the individual and the influences that promote adult competence and personal sovereignty. It misconceives the interdependent manner in which humans relate to each other in economic, social and political realms. These misconceptions result in policies destructive to freedom and order.

At the heart of the liberal agenda's defects is a philosophy of collectivism that ignores the nature of human beings as individuals. That nature cannot be ignored without dire consequences. A careful analysis of human nature and human freedom reveals that a society can sustain individual liberty, economic security and social stability only if its dominant values and institutions are committed to a rational, though not radical, individualism: one defined on self-reliance, voluntary cooperation, moral realism and informed altruism. These claims are the subject of this book.

Basic Capacities

For an elementary introduction to the psychological nature of man, an appeal to common experience will be useful. It is easy to verify that all ordinary human beings can do the following:

- choose among alternatives
- make things happen
- act with purpose
- act independently
- decide what is good and bad for themselves
- run their own lives

These abilities can be labeled:

- Persons who can make things happen are said to have *initiative.*
- Persons who can act with purpose are said to have *agency.*
- Persons who can act independently are said to have *autonomy.*
- Persons who are *competent* to decide what is good and bad for themselves, and who can thus run their own lives, are said to have personal *sovereignty.*

The American tradition of individual liberty has argued that anyone with these capacities–choice, initiative, agency, autonomy and sovereignty—should be entitled to live his life as he wishes. He should be able to live it essentially without interference from others, provided he respects the rights of others to do the same. This tradition argues that so long as a person is competent, his sovereignty—his authority to live his own life by acting autonomously—should not be taken away from him by anyone: not by any other authority, and certainly not by any *government* authority. In fact, the argument for ordered liberty insists that governments should *protect* the individual's sovereignty, not threaten it. That obligation is one of government's most basic functions.

In addition to this *individual* element of human nature, a *relational* element is equally important. Human beings are inherently social animals. They are embedded in relationships with others through economic, social and political processes. Their relatedness to each other emerges naturally in the course of their development from infancy to adulthood. An individual human being is *born* with the potential to become fully human, but he *realizes* that potential only in the course of relationships with others. These relationships occur first with his early caretakers and later with other persons in his community.

These observations on the individual and relational elements or poles of our nature suggest that humans are basically "bipolar" animals: they are, on the one hand, separate, independent sources of initiative who can act autonomously. But they are, on the other hand, inherently relational creatures as well. Indeed, it is clear that individual human beings cannot exist in any normal sense without relating to others even though they retain the capacity to act independently of others.

The Elementary Condition

Capacities for independent action and voluntary cooperation are inherent in human nature. They are evolved functions with adaptive value. A detailed examination of how these capacities operate in complex economic, social and political realms follows in the rest of this book. Before addressing that task, however, it will be useful to review the much simpler circumstances of a physically isolated individual in order to highlight his relationship to himself and his material environment. I appeal here to the Robinson Crusoe story, wherein a solitary individual, as Daniel Defoe imagined, has been shipwrecked on an island unpopulated by other persons.

By the nature of his circumstances, Crusoe's actions must accommodate only the most elementary economic, social and political conditions for the conduct of his affairs. *Economically* speaking, Crusoe is the sole producer, distributor and consumer of goods and services. From a *social* perspective, he can relate only to himself, since his situation neither permits nor requires any type of relationship with others. And from a *political* standpoint, he answers only to himself as the sole source of power and authority in his life.

Under these conditions, Crusoe has absolute freedom to do as he wishes. He also receives all of the benefits and assumes all of the risks in everything he does. He has only himself to depend on for the material needs of his existence. These simple realities define the conditions of Crusoe's life on a deserted island. The hypothetical absence of other persons in this scenario of solitude throws the material and biological facts of his existence into sharp focus. He must accommodate those facts or die.

Quite aside from the physical realities of his situation, however, Crusoe will also confront psychological realities that belong to him as a human being. He may, for example, feel the need for some sort of friendly attachment to animals (assuming there are any) to counter loneliness. He may explore the island to satisfy his curiosity. He may devise some type of recreational activity, create some aesthetically pleasing object, learn something merely for the satisfaction of knowing it, or develop some rituals of worship.

To live as well as possible under these circumstances, he must confront a world that includes his own needs and desires as well as his environment's possibilities and limitations for satisfaction. This principle turns out to be equally valid in the event that Crusoe is joined by a group of persons who are also engaged in meeting their needs for survival and comfort.

The Morality of Survival

In most if not all of his actions, Crusoe will have to make a value judgment about whether something he contemplates doing is worth the effort. He will carefully consider the benefits, labor costs and risks of what he does, because he knows that he can only depend on himself. His judgments and decisions are more critical than if he had at least one partner who might rescue him from some accident or folly of his own. His responsibility for himself creates a standard of value with respect to any non-trivial actions he takes.

This standard of value will be reflected in Crusoe's construction of a scale of good or rational actions, and bad or irrational actions. Good actions for Crusoe will be those that protect his life and safety and increase his comfort. Bad actions will do the opposite. For any individual under similar circumstances, these value scales constitute a morality of living with respect to himself. Absent the development of some very painful physical condition that renders life intolerable, or the onset of a disabling mental disorder, an isolated human being will make very strenuous efforts to survive and improve his lot. He will feel entirely justified in these efforts on the grounds that, for him, the preservation and enhancement of his life is an unambiguously good thing. He will assume a right to pursue happiness. Of course, what any given individual may regard as happiness will depend upon his particular interests and capabilities. But because of certain constancies in human nature, any human being's idea of what it means to live well and to be happy will have a great deal in common with others, whether they live in isolation or in community.

Historically, human beings have gone to very great lengths to secure the conditions which offer them the greatest opportunities for satisfying their needs and desires. Any prolonged indifference to that task leads to a state of chronic frustration, at best, and may well lead to great suffering and death. On this realization, human beings naturally develop a morality of material security and life enhancement based on the most elementary biological and psychological facts of life: their physical requirements and emotional longings, their vulnerabilities to disease and death, their fears of isolation and loss, their innate drive for self-preservation. These are the foundations of what human beings ultimately perceive to be good and bad for themselves, whether remote from others or embedded in multiple relationships with others. The instinctively perceived goodness of life and its enhancement are the rational foundations of all moral codes.

Life in a Group

If a second person, Friday, joins Crusoe on the island and the two men begin interacting with each other, then the scenario becomes much more complicated for Crusoe, as it does for Friday. Crusoe no longer has absolute freedom to do as he wishes. He must consider the possible effects of his actions on Friday, especially the possibility of negative effects to which Friday might react in retaliation. Unless Crusoe can find a way to dominate Friday, a goal with problems of its own, he must develop some mutually agreeable arrangements for cooperating with him.

The new situation requires economic, social and political arrangements for the conduct of Crusoe's and Friday's relations with each other. To be effective, these arrangements must have the character of rules; they must be normative. They must be moral and ethical rules that determine how two or more persons *ought* to behave when they do something with or to each other. To have normative *force*, they must be rules that are held by both parties to be binding on transactions between them. This latter requirement is critical: both parties must be convinced of the reasonableness of the rules and make a moral commitment to them. Only this commitment can provide a basis for peaceful coordination of their actions. Otherwise, intimidation based on the threat of violence, the morality of the mafia, becomes the dominant political principle in their two-person society.

These considerations apply to larger groups of persons, not just dyads. As transactions become increasingly complex, communities of many individuals create rules to regulate their behaviors: the customs, ethics, morals and laws that guide their affairs. These arrangements prescribe what is right and wrong about things people do when they relate to each other. They are expressions of value judgments held by the persons whose lives they guide and govern. Rules for living cannot, by definition, be value-free. They necessarily specify which actions are good and bad, desirable and undesirable, permissible and impermissible. They serve to limit antisocial behavior, however defined. They must be based on some concept of right and wrong, expressed in more or less explicit ethical and moral principles.

The Danger of Government

If informal arrangements fail to control antisocial behavior in the community, for whatever reasons, then a formal system of laws and a judiciary of some sort must evolve in order to enforce the rules for right conduct, resolve civil disputes among citizens, and satisfy the desires of the people to punish wrongdoers. But a system of enforceable laws authorizes a certain subgroup of the community to control the behavior of its members by violence or the threat of violence. With this step, any collection of individuals enters into a potentially dangerous arena of social organization. The danger lies in the fact that power is now concentrated in an agency authorized to use physical force. The likelihood of abuse of that power is invariably high.

When only one such agency has a monopoly on the use of violence to enforce rules, it is called a government. Governments always declare their purposes to be the protection of the people's rights and the maintenance of social order. But even with the best of intentions, governments routinely violate the rights of individuals and disorganize the order they are assigned to protect. Since this disorganization is made possible by a monopoly on force, the most critical problems in political theory may be posed in the following questions: what is the domain of human action over which the state's violence may be applied and how may it be applied against persons who violate the state's rules? What is the proper balance between liberty and restrictions on liberty? By what arguments are citizens capable of independent moral reasoning to be convinced that the reigning government's use of force is acceptable? Answers to these questions, among others, determine the extent to which individual liberty characterizes life in a society.

Although a voice of individual liberty is still quite audible in modern America, it is clear that a distinctly collectivist bias now dominates the whole of western political thought. This bias is destructive to the ideals of liberty and social order and to the growth of the individual to adult competence. Instead of promoting a rational society of competent adults who solve the problems of living through voluntary cooperation, the modern liberal agenda creates an irrational society of child-like adults who depend upon governments to take care of them. In its ongoing efforts to collectivize society's basic economic, social and political processes, the liberal agenda undermines the character traits essential for individual liberty, material security, voluntary cooperation and social order.

2

Rules and Reason

So act as to treat humanity, whether in thine own person or in that of any other, in every case as an end withal, never as a means only.

Immanuel Kant

Rules for Living

The nature of man and the circumstances in which he lives require that certain rules be imposed on the conduct of both citizens and governments in order to ensure legitimate freedoms, maximize the prospects for satisfaction, and minimize the likelihood of social disorder. Notwithstanding the currency of moral relativism in modern western societies, it is evident that those rules must have some rational basis. They must be reasonably well grounded in the biological and psychological nature of man, and in the economic, social and political realities of the human condition. They cannot be arbitrary if they are to have any usefulness in the conduct of human affairs.

On what basis can such rules be constructed? Another look at Crusoe's world before the arrival of Friday will help to answer the question. The only rules that make sense for a man in isolation are those which support a life as materially secure and personally satisfying as possible through his own labors. He can enjoy absolute freedom to do anything he wants. He has no need, and no opportunity, to consider anyone else. Since he has no relationships with other persons, his efforts to produce what he needs economically will have no effect on anyone, good or bad. For the same reason, he cannot have any good or bad social impact on others, either. And since Crusoe is the only source of power and authority in his life, he need not concern himself with any political arrangements or system of enforceable laws in his situation; there are no other persons with whom his or their use of force can be adjudged good or bad, nor is there any police power to apply it.

For Crusoe interacting with Friday, however, the rules for living are much different. Certain things that each man does can affect the other, so any action is a potential source of conflict. Because they share a common material environment with limited resources, and because each will be using that environment to produce what he needs, their actions affect each other economically. Even if both are quite reclusive, they are likely to communicate in some fashion, and thus affect each other socially. To the extent that disagreements arise, they will have to devise some means of resolving their differences; they will therefore affect each other politically. In short, absolute freedom no longer exists for Crusoe or for Friday. To keep peace, each will have to limit what he does to some degree. They will need some rules for relating to each other in activities where cooperation and conflict are the essential alternatives.

The only rational purpose for such rules is to enhance social cooperation and reduce conflict between interacting persons. There is no other reason to restrict individual freedom. Of course, it is implicit in all of this that human life in general, and Crusoe's and Friday's lives in particular, are good things and assumed worthy of preserving. Without these assumptions, all discussions of rules for living are meaningless and so are any discussions of morality. The assumed value of life, reflected in the normal wish to live and to live well, is a necessary basis for any rational morality, and is at least implicit in all religiously grounded moral prescriptions as well.

Good and Moral Things

Good or morally right actions such as cooperation, honesty, love, empathy, understanding, kindness, tolerance, patience, charity, respect for the persons and property of others, and all other virtues, as well as material security and comfort, are good and moral things, not in some existential vacuum but in relation to the nature of man and the human condition. Similarly, bad or immoral actions such as murder, battery, theft, fraud, torture, callousness, selfishness, deceit and all other evils, as well as needless pain and suffering, are bad or immoral in relation to the nature of man and the human condition. Good things produce varieties of happiness (joy, peace of mind, contentment) because of their effects on the biological, psychological and social nature of man and the human condition. Bad things produce unnecessary pain and suffering for the same reason.

Crimes against one's person, such as murder, rape or battery, are evils because, by the nature of man's body, they inflict pain, suffering and death. Crimes against one's property, such as theft or fraud, are evils because, by the nature of man and the human condition, they destroy the control over property that one needs for the preservation and enhancement of life. Civil as distinct from criminal wrongs—certain forms of negligence, for example— are bad because they violate the reasonable expectations of conscientious conduct that people must exercise when living in proximity to each other. More generally, right and wrong acts, and good and bad circumstances, are right or wrong, good or bad, only in relation to the nature of man and the realities of human existence.

The Golden Rule

Crusoe and Friday have a choice between cooperation and combat as the dominant mode of engaging each other. If they choose to cooperate, and if they anticipate that disagreements may arise in their future interactions, then they will agree, at least tacitly, to a set of rules by which they can resolve conflict, avoid combat and relate peacefully. Acknowledging their physical vulnerabilities, each will agree not to use violence against the other. Acknowledging that their lives, safety and comfort depend on each having personal control over material things such as land, houses, clothing, food, tools, personal belongings, etc., they will rule out robbery, trespass and intentional damage to each other's property. Acknowledging their need for predictability in the exchange of things that matter, they will decide to honor certain kinds of agreements between them, especially those involving the transfer of ownership or control over a material good, and rule out breach of contract. By eliminating one unacceptable type of action after another through joint scrutiny and agreement, Crusoe and

Friday can arrive at a set of rules that support cooperation and that are, by agreement, binding on both parties.

Although this rule-making scenario is quite fanciful, we may imagine that something akin to such efforts must have occurred historically among people living in community, and that the ethical principles of various civilizations represent an age-old distillation of experiments in living arrangements. Indeed, the Crusoe scenario becomes less fanciful if we imagine that another shipwreck brings ninety-eight more survivors to shore. With Crusoe and Friday, the island now has a population of one hundred individual sources of initiative. In their interactions they will generate a nearly infinite number of opportunities for cooperation and conflict. The arrangements they choose as normative will determine whether or not this small collection of individuals becomes an orderly society.

The new citizens of the island must create rules governing their actions if they wish to maximize happiness and minimize suffering. Assuming for the moment that all one hundred of them are practical reasoning persons, they will develop a domain of ethical and moral behavior, a moral sphere, consisting of the traditional and now commonly held rules of civilized man: they will honor cooperative behavior based on mutual respect, and they will exclude from their moral domain such behaviors as murder, rape, assault, battery, theft, robbery and fraud, among others. Each person will agree that he or she should not, and will not, commit any of these acts against another person on the island. Any given member of the group will voluntarily submit to these limitations on his belief that all ninety-nine of the other members of the society will do likewise. This agreement will contribute substantially to an environment of individual liberty in which each member of the group will expect to live in relative physical safety from the other. In addition, the group may also agree that each of its members will volunteer such help to others as he is willing to give, but no one will be *forced* to give it or be punished if he chooses not to give it. This last rule would express an ethic of mutual concern but would not coerce anyone directly into service to another.

As a practical moral agent, each member of a group of reasonable persons is likely to conclude that he is better off if he signs on to this elementary social contract. In doing so, he makes a commitment to what has been called the Golden Rule in either of its versions, negative and positive. The negative Golden Rule requires that you do not do to another person anything that you do not want him to do to you. The positive Golden Rule requires that you behave toward other persons as you would like them to behave toward you, and usually implies an ethic of aid and comfort toward them, not just a non-interference pact.

The adoption of both versions of this rule by the group as a whole establishes a basic social covenant–an elementary political system grounded in moral and ethical principles—that aids in the avoidance and resolution of disputes. Although the Golden Rule does not exhaust the topics of morals or ethics, the fact that variations of it span many millennia and cultures worldwide is no coincidence. The Rule reflects the natural, evolved inclinations of rational persons to live in cooperative social groups by agreeing to certain constraints on behavior.

The Intersubjective Perspective

In this review of a desert island scenario, Crusoe and colleagues have been assumed to be practical moral reasoners: persons who are willing and able to arrive at a rational social contract. Certain rules, or laws of relating, in such a contract would define acceptable and unacceptable behavior based on already established moral principles and on the practical consequences of following or breaking the rules. The domain of acceptable (or "lawful") conduct would include all behaviors that either *promote* human well-being or are neutral to it. It would exclude as unacceptable (or "unlawful") all behaviors that are *destructive* to human well-being, especially those behaviors that violate the persons and property of individuals. On these assumptions, societal arrangements are products of rational thought: they are logically derived from valid observations about human interaction and the vulnerabilities of human beings.

A complementary view of human relatedness called the *intersubjective perspective* suggests a different and more fundamental influence in the evolution of arrangements for human relating, one that goes beyond purely pragmatic considerations. This relatively recent concept has been elaborated by Stolorow, Seligman, Benjamin, Atwood and others, and was anticipated by Erikson's theories of biological and cultural interaction in human development. The perspective emphasizes, among other things, the capacity of one individual to "recognize" or fully appreciate the "subjectivity" or consciousness-in-depth of another, that is, the ability to view matters through the eyes of another. This capacity is present in mature individuals who are able to understand and identify with the mental and emotional state of another person: her hopes and fears, joys and sorrows, triumphs and tragedies, strengths and vulnerabilities, her manifest competence and her inner childlikeness.

A capacity for such in-depth appreciation of the other does *not* consist in a mere intellectual realization that human beings have such states. Recognition consists rather in an empathic grasp of what it really is like to have thoughts and emotions of various types. That kind of understanding is a potentially powerful barrier to aggression against other persons, in part because it creates a sympathetic bond with them, and in part because the subject's identification with the other makes aggression against her feel something like aggression against one's self.

It is no surprise, of course, that a complete absence of such recognition is notorious in the sociopath, who is altogether indifferent to the emotional state of the other except for opportunities to exploit it, and who cannot identify with, or relate to, or fully understand the experience of pain or joy in another human being. Among the notable features of the sociopath is the fact that he fails to "attach" to others through an emotional understanding of them. It is in large part the absence of such a connected understanding that allows the sociopath to do violence to his victims in a manner that empathic recognition finds horrifying.

Intersubjectivity and Obligation

By its nature, and in particular by the early developmental process that creates it, the capacity for recognition involves not only identification and empathy with other persons but also sympathy for them. Relevant details of this process are set out in Part II of this book. For the moment, it is worth noting that the element of sympathy in the intersubjective perspective creates a potential obligation to another person, that of taking his subjective experience into account before committing an act that might do harm to him. The problem of the other person' subjectivity is relevant to our desert island scenario. Since any obligation to take Friday into account would intrude on Crusoe's freedom to do as he wishes, it may be useful to ask why he should not simply kill off Friday as soon as possible. With Friday out of the way, after all,

Crusoe could resume the absolute freedom that he enjoyed prior to Friday's arrival, assuming that such freedom has great appeal. Of course the same question can be asked about why Friday should not dispatch Crusoe. In either case, each man, if entirely alone, could enjoy total freedom from all concerns about the other. No burdensome obligations would intrude, and there would be no one else to fear in a solipsist's utopia.

On the other hand, both Crusoe and Friday might decide against homicide for practical reasons. Assuming that neither man is a dedicated recluse, both Crusoe and Friday might reject the idea of killing each other because having a companion feels more satisfying than absolute freedom. Other potential advantages include sharing the burdens of survival, enhanced economic returns from division of labor, and greater defense capabilities against whatever predators may inhabit the island. Each of these possibilities might argue against eliminating a prospective partner by killing him.

These are only practical considerations, however, and none of them address the primary reason why most people in the western world won't take another human being's life: that reason, of course, consists in the moral abhorrence we feel in imagining ourselves committing such an act. The question then arises as to why most of us do in fact feel so strongly against violence toward another person and why such a taboo evolved in the first place as a foundation of human morality.

From a biological point of view it is certain that human beings, like all other surviving organisms, would not be on this earth if some innate tendency to avoid killing each other weren't wired into our brains. The "selfish gene," as it has been aptly called, has a heavy stake in perpetuating itself and not dying out in some genocidal holocaust, either deliberate or careless. But some basis other than biological advantage, economic practicality or religious proscription would surely be of interest, if it exists.

The intersubjective perspective, which may in itself reflect an evolved safeguard against genocide, suggests a possible basis for the taboo against harming other persons that goes beyond those traditions that are usually given credit for it. The basis is reminiscent of Albert Schweitzer's idea of reverence for life, but it consists more specifically in the capacity for recognition of or respect for, if not reverence for, the "subjectivity" of the other. This capacity recognizes a special kind of consciousness in another object that identifies it as a human being and not something else. Recognition in this sense appreciates the fact that another person is a subject very much like oneself, a conscious being with a vast collection of ideas, images, emotions, sentiments, strivings, expectations and longings—and vulnerabilities—that are so universally present in human beings. With these observations, it follows that if you abhor the idea of inflicting pain or death on yourself, then you must, out of identification and sympathy, also abhor the idea of inflicting pain or death on your fellow human, since he is also a subjective self who thinks and feels very much as you do. Viewed in this light, the intersubjective perspective reaffirms the Golden Rule's moral obligation to the other: respect the other person as a conscious, sovereign being, as an independent subject entitled to the same positive regard and the same emotional, and ultimately institutional, protections from harm that you claim for yourself.

Government and the Intersubjective Perspective

The discussion so far argues, first, that the intersubjective perspective perceives the other as a very personal being, as a subject, or self, or soul, in his own right; and second, that this perception leads to a bond with him through empathic and sympathetic identification, including an awareness of his capacity to suffer pain.

But the intersubjective perspective also comprehends the individual's personal sovereignty, his authority over himself, and therefore his right to freedom. This conception contrasts sharply with any view of human beings that depersonalizes or dehumanizes them as mere things to be manipulated. The attitude that human beings are simply objects to be exploited typifies the sociopath in his ruthless efforts to use others as means to his ends. From any rational perspective, intersubjective or otherwise, the use of another person as a thing commits a moral wrong. And when that use—or abuse—becomes severe enough it also becomes a crime.

On a much larger scale, however, governments, too, routinely depersonalize the citizen in their ruthless pursuits of political ends. The liberal agenda, for example, depersonalizes, and even dehumanizes the citizen when it exalts the good of an abstract "all" over the sovereignty of the individual, which must then be subordinated to the collective ends of the state. Indeed, for the government official immersed in collective purposes, human beings are things to be ruled; they are mere means to ends. Only the political agenda really matters, not the conscious experience of the individual it dominates. The liberal agenda's fundamental indifference to the subjectivity of the individual, whose sovereignty is buried in the grand collective—"the General Will," the "Great Society," or "the will of the American People"—allows liberal governments to rationalize unconscionable manipulations of the people they pretend to serve. For all its avowed good intentions, the agenda's political operations are essentially sociopathic. Examples are noted at various points in the text.

The Intersubjective Perspective and Generativity

As already noted, and aside from its origins in a purely moral prohibition, the abhorrence one feels against harming other selves derives its greatest strength from the bond that emerges through empathic recognition. Erik Erikson anticipated this attitude in his concept of generativity. (Erikson 1950) The term denotes a caring concern for the other that emerges in adulthood as a major developmental achievement. Its roots begin in the child who has been loved and understood enough to have acquired an intersubjective perspective toward others, or something very much like it. His growing recognition of the other is not just a cognitive understanding that other persons are like him. In its fully developed form it entails a deeply felt respect for and moral commitment to other human beings. These are attitudes that lie at the foundation of social order. Indeed, when that type of respect and caring are *not* integral to a culture's developmental ideals, then the masses may be seduced by any political agenda that dehumanizes the individual on the way to dominating him or killing him.

3

Dependency and Competence in Community Life

The only liberty I mean, is a liberty connected with order; that not only exists along with order and virtue, but which cannot exist at all without them.

Edmund Burke

The Resolution of Helplessness

All human beings begin life in a state of complete helplessness and dependency. This fact and several others about human growth and development have profound implications for social policy. The central question in this regard is to what extent and in what manner this initial state of dependency is resolved over the course of development, and to what extent is it replaced by competent self-reliance consistent with a given society's social and cultural norms. In a society founded on collectivist principles, the development of individual competence in the population as a whole must be limited in order to preserve a dependent and submissive relationship of the people to a dominant government. *In a free society founded on individualist principles, on the other hand, the proper outcome of child development is an adult person who is essentially self-reliant: he is at least minimally competent to function economically, socially and politically through voluntary cooperation in a community of similar persons under limited constitutional government.* A population of such persons is strongly inclined by nature to establish rules for living that protect individual liberty and property rights, while providing for material security, social affiliation, and the regulation of force and influence among its members.

The Constraints of Conscience

The transformation of a helpless and dependent infant into a competent adult is one of the marvels of human nature. The process is immensely complex and incompletely understood. But it is clear that the child achieves competence by becoming an ethical and moral person as well as a socially and occupationally skilled person. The competent adult has acquired:

- high standards of ethical and moral behavior
- the self-regulatory capacities of a strong conscience
- instrumental capacities to work and relate
- the ability to produce and cooperate voluntarily in a community because he wishes to, not because he is forced to by government authority

The individual liberties celebrated in western civilization since the Enlightenment require for their preservation certain ethical, moral and legal prohibitions on human action. For these prohibitions to function, they must be incorporated into the individual conscience in the course of normal development. This requirement is critically important. If widespread in the population, serious defects in the development of conscience and ethical ideals, including the "work ethic" of economically productive activity, invariably result in the breakdown of social order. Morally and ethically competent individuals, by contrast, can establish through agreement and cooperative effort, and through appeal to the wisdom of history, all of the economic, social and political institutions required to sustain social order and to meet human material and relational needs. Included in these institutions are the formal systems of laws and judiciary required for limiting antisocial behavior in persons whose internal restraints are absent or dysfunctional. Also included are the community functions needed for the care and rehabilitation of persons who are not competent to support themselves. This innate capacity for cooperation is easily observed in the everyday life of competent individuals. It constitutes the natural basis for a free society under limited government. It also refutes the collectivist claim that human beings, by nature, require extensive government intervention for the conduct of their affairs.

Skills for Living

The psychological foundations that enable a competent individual to produce and cooperate are acquired in early childhood. They consist in learned skills and attitudes for the satisfaction of normal needs and desires, and in acquired capacities for the inhibition of pathological impulses, especially those involving sexual, aggressive and acquisitive drives, dependency longings, and impulses toward self-aggrandizement. Capacities for economic production and social cooperation, together with learned ethical and moral inhibitions, become the core elements of the individual's ability to survive in community living. Economic and social skills accompanied by capacities for inhibition, restraint and delay of impulses, become, in the aggregate, the self-regulatory infrastructure of the ordered community.

This concept is important. Unless dominated by a totalitarian regime's Gestapo, social order is a consequence of cooperation, not coercion. Further, a community's ability to regulate itself is based not on some amorphous collective "will," but on the ability of each of its members to conduct himself voluntarily in accordance with accepted standards of behavior. *It is a matter of psychological fact that the locus of administrative responsibility for each person's conduct can only lie within himself, since for any given individual, his brain and only his brain creates, maintains and eliminates all of his own beliefs, attitudes, emotions and value judgments, and initiates, sustains and terminates all of his own actions.* "Society" does not cause an individual to do anything, contrary to the liberal mind's idea of social causation. When one criminally motivated person disrupts the orderly activities of ninety-nine other cooperative persons, he does so based on *his* belief that the odds that he will benefit from and get away with his crime exceed the odds that he will get caught and punished. It is this inner *personal* assessment occurring in the mind of the criminal, not some shared assessment in an imaginary mind of the group, that determines whether the crime is committed.

Ego Strength

The ability to function adaptively under stress is sometimes referred to as ego strength. The ability to recover competence after some loss of function due to severe stress is called resilience. These abilities are by definition adaptive and have the characteristics of habits: they are enduring and persistent tendencies to think, feel, behave and relate in certain useful ways in response to certain kinds of events. Abilities that contribute to ego strength and resilience include a normal capacity to observe facts and to reason about them, to call upon past experience to solve present problems, to tolerate frustration, to delay present or near term satisfaction for future rewards, and to cooperate with others in mutually beneficial exchange. Ego strength is not to be construed as self-esteem but instead denotes the ability to cope under difficult conditions. Resilience is the ability to keep coping and to recover functional effectiveness after serious or persistent misfortune or loss.

These abilities contribute to what is commonly called character, which term also implies dispositions to behave with honesty, integrity, responsibility, self-direction and dependability in interactions with others. Among other things, persons with good character typically keep promises and honor contracts, respect the sovereignty of other persons and their ownership of property, and in so far as possible, take responsibility for themselves by providing for their own needs and the needs of those to whom they have assumed some voluntary obligation. Persons with character do not make legally enforceable claims on the time, effort or material assets of other persons. They do not feel entitled to be subsidized by persons with whom they have no prior personal relationship or contractual duty.

Conscience in the Individual and Society

A free society will function rationally, for the most part, when dispositions of ego strength, resilience and good character are typical of its members. A citizen with these dispositions will be able to make a good life for himself by following the rules for rational economic and social intercourse. To succeed in this effort, he will not need a high level of personality development across the board. To participate effectively in a free and ordered society does not require exceptional social skills, charm, sensitivity or talent, although such personal characteristics cannot but aid in the pursuit of happiness.

What *is* required is a relatively high level development of ethical ideals and conscience that compel honorable behavior in economic, social and political transactions. In this context, "honorable behavior" means that one's dealings with others are characterized by honesty, forthrightness and integrity in representing the terms of any transaction, together with similar behavior in completing the transaction.

Since governments are integral to the functions of society, this requirement for honorable behavior applies to representations made by government to citizens regarding the estimated costs and benefits of proposed policies, and the actual costs and benefits of existing policies. By this definition, however, governments do not typically behave honorably, but instead operate fraudulently by deliberately misrepresenting to the people the real costs and benefits of government programs. Despite claims to the contrary, governments typically fail to obtain the *informed* consent of the people, if they bother with consent at all.

Especially destructive to the pursuit of human happiness is a government's use of fraud or physical force to violate property and contract rights and other legitimate freedoms. The content and scope of these freedoms and their foundations in the nature of man are elaborated elsewhere in this book. For now, it is worth emphasizing again that the destructiveness of governments grows out of the extraordinary concentration of power that develops whenever they are formed. This is true whether that power is seized by conquest and held by tyranny, or authorized by the voluntary but misguided trust of people who, out of ignorance, cede undue authority to others on the illusions of an invalid social contract. In either case, governments inevitably tend to exploit the masses. Regardless of any claims to more noble purposes for the public good, government officials typically act on what they narrowly conceive to be their own self-interest. More often than not, they disregard the long-term welfare of the people they ostensibly serve. For this reason the power of government must be very strictly limited by adherence to constitutional authority.

4

Social Policy
and Childhood
Development

Man lives in a world where each occurrence is charged with echoes and reminiscences of what has gone before, where each event is a reminder of other things.

John Dewey

The American people will never knowingly adopt socialism, but under the name of liberalism they will adopt every fragment of the socialist program until one day America will be a socialist nation without ever knowing how it happened.

Norman Thomas

Socialism and the Modern Liberal Agenda

Although definitions vary in some details, socialism is typically defined as a system of economic, social and political processes in which collective ownership or control over property, investment, and the means of production and distribution figure prominently. For all practical purposes, the term "collective" in this definition denotes a centralized government, despite any idealized representations to the contrary. Beyond this primarily economic definition, however, the modern socialist state also tends to be highly managerial, custodial and parental in its social policy.

A particular expression of this tendency is found in the term "therapeutic state," a label emphasizing the interventionist nature of programs whose intent is clearly remedial. Efforts of this type often use social workers to aid poor children in need of special education, socialization and mental health care. In other arenas, campaigns to achieve more equal distribution of material wealth and to equalize real or perceived disparities in political and social status are associated with the modern socialist state.

Whether these campaigns call themselves socialist or not, however, policies advocated by the modern liberal agenda are fundamentally socialist in their effects. Efforts to establish government controlled ownership or management of major economic and social functions continue to rank high among liberal priorities. Affirmative action laws inject the agenda's politics into employment decisions and college admission policies. A fully socialized health care system remains a key economic objective, and the ethics of political correctness and multiculturalism typify the agenda's intrusion into social arenas. Rules affecting both economic and social conduct in the work place are now common. All of these interventions have been instituted in the name of some collective good. All of these interventions are controlled by government offices. All are basically socialist in nature and in locus of control.

The Liberal Meaning of Government

This socialization of the functions of everyday life directly opposes the philosophy of individual liberty, self-reliance and voluntary cooperation that prevailed for most of the nineteenth century in America, and to a lesser extent in the early years of the twentieth century. Classical liberalism was highly committed to individualism, in contrast to modern liberalism's commitment to collectivism. Under modern liberalism, governments at all levels have assumed control over increasing numbers of economic, social and political functions that were previously entrusted to groups acting voluntarily at community or regional levels. As governments have become more actively custodial, the governed have become more passive and dependent. The reasons for this trend are related to how citizens have come to understand governments in the modern era.

A society's institutions and arrangements, its major rules for living, develop gradually out of meanings attributed by its members to economic, social and political processes. These processes in democracies evolve in large part by the approval of the electorate and the pressure politics of special interests. But electorate approval and the appeal of special interests are both expressions of what government means to its citizens. *The rise to power of the liberal agenda has resulted from a particular meaning that government has come to have for people in western societies, namely, that the state is a proper source from which to gratify the longings of the people for various forms of parental care.* At the invitation of the liberal politician, the people now solicit intervention from the government in every major sector of life: early infant care, day care, preschool and public school education, sex education, employment regulation, occupational safety, product quality and liability, workplace ethics, money and banking regulation, food and drug regulation, health care policy, job security, disability compensation, retirement security, etc. At the urging of the people, government officials have become administrators of cradle-to-grave parental caretaking, protection and indulgence. Politicians who identify with these longings and exploit them in public policy legislation and campaign propaganda have enjoyed great success at the ballot box.

But the cost of this infantilization of the people is a broad based crippling of their competence. Large numbers of the population have adopted a childlike dependency on government welfare programs. The modern state has taken on the role of an apparently benign, generous, omnipotent and god-like parent, who serves as custodian, manager, provider and caretaker, all to the detriment of the people. We have, in effect, parentified our governments in the belief that we will be better off if they take care of us than if we take care of ourselves. We have shifted our assumptions about the human condition from an ethical and religious conception that we must earn a good life through individual and cooperative hard work and responsibility, to a secular and collectivist conception of life as a manipulative competition for the bounty of the state. Rather than praying to a higher power to strengthen and guide us in our personal labors to serve others as we serve ourselves, we plead to our legislators for a place at the public trough and hope that they will do unto us at least as generously as they do unto others. Big government revenue has become in effect the income of a very large family whose many children vie for indulgence, while ready at any moment to protest in the name of egalitarianism if one sibling seems to be getting more than another.

These longings to be taken care of, to be relieved of the responsibilities of adult life, have their origins in infancy. They are properly satisfied in the dependent attachments of children to their parents. They are not properly satisfied in the dependent attachment of adults to the state. Instead, the gradual replacement of the dependency longings of the child with mature capacities for competent self-reliance and cooperation with others, as opposed to parasitism on the state, is a critical developmental goal. Whether or not that goal is achieved has profound implications for the nature and extent of government in a given society.

The Child's Growth to Competence

The adult citizen's dependent attachment to government comes at an enormous price: the constant growth of the politician's power to gratify his constituents is paralleled by a constant growth in his power to dominate them. Unfortunately, the resulting decline in the citizens' freedom is gradual enough to avoid alarming them. The liberal agenda's favors seduce the people a little at a time, always playing on their regressive longings to be indulged. Favor by favor, accompanied by the constant drumbeat of entitlement propaganda, the otherwise intelligent citizen is led to an increasingly erroneous conception of the proper role of government in a free society. Like a child molester, the liberal politician grooms his constituents until their natural cautions against yielding power in exchange for favors dissolves in reassurance.

Why do people allow themselves to be so duped? Answers to this question can be found in many areas: in the gullibility of the child that persists in the adult, in the wishful thinking intrinsic to human nature, and in the distortions of understanding that grow out of the dynamics of the mind. Despite a general tendency toward increasingly realistic perceptions of the world as they grow up, children easily acquire misconceptions about human nature and the realities of human life, about the nature of government, and about the economic, social and political processes that characterize modern societies.

Some of these misconceptions can be attributed to simple ignorance. But some of them arise from neurotic and other irrational mental processes, and not from lack of knowledge per se. These irrational processes consist in maladaptive ways of thinking, emoting, behaving and relating. Some are characterized by envy and jealousy, some by feelings of inferiority, some by strivings for power, domination and revenge. Some are driven by misguided instincts for nurturing. Some consist in paranoid perceptions of victimization, or obsessive pursuit of control and regulation. Some are characterized by delusions of grandeur, or infantile claims to entitlement, indulgence and compensation.

It is clear, of course, that any of these potentially severe states of mind can drastically disrupt an individual's ability to cope with the challenges of everyday life. But they may also affect his ideas in a more general manner; they may influence his notions about how people ought to relate to each other and what roles governments should play in the conduct of human affairs. Even when not seriously disorganizing, irrational thinking may distort the citizen's ideas about how society ought to be organized, what its rules should be, and how much value to give to individual freedom, responsibility and cooperation.

Early influences on personality formation are especially important to a person's later ability to think rationally about his world and the manner in which people interact. Those influences come from many sources, beginning in one's formative years. A child will, for example, be affected by watching others go about the routine business of living. He will see directly how individuals relate to themselves and to others, and to social institutions. He will observe that some are self-sufficient and cooperative, some dependent and manipulative, some hostile and exploitative, some reliable and honest. He will learn through his parents and teachers about how people relate to their world. He will listen to descriptions and value judgments about how others live their lives. He will be told how to understand what people do, how they think, how they feel and what their motives are. He will be told what is good and bad in the habits of human beings.

In addition to these influences, the growing child's own trials and errors, his own countless interactions with others, will contribute to whether he eventually achieves adult competence—that is, a well-developed capacity to provide for himself, assume responsibility for his life and well-being, work with others, act with moral integrity, and solve the problems of daily living through voluntary cooperation and without appeal to the force of government. The sum of all developmental influences over the course of the child's growth will determine whether, as an adult, he will have acquired a capacity for personal initiative and industry, learned to respect the property rights of others, managed to reject childish feelings of entitlement, and grown to understand that what he does must please others if he expects them to reward him for it.

Thus the adult individual's understanding of his world begins in childhood and affects both his basic conceptions of the human condition and his ability to function as a competent adult. That understanding will also eventually influence his preferences for particular economic, social and political programs. His personality acquired from parental caretaking and from the climate of values and beliefs in his community will have an impact on whether or not, as an adult, he will vote for policies that maximize his and others' individual liberty in a manner consistent with social cooperation, or for policies that forfeit a great deal of that liberty in return for government promises of protection or subsidy. His votes will reflect his perceptions of the world, especially those that affect his understanding of personal freedom, cooperation, responsibility and obligation. His perceptions will influence social policy through his demands for government services. If he happens to be poorly equipped to function in the general market of goods, services and relationships, he may be tempted to exploit the power of government in order to compensate for his deficiencies at the expense of others. He may then make persistent attempts to increase government power to the level of tyranny, including the tyranny of the majority. More generally, to the extent that persons with such defects advocate, administer, benefit from or vote for government programs, either liberal or conservative, their psychopathology will affect social policy.

Aspects of Development: Competence

If all goes well enough in the course of a child's growth, the end result will be a competent adult. As noted earlier, the word competent is intended to refer to individuals in whom certain instrumental and social skills, together with certain capacities for the regulation of impulse, emotion and behavior, have been firmly installed in the psyche, along with the ability to cooperate with others for constructive purposes. These capacities permit a relatively high degree of effectiveness in meeting one's own biological, psychological and social needs. In this sense, competence reflects an ability to solve the problems that characterize ordinary human life. The competent adult relies on his own abilities to observe his environment, assess its significance, and respond to it logically in light of whatever rational goals he has in mind, tempered by the appropriate prohibitions of conscience and the constraints of civility. He may readily accept the guidance of others, and he may enjoy being taken care of for relatively short periods—when on a vacation or in emergency situations, for example.

But in providing for his own material and interpersonal well-being, and the well-being of those for whom he has assumed responsibility, the competent person has no need of parental services. While always humanly fallible and vulnerable, and always subject to failure and loss, his efforts to run his life through his own initiative ordinarily suffice well enough and are personally satisfying in their own right. In particular, he has no need or desire for the government to assume a task that he is able to perform for himself, with or without the assistance of others. Beyond certain very limited though critical government functions, such as the protection of property and contract rights, military defense against other nations, and the coordination of those relatively few matters best regulated as public goods, the competent man desires only to be let alone by the government in order that he may continue to live his life as he chooses—while he honors the rights of others to do the same.

5

Altruism and the Competent Self

*In the end, more than they wanted freedom, they wanted security.
When the Athenians finally wanted not to give to society but for society
to give to them, when the freedom they wished for was freedom from
responsibility, then Athens ceased to be free.*

Edward Gibbon

Competence and Altruism

Competent individuals have achieved capacities for autonomy, mutuality and cooperation. They have also achieved capacities to empathize with others, to *recognize* others, in intersubjective terms, and to respond *altruistically* to others who are in need or in pain. Responsive empathy of this sort derives in part from conscious identification with other persons: a sense of being fundamentally like other human beings in a manner that not only opposes any thought of harming them but also fosters compassion for persons who are already suffering.

The opportunity to acquire this capacity and then exercise it is dependent upon certain societal values, including genuine altruism as a moral ideal. In this regard it would be reasonable to expect altruism to play a major role in the philosophy of collectivism, and in theory it does. But in the world of real politics, and in spite of constant propaganda about the importance of "giving" to the poor, the liberal agenda undermines the development of genuine altruism at individual and community levels, first by usurping their caretaking activities through centralized welfare programs, and second, by sending a message, between the lines, that in effect discourages individual and community altruism. The message is roughly the following:

You, the individual, and your neighbors around you do not have to take care of the hungry, needy, diseased, disabled or homeless persons in your community, because we, your elected government officials, will plan and administer the programs needed for that purpose from our central offices. These programs, designed by intellectuals, directed by bureaucrats, and funded by your tax dollars will resolve the difficulties in your area. The programs are already in progress. As we continue taking over the welfare functions that you and your neighbors used to perform by yourselves through your churches, civic organizations and neighborhood groups, here are a few cautions to keep in mind:

First, do not believe critics who say that welfare programs should originate locally in order to be effective, and that only locally run programs can provide the incentives, rewards, monitoring or relationships needed for success. More specifically, do not believe that you have to organize yourselves into local groups for those purposes, or coordinate your efforts using local personnel and local resources, or create programs of your own tailored to the special problems of your community. None of that is necessary. With our generic plans and programs and our dedication to your community's welfare, we in the government will take care of all of your problems from our central and satellite offices.

Second, you need not attempt to rehabilitate persons in your community who are unable to care for themselves. We will subsidize their disabilities for an indefinite period. And speaking of that problem, do not believe critics who claim that our government programs only offer to feed the hungry but fail to help them become self-reliant enough to feed themselves.

Third, do not worry that our welfare programs will rob you of opportunities to feel good about yourself when helping others or undermine the enhanced sense of community that you and your neighbors feel when helping others jointly. Do not concern yourself that your community will become less cohesive without the shared charitable activities that reaffirm bonds of social cooperation.

Above all, do not believe the critics when they say that we actually want to keep you, your community, and the welfare class dependent upon government services as a way of maintaining our power. That allegation is grossly unfair. We never have such motives. We are your government officials, and we only wish to help you by taking care of all those problems that you can't take care of yourself.

The Intrusions of Government Welfare

These implicit messages to the population as a whole, combined with the state's overt intrusions into local welfare functions, undermine society's understanding of altruism as both a moral ideal to be realized through individual and cooperative action and a developmental achievement with important effects on personal identity and social harmony. The fact that any welfare program already initiated and run by the state cannot be initiated and run by individuals in their communities undercuts local analysis, local choice and local commitment. Initiatives needed to solve welfare problems where they exist—awareness of local needs, analysis of the types of services required, plans for remedial programs, innovations for special problems, local coordination of time, effort and funds—all of these initiatives as well as the persistent labors of local citizens to sustain their programs over time are preempted by centralized welfare agendas.

In pursuing these agendas the state undercuts the development of altruistic activities at ground level and thus undercuts a major form of social cooperation central to community cohesion. But in fact, this type of interference is typical of all government intrusions into the affairs of the people, not just its welfare programs. Aside from their destructive effects on the problems of altruism *per se*, the state's initiatives always invade the freedom of individuals to cooperate among themselves in the solution of social problems. Stated more broadly, all choices made by the state, whether they involve welfare programs or something else, are choices that the individual and his community cannot make for themselves, thus reducing their agency, autonomy and initiative. Even setting aside the inevitable inefficiency, excessive cost and adverse effects on recipients of nearly all government programs, their presence in the lives of the people degrades individual liberty by interfering with freedom of choice at individual and community levels. The state's rules, regulations and taxes invariably intrude on the time, effort, goals, decisions, peace of mind and material wealth of citizens who are attempting to run their own lives and cooperate with each other voluntarily.

The Competent Self

Unfortunately altruism is only one of the casualties of the collectivist state, and it is not the most serious one. The extraordinary intrusion of the liberal agenda into the lives of citizens interferes with the most basic development of the self in its central functions of agency, initiative, autonomy, sovereignty, self-determination and identity. In the collectivist state, the individual's quest for competence, let alone a thorough development of his unique gifts, cannot be fully realized through the exercise of free choice, because the state's choices trump the individual's choices, and because the state, in its efforts to increase the population's dependency, always has an interest in limiting competence. To the extent that the state's choices are dominant, to that degree the individual self is disempowered, enslaved and effaced. The young person's natural thrust toward individuation in these environments, even to the level of minimal competence, is thwarted by the collective mission. Under the liberal agenda, collectivism overrides individualism, and the person who is not among the government's ruling elite becomes and remains a merely fungible part of the whole.

Absent this suppression, however, and given adequate love and guidance in the formative years, the natural course of human development is the flowering of the bipolar self: the achievement of coexisting capacities for autonomous action in the service of self-fulfillment, on the one hand, and cooperative and altruistic behavior in the service of social order, on the other hand. The emergence of mature competence in these fortunate cases permits solitary absorption in pursuits of one's own choosing, but also collaborative engagement and charitable concern with the lives of others. The pursuit of self-fulfillment through work in a free society almost always results in benefits to others, as one's efforts to gratify himself personally and financially result in goods and services that also gratify his customers. Where the state protects individual liberty in general and free markets in particular, self-interest and other-interest are united.

Between these two poles are an infinite number of variations in the nature and purpose of relations with oneself and others. Proportions of self-interest and other-interest vary even from moment to moment. A competent individual always remains a unique and lifelong cause of his own experience, with innate capacities for awareness, choice and initiative that serve him in his quest for self-fulfillment. This pole of his human nature justifies a life lived in freedom, one that reflects his exercise of personal sovereignty. Depending on his level of maturity, however, he will also commit himself voluntarily to the well-being of others and find that commitment rewarding in its own right. When not lost in the torment and dysfunction of mental disorder or discouraged by the oppressive hand of government, charitable service to others feels inherently gratifying and even fulfilling, not burdensome, to the mature adult. This altruistic pole of human nature, a rational expression of a biologically determined nurturing instinct, is one of the pillars of social order.

A full development of a bipolar self, with its unique sense of identity, self-determination and benign relatedness to others, can be realized in a particular individual only if adequate nurturing factors from parents and family combine with cultural and community factors to facilitate the inherent tendencies of human beings to care for themselves and each other. In a free society where the innate potential for growth to competence is permitted, the natural outcome of child development is the self-directing/interdependent adult who is able to meet, through his own efforts or in voluntary cooperation with others, all of the essential biological, psychological and social needs relevant to the human condition, including the functions of parenting children to a similar degree of competence. This is the natural result of the human life cycle when allowed to proceed under good enough parenting and good enough community and cultural support. The *competent* person that emerges from this process can determine his best interests and direct his life accordingly, while he cooperates with others and benefits them whether he intends to or not. His *altruistic* impulses propel him beyond the level of unintended benefit to respond compassionately to those who are disadvantaged.

The Strength of Community

It is important to emphasize here that the process of growth to competence does not produce a solitary adult who is callously indifferent to his fellows. By definition, competence implies capacities not only for self-determination but for compassion as well. Especially important is the tendency found in all such persons to sympathize with those who are disadvantaged and to volunteer some type of help to them on at least some occasions. A more complete discussion of the origins of altruism follows in another part of this book, where this virtue is seen to be an outgrowth of the child's early experience of empathic tenderness from caretakers and an expression of an innate instinct for reciprocal nurturing.

For the moment, it is worth observing that *the combination of individual self-reliance, cooperation and charitable service to others in competent individuals is the strength of the community and the ultimate source of security for the disadvantaged population. It is this strength, among others, that is stifled by liberal government's usurpation of the community's welfare services to its members.* Relieved of the destructive coercion and bureaucratic waste that characterize all big government efforts to solve the dilemmas of the disadvantaged, the community of competent persons, whether rich or poor, will not only take care of its handicapped members but, more important for the long run, will maximize the possibilities for their restoration to self-reliance. They will achieve these benefits through individualized, locally delivered rehabilitation programs consisting of evaluation, treatment, instruction and support, tasks totally beyond the bureaucracies of government. Most important, this community of persons under limited government will tend to raise similarly mature children whose growth to self-reliance and mutual concern for others is not aborted by the liberal agenda's constant invitations to dependency.

6

The Innate Character of Choice

The origin of action—its efficient cause, not its final cause—is choice, and that of choice is desire and reasoning with a view to an end.

Aristotle

The dispute between the theory of a predestined future and the theory of a free future is an endless dispute. This is so because both theories are too literal, too rigid, too material, and the one excludes the other. These opposites are both equally wrong because the truth lies in a unification of these two opposite understandings into one whole. At any given moment all the future is predestined and existing—provided no new factor comes in. And a new factor can only come in from the side of consciousness and the will resulting from it.

P.D. Ouspensky

Freedom and Choice

The ability to choose is inherent in the operation of the human psyche, appearing spontaneously and early in the child's behavior as a natural response to his environment. At every moment of waking life, and to the extent that he is able, the child engages the world with interest and curiosity, to explore it, understand it and act on it. These responses arise naturally as a result of the brain's processing of information from its surroundings. It has evolved to do this in order to survive.

The act of choosing in this process is innate, automatic and free, i.e., unimpeded, in the physically normal individual who is not ill with obsessions, compulsions, phobias, paranoid fears and other serious disorders of the mind. From earliest childhood, the mind automatically scans the world of physical and interpersonal circumstances, processes information through perception and association, formulates responses, and initiates whatever actions are appropriate to purposes already in mind. Whether conscious or unconscious, deliberate or spontaneous, choice is operative at every step, including the choice to ignore the reality of whatever circumstances are immediate and present, or to dissociate whatever element of the process is too disturbing or trivial to be reported to consciousness.[1]

Choice always takes into consideration some type of information, true or false, relevant or irrelevant, adequate or inadequate to the task in question. A particular choice of one alternative over another is determined by several factors: the mind's level of awareness and deliberation at the moment, its ability to imagine novel arrangements of conditions and events, the influence of past experience, the circumstances of the environment and the goals at hand. The mind's capacity to process information is subject to normal doubt and uncertainty, to the ambiguity of real or imagined situations, to fatigue and arousal factors, and to matters of caution and prudence. *The assessment of information relevant to some biological, psychological or social purpose, and the production of a selective response to that information, is precisely what the mind has evolved to do*. The capacity to choose comes with the package, at no extra cost.

Determinism, Strict and Otherwise

Choice is thus determined in the sense that it is *limited* by and *contingent* upon factors which affect it, influenced by the degree of awareness of the chooser, and subject to his purposes. But careful observation—not to mention everyday experience— argues against the idea that choice is *strictly* determined. Indeed, researchers quip that "experimental animals under carefully controlled laboratory conditions will do just as they damn please."

This maxim is infinitely more true of humans, who often do just as they please—by choice—contrary to all predictions.

To the careful observer, in fact, it appears that choice is routinely subject to highly *unpredictable* influences such as imagination and fantasy, novel ideas and new insights, the urges of emotion and mood, and the prompting of unconscious impulses. To date, no theory of strict determinism can account for the scientist's original insights, or the artist's new forms, or the common man's daydreams, or the child's imaginings. To assert that these creations are the strictly determined consequences of past events requires a very strained argument.

Imagination, invention and creativity are in fact commonplace in human thought, but neither their content nor the time and place of their occurrence can be predicted. Whether mundane or sophisticated, new ideas, images and fantasies routinely occur in the adult mind, much as spontaneous musings occur in the child's mind: they "happen out of the blue," as it were, in the free play of the mind with or without conscious intent and often without prompting. These characteristics—spontaneity, creativity and originality in human mental activity at any moment—liberate human thought from the bonds of strict determinism, though not partial determinism, and distinguish its essential freedom. Indeed, the human mind's ability to combine its representations of the world and of itself in new ways introduces a variable and unpredictable force into the universe of cause and effect.

Practical Determinism, Morality and Freedom

Some reflection on whether and to what extent human choice is free or determined, or both, is not a mere academic exercise. A grasp of these matters can aid in understanding the dynamics of human behavior as they relate to society's rules for living. It can aid in understanding how much freedom a society allows its citizens to live as they choose and to what extent its rules determine how they live.

It is assumed in ordinary conversation, for example, that principles of practical determinism apply when attempting to explain why a person commits a particular act on a particular occasion. It is assumed that a particular action is determined by an interplay of psychological forces: those that compel action–appetites or desires, for instance—and those that inhibit action, such as fear of shame or guilt or punishment. All efforts to explain behavior routinely employ the language of goals, motives and emotions, among other mental processes. All such efforts assume the logic of practical determinism.

An example of this type of explanation can be found in the analysis of criminal responsibility, where it is generally assumed that a man commits a wrongful act because:

- he has a conscience, but ignores its dictates at the time of the offense and makes a deliberate choice to do a wrongful act for some criminal gain;

- he has a conscience, but a mental disease or defect impairs it and renders him unable to understand the wrongfulness of his acts, or unable to restrain himself from wrongful behavior, or both;

- he has no conscience and feels no internal opposition to doing criminal acts.

These explanations imply that some type of mental mechanisms, including the mechanism of choice, or impaired choice, determine a criminal act, and that among the determining causes is the presence or absence of a conscience.

The convicted criminal is assumed to have the mental capacity for legally responsible behavior even though on the particular occasion of his crime he chooses to do a wrong act anyway. The offender found not guilty by reason of insanity, on the other hand, is said to have committed an offense because his illness prevented him from choosing not to do a wrong act. And the sociopath is assumed to commit a crime because he has never developed a conscience to oppose his criminal impulses in the first place. All of these propositions entail a practical determinism. They explain criminal behavior based on common sense notions of psychological cause and effect.

These observations imply that a human being's capacity for ethical and moral behavior is dependent on the presence in the psyche of ethical and moral ideals and on the prohibitions of conscience: that is, on the presence of enduring, reliable constraints against doing wrongful acts, especially those criminal acts that arise from sexual, aggressive and acquisitive impulses. It is clear in fact that the child's experiences during his formative years determine whether or not he acquires a proper understanding of right and wrong and whether or not he develops the will to behave according to law and moral custom.

This is not the whole story, of course. It is also common knowledge that the vast majority of well behaved persons, who may be assumed to have intact ideals and a functional conscience, may nonetheless yield to temptation on occasion and knowingly choose to do wrong. Perhaps this fact indicates that the functions of conscience are not always, or even usually, fully installed even after some years of adulthood. But it more likely points to something inherently imperfect in the ethical and moral nature of man no matter how adequate his rearing. Indeed, given the obvious susceptibility of all persons to commit wrongful acts when strongly tempted by their own longings and by the urgings, seductions and exhortations of others, it is reasonable to conclude that the functions of conscience can be compromised by many factors: the messages of the moment, the fads and propaganda of the times, the constant barrage of stimuli that tempt us to do what we should not do. It is evidently part of human nature that impulses toward egotism, hostility, sexuality, acquisitiveness and power, among others, forever seek indulgence.

It appears, then, that the contest between forces that *urge* immoral choices and forces that *limit* immoral choices is affected not only by inner ideals and prohibitions but also by the community's dominant values and expectations. The autonomy of conscience has its limits. The values and expectations of the individual and his community are in some kind of reciprocal relationship with each other: each can inspire and reinforce, or corrupt and undermine, the other.

Thus, a society's values and expectations about what is right or just influence the citizen's moral choices in economic, social and political arenas at any moment. *If society honors the principles of rational individualism, the citizen's choices will be influenced by ideals of individual liberty, self-reliance, personal responsibility, voluntary cooperation, moral realism, and respect for the rights and sovereignty of others. If, on the other hand, society honors the liberal agenda's principles of coercive collectivism, then the citizen's choices will be influenced by ideals of entitlement, welfare dependency, state regulation, moral relativism, and the socialization of major categories of human action.* These two views differ drastically on whether a society should allow its citizens to live as they choose largely by their own initiative and by mutual consent, or whether the rules of the state should control how they live and to whom they relate. These are competing visions about individual freedom to choose and cooperate. They are competing visions about what values should determine everyday choices, and about whose will, the individual's or the state's, should prevail in the real worlds of everyday life.

Intrapsychic Threats to Individual Liberty

Whether the human will is free and to what extent choice is determined have long been argued among intellectuals. The fallout from this debate has fueled additional questions as to whether human beings can be, or should be, free in a political sense. B.F. Skinner promoted the radical behaviorist argument that proper social "reinforcement", i.e., government administered rewards and punishments, can determine a harmonious social order. He suggested that we should get beyond illusory ideas of human freedom and human dignity based on individual sovereignty. Human behavior can be and should be "shaped" by appropriate stimuli provided by the environment.

But this line of thought deeply misconstrues human nature and the human condition from every conceivable psychological perspective. And it is surely obvious by now that Skinner's conception is bizarre, if not monstrous, from a political perspective, since it amounts to a prescription for totalitarian rule under a regime of psychologists and social engineers. The fact is that human beings can, and typically do, directly perceive the realities of their freedoms and the dignity of their own lives if those instincts are not suppressed by authoritarian rule. History documents man's heroic efforts to secure the conditions needed to enjoy both of these realities as natural rights. Freedom is derived from the sovereignty of the individual. Dignity arises from the perception of the inherent value of one's life. Normal human beings will not, and indeed by their nature cannot, rationally give up their freedom or dignity, least of all for some imaginary behaviorist utopia.

But the real obstacles to human freedom do not involve doubts about whether choice and will are free or determined. The real threats to freedom are readily identifiable: those from within the psyche in the form of mental impairments, and those from without in the form of political oppression and ordinary crime. Later sections will have more to say about threats to freedom of choice and individual liberty that arise from within the mind itself. Those threats come not from a strict determinism that overrides the healthy mind's capacity for creativity and invention, but from pathological processes which generate irrational fears and doubts, compulsive thoughts and behavior, severe impairments of emotional control, paranoid beliefs, and other disorders of reason that destroy the capacity of the mind to observe the real world of persons and things, comprehend it, and choose freely among rational alternatives for adaptive purposes. When the mind is so afflicted, then its freedom in any meaningful sense decreases sharply or disappears, and so, incidentally, does the likelihood of predicting its choices or assessing any determinants of those choices. Minds afflicted with severe disorders do not exercise free choice or free will in any ordinary sense of those terms.

[1] My use of the word choice as equivalent to selective response is intentionally broad. The driver of a car is constantly making choices that are largely if not entirely automatic, and he is almost wholly unaware of doing so. The same driver is capable of very deliberate and reflective choices that arise from careful and conscious reasoning. Thus our intuitive ideas about choice are themselves quite broad. We may at times attempt to specify the extent to which a choice is consciously made, although this is usually very difficult and often impossible. But in a discussion of social philosophy, there is no reason to narrow the concept of choice with respect to the degree of awareness or deliberation with which choices are typically made.

7

Competence and Collectivism

Mankind is at its best when it is most free. This will be clear if we grasp the principle of liberty. We must realize that the basic principle of our freedom is freedom to choose, which saying many have on their lips but few in their minds.

Dante Alighieri

By liberty, then, we can only mean a power of acting or not acting, according to the determinations of the will: that is, if we choose to remain at rest we may; if we choose to move, we also may. Now this hypothetical liberty is universally allowed to belong to every one who is not a prisoner and in chains. Here, then, is no subject of dispute.

David Hume

The Ideals of Autonomy and Cooperation

The ideal of *personal autonomy,* as evidenced in the capacity to act independently through responsible self-direction, and the ideal of *social cooperation*, as evidenced in the ability to work with others in pursuit of shared goals for mutual benefit, are threshold developmental achievements in the child's growth to competence. In a society committed to individual liberty, individual responsibility and individual assumption of risk, and in the interest of minimizing actions that encroach on the persons and property of others, social order requires that children be raised with at least minimal capacities for self-direction and collaborative effort. *Expectations that the mature citizen will take care of himself and not coerce others into that duty are consistent with a principle basic to freedom: that in a free society, no one is born into the world with a legally enforceable obligation to take care of persons other than his own children, especially persons whom he has never met. Citizenship in a free society should not entail a legal duty of care to strangers: that is, a statutory mandate that you adopt one or more persons deemed deserving by government officials.*

But these core ideals of freedom contradict the basic tenets of the liberal agenda. Citizenship in modern liberal America means, among other things, that as soon as you become economically productive, you must, on penalty of imprisonment, work for several months of the year for others. These others, whom you don't know and with whom you have no voluntary relationship, include sick, elderly, disabled and unemployed persons, as well as habitual criminals and other character disorders, all of whose adverse circumstances are no fault of yours. But your innocence in their misfortunes is irrelevant in the liberal mind's view. The liberal agenda legally requires that you support these persons at the expense of your time, effort, assets and abilities—at the expense, that is, of your freedom to live your life as you wish.

These facts have critical implications for the rearing of children and the general thrust of the child's growth to adulthood. The free but lawful and morally responsible society that honors the sovereignty of each citizen by forbidding anyone from indenturing his time, effort, abilities and assets to others, rewards parents for rearing their children to competence. A society dedicated to freedom and order places a premium on learning to choose responsibly. Collectivist social policy, by contrast, preempts individual choice with countless regulations and prohibitions, then rewards incompetence through its standing invitation to dependency upon an indulgent and overprotective parental government. Collectivism drastically reduces incentives and opportunities for the growing child to choose self-responsibility and productivity as core ideals of development. Indeed, collectivist morality implies that you, the average citizen, need not make rational choices that protect your livelihood or safety, need not secure access to health care with medical insurance, and need not provide for your children's education or save for your old age, because the government will do it all for you at someone else's expense. Collectivism declares that these and numerous other aspects of your welfare are the joint responsibility, but not the free choices, of countless persons who do not know you and do not have any reason to care about you.

The core tenets of individualism, on the other hand, protect your freedom to live as you wish but charge you with an inescapable moral responsibility: that of providing for your own material welfare, unless you are occupationally disabled. The minimalist social policy of rational individualism will not burden you *legally* with the care of any other persons except your children, but if you choose to help others out of altruistic concern for them, then you may do so (with their consent) to your heart's content and without any lawful interference. As already noted, however, the capacity for altruism, expressed in charitable acts toward others, is a developmental achievement that ranks high among the underpinnings of social cooperation. In this respect altruistic behavior, though not a legally enforceable demand, is nevertheless a *moral ideal* directed toward others. It compliments the citizen's moral imperative to take care of himself.

Choice and Competence

Unless rendered incompetent by some disease of mind or brain, an adult is assumed to have not only the rationality but also the authority to live his life as he sees fit, to decide what is best for his life among countless alternatives. His decisions include such matters as what goes in his mouth, when he goes to bed, what may be injected into his body, and whether or not he should buy a house, write a poem, play a game or sign a check. All of the historical quests for individual liberty and their revolutions against oppression of all kinds have grown out of man's increasing appreciation of the fact that he is, individually and by nature, not only a maker of choices but also the only proper source of decisions about his own life.

In fact, guardianship statutes formalize this understanding. It is reasonably assumed, until proven otherwise, that a chronological adult is the single most knowledgeable person about himself and the only person with legitimate authority to administer his life. For a given individual, that authority is assumed valid under the law unless some type of incapacity destroys his competence to manage his own affairs or renders him imminently dangerous to others. Then, and only then, can another party, the state, legitimately entertain the possibility of overriding his sovereignty by incarcerating him or forcing him to submit to a guardian of his person or property. Only then, through due process, can his authority over himself be legitimately questioned and nullified to the extent that he is deprived of control over his body and material assets and dominated by a fiduciary caretaker.

But under the liberal agenda, the population as a whole is not so respected. Under claims of fiduciary commitment to the general welfare, liberal government consistently arrogates to itself the status of guardian over able and sovereign citizens, then dominates and exploits them through its regulations and taxes, despite the fact that the people have not been adjudicated incompetent. The government's endless intrusions under this fraudulent authority always invade the sovereignty of the competent individual, constantly restricting his freedom with obsessive regulations, and stealing his time, energy, talent and effort by means of confiscatory tax laws. All of this is done under threat of imprisonment, which if resisted, results in additional threats of bodily injury and death. All modern liberal governments thus enslave, to one degree or another, the people they serve. And all forms of enslavement, whether by individuals or governments, are evil precisely because they deny the individual's competence, invalidate his agency, and stifle his natural expressions of freedom in the sovereign and legitimate acts of choosing how to live his own life.

Individual Sovereignty and Government

Opportunities for choice in daily life depend on countless personal and environmental factors: abilities and disabilities, material and social circumstances, economic and political conditions, prevailing religious and cultural proscriptions, and so on. Whatever the givens and whatever the particular assets and liabilities with which one is empowered or impaired at any moment, a person may choose among available alternatives only if he feels *psychologically* free to do so and is also *actually* free to do so because societal arrangements *permit* choice. The *feeling* of freedom is an internal matter, a function of one's personal psychodynamics, preferably unhindered by pathological fears and inhibitions. But one's *actual* freedom to choose among real world opportunities in critical areas of adult life strongly depends on the reigning values and institutions of local communities and the society at large and, in particular, on government policies in economic, social and political realms.

Properly grounded in a philosophy of merit and desert, a free society promotes self-actualization based on how well an individual performs in relevant tasks and on how well he relates in voluntary associations. When his efforts are not stifled by government policy but are instead allowed to flower as fully as possible through personal choices among real world opportunities, the individual's life becomes a unique story, written as it is lived, and rewritten creatively as fate and fortune demand. In very gifted persons, as Erikson saw, opportunities for such self-actualization give rise to the creative geniuses of history. With all persons, society's rules for living determine the freedom with which an individual can combine his genetic endowment and the legacy of his childhood with life's accidental events. When those rules give him the freedom to identify, pursue and realize his dreams through his own efforts, the life he creates is his unique achievement. The identity he creates is his own, worked out through voluntary interactions with others. The song lyrics, "I Did It My Way," have meaning in this environment. They cannot have the same meaning under modern liberalism. Affirmative action programs, for example, assume that the recipient of a certain race or other minority is too inadequate or too disadvantaged to make a good life for himself. He must instead have it given to him by the state. But surrender to this mandate carries a heavy cost. Any affirmative action program disconnects the citizen from the opportunities and resources of his community, puts him in a passive-dependent relationship to government officials, undermines his effort to construct an identity of his own, and forces employers and schools to submit to the will of the state. "I Did It the Government's Way" are the lyrics in this song. Meanwhile, those who have been rejected by the program in favor of the recipient are supposed to feel good about themselves for submitting to the state's power over them.

The Administrative State

Modern liberalism rejects, to one degree or another, the competence and sovereignty of the common man and subordinates him to the will of governments run by liberal elites. The western world's twentieth century capitulation to this philosophy is obvious—and the implications for liberty are ominous. But the history of the world also documents the heroic struggles of human beings to escape from tyrannies of all types, whether imposed by the brute force and declared entitlement of a dictator, or falsely justified by economic, religious or political sophistries. The science fiction of Marxian economic evolution, the grandiose fantasy of a New World Order, the utopian dreams of The Great Society, the myth of the divine emperor, have all had their turns on center stage in irrational man's attempts to legitimize government control and deny individual liberty. The realities of the human condition, especially the inherent sovereignty of individuals and their inevitable differences in choice and preference, render all collectivist doctrines absurd. A rational biologist will not transport a mountain goat to a prairie and declare a match between organism and environment. A rational social policy theorist will not create an environment of rules for human action that dismisses individual differences, ignores the critical roles of free choice, morality and cooperation, and otherwise distorts and violates the nature of man, and then announce that utopia has arrived in a workers' paradise. Of course, modern western collectivism stops short of the psychotic delusions of full-blown communism. But the liberal agenda still denies the individual's full ownership of himself; denies his sovereign control of his person and property, and declares that a very great deal of his time, effort and assets are the disposable property of the state, to be redistributed to others at the discretion of government officials. On this premise, the liberal mind assumes the right to tax and regulate the citizenry, but denies that these activities are theft and domination. Similar criticisms apply to the liberal agenda's intrusions into the world of contractual agreements and social relationships. The entire liberal enterprise is rationalized as beneficent, while the people, who have lost sight of America's original vision of individual liberty and individual responsibility, are duped into voting for manipulators masking as statesmen with noble purposes.

The Intrusions of Government

The economic, social and political arrangements of a society reflect the extent of government's intrusion into the general markets of goods, services and relationships, and the freedom with which its citizens can assume responsibility for their lives. It is government at all levels that either impedes or protects the freedom to work and to relate to others as one wishes. It is government policies, because of their effects on the costs of doing business and engaging in relationships, that too often determine the success or failure of a particular venture, be it economic or social. Opportunities for individual choice and production of wealth for the community are severely limited in an economic environment burdened with government-imposed licensure requirements, wage and hourly work requirements, occupational safety and health regulations, employment discrimination policies, benefit and insurance requirements, environmental impact restrictions, family leave mandates, Social Security and Medicare taxes, political favoritism and union violence, pork barrel and monopoly effects, manipulation of credit and money supplies, duties and tariffs on trade, and taxes on sales, income and estate transfers.

Social and political prohibitions affecting private clubs and organizations based on gender or ethnic exclusivity, prescriptions for politically correct speech, and membership quotas based on racial or ethnic proportions in the general population all interfere with voluntary and competent relationships and with associations based on personal preference, merit, or shared interests. Under these circumstances, the individual committed to running his life as he sees fit by choosing the directions of his economic and social endeavors, and by honoring identical rights of choice for others, suffers needless limitations in his personal freedom.

8

Parenting and Culture

The child is father of the man.

Wordsworth

The Individual in Society

Family influences, especially those arising from personality characteristics of parents, are obviously critical to a child's growth and development. They will, in and of themselves, reflect the broader cultural ideals, values and prohibitions of society at large. Conversely, a given society's institutions will reflect its child-rearing practices and their relative emphasis on autonomy or dependency, cooperation or opposition, morality or immorality. Of special interest is the extent to which all of these influences forge an ethic of self-reliance and personal responsibility, or an expectation that the citizen will become a ward of the state. At stake are not only the rules that affect individual autonomy versus dependency on government, but also the possibilities for an individual to write the story of his own life. Some years ago the U. S. Army ran a television advertisement inviting youngsters to join the service and "Be All You Can Be." Notwithstanding the fact that the ad was run by a highly regimented government agency, it appealed to a great American tradition, which in another time and medium might have been stated in the call, "Go West, Young Man, Go West!" The philosophy behind both urgings is, of course, the belief in self-actualization, the pursuit and realization of one's personal dreams. Whether military life or the western frontier is the place to realize a particular dream is open to question, and not, of course, the point of these remarks. Only a few persons will find the highly structured, authoritarian life of the military to be the best environment in which to realize their dreams or write and rewrite the stories of their lives. But I mention the tradition of "becoming all one can become" in order to emphasize the fact that such self-actualization, for the vast majority of persons, can occur only in a free society, that is, only in a milieu that allows maximum opportunities for freedom of choice.

The Irrational Self-interest of Narcissism

To anticipate an objection to the ideal of self-actualization, it is worth digressing briefly to make a distinction between rationally self-interested efforts to realize one's goals in the pursuit of happiness, on the one hand, and the behavior of persons with certain forms of pathological narcissism, on the other hand. The narcissist, or pathologically self-centered person, exemplifies a particular genre of personality disorder in which multiple capacities for relatedness to self and others are impaired. His disorder may not impair his ability to function in the economic market. Indeed, many highly productive persons are extremely narcissistic in the pathological sense and yet contribute mightily to the world's wealth as artists, inventors, scientists, entrepreneurs, entertainers and the like. The idea that the individual is sovereign and significant in his own right, however, and entitled to become what he may through his own efforts, is a much different matter and has nothing to do with the pathology of self-centeredness.

Freedom's claim on behalf of the sovereignty of the individual simply recognizes his undeniable existence as an agent of choice and initiative and asserts further that there is no justification for his enslavement by anyone else, including a government. *The efforts of any citizen to pursue his personal dream while respecting the equal rights of others to do the same is not narcissism or selfishness or greed, but an expression of rational self-interest consistent with the nature of man. In fact, in a free society, rational self-interest strongly recommends consideration of others, since it is in one's self-interest to please others and to serve them well.* The entrepreneur who realizes his self-interested dream of a business empire does so by pleasing customers with products as he pleases employees with jobs.

Similarly, the individual in search of gratifying relationships seeks to please others as he pleases himself. The long term congruence of rational self-interest and community interest is inherent in the human condition, as Hazlitt has so forcefully argued.

Thus, the drive to self-actualization and the commitment to mutuality combine to satisfy the bipolar nature of man. Both individual sovereignty and embeddedness in relationships with others are integrated in the self-interested pursuit of happiness that also benefits others. Long ago, Alfred Adler emphasized the development of social interest in the child as an antidote to the power-seeking of those who misconstrue relationships as opportunities for domination, exploitation and personal aggrandizement. Recalling the meaning of competence, then, it is evident that a major goal of child-rearing is the development of rational self-interest that includes mutuality and cooperation as essential elements. With these ideals complimenting those of individual liberty and self-responsibility, adult attempts at self-fulfillment honor both the individuality and social relatedness of human nature. The child's growth to adult competence, which pursues self-interest while respecting the rights of others, and which rejects exploitation of others through claims of economic and social entitlement, is a powerful antidote to the pathology of narcissism.

Early Mental Representations

The journey to adult competence begins in the helplessness of the newborn infant, whose brain is so immature as to barely manage feeding, eliminating and crying. Within some hours after birth the newborn brain may dimly register the mother's face and voice, but for at least a few more months, it will not generate much that resembles a mind. Once that process begins, however, the most remarkable transformation in all of biology, the emergence of a personality, begins with it.

It is not possible, of course, to know the subjective experience of the infant for the first several months of his existence. His mental representations of his world are no doubt vague, perhaps surreal and surely inexact. But it is possible to extrapolate backward from his later behavior and imagery in play and drawings, from his reports of fantasies and dreams, and from the nature of his habitual interactions with others, and conclude that, in the later infancy and early toddler phases of life, the child begins to register in some coherent way both the fact and the nature of his existence. In particular, he must, as a part of the structuring of his psyche, create secure representations of himself and significant others in his life. He will also represent his experience of recurrent interactions with these persons. By these processes he acquires a more or less coherent mental mapping of his world, especially those events involving relations with his caretakers. These are typically not emotionally neutral representations but instead carry intense emotional charges ranging over a continuum from extreme terror to extreme joy. When patterned at very early ages, they also include a powerful visceral component; any reactivation of these relational representations at a later time in life stimulates strong physical experiences, not just emotional ones.

These observations on the early representational functions of the psyche have important implications for later participation in the community. Essentially all phases of personality development can, and often do, go awry. The resulting distortions and deficits can have highly maladaptive effects on the manner in which persons who suffer from them participate in economic, social and political processes. In large numbers, such persons can have major effects on social policy, not only by their personal conduct, but also through their influence in the voting booth and opinion poles, in their rearing or teaching of children, and in their tenure in public office. These effects, in turn, can alter not only the rationality of the society as a whole but also influence future generations of individuals and their conceptions of social processes. What we do as individuals matters in the aggregate. What we do in the aggregate defines our rules for living and our society's legacy of values.

The Primitive Experience

A mother's care of her child is his first and most primitive social encounter, an interaction that will lay the foundation for his eventual relatedness to others. His earliest experiences in that relationship strongly influence which of many possible dispositions, adaptive and maladaptive, he will bring to his life as an adult. These include, as examples:

- A buoyant and hardy optimism that life will go well and reward his efforts; or a fearful pessimism that circumstances will eventually defeat him

- Autonomy, rational choice, and a firm sense that he is a good person who deserves to run his own life; or inhibition based on crippling self-doubt or a conviction that he is unavoidably controlled by powerful, ruthless and malevolent others

- Confident self-reliance coupled with adequate social skills for affiliation and cooperation with others; or enduring patterns of helplessness, pathological dependency and neediness as a fundamental mode of living

- Authentic concern for other persons based on empathy, identification, mutuality and compassion for all human beings, especially those who are disadvantaged; or an ostentatious concern for the welfare of others that masks essentially predatory efforts to manipulate, dominate and exploit them

These examples illustrate only a few of the myriad combinations of attitudes and dispositions that the growing individual brings to his encounter with the world. Immersed in a tide of cognitive, affective and behavioral experiences over the course of his development, the child is confronted with the interpersonal stuff of life and attempts to make sense of it.

The Mother-Child Relationship as Social Process

The child's earliest experience of the world in the presence of his mother is economic, social and political in most of its essentials. The newborn baby protests his rude change of residence, but acts immediately and instinctively to meet his material needs: he cries, he breathes, he roots for the nipple, he sucks to satisfy the biological imperative. Whatever his genetic endowment, however gifted or impaired he may be, he must do at least these primitive things to survive. They are his first economic actions in seeking the most basic of economic goods. This is only a beginning, of course. Under his mother's care, he rapidly expands his desires for other goods that he cannot provide for himself, especially her touch, her gaze, her voice, her person. She carefully enlarges his world to include other persons and things. Her satisfaction in seeing him grow and thrive, and her experience of his deepening love for her, are her compensation, her wages, for meeting his most essential needs.

But as her child grows, a wise mother makes increasing demands on him to consider *her* needs and desires, not just his, when he tries to get what he wants. In requiring certain actions from him in return for her services, she gradually resolves his self-centeredness by requiring him to trade with her, not just take from her. She makes him aware of her personhood and instructs him in the manners of mutual exchange. By the end of the first eighteen months or so, his interactions with her are, or should be, a two-way affair, not unilateral giving. If they become and remain for the most part reciprocal, then the child will eventually learn to satisfy his needs and desires through cooperation, first with his mother and later with others in the general market of goods, services and relationships.

The mother-child relationship is not just economic, however. It is also highly political, a fact evident in attempts by both parties to influence each other in some desired direction by persuasion, manipulation, compromise and power plays. What the infant lacks in weight and physical prowess he makes up for in vocal power and facial expression. He leverages his mother's primary maternal preoccupation with him, her loving tenderness, and her nearly unlimited moral imperative to see that he thrives, no matter what the personal cost to her. She, on the other hand, requires him—or should require him—to nurse, smile, cuddle, talk, return her gaze and adjust, as best he can, to her need to change his position, delay his feeding, cool his fever, put him to bed and allow her to meet her own needs. Within the mother-child dyad, politics and economics merge in the endless opportunities for cooperation and conflict. Beyond that dyad, opportunities rapidly expand as the infant's world includes his father, siblings, extended family and others to whom he can turn to get what he wants by whatever means, from pleading to power plays, the family rules allow.

If this earliest experience is economic and political, it is certainly social in the most profound sense. The two-person society of mother and infant begins, of course, in those processes needed to meet the biological imperatives of human life. But infants who are merely well fed in a physically protected environment fail to thrive in the absence of some minimum maternal care. The tactile experience of being held, the visual imagery of a human face, the smell of the mother's body and the sound of her voice all mediate the release and coordination of some unknown but essential humors without which the infant's journey to adulthood, or to simply survive, is derailed. Something about human nature makes social relatedness imperative in its own right from the very beginning.

Equally important is the fact that the quality of this early maternal experience lays the groundwork for the child's later interaction with the larger social order. A critical aspect of this experience consists in the mother's gradually increasing insistence that he recognize her as a subject, not a mere object, and respond to her as a sovereign person in her own right, not a mere extension of his will or servant of his desires. It is difficult to overestimate the significance of her efforts in this regard, because her success or failure will affect his later ability to relate *mutually* at a personal level–in a marriage for example—and *cooperatively* with society as a whole. These observations are illustrated in the problems associated with pathological narcissism. Narcissists treat others as objects to be manipulated, not independent subjects to be respected, and this type of relating can disrupt effective cooperation at every level of human endeavor. That unfortunate outcome is avoided, however, in the child who has grown up with an understanding that his parents have their own needs and desires that he must respect and accommodate. In the course of that accommodation he learns first with family members, and later with others, that negotiation for mutual gain, not deception or threat of harm, are the proper ways to relate to the world.

There is an added bonus from these observations: the capacity for recognition of the other person as a sovereign subject can serve as a premise for political equality and a foundation for moral equality. On this understanding, the other person is never to be used to his disadvantage, not for personal gain and not for a political agenda. He must instead be honored as a legitimate source of agency; he must be recognized as an end in himself.

Thus the mother-child relationship, understood here as economic, social and political process, deals with matters critical to a rational society's rules for living. Whether or not the child develops virtues of self-reliance, mutuality, and recognition— initially with his caretakers and later with peers—has everything to do with his eventual ability to relate to others by voluntary consent instead of government coercion. These virtues are missing from the liberal agenda and from the liberal mind that gives rise to it. Their absence permits the agenda to degrade the importance of the individual relative to the state and to undermine the critical role of social cooperation.

9

The Ideals and Imperatives of Development

Liberty means responsibility. That is why most men dread it.
George Bernard Shaw

It is only the novice in political economy who thinks it is the duty of government to make its citizens happy—government has no such office. To protect the weak and the minority from the impositions of the strong and the majority—to prevent any one from positively working to render the people unhappy, (if we may so express it), to do the labor not of an officious inter-meddler in the affairs of men, but of a prudent watchman who prevents outrage—these are rather the proper duties of a government. Under the specious pretext of effecting "the happiness of the whole community," nearly all the wrongs and intrusions of government have been carried through. The legislature may, and should, when such things fall in the way, lend its potential weight to the cause of virtue and happiness—but to legislate in direct behalf of those objects is never available, and rarely effects any even temporary benefit.
Walt Whitman

Freedom and the Origins of the Psyche

The biological imperative to survive and the psychosocial imperative to relate to others meet jointly and for the first time in the mother-child relationship. Each imperative facilitates the other. Individuals survive and mature biologically, and become whole selves psychologically, only in the context of an initially primitive and later increasingly complex parent-child relationship. The outcome of this process is determined by the physical and personal characteristics of both mother and child, and affected by the real world conditions in which they exist. Without dismissing what is now appreciated as the important contributions of inherited personality traits, it is clear that virtually every aspect of an individual's adult life—occupational, social, sexual, marital, parental, political, recreational and spiritual—is influenced by childhood experiences, especially those repeated interactions with parents, siblings and other significant persons during his formative years. The core of the child's psyche, forged in his immature brain, becomes empowered or impoverished by interactions with the primary figures who nurture him or neglect him, protect him or traumatize him. In particular, his capacities for love and hate, affection and indifference, cooperation and opposition—all the qualities that define his humanness and enable him to participate in the human community—arise in his early interpersonal experience, first with his mother and later with others. They prepare him, or fail to prepare him, to live in freedom and harmony with others.

Preparation for life in a society of ordered liberty requires a great deal from both parent and child. Ideally, their joint efforts, sustained over the first twenty years of life, teach the child to:

- Acknowledge the value of individual lives
- Respect the sovereignty, agency, autonomy and freedom of other persons
- Honor certain values essential to social cooperation
- Recognize the right to be let alone as fundamental to individual liberty
- Earn a living through self-reliance and voluntary exchange with others
- Honor the obligations of promises, contracts and property rights
- Relate with integrity to other persons who can act similarly

- Treat others with thoughtfulness, decency, and courtesy
- Relate lovingly and sympathetically toward others where appropriate
- Take care of children and the chronically ill or disadvantaged.

These lessons restate the principles central to rational individualism: self-reliance, voluntary cooperation, moral realism and informed altruism. These are the cornerstones of a society able to sustain individual liberty, economic security and social stability.

Development and the Embrace of Freedom

Beyond our earliest formative experiences, our ideas about the social world are acquired gradually through complex socializing processes which shape our adult dispositions. Countless interactions with others establish in the child's mind enduring conceptions of the world as benign, neutral or malevolent, interested or indifferent, receptive or rejecting, collaborative or oppositional, validating or invalidating, manageably competitive or dangerously combative. Beginning in infancy and continuing through the formative years of childhood and adolescence, these and other conceptions determine the individual's eventual ability to cooperate with others as an adult. Myriad cultural messages—ethnic traditions, social conventions, peer pressures, moral imperatives, political propaganda, the effects of advertising, the ideals and standards of religion—all affect the growing individual's capacity to live his life effectively in the pursuit of happiness, and to do it cooperatively within the rules that structure a free society.

In present day American political forums, the adult citizen may choose between competing political arrangements: those that are characterized by strictly limited government, rigorous protections of property and contract rights, maximum freedom of economic and social choice, and maximum individual responsibility, on the one hand; and those that are based on large, coercive governments that intervene extensively in the lives of citizens and which engineer and regulate fundamental economic and social processes, on the other hand. The first arrangement permits the widest range of opportunities for personal fulfillment and effective cooperation;

the second markedly reduces the range of economic and social cooperation and opportunities for personal fulfillment.

The choice for maximum freedom honors the sovereignty of individual persons and their innate tendencies toward mutual cooperation. Empowered by fundamental property protections, this choice recognizes a natural and complementary harmony of individual and societal interests that are mutually reinforced by the economic effects of Adam Smith's "invisible hand" and by the social effects of spontaneous empathy, compassion and altruism.

To the person who chooses a system of large and coercive central government, on the other hand, such arrangements represent a cruel and illusory fiction that rewards exploitation of the masses by "the rich" or by sinister "capitalist" forces. These forces, it is argued, control the major dynamics of society. They must be overridden by interventionist government, since only then can the masses be protected from a world that is fundamentally unsafe for them.

The choice for maximum freedom assumes that under the rule of certain laws the world can be made safe enough that individuals can be trusted to live self-fulfilling as well as socially harmonious lives through voluntary cooperation with each other. The mission of government under these assumptions is to guarantee, in so far as possible, equal and identical economic and political freedoms to all citizens by protecting their persons and property against criminal acts from any source and by strictly prohibiting enforced surrender of any citizen's time, effort and assets to the purposes of the state, regardless of intent. The choice for interventionist government, by contrast, sharply limits individual liberties, especially economic liberties, as a consequence of the state's commitment to redistributing material assets from persons who produce to persons who don't, and its unequal and disproportionate award of political and legal indulgence to persons deemed disadvantaged.

Wards of the State

The cumulative effects of these choices in a democracy are critical for the nature and extent of its government. Majority votes become destructive when the dependency longings of the people override their commitment to individual liberty, when they misconceive government as a parental caretaker rather than a protector of freedoms, and when the constraints of a constitution designed to prevent the excesses of government are emasculated by judges and legislators who fail to uphold them. The regressive choices of the electorate in favor of the state as *parens patriae*, together with the seductions of position, power and wealth that inhere in the offices of big government, mutually reinforce the decline of the free individualist society into the regulated socialist society, the utopian ideal of the liberal mind.

More specifically, the usurpation of fundamental economic, social and political functions by the collectivist state alters the climate of individual development in the society, frustrates the achievement of adult competence, and leads to increasing numbers of citizens who choose to remain pathologically dependent on the state, childlike in their submission to its authority, and stunted in their character development. Under the modern liberal agenda, the people fail to develop normal capacities for adult autonomy, self-reliance and local community responsibility that are the necessary foundations for both individual happiness and social order. The electorate's decisions in favor of parental government ignore the penalties that must be paid: the liberal agenda eventually undermines the integrity of economic and social processes; disrupts community identity, cohesion and support; disorganizes family structure and function; and induces large portions of the citizenry to become wards of the state. Ultimately, as Hayek observed, choices in favor of interventionist government put society on the road to serfdom.

The Tools of Survival

All competent persons perceive directly that a real material world exists, that it is populated by other persons, that it is capable of being understood, and that it is, for the most part, manageable. An intact ability to perceive and interpret the significance of a moving truck or the attitude of another person is essential for life and represents a normal capacity to test reality. The ordinary mental functions required for the appreciation of reality include the following:

- Attention, concentration, perception and registration of the environment and events occurring within it
- Association to prior categories of events and contexts to identify and evaluate the present environment and the significance of relevant events for possible action
- Memory, reasoning and judgment in these processes
- Formulation of goals and plans to implement them

- Action initiated to reach those goals, monitoring of results, reassessment, changes in plans and goals, etc.

These and numerous other functions are the tools with which competent persons attempt to sustain life and enhance its quality. They do this on the understanding that the worlds of material objects and social interactions are real, causally ordered and knowable. Competent human beings understand that they must respect facts and think logically about people and things. They understand that actions have consequences, that certain actions make their lives better or worse, and that certain rules must govern the behaviors of persons in order to allow for individual freedoms and the preservation of social order.

In his effort to succeed, the competent adult assesses a social reality populated with persons other than himself. He perceives his own body and psychological self, and by observation and empathy the psychological selves of others. He is able to perceive the nature and significance of his relationships with others well enough to function in the community, and he can ordinarily do this in a manner that meets his own needs and the needs of others without disrupting social order. In the course of his interactions with others, his own body and psychological self, and the bodies and psychological selves of others, impose various demands on him. These are, first and foremost, biological demands for food and shelter, and second and ordinarily less urgent, psychological and interpersonal demands. Competent individuals are able to meet these demands reasonably well, assuming an environment of rational economic, social and political arrangements.

Rational Arrangements

At every point in these efforts, competent persons realize that freedom to seek facts and explore possibilities, experiment with alternative solutions, learn by trial and error, and take corrective action are the keys to eventual success in the pursuit of happiness. The possibilities for that success are established by economic, social and political arrangements that accommodate certain realties of the human condition. These arrangements, when derived from the wisdom of history and expressed in appropriate laws, customs, ideals and morals, set proper limits on the choices that people can reasonably make and outcomes they can reasonably expect. If the rules too greatly restrict their choices or narrow the range of outcomes, or on the other hand allow for so much latitude that social order is lost, then the likelihood of achieving happiness is also reduced. If the rules are consistent with human nature and the material conditions of human existence, then the reasonably functional individual can use his faculties effectively, as his abilities permit, in the pursuit of happiness. He can make choices that stand a good chance of success by choosing realistic goals and respecting the logic of cause and effect.

Economic, social, and political arrangements thus constitute a "holding environment," an existential ether, in which human beings are embedded. But this environment has to be invented—there is no system given to us in advance. Indeed, the history of mankind is a series of experiments in these arrangements, developed through trial and error, and consisting of countless variations in rules for living at every level of human action. Not all such arrangements have respected the biological and psychological nature of man or the fundamental conditions of human existence. Not all arrangements have permitted human beings to grow into competent adults, to live as their human nature enables them to live. For the most part, in fact, historical arrangements have been antithetical to the security and contentment of the persons living under them. The arrangements that gave birth to the United States were an exception.

The Invitation to Regress

For well over a century after the founding of this nation, the remarkable appeal of the American way of life was grounded in the historically unprecedented freedom with which individuals were able to pursue their lives unencumbered by kings, emperors, politically tethered priests, and other tyrants of every stripe. Those who immigrated to America willingly accepted complete responsibility for their own lives and those of their families, and they gladly assumed all of life's risks as the proper cost of individual liberty. With the liberal agenda's ascendancy over the past hundred years, however, America has witnessed a substantial retreat from its ideals of individual freedom, individual responsibility and individual assumption of risk. Under collectivist values, the liberal transformation has induced a developmental regression in the people of the nation to a childlike state of dependency on parental government and a childlike submission to its authority.

The enormous expansion of caretaking and managerial functions in modern government has resulted in an endless series of oppressive laws and a massive surrender of personal freedoms. Government as *parens patriae* has eroded the character of the people by excusing them from responsibilities for themselves and voluntary obligations to others. Liberal government offers a standing invitation to ignore the realistic assessment of risk and the consequences of irrational decisions: the people continue to live in a flood plain, make foolish investments, omit preparing financially for disability or old age in the correct belief that government will bail them out. Liberal legislators write laws that encourage the people to sue each other for even trivial insults and to hold each other legally accountable for every imaginable misfortune. Indulgent judges dismiss contractual obligations while federal bankruptcy laws sanction financial irresponsibility. The liberal agenda thrives on the dependency of the people and encourages them to remain childlike, heedless to the ominous implications for societal madness.

American Cultural Decline

It is no coincidence that modern American society has become increasingly irrational as the liberal agenda has enlarged its influence on social policy and on the attitudes of citizens. By any reasonable measure the country has been in a process of cultural decline for at least several decades. In economic, social and political domains, substantial portions of the population have become increasingly dysfunctional despite the fact that among our citizens the reservoirs of talent, inventiveness and determination, together with access to information and material resources, exceed those of every other country in the world. To understand this decline is to understand the dynamics of the liberal mind's overthrow of the individualist/libertarian tradition that guided America's founding fathers.

In fact, the United States created in substance—but then largely abandoned in spirit and practice—the necessary moral traditions and constitutionally based legal standards required for a sane society. When those traditions and structures were operative, as they were for most of the nineteenth century, the opportunities for an individual to improve his standard of living in this country became unique in human history. The arrangements necessary for individual liberty were unimpeded by government policies that violated the principles of rational societal organization. Maximum freedom of choice allowed communities across the country to benefit from the natural tendencies of human beings to produce and exchange voluntarily with each other under the rule of law. Within this otherwise beneficent environment, the enslavement of blacks remains, of course, the greatest tragedy of American history. But that tragedy illustrates just the kind of evil that inevitably arises when human beings are excluded from the benefits of a free society, or in the case of slave owners, exempted from the rules that sustain a free society.

In the early United States, the philosophic and pragmatic foundations for the natural cooperation between individual and community emerged from an intuitive, as well as explicit, understanding of what it takes to be a human being living in peace and safety with others. An innate compatibility between the individual and his community was clearly understood by the nation's founders to rest on the twin pillars of individual sovereignty and voluntary cooperation. But the emergence of this compatibility required a context of moral rectitude that protected social order and statutory rules that protected property rights. The latter rules severely limited the power of government to intrude into the lives of the people. For the sovereign and self-responsible individual under these protections the community then became an economic and interpersonal domain in which he could make a living and relate to others as he and they freely chose. In this setting his responsibility to the community was to respect the rules essential to order and cooperation: he had to respect the prohibitions against encroaching upon the persons or property of others, and he had to honor any contractual obligations to which he committed himself. To the extent that he and other citizens adhered to these and other basic rules of economic and social intercourse, including those urging charitable caretaking of the truly needy, the community could serve its equally basic function of providing a general market of goods, services and relationships needed for the pursuit of happiness. Out of respect for individual sovereignty and responsibility, early American society's prohibitions against government intrusions fortified the people against the tyranny of collectivism. This environment has not endured under the onslaught of modern liberalism.

Effects of the Liberal Agenda

All forms of the liberal agenda interfere with the rational relationship between human action and the conditions of life by disconnecting outcomes from adaptive behavior. Government welfare programs of all kinds disconnect the receipt of material benefits from productive behavior and voluntary exchange, and from those normal developmental processes that lead to adult competence. Social Security, Medicare, Medicaid, and all other federal and state welfare programs divorce an individual's material security and emotional well being from his economic and social connections to his community, and replace them with a marriage to government officials. In particular, welfare programs disconnect the individual's security and well being from two of his most reliable resources: his own initiative in producing and exchanging with others, and his social bonds to members of his family, church, neighborhood or village. The liberal agenda's takeover of countless individual and community functions, from early education to care of the elderly, has had the effect of alienating the individual from his community and robbing both of their essential mutuality.

In the economic sphere, especially, the liberal agenda's rules have become strikingly irrational. Countless restrictions dictate what the ordinary businessman and professional may or may not do regarding hiring procedures, sales and purchasing, health insurance plans, retirement plans, safety precautions, transportation policies, racial and ethnic quotas, immigration matters, liability rules, and provisions for the handicapped. Endless paperwork adds to the already crushing burden of confiscatory taxation. Licensure requirements needlessly prevent workers from entering new fields in which they are willing to work hard and risk much in order to make life better for themselves and their families. Unnecessary and unjust restrictions in the freedom with which individuals can run their economic lives are the hallmarks of the liberal agenda.

But the social pathology of collectivism extends well beyond the economic realm. While children can be happy in dependent relationships with parents, adults cannot be happy in any mature sense in dependent relationships with government welfare programs, no matter how well intentioned or administered. The reasons for this are developed more thoroughly below and occupy a major portion of this book. Stated briefly, however, the large-scale dependency of the adult citizen on governments is always inherently pathological and always profoundly detrimental to his growth to maturity. The full development of occupational and social skills that enable an individual to provide the material security and interpersonal life that he needs for adult happiness is derailed by the infantilizing effects of liberal social policy.

In addition, and beyond their regressive consequences, these policies adversely affect social order by generating, among other negative conditions, various degrees of class conflict between the recipients of welfare benefits and the productive individuals whose assets are confiscated to support them. Examples of this type of conflict include ongoing disputes over the funding of welfare, Medicare and Social Security programs. Liberal government policy pits producers against non-producers, the well against the sick, the young, against the old, and one race against another as the liberal agenda's federal programs usurp the community's authority and preempt its resources for charitable assistance to its own poor, sick and elderly citizens through voluntary efforts. What is promoted as "compassionate" in these programs can be seen in reality to be divisive and destructive, as the politicians incite conflict with the propaganda of victim-hood, all the while alienating the citizens from their own community's resources and discouraging voluntary cooperation.

10

The Signs of Decline

A great civilization is not conquered from without until it has destroyed itself from within. The essential causes of Rome's decline lay in her people, her morals, her class struggle, her failing trade, her bureaucratic despotism, her stifling taxes, her consuming wars.

Will Durant

In the fall and sack of great cities an historian is condemned to repeat the tale of uniform calamity: the same effects must be produced by the same passions; and when those passions may be indulged without control, small, alas! is the difference between civilized and savage man.

Edward Gibbon

The Symptoms of Societal Disorder

Specific indications of madness in America are easily observed in overt signs and symptoms of progressive social disorganization, now well developed and badly in need of remedial measures. In his book, *When Nations Die*, J.N. Black describes the general indications of cultures in decline. He then observes the particular indications of disintegration in American economic, political, and social institutions which have historically predicted the demise of great nations:

- rise in lawlessness
- loss of economic discipline and self-restraint

- expansion of taxation, government bureaucracy and regulation
- decline of education
- weakening of cultural foundations and loss of respect for tradition
- increasing materialism and immorality
- devaluing of human life

All combine to undermine and disorganize the infrastructure of social cooperation. Black cites researchers Joad and Parkinson, who have included the following factors as key determinants in the downfalls of previously successful societies:
- Over-centralized government
- Inordinate growth in taxation
- A top-heavy system of administration
- The urge to overspend
- The effects of superstition and preoccupation with self
- The influence of popular attitudes on social policy over those grounded in sound moral and social judgment

Observing the clear indications in the United States of deterioration in all of these categories of economic, social and political functions, Black finds us confronted with "a level of social disintegration that exceeds anything we have ever experienced before in this nation." He cites Bennett's Index of Leading Cultural Indicators:

> "The index shows that the United States is at or near the top of all nations in the industrialized world in the rates of abortion, divorce and births to unwed mothers. We lead the industrialized world in murder, rape and violent crime. In elementary and secondary education, we are at or near the bottom in achievement scores."

Bennett himself notes that since 1960, annual spending on welfare (measured in 1990 dollars) soared from just under 144 billion to nearly 800 billion, and that more than one child in eight now receives a welfare check in America. He notes further that since 1960:
- Illegitimate births are 400% greater

- The number of children living in single parent homes has tripled
- Teenage suicides have tripled
- Violent crime has risen 500%

The consequences of welfare statism in the U.S. have been remarkable. As Bennett observes, welfare has not only failed in its economic purpose, it has also eroded the nation's character with an anti-family social policy in which, until the mid-1990's, a single mother had to meet two conditions to get her welfare check: 1. she must not work, and 2. she must not be married to an employed male. This arrangement, a classic example of the destructive effects of the liberal agenda, paid a woman to have children out of wedlock and discouraged her from creating and maintaining a two-parent nuclear family. The resulting increase in births of children who have no fathers and who are psychologically and socially aberrant is a major source of the rapidly developing American underclass phenomenon, already dreaded with good reason and ominous for the nation's future.

The signs and symptoms of American social disorder are published and broadcast every day in the media and can be observed in nearly every community in the country. The Kiplinger Letter, which tracks economic, social and political trends across the nation, observes the decline in the social well-being of American youth (and in the society at large) as part of a trend away from taking responsibility for actions and toward playing the victim, always blaming problems on someone or something outside of one's self. The Kiplinger editors write of the "breakdown in families, schools and communities (that) affects everyone, including business people, who need honest, responsible workers, and who understand that the future of this country lies in its youth." (Kiplinger 1995)

The Kiplinger editors cite cheating, violence and theft in schools, along with adolescent suicides and homicides, as signs of social breakdown. They note that out-of-wedlock births now account for about 30% of all newborns, more than two thirds of black childbirths and nearly a fourth of white childbirths. Illegitimate births are rising faster among middle class white teens, consistent with sociologist Charles Murray's fears that the growing white underclass represents another menacing social development in this country. (Murray 1984)

But no formal study is needed to establish the fact of social deterioration in the U.S. Business man James R. Cook observes it informally. He poignantly tells it as it is:

> You can see the blueprint for America's future in the littered inner cities, the stark and lifeless reservations, the junk strewn rural shacks and the gleaming towers of the social welfare bureaucracies and government agencies ... (in a nation) where self-indulgence, bizarre behavior, over-consumption, gambling, stimulants, narcotics, mindless entertainment, marginal integrity, and crime are commonplace. Everywhere you look in America there is dependency, financial excess, profligacy, intemperance, grossness, indolence, bad manners, arrogance and incivility. (Cook 1995a).

Cook indicts a social policy that encourages the role of victim as it embraces welfarism, redistribution, government paternalism, political correctness, socialist economics and a de-emphasis on merit. Commenting on the economic consequences of the liberal agenda, he notes "the shocking structural changes in the foundations of the U.S. economy, its low savings, over-consumption, dollar weakness, disastrous liquidity trends, trade deficits, high speculation and astronomical public and private debt." He writes:

> This is the age of excess: a nation of overweight citizens on a runaway consumption binge; a failing educational system; the dumbing down of youth; bizarre zombies in public places with orange hair and rings in their tongues; a staggering boom in fun, self-indulgence and entertainment; endless examples of bad taste and vulgarity; and shameless citizens sharing degrading personal revelations on TV. (Cook 1995b)

He continues:

> Along with these extremes, a plague of runaway crime. In today's cities, murders barely make the news. Nasty examples of theft such as shoplifting and stealing cars get no more punishment than a

traffic ticket. Drug violations are the common cold of a sick court system, and ten or fifteen drunk driving charges may get you a year in jail with nine months suspended. (Cook 1995b)

"The wealthiest nation in the world," says Cook, "has become the most dysfunctional."

Lest the reader think that these types of observations are only the biased ranting of reactionary conservatives, the late liberal luminary and U. S. Senator, Daniel Patrick Moynihan, wrote more than forty years ago that the rising rate of broken homes and illegitimacy in black families was undermining their community. While working for the Department of Labor he published a report that read in part:

> From the wild Irish slums of the nineteenth century eastern seaboard to the riot torn suburbs of Los Angeles, there is one unmistakable lesson in American history: a community that allows a large number of young men to grow up in broken families, dominated by women, never acquiring any stable relationship to male authority, never acquiring a set of rational expectations about the future—that community asks for and gets chaos. Crime, violence, unrest, disorder—most particularly the furious lashing out at the whole social structure—that is not only to be expected; it is very nearly inevitable. (Moynihan 1965).

Social Decay and the Family

It has been clear for many years that the breakdown of family stability in a population reflects on its general character, on its ability to rear children to competence, and on the nature and problems of its social pathology. A number of writers (e.g., Keyes 1995, Sowell 1995, Murray 1984, and Wilson 2002) have analyzed the deterioration of the family in America. Their findings are interesting, especially when viewed in the context of modern liberalism's increasing influence over the past hundred years. Keyes observed that in the late nineteenth and twentieth centuries, black families had remained largely intact despite the legacy of slavery, despite continuing economic, social and political prejudice, despite the social dislocations associated with migrations to large cities, and despite the growing secularism and welfarism of the succeeding decades. Sowell (1995) notes that between 1890 and 1950, among both blacks and whites, an *increase* occurred in the proportion of both men and women currently married. Between 1920 and 1960, he writes, "at least 60 % of all black males from age 15 on up were currently married" and "the difference between black and white males in this respect was never as great as 5 percentage points during this entire era." Keyes attributes this strength to strong black religious and moral traditions that were later undermined by modern liberal political movements.

In the decades since 1960, and coinciding with the accelerated influence of modern liberalism, the institutions of marriage and family, both black and white, have not fared so well. Sowell observes that by 1980 less than half of all black males in the 15-plus age brackets were married, and the gap between black and white males widened further by 1992. Predictably, black illegitimacy also increased rapidly over this period. So did illegitimacy in whites. By 1965, the black illegitimacy rate had climbed six-fold, from its 1930 level, to 25%. By 1993, the white illegitimacy rate had grown to 22% nationally, and by 1997, the overall rate was approximately 30%. Among blacks the rate in recent years has approximated 65%. The number of fatherless children has risen accordingly. In his book *Fatherless America*, Blankenhorn (1995) reported that 40% of U.S. children live without a father in the house and that more than half of American children can be expected to spend most of their childhood without a father. Indeed, the absence of parents in the home is emblematic of our welfare culture. Journalists in major American cities repeatedly document a typical welfare home scene: with parents largely absent or inattentive, the children do whatever they wish to each other or sit mindlessly in front of a television set watching programs on sex, crime and violence. Also apparent is the fact that poverty has tracked the breakdown of the family. It is now a cliché that the surest route to financial hardship is early single parenthood. These and other observations support the fact that modern liberalism's growing influence, especially since the sixties, has eroded the character of American culture, both black and white. This effect is purposeful, not accidental. Liberalism's fundamental values of personal permissiveness and institutional welfarism have perverted the ideal of individual liberty into an ethic of self-indulgence, replaced self-reliance with an ethic of government dependency, and promoted self-gratification over the traditional obligations of church and family. All of these influences have undermined the family as a social institution.

The Madness of American Government

The madness of American society is reflected in the madness of its liberal government policies. Whether in economic, social or political realms, the irrationality of the collectivist agenda is painfully evident. Its *economic* operations are strikingly irrational, since they routinely ignore the most elementary principles of business and financial management. Governments invariably spend more on social programs than they collect in revenues, then finance the shortfall by excessive borrowing, taxation or expansions of the money supply. Government borrowing in the credit markets increases the demand for money, raises interest rates, increases the cost of capital, and competes with private individuals and businesses that need funds to create new products, services and jobs. Government tax laws violate the property rights of all citizens, reduce their return on production and investment, reduce incomes to individuals and families, and raise the costs of goods and services to consumers. Government control of central banks expands credit and inflates money in circulation, debases the currency, increases the price of goods and services, and misallocates investment capital through its lending programs. Government subsidies to industry cause comparable distortions in markets at all levels.

During the late 1990s in America, when the enormous productivity of the information revolution expanded tax revenues over expenditures for the first time in several decades, the US Government made perfunctory gestures in paying down the national debt, but expenditures continued to rise as usual. The arrival of the twenty-first century has seen still greater expansions of federal programs under both Democratic and Republican governments, together with ostentatious pretensions to secure long-term funding for Medicare, Medicaid and Social Security. But these programs remain on track for bankruptcy within the next generation. The year 2001 saw Washington throw a few crumbs to the masses in the form of miniscule tax refunds and marginal tax rate reductions.

The record is no better in the realm of government *regulation*. Here especially, the massive intrusions of the politicians' will into the lives of the people encroach on fundamental freedoms. Nearly all such intrusions interfere with the rights of persons to make mutually consenting agreements and enjoy their benefits. Regulations discourage the start of new businesses, increase the risks and costs of expanding old ones, and burden all production and employment with massive paperwork obligations. In the regulatory domain, in particular, government is notorious for imposing waste and inefficiency, exercising political favoritism and capitulating to special interests for make-work, patronage and pork barrel projects, all the while burdening the common man with its bureaucratic arrogance and obstinacy, its graft, corruption and self-indulgence.

By these and many other violations of the rights of the people to be free of unnecessary intrusions into their lives, and to keep or trade what they produce and lawfully acquire, government always interferes massively in the lives of the people, inevitably defaults on its primary obligation to protect their rights, derails their efforts to cooperate peacefully, and ultimately reduces their ability to increase their material wealth. No rational person, family or company attempts to manage his or its economic affairs as governments do.

Government *social* policy has been only slightly less expansive and criminal, but no more rational, than its economic and regulatory policies. The Great Society programs of the sixties under the Johnson administration, the attempt to nationalize the U.S. healthcare system under the Clinton administration, and the "war on drugs" under several administrations, all exemplify the extraordinary arrogance, incompetence and grandiosity of government social engineering. These programs illustrate the madness of egalitarianism, protectionism and welfarism as the social engineers pass laws that ignore the individual's sovereignty, restrict his freedom of choice, invalidate his responsibility for himself, corrupt his morality, and invade his material assets through redistributive tax policies, all the while creating massive bureaucracies and the disastrous economic and social consequences of drug trafficking and welfare dependency.

These policies are painful illustrations of the liberal agenda's profound misunderstanding of what human nature and the human condition actually require of social policy in order to facilitate the pursuit of happiness. The agenda's primary misconceptions center around its projections of a childlike need for parental caretaking onto the general population, its delusions that the people need direction and support instead of protection of their persons and property, and its denial of the average citizen's competence to manage his affairs through voluntary efforts with others. All of these represent the liberal mind's misconception of the proper role of politics in the human enterprise. That proper role is to maintain a secure arena in which the human drama can be played out freely and responsibly by all of the people, not to create a grand theater in which government is the playwright, director and lead actor, with the people as "extras," or captive and paying audience.

The fact that many people will use government services or approve of them is not proof of their necessity or desirability. Government laws often prevent the use of competing services. In nearly all government programs, economic costs in the form of impaired production and higher prices, social costs from increased conflict and lower moral standards, and political costs as a result of diminished freedom and increased bureaucracy are typically misrepresented: downside risks are ignored or denied, and adverse consequences are covered up. In particular, the costs of government with respect to the citizen's growth to individual competence are unacceptably high by reason of its constant seduction of the people into childlike dependency.

Of course, government's own politics, its own use and abuse of influence, power and coercion, constantly add new chapters to the long history of reasons for the cynicism with which rational persons eventually come to view its operations. The news media recount each day the ongoing fraud, graft, embezzlement, collusion and violence of government officials at all levels. Luxurious office buildings and bloated office staffs reflect the politician's narcissism, the endless extravagance of government's own greedy materialism, its rationalizations of its salaries as brokers' fees for services to the "needy," its preaching of self-sacrifice to the taxpayers, and its reproach against them for not wanting to "give" more. But our government officials with their "perks" and plush offices are merely the modern analogues of historic monarchs with their lackeys and castles. Modern intellectuals serve them just as the priests of the past did, justifying government policy with the sophistry of collectivism.

The Political Inequality of the Liberal Agenda

In all of this, America illustrates a breakdown of the principles and ideals that safeguard order in any rational society. Given religion's historical role as an ultimate justification for and constant reminder of the rules of goodness in man's relations to himself and his world, it is probably no accident that this social breakdown has occurred along with a decline in traditional religious values. But religious justification, as critical as it is to society's moral foundations, is not the only basis for social order. An argument for rational laws governing human life and its communal organization is accessible through reason. In fact, as soon as the history of tyranny is understood, and as soon as the ideals of individual sovereignty and political equality are acknowledged, i.e., that no individual may be used against his will for the benefit of another, then the laws protecting person, property and contract follow logically.

But the modern liberal agenda shamelessly violates the ideals of sovereignty and political equality. If, for example, I become a government-entitled welfare recipient and you are a taxpayer, we are no longer political equals. The liberal politicians that I have voted for have passed laws that override your natural right to be let alone. Under these laws you no longer have a right to refuse my demands for your money. The state can now compel you to assume the burden of my welfare because I am now lawfully entitled to some portion of what used to belong to you alone. Empowered by the liberal agenda's "compassion" for my needs and desires, I am politically your superior: I can see to it that you do as I wish and not as you wish, regardless of your commitments to others or to yourself, and regardless of your sentiments, if any, toward me. To whatever extent the government permits, I am your master. The law now permits me, however indirectly, however deviously, to use you, exploit you and subjugate you for my purposes. Your protests will not prevent me from taking what I need from you because I am entitled to it under the liberal agenda. With the power of welfare and regulatory statutes behind me, I can intrude forcibly into your life in violation of your sovereign right to live in freedom and in violation of your right, if you so choose, to have nothing whatever to do with me. If you do not surrender to my demands, the government that takes care of me will punish you by imprisonment or fines or both. If you resist its punishment, the government will force you to comply. If you resist its force, it may have to injure or kill you as a lesson to others.

The Fraudulence of Government

For those not seduced by its sophistry, the liberal agenda's fallacies, failures and fraud have led to increasing distrust of government at all levels and a correct belief that the principles of freedom and responsibility on which America and its Constitution were constructed have been defiled. Having set itself above the law and moral accountability, liberal government steals the time, effort, assets, and lives of the people through taxation and graft. Having exempted itself from the disciplines of profit and loss in the marketplace, and accumulated a monstrous national debt now exceeding six trillion dollars, liberal government argues that it can spend the people's money more wisely than they can—and then proceeds to waste it.

Having demonstrated for decades that it cannot administer its own offices—witness the massive computer system failures of the IRS, the ludicrous costs of military defense programs, the economic debacle of Amtrak, the inefficiency and incompetence of the U. S. Post Office, the imminent bankruptcy and rampant fraud in Social Security, Medicare and welfare programs—liberal government meddles obsessively in the lives of the people by prescribing and regulating the food we eat, the chairs we sit in, the toys we play with and the cars we drive. Liberal government presumes to tell us what we can say to or ask of others, whom we can hire or fire, how we can configure our offices and buildings, what medications we can use, and from what foreign country we can make a purchase and at what price. With an incomparable record of flawed analysis, faulty solutions and destructive consequences, liberal government grandly proclaims itself indispensable and presumes to regulate and administer our lives from the business office to the bedroom. The inherent potential for madness in all human beings—our tendencies toward grandiosity, overestimation and extravagance; our impaired judgment, distortions of fact, misunderstanding of cause and effect and resistance to learning from experience; our lack of perspective and obsession with irrelevant details; our foolish goals, paranoid fears and irrational counter-aggression; our power-grabbing and criminality—all are writ large in the madness of liberal government. Its policies and operations are a study in the psychopathology and sociopathology of human nature.

11

Recap of Part I

The first ten chapters of this work have touched on a number of matters connected with human nature, individual liberty and the liberal agenda. Relying on the reader's intuitive understanding of relevant ideas, I have remarked on some broad implications of the biological and psychological nature of man as it manifests itself in the economic, social and political realms of human action. Here is a recap of some basic ideas.

1. In their abilities to choose and act independently, it is in the nature of competent human beings to run their own lives and pursue self-fulfillment through responsible self-direction. In these abilities the competent individual possesses the virtue of autonomy. In interacting with others voluntarily and within the constraints of adult conscience, the competent individual has the virtue of mutuality. The rational self-interest of the competent individual living his life as he chooses, and the rational social interest of a society committed to ordered liberty, are reconciled through social cooperation, i.e., the combined voluntary efforts of many persons pursuing shared goals for mutual benefit. In defiance of all this, the liberal agenda exploits the force of government to undermine liberty and virtue, violate the sovereignty of the individual, and preempt the natural inclinations of the people to cooperate.

2. As social animals, human beings are embedded in multiple relationships with others and are mutually interdependent with them. These social relationships serve needs for attachment and relatedness while facilitating economic production and exchange.

The economic, social and political arrangements of a society constitute the holding environment for human action.

3. An individual isolated on a desert island has complete freedom to do as he wishes. But if his actions encroach on the persons or property of others, then he does not have complete freedom to do as he wishes. To achieve his goals, his interaction with other persons in economic, social and political realms constantly confronts him with a choice: to cooperate by mutual agreement or dominate by force or fraud. But no valid argument justifies the domination of one man by another. This principle imposes a rational morality on all persons to limit their actions in certain ways. These limitations cannot rationally favor some persons over others, but must instead be universal: they must apply equally to all persons.

4. The ability to choose is inherent in the operation of the human psyche, appearing spontaneously and early in the child's behavior as a natural response to his environment. At every moment of waking life, and to the extent that he is able, the child engages the world with interest and curiosity, to explore it, understand it and act on it. These responses arise naturally as a result of the brain's processing of information from its surroundings. It has evolved to do this in order to survive. The act of choosing in this engagement process is innate, automatic and free, i.e., unimpeded, in the physically normal individual who is not ill with obsessions, compulsions, phobias, paranoid fears and other serious disorders of the mind.

5. A society's messages to its people about what matters, its attitudes and sentiments about what is right or just at every level of social interaction, must, in fact, influence the citizen's moral choices in economic, social and political arenas at any moment. If those messages honor the principles of rational individualism, the citizen's moral choices will be influenced by ideals of individual liberty, self-reliance, personal responsibility, voluntary cooperation, moral realism, and respect for the rights and sovereignty of the other. If, on the other hand, society's messages honor the liberal agenda's principles of coercive collectivism, then the citizen's moral choices will be influenced by ideals of group entitlement,

welfare dependency, state regulation, moral relativism, and the socialization of major categories of human action.

6. As practical moral agents, men agree to a fundamental social (moral) contract that says among other things: do not do to others what you do not want done to you. This moral principle is properly defined on the biological and psychological nature of man and the natural circumstances of human existence. The nature of man includes his vulnerability to suffering and death as well as his capacity for choice and moral responsibility. The circumstances of his existence include the material conditions of the earth and the fact that he must cooperate in production and exchange to live beyond a level of minimal subsistence. These considerations lead logically to certain moral and legal constraints on his actions.

7. From a state of complete helplessness at birth, the thrust of all human growth is the achievement of adult competence. At a minimum, this implies the ability to participate voluntarily in the general market, manage one's material affairs and meet ordinary needs for relatedness. The competent person assumes full responsibility for himself, respects the property rights of others and avoids intruding unnecessarily into their lives. He also responds with empathy and compassion toward others who are disabled, and where indicated, intervenes altruistically.

8. Morally and ethically competent individuals can establish by agreement and cooperative effort, and by appeal to the wisdom of history, all of the economic, social and political arrangements required for material and relational needs and the maintenance of social order. These arrangements include formal systems of law and judiciary required for limiting and punishing antisocial behavior in persons whose internal restraints are absent or dysfunctional. Also included are the community functions needed for the care and rehabilitation of disabled persons. The psychological foundations for these social arrangements, including the motivations to establish them, lie in behavior patterns acquired in early childhood. These give rise to learned capacities for the appropriate satisfaction, inhibition and delay of impulses and desires, especially those involving self-aggrandizement, dependency longings, and sexual, aggressive and acquisitive drives, and to learned capacities for compassionate actions for the benefit of others. These core

elements of conscience, ethical ideals and social responsiveness become the regulatory infrastructure for social order.

9. Developmental influences in childhood affect the behavior of adult citizens who create and implement the economic, social and political institutions of society. Conversely, the enduring institutions thus created affect the development of the child. In the course of this development, the child observes multiple modes of relating to the world of persons and things. His experience strongly affects his eventual capacity to provide for himself, assume responsibility for his life and well-being, cooperate with others, and solve the problems of living without appeal to government authority.

10. The child's early conceptions of human relationships determine his later readiness to live under certain economic, social and political arrangements. As an adult, these conceptions lead him to choose between competing economic, social and political systems: those characterized by strictly limited government, rigorous protections of property and contract rights, and maximum freedom of economic and social choice; or those with large and coercive governments which intervene extensively in the lives of citizens and strongly regulate economic and social processes. The choice for maximum freedom honors the sovereignty of human beings and their innate tendencies toward mutual cooperation. The choice for interventionist government sees the masses as helpless in the face of exploitation by powerful "capitalist" forces that control the major dynamics of society. This choice insists that big government is essential for the protection of the people in a world that is fundamentally unsafe for them.

11. The egalitarianism and welfarism of modern liberal government are incompatible with the facts of human nature and the human condition. But the rise to power of the liberal agenda has resulted from the fact that the people of western societies have irrationally demanded that governments take care of them and manage their lives instead of protecting their property rights. This misconception results in massive violations of those rights while permitting government officials to act out their own and their constituents' psychopathology. The liberal agenda gratifies various types of pathological dependency; augments primitive

feelings of envy and inferiority; reinforces paranoid perceptions of victimization; implements manic delusions of grandeur; exploits government authority for power, domination and revenge; and satisfies infantile claims to entitlement, indulgence and compensation.

12. Under the liberal agenda, governments at all levels have assumed control over economic, social and political functions previously entrusted to individuals or groups at community levels. Modern liberalism's socialization of these functions has altered the climate of personal growth and development in our society. This has led to increasing numbers of citizens who become and remain pathologically dependent on the state, childlike in their submission to its authority, and stunted in their character development. The spread of collectivist values has undermined the integrity of economic and social processes; disrupted community identity, cohesion and support; disorganized family structure and function; and vastly increased governmental intrusions into the lives of citizens.

13. Liberal government consistently arrogates to itself the status of guardian over able and sovereign citizens, then dominates and exploits them through its regulations and taxes despite the fact that the people have not been adjudicated incompetent. Liberal government invades the freedom of the people to cooperate while it denies individual agency and autonomy. No one in a truly free society is born into the world with a legally enforceable obligation to take care of other persons, especially persons whom he has never met. That obligation is the antithesis of freedom. The genuinely free and morally responsible libertarian society honors the sovereignty of each citizen by forbidding anyone to indenture his time, effort, assets and abilities. This protection is among the most fundamental expressions of property rights. It is the necessary foundation for individual liberty.

14. All forms of the liberal agenda interfere with the rational relationship between human action and the conditions of life by disconnecting outcomes from adaptive behavior. All welfare programs divorce an individual's material security and emotional well-being from his economic and social connections to his community and replace them with a marriage to government

officials. The liberal agenda's takeover of countless individual and community functions, from education to the care of the elderly, has had the effect of alienating the individual from his community and robbing both of their essential mutuality.

These ideas represent the major thrust of the first ten chapters of this book. They and other ideas are developed further in Parts II through IV.

PART II

Preface To Part II

Part II of *The Liberal Mind* examines more closely the relationship between personality and the rules that govern social process. Because psychological concepts figure prominently in this analysis, their scientific status is reviewed in some detail. Two conclusions follow from this review: first, that explanation in the psychological sciences is a systematic extension of the mind's ordinary capacity for observation and inference in everyday life, and second, that conclusions reached by this process may constitute legitimate knowledge provided they are verified by methods that separate genuine understanding from mere folklore.

The discussion then turns to early childhood development with emphasis on the role of such psychobiological drives as sexuality, aggression, acquisitiveness and narcissism as givens in human nature, and on the role of the child's early attachments in determining his later behavior. Special attention is given to the significance of pathological dependency. Subsequent chapters contain a more explicit discussion of certain dichotomies of development, leaning heavily on the ideas of Erik Erikson and expanding on their significance for social process. The analysis then returns to earlier ideas of maturity and relates them to a particular example of modern personality theory, that of Cloninger and Svrakic. Underlying this analysis is an assumption that psychological explanation is only as good as the factual and logical foundations on which it rests.

These efforts are intended to strengthen the argument that human personality development is reciprocally related to social institutions in ways that profoundly affect individual liberty and social order. It becomes apparent, again, that under appropriate child rearing conditions, certain innate behavioral dispositions emerge in normal human development that support individual liberty and voluntary social order. It becomes equally apparent that the modern liberal agenda systematically undermines these dispositions.

12

The Scientific Status of Behavioral Descriptions

The whole of science is nothing more than the refinement of everyday thinking.

Albert Einstein.

Hard and Soft Science

Psychological theories have often been criticized as "soft science" on the grounds that they are not "objective." They are said instead to be "subjective" because they depend, to an important extent, on introspective reports about conscious states of mind. Psychology has been compared unfavorably with the "hard sciences," such as physics and chemistry, which are said, by contrast, to be more rigorous and quantitative. Although this is not the place for a thorough debate on the matter of comparative rigor among the sciences, a few remarks on the truth value of psychological theories are in order before elaborating further on a theory of psychology and social process.

First, psychology is scientific to the extent that it attempts to make sense of certain kinds of observable phenomena and is self-critical in the process. To "make sense" in this case means to arrive at certain inferences about the nature and causes of psychological events. Inferences of this type must be logically related to observable facts, must be grounded in observations that can be verified by the scientific community, and must be capable in principle of being refuted by some logical or empirical means.

Second, it is routine that human beings make useful observations and inferences about psychological phenomena in everyday life. We notice *what* people say and do, and we draw at least tentative conclusions about the meanings of their words and deeds. We also notice *how*, or in what manner, people say and do things and, again, attribute at least tentative meanings to those observations. With the opportunity to observe a given individual over time, we notice that he repeats certain types of behavior in various situations. Based on those observations, we may draw some conclusions about his "nature" or "character." Knowledge of certain influences during his "formative years" may allow us to explain to ourselves—and perhaps to him—some reasons why he thinks and behaves as he does. Not only do human beings ordinarily engage in this type of thinking about particular individuals, we also make similar observations and inferences about large groups of persons.

Third, it is important to note that what distinguishes the professional scientist from the lay person in these pursuits are refinements of logic, method and quantification, not some mental mechanism unique to scientists. The disciplined researcher uses the same cognitive apparatus as the man on the street. The differences in applying that apparatus lie in the fact that the scientist's methods of observation and analysis are much more systematic than those of the lay person, and they are more self-consciously intended to eliminate error. The scientist is especially concerned about whether his impressions are reasonable and consistent and whether others have made similar observations and arrived at similar impressions. Here it is worth noting again that our own inclinations to compare impressions with others in the course of casual inquiry and the scientist's mandate to do so in formal research investigations point to the fact that coming to know things reliably about our world is, ultimately, a cooperative process.

The present work intends to proceed along similar lines: that is, to understand the relationship between human psychology and social process by staying close to observable human behavior, drawing what inferences are reasonable from what people can tell about their subjective experience, and submitting the results to formal and informal scrutiny. It is obvious, of course, that in this endeavor the quantitative methods of physics do not apply. But that fact does not remove such efforts from the realm of scientific inquiry nor preclude the acquisition of real knowledge on which to construct a bona fide science of man. Though different in their domains of inquiry and in their methods, the sciences are unified in respect to their systematic, self-critical search for verifiable truth.

A final comment on the affiliation of scientific inquiry with other forms of knowing observes that the systematic search for truth is characteristic of the sciences but not limited to them. Decisions in the business world, for example, typically rely on verifiable facts about supply, demand, price levels, interest rates, marketing demographics, delivery costs, market share and the like. Similarly, decision making in the practice of law is heavily dependent upon whether certain facts can be verified and whether they will count as evidence in a courtroom. Making observations and drawing conclusions are natural activities for human beings. Moreover, these activities readily lend themselves to the study of human behavior in all its forms.

Inference in Human Behavior

Psychology and related disciplines of social psychology, anthropology, economics and political science all attempt to make sense of the ways in which human beings act and to ground general propositions about human nature and human action in relevant facts. Of special interest is the fact that the behavioral sciences, like all others, distinguish themselves from non-scientific belief systems by attempting to prove their own assertions wrong. This commitment to self-correction, the supreme virtue of science, has arisen from its origins in western philosophy—its origins, literally, in the love of knowing. Indeed, it is only the self-critical search for truth for its own sake, as opposed to the manipulation of belief for other reasons, especially political reasons, that counts as authentic science. The purpose of these remarks is to anticipate criticism that the propositions set forth in this book about human nature, the human condition and modern liberalism are invalid because they are the product of mere speculation and do not have the character of factual statements about real phenomena. Liberals have argued, for example, that there is no such thing as human nature; that therefore no valid inferences can be drawn about human nature; that human nature, if it exists, is almost infinitely malleable and can flourish under liberal social policy; and that, in any case, there can be no valid objections to the liberal agenda based on psychological theories or facts, especially those that relate to the individual's participation in social process. These objections rely on assertions that the science of psychology cannot be used to critique the liberal agenda.

Of course, the modern liberal rejects any arguments on any grounds that might contradict his primary political purpose, which is the maximum socialization of society's major functions. His indifference to psychological facts that contradict that purpose is certainly to be expected. In particular, his assertion that there can be no factual basis in human nature or the human condition for objecting to his agenda leaves him free of any rational constraints that might oppose his programs for regulating the masses by means of government coercion. In his denial of certain realities, he can fervently recommend for political purposes what will not work for factual reasons and should not be attempted for moral reasons. He will then further deny that any adverse consequences will follow.

But if the modern liberal rejects the propositions in this book on methodological grounds, he must also discredit the same methods, those of careful observation and logical analysis, by which we and he gain real knowledge about everything else. If he does this, he ends up preaching epistemological nihilism. Indeed, the liberal's resistance to a valid science of human behavior and its relationship to social process explains his vigorous embrace of relativism and deconstructionism. Both of these philosophies blur distinctions between arbitrary fantasy and verifiable reality by asserting that anything may work and nothing can be objectively or morally certain. Most importantly, the liberal mind continues to ignore the fact that our accumulated understanding of human psychology thoroughly contradicts his perverse overestimation of the socialist state and his refusal to recognize individual liberty as the only valid *primary* political ideal consistent with the realities of human existence. In this denial, the liberal agenda puts human freedom and social order in constant jeopardy.

13

Challenges of Development

If the intrinsic properties of personality become the object of inquiry, then consciousness and freedom, their different modalities, their role in the overall functioning and their importance to the individual, will also become manifest.

Augusto Blasi

Personality and Society

The following chapters explore certain disruptions in the child's growth to adulthood and the effects they have on his achievement of competence. In fortunate individuals, such disruptions do only minor damage to the personality, but in many cases the damage is severe and in some it is catastrophic. When such developmental failures occur, they can often be traced to deprivation, neglect or abuse in various phases of childhood. Serious depression, loss of self-esteem, faulty judgment, impaired autonomy, or the emergence of paranoia may be the painful legacy of those failures. In the psychopathology of everyday life, hatred may overwhelm love, narcissism may erase mutuality, temptation may corrupt character, demandingness may override consent, and despair may trigger dangerous gambles to relieve torment.

Distortions of these types affect human action in matters ranging from mundane to monumental. Beyond the individual and family tragedies that play out in such dramas, the central question in a larger social context is whether a *society's* child rearing practices can limit the emergence of undue destructiveness in its citizens and, at the same time, inspire them to appreciate individual liberty as the highest political good. Those tasks require the citizen to embrace the responsibilities and risks on which freedom depends and to honor moral virtue as the primary safeguard against the dangers of primitive impulses.

The complexity of human development has everything to do with the transformations that occur between the child's initial state of helplessness and his ultimate ability to cope with adult life. In his march to adulthood, changes in the child's functional capacities (cognitive, emotive, behavioral and relational) in multiple domains (economic, social and political) provide countless opportunities for coordination or conflict, success or failure. It is possible to analyze certain elements of that process and explore their implications for the achievement of adult competence. The central question just posed can be set out in more detail:

- What developmental functions are institutionalized in the economic, social, and political arrangements of a society? What laws, rules, customs, and social policy have emerged in response to the multiple desires and needs that characterize human nature? How do these arrangements meet human needs for food, clothing, shelter, health care, education, transportation, police and judicial services, protection and defense functions, environmental management, etc., and how do they accommodate the countless rituals of social, religious, and family interactions that characterize communal life?

- What are the effects on the child's growth to competence of the institutions that characterize the liberal agenda, as opposed to the institutions that characterize a lawful and virtuous libertarian society? Do the rules of society enable persons to meet the challenges of adult life, or on the contrary, do they interfere with that endeavor and even make success impossible?

An effort to answer these questions begins by first considering some fundamental aspects of human nature and the human condition.

Drives, Instincts and the Tasks of Living

Human nature and the conditions of human life require a person to relate to himself, to other persons and to his physical world, all within certain limitations. He must relate to his own biological nature by providing the material means of physical survival. He must relate to his own psychological nature by meeting the conditions for mental and emotional well-being. He must relate to others by means of similar accommodations to their biological and psychological natures. He must relate to his material world by accommodating the physical laws that govern the use of land, air, water and the myriad objects of human invention. Failure to accommodate these realities has consequences that range from trivial to catastrophic. The biological and psychological nature of man imposes certain limitations on what he can reasonably do. These limitations set boundary conditions on behaviors that allow for cooperation while permitting individual freedom.

The Integration of Drives and Needs

In the course of his development, the child acquires ideas about his world that determine how he confronts the tasks of living as an adult. At a fundamental level, those ideas determine whether he attempts to dominate a world he views as threatening, or to cooperate in a world he sees as benign, to cite only two of countless possibilities. Our modes of coping are laid down in the earliest years of development. In the process, certain innate needs and drives must be incorporated into fundamental behavior patterns. The most familiar of these are the instincts for self-preservation, sexual satisfaction and aggressive behavior. But dependency and relational needs, nurturing impulses, acquisitive impulses and narcissistic needs also affect human motivation with equal urgency, and they may well dominate all other factors in determining particular instances of human behavior. The nature of these forces and their ordinary expressions in the course of development are described in detail below. The manner in which they are integrated into an individual's repertoire of behaviors determines whether his actions are adaptive or destructive to himself and the human enterprise.

The power of these forces to motivate human behavior for good or evil purposes cannot be overestimated. From personal experience, all of us are familiar with intense sexual impulses as early as adolescence, and all of us are likewise familiar with rage in response to injustice. Depth psychology typically understands self-preservation, sexual appetite and aggression as primitive instinctual drives in the most elemental sense of the term. The extraordinary force of these drives is related to their original biological functions in reproduction and in defense against rivals and predators. Depending on how they are channeled, any of them may act as a force of nature, generating actions that range from noble heroism to unthinkable atrocity. But dependency, nurturing, relational, acquisitive and narcissistic needs are equally primitive and can be equally compelling—for better or worse. To get a clearer perspective on this matter, we turn now to a review of functions mediated by the most primitive portions of our brains.

The Lizard Brain

Evolution has generated in human beings a brain of much greater complexity than those of lesser animals. This result puts at our disposal an almost unlimited range of higher functions, but still preserves primitive impulses associated with feeding, defending, reproducing and nurturing. These latter functions first emerged in the brains of reptiles, and it is no coincidence that neuroscientists refer to certain portions of the human brain by the term "reptilian" in order to emphasize a number of structural and functional similarities between us and our lizard-like ancestors. It should not be a surprise that the actions of men and reptiles, at least at a very basic level, are remarkably similar.

Imagine a lizard as he encounters another object. The object may be another lizard, an insect, a larger animal that likes to eat lizards, etc.—the possibilities are, of course, many and varied. How does the lizard respond to what he encounters? His brain provides him with certain behavioral options basic to lizards. Depending on what object is before him, the lizard may eat it, attack it, flee from it, protect it, get food for it, mate with it or ignore it. His primitive drives involving sexual, aggressive, nurturing, territorial, and other impulses energize his behavior in various situations. His responses are essentially self-preservative and reproductive, and they are wired into his reptilian brain.

But comparably primitive responses are also wired into human brains. When a human being encounters another object, he also, like the lizard, has the primitive options to eat it, attack it, flee from it, protect it, get food for it, mate with it or ignore it. These responses remain potent in human beings: they are the original reptilian sexual, aggressive, nurturing, territorial, protective and defensive behaviors that serve basic life functions. When well regulated and well integrated, they energize human behavior adaptively: primitive nurturing and protective impulses, for example, energize reproductive and child rearing behaviors; primitive aggressive, defensive and territorial impulses energize resistance against enemies; primitive attachment and dependency impulses energize cooperative activity at all levels.

When primitive impulses are *not* well regulated or integrated into adaptive behaviors, however, they may have profoundly destructive effects. The most obvious examples occur in those actions motivated by frankly criminal intent: pathological combinations of aggressive and sexual drives, for example, when coupled with defects in conscience, lead to crimes of rape and lust-murder. Pathological combinations of aggressive and acquisitive drives, when coupled with defects in conscience, lead to crimes such as theft, robbery, embezzlement, fraud and larceny. Pathological dependency combined with unrestrained acquisitive impulses creates the con man who exploits public programs to gain unearned compensation, free medical care, subsidized housing and the like.

But we need not look at such extreme examples to see the enduring effects of the lizard brain. Primitive dispositions and their derivative behaviors can easily influence all human activities, including all economic, social and political processes, drastically altering individual motives in complex situations. Indeed, in the human brain, the array of primitive dispositions expands from basic sexual, aggressive, dependent, nurturing and acquisitive impulses to include intense drives to power, domination, competition and ego-enhancing goals that affect everyday life. In economic and social settings, for instance, neurotic and even psychotic drives to dominate, defeat, depend on and exploit others often compel disturbed personalities to act destructively. In political arenas, neurotic individuals falsely believe they are victimized, seek control over others for material security, exploit subordinates for sexual favors, or seek office for self-aggrandizement. In international politics, pathological narcissism, aggression and acquisitiveness in various combinations generate dictators who exploit entire countries for personal gain.

Whatever the arena, the effects of primitive processes, including emotions such as fear, hatred, jealousy, envy and humiliation are common at conscious and unconscious levels in all persons who act in ways destructive to themselves and others. The aggregate effects of these processes depend on the manner in which they are integrated into behavior patterns in particular individuals, and on how a given society's institutions set limits on certain behaviors. The effects are not trivial. The most destructive men in history, the Hitlers, Stalins, Husseins and Pol Pots of the world, have been driven by motives both primitive and deviant: sexual, aggressive, dependent, self-preservative, acquisitive and narcissistic impulses unrestrained by the normal prohibitions of conscience and acted out in societies whose institutions were inadequate to prevent their crimes. The power of these processes derives in part from the fact that they evolved originally to preserve life against the most lethal dangers and in part from the fact that they typically combine to reinforce each other. In combination with other drives, the power of any one primitive disposition in motivating human action is augmented to a degree far beyond what would otherwise be expected. For these reasons, it is critical that the human developmental process generate benevolent forces in the child's personality: those positive attitudes, sentiments, constraints and virtues that oppose the expression of destructive tendencies. Only then can evil be limited.

14

The Dichotomies of Development

Our claim is, rather, that the very properties of concepts are created as a result of the way the brain and body are structured and the way they function in interpersonal relations and in the physical world.

George Lakoff and Mark Johnson

The Goals of Parenting

At this point it will be useful to review certain functional capacities that must be acquired by the child in preparation for adulthood. Capacities for economic production, social cooperation, personal intimacy and moral behavior, to note a few, are acquired in varying degrees by nearly all persons. Among other ideals, reasonable parents in western cultures want their children to become economically self-sufficient adults with marketable occupational skills, not recipients of private charity or government subsidy. Reasonable parents also want their children to become socially competent adults, able to enjoy constructive relationships and capable of the intimacy and cooperation needed for marriage and the rearing of children. They do not want their children to become reclusive, antisocial or otherwise marginal adults lacking positive connections to other human beings.

The individualistic ideals of western societies are consistent with these parental goals. They value initiative instead of inhibition, autonomy instead of dependency, industry instead of passivity, honesty instead of dishonesty, productivity instead of parasitism, forthrightness instead of fraud, mutual consent instead of coercion, altruism instead of exploitation. These and other ideals reflect an intuitively correct understanding of what is required for individuals and societies to flourish. Careful examination reveals that the liberal agenda undermines these and other ideals of normal development, substitutes maladaptive ideals of dependency and manipulation, incites class warfare, invites competent adults to regress in the service of the state, and threatens the cohesion of society by its use of coercion. It does all of this by an ongoing campaign of propaganda that misrepresents human nature and the conditions of viable human relatedness. Illustrations of these effects can be found throughout this book.

Functional Dynamisms and Dispositions

Over the course of his development, the individual's countless experiences in relating to others are organized into complex patterns of thinking, feeling, behaving and relating. These patterns serve the pursuit of satisfaction, defend against painful emotional states, define personal identity, and assist in meeting the challenges of adult life. These adaptive–or maladaptive—patterns are known as functional *tendencies, dispositions or dynamisms.* The latter term, after Sullivan, underlines their organic and goal directed nature: they are enduring patterns of coping and defending that are readily observable in individuals acting over time. The largest of these dynamisms is the personality itself: an overarching aggregate of processes that attempts to integrate all aspects of the individual and his experience for adaptive purposes. All dynamisms evolve over the course of childhood, then tend to stabilize in later years. If they are grounded in early childhood they are likely to resist change later; they tend to become permanent personality traits. A few examples of such dispositions, together with their dysfunctional counterparts, were noted in Part I. They are repeated now in order to reintroduce some relevant ideas and to orient the reader more generally to what lies ahead. The developing child may acquire, for example:

- A disposition to active optimism: energetic initiative based on expectations that life will go well as a result of one's persistent efforts, as opposed to inhibited initiative based on fears that inherent inferiority will lead to failure or that retaliation will punish success.

- A disposition to autonomous self-direction: a firm sense of self-worth and freedom to direct one's life, as opposed to a guarded submissiveness based on a fearful conviction that one's life is unavoidably controlled by powerful and exploitative others.

- A disposition to confident self-reliance and self-responsibility coupled with adequate social skills for economic and social cooperation with others, as opposed to an enduring pattern of helplessness, neediness and pathological dependency as a fundamental mode of living.

- A disposition to mature mutuality: an authentic concern for other persons based on empathy, identification and compassion toward all human beings, especially those who are disadvantaged, as opposed to an ostentatious but false concern for others that masks essentially predatory efforts to manipulate, dominate and exploit others.

These are only four examples among an almost infinite variety of functional dispositions that can develop in an individual by the time he reaches adulthood. They are presented here as rough dichotomies in order to highlight the contrast between adaptive and maladaptive patterns of behavior. Comprehending human behavior in this manner was first elaborated by Erik Erikson in various writings, beginning with *Childhood and Society* in 1950. In that work he described eight phases of development over the human lifespan. Stated in his original dichotomies, they are:

1. Basic trust versus basic mistrust
2. Autonomy versus shame and doubt
3. Initiative versus guilt
4. Industry versus inferiority
5. Identity versus identity diffusion
6. Intimacy versus isolation
7. Generativity versus stagnation
8. Integrity versus despair

The first term of each dichotomy represents a developmental task: a functional capacity to be acquired in preparation for adult living. The second term represents a developmental failure: a dysfunctional outcome with potentially grave consequences for the quality of one's life. Explored below are the functional and dysfunctional implications of each pole of these and several other dichotomies of development, beginning with that of basic trust. Their relationship to society's economic, social and political institutions are then reviewed in some detail. Prior to that undertaking, however, some introductory remarks will point out the general relevance of these concepts.

Dichotomies and Development

Erikson's dichotomies of development—trust vs. mistrust, autonomy vs. shame and doubt, etc.—incorporate fundamental attitudes toward one's self and others. The developmental outcome of a particular dichotomy is never a pure expression of either pole but is instead a net tendency arising from their interplay. That is, between the poles of each dichotomy are continuums representing the extent to which a given individual tends toward one disposition or another: toward trust or mistrust, toward autonomous action or shameful self-effacement, toward constructive initiative or guilty inhibition, toward industrious effort or immobilizing feelings of inferiority, and so on. In addition, Erikson's several dichotomies may combine with many others to produce the complex structure of attitudes, dispositions and dynamisms that make up the adult personality. These dispositions strongly influence the manner in which persons participate in the economic, social and political arrangements of society.

My debt to Erikson's concepts will be obvious to the reader familiar with his work. His influence will be especially evident in discussions of how developmental dichotomies relate to society's institutions. But there is, of course, nothing sacred about the use of dichotomies in understanding human nature. Erikson's list and those added in this book are employed here because they are useful conceptual tools, not because human behavior exists only in pairs of polar opposites. Matters are clearly much more complicated than that. The achievement of autonomy, to note just one example, may be aborted in favor of not just one but several dysfunctional outcomes that defend against shame and doubt. Instead of healthy autonomy, a child may develop predominantly rebellious and defiant, or passive-aggressive, or obsessive-compulsive traits on his way to adulthood; or he may develop some combination of these and other dispositions. As will become clear below, each developmental task—trust, autonomy, initiative, industry, etc.—is associated with many other processes that shape personality for adult life. The complexity of human nature cannot be denied, nor can it be condensed into a single conceptual framework.

In Further Defense of Dichotomies

It is worth noting at this point that the use of dichotomies in scientific and philosophical discourse has been criticized by certain postmodern scholars as arbitrary and misleading, especially by those identified with deconstructionism and feminist critiques of western thought. Critics cite elementary polar opposites— love and hate, life and death, good and evil, etc.,—as examples of "binary" thinking. They hold that such narrowly conceived categories improperly permit arguments in favor of what is already desired based simply on prejudice and on culturally conditioned assumptions. They assert, in addition, that the underlying goals in the use of such dichotomies as good and evil, or right and wrong, are not really bona fide efforts to seek truth but only devious efforts to gain economic, social, and political power and establish male dominance. Furthermore, the critics say, the whole idea of "objective truth" is highly suspect in its own right. The best we can really do in our efforts to learn about the world, they claim, is to reach a social "solidarity" about how we think things might be, a kind of community consensus or sharing of useful myths but not a legitimate convergence on anything that approaches epistemological certainty.

This is not the forum in which to debate the matter at length, but a few words from the point of view of biology and cognitive science may provide some perspective on these criticisms. Lakoff and Johnson most recently, and others before them, have set out an elegant argument for human cognition as an evolved mechanism for processing certain kinds of information basic to survival of the species. Our physically embodied minds must, first and foremost, comprehend the real three-dimensional space and one-dimensional time continuum in which we live as biological organisms. To that end, we have to relate to such fundamental spatial categories as up and down, left and right, back and forth, inner and outer, and the like, and to such fundamental time dimensions as past and present, sooner and later, before and after. Brains that originally evolved to process this type of information about the inanimate physical world later evolved to process other types of information about the world of living things. Higher animals learned to discriminate between things nourishing or toxic, things dead or alive, things protective or threatening, and things of one's own kind or a different kind.

The mammalian brain thus evolved mechanisms to conceptualize the world in dichotomous terms, because much of the world it had to comprehend presented itself in such contrasts. Our human brains have adapted these mechanisms still further in order to reason about aspects of the world that are not so concrete as up and down, left and right, or now and later, but which still have polar characteristics. Building on the cognitive abilities of our ancestors, we have learned to reason about more abstract matters by means of metaphors built on elementary concepts of space, time, material realities and bodily processes. Through our more complex brains, the primitive mechanisms that comprehend these realities have given rise to metaphorical conceptions that help us to understand more abstract ideas. Thus we speak of ideals that are high or low, goals that are lofty or base. We speak of moving up in the world or falling down into bad times. We grasp or fail to grasp concepts with our intellects instead of our hands, nourish or poison our minds with ideas instead of food, cultivate or reject our friends, elevate or lower our morals, digest information, devour facts, expel wrong doers, give birth to new communities, penetrate mysteries, crush our opponents, embrace principles, and on and on. Crude dichotomies about space, time and material realities become the bases for metaphors on less tangible processes. Eventually human minds invented ways of thinking about psychological events and about economic, social and political processes.

With these observations in mind it is not a very drastic climb up the scale of abstractions to move from talk about inanimate spacio-temporal dimensions, such as up and down or past and present, to biological talk about birth and death or sickness and health. From these physical conceptions it is only another short step to ideas about how human beings naturally relate to each other. With a few more steps in the evolution of thought, purely psychological constructs, such as trust and mistrust or dependence and independence, emerge in the realm of human ideas. Thus the physical worlds of our senses and bodies, the psychosocial worlds of our personal experience, and the myriad processes of development from childhood to adulthood can all be usefully described in terms of metaphor, polarities and continuums. Thinking in such terms is an important cognitive method of processing information about our world and our selves. Our minds function like that because our brains have evolved that way.

Accordingly, my use of dichotomies in this book is an earnest effort to understand the human condition, not a manipulation of language for sinister purposes. Thinking about human nature and its development with the help of dichotomies is, in fact, a rather elementary application of innate reasoning mechanisms to mental and physical phenomena that happen to be understandable in terms of polarities and continuums. Of course, some critics, notably the deconstructionists, will argue that *any* reasoned defense of modern philosophical and scientific methods of seeking truth is just another example of word manipulation. But then all rational discourse ceases on that argument. In fact, if deconstructionism is applied to itself, the ultimate emptiness of its doctrines becomes obvious. Persons with inquiring minds can then return to a more important task, that of making sense of the world, wherever that may lead.

The Relevance of Dichotomies

As a final note on the matter of developmental dichotomies, an argument that is quite elementary can be made for the mundane reality of such dispositions as basic trust, autonomy, initiative, industry, identity, intimacy, generativity and integrity. It depends on the simple fact that in everyday life we usefully describe persons in terms of dispositions, dynamisms and dichotomies. We observe, for example, that some persons are predictably *trusting* in relationships; others are suspicious and mistrusting. Some persons consistently act *autonomously*, while others need a great deal of encouragement, support or direction. Some persons readily show *initiative,* while others remain passive. Some typically work *industriously,* while others remain idle.

In respect to the dynamism of *identity,* one can observe persons who seem to sustain definite perceptions of themselves: they have clear ideas of who they are, what they hold dear, what they want to do with their lives, and how they can live comfortably. Others, by contrast, relate only superficially, even vaguely, to themselves and their neighbors. They seem shallow and lacking in values beyond the whims of the moment. They tend to drift passively through life without much purpose. A definable identity is difficult to discern in these persons.

Again, with enough information about a given individual's adult life, it is usually possible to determine whether he has developed a capacity for emotional and physical *intimacy* with others, or whether he remains isolated and estranged from them. By middle age, typically, one can also determine whether a person has reached the stage of *generativity* in his development—a capacity for caring about and parenting either his own off-spring literally, or some portion of his community figuratively—or whether he has instead remained pathologically self-absorbed, stagnant in a world of his own and indifferent to the world at large.

Once established in adulthood, these patterns strongly resist change. They tend to remain typical of a given individual over long periods. They are often called *characterological* responses in order to emphasize their entrenched nature and their tendency to appear repeatedly in diverse situations over time. Their expressions in everyday life are notably persistent even when they repeatedly cause problems.

Finally, with sufficient inquiry, it is possible to observe among elderly persons whether a given individual has achieved a sense of *integrity* in his life: an enduring conviction that he has lived life well enough considering what was given to him, or whether, on the other hand, he has come to believe that his life has been tragically flawed, that he has failed himself or others, or that others have, in some fundamental way, failed him.

With concepts of this type it is possible to characterize the psychosocial dimensions of human nature, sometimes in ordinary language and sometimes in the technical jargon of the social scientist. These characterizations are grounded in facts that can be verified by other competent observers. When systematically developed, they constitute reputable scientific knowledge about human behavior and the dispositions that define it. Moreover, these characterizations can be usefully related to the economic, social and political arrangements that guide our lives.

15

Child Development
and Social Process

My opinion is that the future good or bad conduct of a child depends entirely upon the mother.

Napoleon I

Human Nature and Freedom

Chapter 12 of this book began with remarks on the scientific status of behavioral explanations, then reviewed certain biological characteristics of human nature that must be taken into account when trying to understand personality and its relationship to social institutions. The instinct for self-preservation and the sexual and aggressive drives were acknowledged as fundamental to any conception of human nature, but the power of other dispositions, especially those related to attachment, nurturing, narcissism, acquisitiveness and dependency was recognized as well. The preceding chapter suggested that the material, relational and developmental worlds of human experience can be understood in terms of metaphor, polarities and continuums. The developmental dichotomies of Erikson are particular examples of this kind of thinking: his conceptions of basic trust, autonomy, initiative, industry, identity, intimacy, generativity and integrity are obviously polar continuums. Finally, the discussion so far has noted in a general way that the child's early relationships to his caretakers determine the manner in which his biological drives are integrated into psychological dispositions: that is, into patterns of thinking, feeling, behaving and relating that characterize his particular development and the unique self that emerges from it.

With these ideas in mind the focus turns now to a review of the child's early relationships and his most basic interactions with caretakers. These interactions concern his developing self, the significant others that frequently relate to him (especially his mother in the earliest years), and the larger world to which he has increasing access by virtue of rapidly expanding abilities. The goal here is to characterize certain processes in the child's development and relate them to his eventual capacity to meet the challenges of adult living.

Of particular interest is the manner in which behavior patterns acquired throughout childhood affect an individual's later encounter with society's rules for living. Common experience suggests that with normal intellectual endowment at birth, the natural result of good enough caretaking in childhood is an adult individual who seeks economic, social and political freedom for self-fulfillment and who cooperates voluntarily with others in order to maintain social harmony. This outcome results from the positive influence of adequate nurturing on the wired-in social instincts of human beings. Evolution has programmed the human brain to facilitate social relatedness for survival and reproductive purposes. That program includes innate tendencies toward attachment, trust, affiliation, empathy, sympathy, compassion, altruism and other forms of social cooperation that emerge spontaneously when individuals live in community. *Common experience suggests further that the natural result of good enough care taking is not an adult individual who seeks government control over his own economic, social and political activities, or government limits on his ability to make voluntary, informed and mutually consenting agreements with others. Nor is the natural result of good enough care taking a government owned taxpayer who approves the confiscation of his assets and their anonymous transfer to beneficiaries of the government's choice even if it is rationalized by misleading labels of "compassion" and "altruism."*

In any case, there can be no reasonable doubt that human beings do in fact acquire certain capacities for trust or mistrust, autonomy or shame and doubt, initiative or guilt, industry or inferiority, intimacy or isolation, etc., that Erik Erikson described in *Childhood and Society*. Nor can there be any doubt that human beings may be usefully described by common labels such as hopeful, hostile, willful, oppositional, faithful, competent, dependent, acquisitive, devious, loving, grandiose and caring, to name a few. All of these terms describe more or less enduring behavioral tendencies intrinsic to human beings. All of these tendencies are routinely observed in everyday social intercourse in varying degrees. The question at hand is how these and numerous other dispositions acquired in childhood also interact with society's broader rules for living. To begin to answer this question more precisely, the discussion must once again return to the mother-child relationship.

The Mother-Child Relationship

The mother-child bond is the crucible in which the foundations of the psyche are formed, subject to whatever genetic and congenital influences are relevant. The newborn infant enters the world in a totally helpless state. All of his perceptual functions—vision, hearing, touch, smell, taste—are operational in only a rudimentary sense, and they are incapable of registering any useful information to a brain that is equally unable to process it. The infant is incapable of orienting himself in the most elementary way: he does not know where he is (he has no concept of location), he does not know what time it is (he has no concept of the sequence of events or the continuity of existence), he does not know who he is (he has no concept of himself), and he does not know what situation he is in (he has no concept of his interaction with the physical world or other persons). He cannot feed, clothe, or shelter himself, and he cannot maintain personal hygiene, regulate his body temperature, or control his eliminative functions. The newborn infant has no will and no ability to choose in the ordinary meanings of those terms. He is in a largely vegetative state, and he is totally dependent on others for his survival. From this humble beginning, the proper mission of his caretakers is to guide him into adult competence. Any outcome short of competence represents a failure in one degree or another of the developmental process.

The most important caretaker in the infant's world is his mother. It is her task to provide him with the mental and emotional foundations on which to become an autonomous, economically productive, self-reliant and socially cooperative adult who plays by the rules and respects the rights of others. This is the intuitively evident endpoint of her efforts. *Equally evident is the failed outcome at the other extreme: an economically and socially dependent adult child who claims to be victimized, blames others for his failures, seeks parental surrogates, attempts to manipulate the political system, and feels entitled to coerce goods and services from others while ignoring their rights to refuse his demands.* Between these extremes lie an essentially infinite number of combinations of socially adaptive and maladaptive tendencies that impact on social processes.

The mother bends to her task by offering her child extraordinary services including those that make the difference between life and death in the first dozen or more years of his life. In later years the effects of her care become apparent in patterns of behavior that prove to be adaptive or maladaptive, as the case may be. In fortunate cases, the child learns to approach life with skill, courage and determination, fortified early on by his mother's love, guidance and encouragement. In less fortunate cases, the foundations of the personality become so weakened by defects in the mother-child bond and by other adverse influences that powerfully destructive tendencies ensue: self-destructive tendencies that may impel the individual to a tragic personal end, or other-destructive tendencies that wreak havoc on society, or both. Again, an infinite number of combinations of adaptive and maladaptive dispositions may develop in cases between these extremes.

Whatever the eventual outcome of her efforts, the mother's job description is astonishingly complex and difficult, in part because her child's physical vulnerability puts his life at stake, in part because his emotional vulnerability puts his sanity at stake, and in part because the functions which she must perform in order to compensate for his helplessness require extraordinary energy, sensitivity and patience. These critical maternal functions are, of course, missing or seriously compromised where the child is the victim of neglect, deprivation or abuse from whatever source. Wounds from such early traumas leave lifelong scars that may affect later efforts to live in a free and orderly society. But even in the absence of obvious trauma, more subtle but nevertheless serious difficulties in the mother-child bond and in the child's interactions with others may affect later capacities for self-reliance and willingness to cooperate.

Varieties of paranoid pathology, for example, may generate perceptions of victimization in political and social arenas, and sociopathic tendencies can lead to exploitation of others in political and business arenas. Especially problematic for a society based on liberty is the pathologically dependent and manipulative adult who, with an attitude of entitlement, seeks through the political process to force others into providing for him what he cannot or will not provide for himself. Of course, most other persons will promptly refuse such demands if they are made in person one-to-one. They will refuse him on the grounds that they do not know him and do not have a moral obligation or a legal duty to do as he demands. In a group effort with other similarly demanding individuals, however, and empowered by liberal social policy, large numbers of pathologically dependent persons can find government officials who are ready to serve their joint and coercive interests. If their numbers are large enough, they may succeed through the electoral process in imposing a tyranny of special interests, with dire consequences for everyone's liberty.

The General Nurturing Functions of Mothering

What is required of a mother to raise her child to competent adulthood? Certain nurturing capacities that are most likely to protect against serious defects in development and most likely to secure the foundations of growth to competence easily come to mind:

- Maternal love: an intense affectionate reverence for the child
- Maternal tenderness: a deep appreciation of and sympathetic response to the child's emotional and physical vulnerability
- A fierce determination to protect the child from undue harm
- An ability to engage him in mind, mood and spirit
- An ability to understand what he perceives, identify it, validate it and correct it
- An ability to instruct the child in relating rationally to himself and to others
- Abilities to instruct him in the morality of human relationships, to validate his increasing real mastery of himself and his world, to affirm his personal worth on realistic grounds, and to insist on his respect for the individual sovereignty of other persons

It is these nurturing capacities that establish the foundation for later development. When adequate, they install the emotional infrastructure for the eventual achievement of basic trust, autonomy, initiative, industry, identity, intimacy, generativity and integrity.

16

Attachment, Detachment, and Trust

Where love rules, there is no will to power, and where power predominates, love is lacking. The one is the shadow of the other.
Carl G. Jung

Mother and Child

The mother-child bond is the holding environment in which the foundations of the psyche are laid down subject to whatever genetic and congenital influences happen to apply. This bond is a natural instinctive development when mother and child are normally endowed, but its realization in a particular infant-mother couple is not automatic. The brain-impaired autistic child does not seek or permit attachment. The mother who has withdrawn into a world of paranoid delusions or depressive ruminations is unable to bond with her infant initially or sustain a healthy engagement with him later on. Between healthy attachment at one end of a continuum and essentially non-existent attachment at the other end lie countless variations in the nature and quality of the mother-child relationship. Within this complex interaction, basic life sustaining processes evolve to protect the infant. Emerging at the same time are his first experiences of cooperation and conflict. As the foundations of his personality are put in place, he begins the transformation from passive suckling to active instigator of human events.

Early interactions with the mother give rise to the child's first and most primitive experience of self and other, self and world. Within the first two years of life, fundamental modes of representing all types of experience are installed in the child's psyche. They may be adaptive, maladaptive or both. Based on his experience over the first twenty years of life and subject to genetic predispositions, the child will grow up feeling basically trusting or mistrusting, receptive to the world or wary of it, emotionally connected or disconnected, solid in his own being or doubtful about it, and convinced of a knowable reality around him or skeptical that things others perceive as evident are mere illusions. Depending on the nature and quality of his earliest experience, he will tend to feel secure or insecure, contented or anxious, tranquil or agitated, cohesive or fragmented, full or empty, gratified or deprived, effective or helpless, engaged or estranged. His earliest sense of connection and relatedness to others; his sense of predictability, order, reality and safety in the world; and his faith and optimism about the future all grow out of the child's earliest attachment to his mother or her surrogates.

The child's earliest experiences in all of these modes contribute to later mental representations of himself and the world of persons and things. They establish the foundations of his attitudes about himself and others. Erikson observed in this period the precursors to later tendencies toward demandingness or cooperation, generosity or greed, receptivity or rejection, relaxation or tension, confident optimism or anxious worry. Sentiments about one's self as basically good or bad, valuable or worthless, significant or insignificant begin in the child's first encounters with life. And his later capacity for spiritual experience surely emerges from his earliest experience of communion-like rapport with his mother, who appears to him as the first omnipotent creator in his world. Later perceptions of the world as predictable, stable, comprehensible, friendly, accommodating, embracing and gratifying as opposed to unpredictable, chaotic, confusing, indifferent, cold, abusive and painful have their origins in infancy.

The contributions of these primitive experiences cannot be ignored if the human condition is to be understood. Notwithstanding the effects of genetic influences and the aggravating and mitigating circumstances of later life, any analysis of adult behavior and social process has to examine early development. *The child's earliest experience of deprivation or satiety, contentment or alarm, loving response or callous neglect and other states of mind will affect his later estimate of how much material wealth he needs in order to feel secure, how much responsibility he should assume for himself, and how much caretaking by others can be obtained by the use of force, including the force of government.* His first experience of himself as the repeated object of his mother's tender embrace or cold indifference, of her willingness to accommodate or frustrate him, will impact later on his expectations that others will cooperate with him or thwart him. *The child's earliest experiences with caretakers in accommodation or conflict will determine in part whether he will choose in adult life to cooperate with others as political equals in a free society or attempt to make them dutiful servants in a coercive society.* All of these alternatives depend on how the fundamental drives toward self-preservation, dependency, acquisitiveness, narcissism, aggressiveness, sexuality, nurturing, and relatedness are integrated into the psyche. These integrations begin in the child's first attachments to his mother. They initiate his development into an economic, social and political being who chooses to trade or take, coerce or cooperate, participate or withdraw.

Social Institutions and Attachment

What does a society institutionalize in its rules for living based on these fundamental aspects of our human nature, and at what cost? As already observed, modern western societies have institutionalized maternal caretaking functions, first and foremost. The terms "nanny state" and "cradle-to-grave welfare" reference this development throughout most of the twentieth century. Indeed, we have institutionalized in our political rituals even the loving and caring attitudes of mothers. The liberal politician emphasizes his personal devotion to his constituents, assuring them that he feels the pain of their struggles and their need for rescue. He tells them that they are not alone, that he cares for them, that he is devoted to them, and that he will not rest until he can relieve their burdens with benefits far beyond what they can provide for themselves. Campaign rhetoric is invariably passionate in its guarantees of safety and security. The task of providing for all of life's uncertainties, from prenatal and early child-care through education and housing, to medical care and retirement security is now considered the proper function of government. Government has become the "essential (m)other" of first and last resort. The people have become permanent wards of the state.

But in providing all things to all people modern liberal government also seeks to control them to an extent far exceeding what is needed for individual liberty, community security and social harmony. The liberal agenda urges the citizen to place his basic trust in government, to see it as the mother of all providers, and to mistrust those with whom he would have to trade voluntarily in order to get what he wants. In doing this, the politician seeks to redirect to government offices the trust which can and should empower the individual to run his own life through voluntary cooperation with others. Government programs appeal to the citizen's passivity by implying that he need not provide for his own health care, housing or retirement. And he need not cooperate with his fellows for these purposes either. Instead, he is told, he need only trust the government to make available to him whatever he needs and to implement that trust by ceding to its officials the power to tax the people and regulate them for his benefit. In short, the government invites the citizen to vote for the candidate who promises what a parent gives a child. It invites him to assume the dependent role of the child, to surrender his personal sovereignty to the state, to ignore his existential obligation to take full responsibility for his material and social welfare, and to empower government officials as his guardians.

Politics and Pathological Dependency

In its widespread socialization of the most basic of human needs at the expense of individual liberty, individual responsibility and individual assumption of risk, the entire liberal agenda is a prescription for pathological dependency. Because all adults begin life as helpless children the appeal of this prescription is recognized and exploited world wide. Our early history of total dependency leaves us with residual infantile longings for a return to effortless gratification in the care of an omnipotent benefactor. From the perspective of the infant, the mother is, or should be, just that kind of benefactor: an omnipotent provider who has the power to give him whatever is needed whenever it is needed, and to protect him from all risk. He rightly assumes that her intentions are benign and loving, and he surrenders himself to her willingly—and because he has no other choice. Cost, including all of her extraordinary time and effort on his behalf, is no object from the point of view of the very young child.

If not opposed by the ideals of principled self-reliance, an ordinary citizen's primitive dependency longings easily become his entitled demand for government largesse. The liberal politician's invitations resonate strongly with the people's longings to get something for nothing, to live off of someone else's labors. The unwary citizen who feels needy for any reason, who remains ignorant of the economic implications of the welfare state and who retains a childlike disregard of the property rights of others takes the political bait just as naturally as an infant accepts his mother's feeding. Of course, that type of response is appropriate for an infant. But it is not appropriate for an adult in a free society. The child's total dependency on the mother is an unavoidable reality and a necessary condition for his survival. His willingness to trust her completely to provide for him in every way is essential to his growth to adulthood. But the citizen's contract with a parental government is a choice he can make in a voting booth. Too often, he is ignorant of the implications of that choice and succumbs to the seductions of the liberal agenda.

The historic ascendancy of the liberal agenda in the western world has been strongly fueled by the latent longings of the masses to re-experience the guaranteed security of an idealized parent's care. These longings are largely unconscious. If confronted with them, the dependent individual will deny their true significance and even their existence. In response to those longings the welfare programs of collective government promise to provide what the small child enjoyed, or should have enjoyed, in the first few years of his life: the loving generosity and protection of an all-powerful mother. The liberal politician exploits whatever developmental deficiencies remain from those years by promising to allay our most basic fears; we need only give him enough power and money to do so. It is by this route that the politicians of the nanny states of Europe and the Americas have been empowered by the wishes of the people to be adopted. Without exception, the major populations of the western world have invited governments to assume the most fundamental nurturing functions of the nuclear family. In so doing, however, they have also delegated to governments the power of parents over children.

Institutions and Values

What has in fact been institutionalized in any democratic state is an expression of what its people value most deeply, either wisely or foolishly. More generally, what is institutionalized in a democratic society's arrangements for living depends on what longings and fears the electorate believes should be addressed by the state. If the electorate's ideals are individual liberty, self-responsibility, self-actualization and voluntary cooperation, and if the fears to be addressed are those related to invasions of one's person and property or to violations of binding contracts, then society's rules will protect the rights of private ownership and the performance of enforceable agreements. If, on the other hand, the people yearn for the illusions of egalitarianism, guaranteed material security and wide-spread regulation of each other, if they long for indulgence and fear uncertainty and their own envy and inadequacies to a sufficient extent, then they will reject the ideal of freedom. They will, instead, create the modern managerial state and empower it to regulate, compensate, tax and redistribute under the excuse of social justice.

A freedom loving society, by contrast, will not institutionalize government programs that attempt to substitute in the life of the adult citizen the functions of parenting appropriate to childhood. The rules protecting freedom must not permit persons who in fact have the ability to take care of themselves through gainful employment, even if only at a subsistence level, to parasitize their fellow citizens by appeals to social or economic equality, envy of better circumstances, a grandiose sense of entitlement, a wish to be adopted, an indignant refusal to do menial labor, or just simple laziness.

For those persons who do, in fact, lack the capacity to care for themselves, the community's charitable organizations can—and to preserve society's freedom must—voluntarily provide the resources necessary to rehabilitate their deficiencies, or else compensate for them if they are incurable. On this matter it is critical to note that, for the preservation of individual liberty as an ultimate political ideal, the voluntary provision of charitable services by local communities is the only way to avoid the inevitable invasions of liberty that occur when governments assume responsibility for the disabled. In its innate sympathy for seriously disadvantaged persons, the population at large is incapable of ignoring their plight for very long and will insist that something be done for them by someone. The question is always whether it will be done voluntarily and therefore freely by able persons in the community, or whether it will be mandated by government and become one more opportunity for coercion to undermine freedom. *Any government with the power to mother its citizens also has the power to dominate them and steal from them: to overtax them, confiscate their property and override their binding agreements.* For this reason, the legally enforceable institutions of society must be very limited, lest the government charged with protecting the people against tyranny and theft becomes itself the most dangerous tyrant and thief.

17

Trust, Mistrust and Social Process

Hope helps man to approximate a measure of that rootedness possessed by the animal world, in which instinctive equipment and environment, beginning with the maternal response, verify each other, unless catastrophe overtakes the individual or the species.
Erik Erikson

The Fundamental Importance of Trust

Recent chapters have explored certain implications that early maternal deprivation and abuse have for cooperation in a free society and have alluded to the impact of such trauma on the foundations of basic trust. The present chapter offers some additional perspectives on trust and its relevance for societal arrangements, beginning with the observation that basic trust is simply a precondition for engaging the world. Based on his belief that he can depend on his own mind and body, on his faith that the world is sufficiently benign, and on his conviction that he can effectively relate to others, the healthy adult in a healthy society engages life in the expectation that he and others can interact to the benefit of all by doing what they have agreed to do and by behaving according to commonly accepted rules.

An expectation of trust in the ordinary sense of the word is typically implicit in any agreement to do something jointly. Most transactions begin on the assumption that participating parties will behave appropriately: they will respect each other's persons and property, honor the terms of an agreement, and keep whatever promises were made in good faith. Trust permits persons to make arrangements with each other, to relate without the use of force, and to achieve individual and group goals that facilitate the pursuit of happiness. Freedom in an orderly society is heavily dependent upon trust and its obverse, trust-worthiness. The latter is an enduring disposition toward authentic good will, honesty, fairness, mutual consideration and dependability in both personal and financial transactions. The capacity for basic trust is central to all relationships founded on mutual consent, not on coercion.

I note here with special emphasis, however, that the goal of normal development in a free society is not to instill in the child a "trust" that the government will take care of him as an adult. Erikson's concept of basic trust does not countenance a citizen's expectation that a significant portion of his life will be subsidized by the state or by anyone else. Unfortunately, that is precisely what the liberal politician invariably promises to his constituents: that they can and should trust a government program to guarantee their material well-being. Since an expectation of this type clearly entails a dependency appropriate only to childhood, its persistence into adulthood necessarily undermines growth to competence. Even more critical to a rational concept of trust, however, is the fact that any relationship in which the government adopts its citizens is not really a relationship of trust at all. It is instead a Faustian bargain based on the citizens' pathological dependency and the politician's willingness to exploit it. "Trust" that government will subsidize one's living is obviously not what Erikson or any other psychologist has in mind as a developmental achievement, nor can such an attitude of entitlement be what any political thinker committed to freedom means by the social concept of trust. Economic considerations alone contradict any conjunction of trust and government subsidy: the realization of individual liberty is not compatible with enforced transfers of wealth. In genuinely free societies wealth is transferred only through voluntary exchanges among those who buy, sell and trade in free markets, or through inheritance, or through charitable donations to recipients selected by the donor.

Of course, economic exchange is just one category of countless freely chosen interactions that provide the substance of social process in a free society. In these interactions, trust can play its critical role as an enabling force for voluntary cooperation only if it remains uncontaminated by the intrusion of government coercion beyond that needed to protect basic liberty rights. Trust requires that that the terms of binding agreements, whether economic or social, will, in fact, be enforced. Even in these transactions, however, trust is based in the first place on the assumed honesty and integrity of all parties. Basic trust in the Eriksonian sense of an a priori optimism about life lies at the heart of social process in a free and orderly society. In any overarching conception of individual liberty, the developmental achievement of basic trust is an indispensable preparation for the adult world of voluntary transactions.

Liberal Mistrust and its Consequences

To the extent that the liberal politician succeeds in his intrusive regulation and in his enforced transfers of wealth, he undermines the people's incentives and preempts their opportunities to solve their social problems through voluntary cooperation. This is, in fact, a central strategy in the liberal agenda: to foster doubt and fear in the minds of the masses in order to prepare them for additional governmental intrusion into their lives. The liberal agenda regularly attempts to promote mistrust in the people by convincing them that local solutions to problems are inadequate and that local attempts at solution must be regulated by a government bureaucracy, else the attempt will fail. The government's efforts just as regularly fail in their own right, however, whereupon the bureaucrat proposes still more government intervention. Despite his long record of policy failures, the liberal politician and his fellows assure all who will vote for them that under their programs the people can "trust" that education, housing, health care, Social Security, and myriad other "needed" benefits can and will be provided *without any adverse consequences*. In fact, however, the real world of such programs abounds in adverse consequences.

One of the worst of these is the corruption of the moral fiber of the people. Note, for example, that the average citizen, even when duped into believing that government subsidy is legitimate public policy, would not even think of demanding comparable support from a next door neighbor or from anyone else in his own town, or from any particular person in any other town. It would not occur to Smith, for example, to tell his neighbor Jones that he has selected Jones to subsidize one of Smith's expenditures—and would Jones please make out a check in the specified amount. Aside from the fact that Smith would, on moral grounds, feel too ashamed to make such a demand, he also knows with great certainty that any such demand would be met with disgust and flatly refused by Jones. If Smith then tried to force a "contribution" from Jones, his behavior would at that point become criminal, not just shameful. In this scenario Jones would properly call the police to report Smith's attempt to extort him.

Note that the morality of this situation would not change if Smith were joined by several other persons in the community to make a group demand on Jones for the same subsidy that Smith made individually. Imagine, for example, that Smith and a dozen other persons present themselves at Jones' door and demand as a group what Smith had demanded by himself. Jones would, of course, still be as rightfully disgusted, if not more so, with the group demand as he was when Smith made it alone. And if the group tried to force Jones to comply, then again, shameful behavior would escalate into criminal behavior. But note also that if the group that demands Jones' money is the government, the argument is not altered. If it is the IRS that knocks on Jones' door, Jones is still rightfully outraged at the demand that he subsidize somebody he doesn't know or care about. Theft is theft, extortion is extortion, regardless of who is perpetrating the act. The immorality and criminality of such actions, whether they are perpetrated by individuals or by governments, or called robbery or taxation, are clear to any reasoning person. But the liberal agenda's welfare propaganda has succeeded in clouding the average man's sense of right and wrong when the government commits the crime.

Seduced by liberal welfare policy, the would-be seeker of subsidy goes not to his neighbor, who would refuse him, but instead to his congressman, who assures him that he deserves an enforced government transfer of something that no one else will give him by choice. The congressman exploits the fact that in this transfer, which is in fact a mediated theft, neither recipient nor taxpayer knows each other. This maneuver bypasses the potential for moral outrage and indignant refusal inherent in the usual relationship between neighbors. The anonymity of the theft circumvents the neighbor's social disapproval and shields the recipient from public shame. Those who subscribe to this conspiracy are corrupted. Those who don't are demoralized. The foundations of basic trust in voluntary cooperation are weakened in both cases.

Additional Implications of Basic Trust

Notwithstanding liberal efforts to undermine the role of trust in voluntary transactions, the idea of basic trust, when understood beyond immediate personal relationships, has everything to do with matters of social process at all levels. Trust in all forms of social intercourse develops where individuals consistently exercise a principled respect for the persons and property of others and honor the terms of bona fide agreements. Such respect avoids the powerful and often dangerous emotional reactions that develop when trust is betrayed. Breach of contract, property trespass, civil rights violations, default on debt, defiling of social conventions, desecration of religious rituals, and contraventions of political treaties are routinely perceived as violations of trust, and they routinely evoke emotions and actions that disrupt social harmony. Such betrayals generate intense personal and social conflict on a limited scale and may well lead to war on a larger scale. In the limited domain of a marital relationship, for example, the emotional injury that typically occurs with sexual infidelity may completely disrupt and ultimately destroy both the marital union and, at least temporarily, the functional abilities of the parties involved. On a much larger scale, profound social disruption is typically seen among nations and ethnic groups when territorial agreements or religious rituals are violated. In every case of betrayed trust or the perception of betrayed trust, whether interpersonal or international, the threat of retaliation and social upheaval is never very far away. Individual and group emotions activated in these situations—fear, rage, jealously, heartbreak, and despair, coupled with reactive behaviors that emanate from them—are notably similar from one case to another.

The importance of trust becomes even more obvious when its opposite, mistrust, characterizes the expectations in a transaction. In the extreme case, two paranoid individuals are so mistrustful of each other that negotiations never begin or else rapidly deteriorate and no transaction occurs at all. (The opposite extreme, a blind faith that others will always have one's best interests at heart, may risk life, limb, and property). Of course, in those cases where fraud, trespass, breach of contract or other violations are actually present, mistrust is entirely appropriate and should lead to prompt termination of the relationship. Mistrust in these cases is clearly not irrational and does not represent a developmental failure. In legitimate transactions, on the other hand, trusting but responsible individuals honor the terms of agreements. Such persons expect cooperation from each other but take appropriate precautions to ensure that each party follows whatever rules apply. Based on realistic expectations of trustworthy behavior, but tempered with caution, the competent individual's position is neither childlike naivete nor paranoid avoidance.

With these observations in mind, the importance of trust in the lives of both individuals and local communities is difficult to overstate. Since one's individual pursuit of personal goals in a free society invariably requires cooperation with others, transactions grounded in genuinely trustworthy behavior are critical to self-actualization. But given the dire consequences of betrayed trust at all levels of group interaction as well, it becomes equally clear that the rational society's overall pursuit of economic, social and political order is critically dependent on an ethical environment that supports the achievement of basic trust in its citizens. For these reasons a society's s commitment to trustworthiness at all levels is essential to its moral fabric. Trust is foundational in the life of man.

18

Autonomy and Social Process

The makers of our Constitution undertook to secure conditions favorable to the pursuit of happiness. They recognized the significance of man's spiritual nature, of his feelings, and of his intellect. They knew that only a part of the pain, pleasure, and satisfactions of life are to be found in material things. They sought to protect Americans in their beliefs, their thoughts, their emotions, and their sensations. They conferred, as against the Government, the right to be let alone – the most comprehensive of rights and the right most valued by civilized men.

Justice Louis Brandeis

Personality develops by acquiring successive freedoms.
Jane Loevenger

Individuation and Autonomy

To address the second of Erikson's developmental tasks, an exploration of the early foundations of adult autonomy is now in order. As already noted, the term autonomy means, literally, self-law or self-governing. It stipulates to an internalized control of certain functions essential to rational living. The foundations on which normal adult autonomy eventually comes to rest are laid down in the first several years of life. They consist of massive transformations in the child's mental, emotional and physical makeup. The overall process by which these changes occur is commonly called individuation: it is the process of differentiating and integrating one's person into a distinct, unitary and sovereign self. Individuation is fundamental to any society grounded in the principles of individual liberty.

Autonomy as a Developmental Achievement

The achievement of autonomy is critical to adult functioning. Assuming that the child has acquired a modicum of basic trust, the individuation process begins with the toddler-age child's growing ability to perceive the world, to control his motor behavior and toilet functions, to identify what he wants, and to make more or less deliberate as opposed to merely impulse-driven choices. As the toddler emerges from the helplessness of infancy, he begins to construct a self through the exercise of his emerging will and an increasing awareness of himself as a person distinct from others. The process continues through the remainder of childhood and, indeed, throughout the life cycle, if all goes well enough. The hoped for outcome of individuation is a self-reliant but cooperative adult with a robust conviction that he is entitled to run his own life and to relate voluntarily with others. Unfortunately this process can have undesirable outcomes, some of which are noted below. Among them are those patterns in which one's freedom to act autonomously is impaired by deep-seated shame or doubt, by paranoid fears of control by others, by the conviction that one's adult life must be directed by parents or their surrogates, or by the need for pseudo-independence through arbitrary defiance.

The autonomous individuated adult correctly assumes his right to life, liberty and the pursuit of happiness. He assumes that right as a moral conviction: he has a proper sense of entitlement to a life of his own, to live as he sees fit and not as someone else directs. But mature autonomy does not consist in a belief that one should be able to do or have anything that one wants without regard for others and without earning it. It does not imply entitlement to goods or services from others simply because one demands it or needs it. That is the attitude of a dependent child. But the mature independence that characterizes adult autonomy is also not the false independence of the narcissist. It is not the callous disdain for the other that is always present in pathological narcissism but often concealed by superficial charm. Mature autonomy does not lead to a conviction that others have a duty to admire one's person, indulge one's wishes or submit to one's will.

The truly autonomous person learns in contrast to the narcissist that every other person is also an autonomous agent in his own right, not a mere object to be exploited. Of particular importance is the fact that the normal development of autonomy also requires the normal development of mutuality. The truly autonomous person readily acknowledges that the dignity with which he invests his own life belongs to the lives of all others as well. In intersubjective terms, he recognizes the other as a subject and not merely an object. On this acknowledgment, the truly autonomous person honors the sovereignty of other competent persons and respects their right to live lives of their own. These insights are critical to participation in a free society. They ground our conceptions of individual liberty, lead to prohibitions against encroaching upon the persons and property of others, and establish the attitudinal foundation for equality under the law.

Individuation

Individuation has been called a second birth, a kind of psychological emergence analogous to physical delivery from the womb. Its early overt expression becomes apparent around the age of fifteen months and continues at an especially rapid pace over the ensuing two years. The process is strongly associated with major advances in cognitive development and physical mobility. It is energized by innate drives to explore the world and gain mastery over it. The child is programmed to learn as rapidly as possible about his environment: the spatio-temporal world of mass, motion, force and energy, and the interpersonal world of human relationships. The long-term developmental goal of this process is a competent, self-reliant, self-directed, self-actualizing adult who respects the personhood of others and interacts with them through voluntary cooperation, not coercion.

Unless these early experiments in autonomous action and mutuality are met with some form of retaliation from others, the child will, over the course of his life, seek conditions of freedom and cooperation in which to pursue his goals. His increasing competence will validate his image of himself as an independent agent who can act effectively in his own behalf. But his growing perception of the sovereignty of others and increasing respect for their rights will constrain him to act only within certain moral and ethical boundaries. He will know from experience the satisfaction of acting freely in pursuit of personal fulfillment, subject to the rules of cooperation needed to insure the same opportunity for others.

The child's earliest experience with caregivers will strongly determine whether or not he becomes a free, effective, legitimate, cooperative and mutual actor. The following are among the more important changes that characterize the early foundations of autonomy:

- Enhanced capacities for attention, concentration, perception, recognition, reasoning and memory
- Expansion and elaboration of conscious experience with increased differentiation of emotional feeling and expression
- Acquisition of language and non-verbal communication skills
- Enhanced control of eating and eliminative functions
- Major increases in strength, body control, curiosity and exploratory behavior
- Emerging capacities for choice, will and agency
- Increasingly unified and stable self-representations with developing functions of identity, agency and relatedness
- Increasingly stable and unified representations of the mother as both gratifying and frustrating object
- Increasing appreciation of the mother as an independent and sovereign self
- Increased interest in and tolerance for physical separation from the mother
- Intensified loving attachment to the mother and her surrogates
- Increasingly accurate perceptions and representations of others as separate and sovereign selves

Individuation is thus a complex process involving major progress in the child's physical and intellectual maturation. This process is strongly influenced by the behavior of his caregivers and heavily dependent upon whether he has acquired the foundations of basic trust in the first twelve to fifteen months of life. Societal support for individuation is critical to the realization of economic, social and political freedom. The autonomous individual who is able to define, set and pursue his own meaningful goals naturally seeks the freedom to achieve them as he respects the rights of others to do the same. Indeed, the more the individual is able to govern himself, the less his need to be governed by others. The more government regulation is imposed upon him, the less freedom he has to govern himself, and the less incentive and opportunity he has to achieve self-government. He will then look to government to compensate for his deficits.

19

Biology and Autonomy

The acceptance of an ontology is, I think, similar in principle to our acceptance of a scientific theory, say a system of physics; we adopt, at least insofar as we are reasonable, the simplest conceptual scheme into which the disordered fragments of raw experience can be fitted and arranged.

Willard V. Quine

The Biological Foundations of Autonomy

The foundations of autonomy begin in the biological realities that define human nature and the nature of human relating. Among these realities is the simple fact that each individual is an organism with one body, separate from all other bodies, whose contents are enclosed in an envelope of skin and whose actions are directed by an inner self. The critical reality here is the fact that each human being, upon his delivery into the world, is a separate and distinct entity. Each human being, at birth and forever after, is an objectively real physical thing different from all other physical things in the universe. Over the course of development, each body becomes for its owner the material referent for a unique objective "me." It is also the only residence of a unique subjective "I." So long as it is alive, the body and the brain/mind it contains (the objective me) are discontinuous from the rest of the world. So long as it is alive the brain/mind and the mind/self it contains (the subjective I) are also discontinuous from the rest of the world.

Just as an individual human being is an objectively different *entity* from everything else in the world, it is also true that his subjective *experience of himself* is different from his subjective experience of everything else. Note that by simple introspection, each of us can identify what has been called a "subjective self" or "narrative self." This is the self about whom I am speaking when I say that *"I feel this," "I think this," "I want that,"* or *"I did that."* Clearly, my awareness of this "I" is very different from my awareness of everything else. Note also that by simple introspection and observation, each of us can identify an "objective self" or "empirically observed self." This is the "me" that is my body and my stream of consciousness. It is all of the things that I identify as "me:" the various parts of my body, their functions and appearance, their connection to the rest of me, their history with me over time. Taken together, my subjective self (my "I") and my objective self (my "me") constitute the unique core of my *self-experience.* Note further that the uniqueness of this experience arises as a result of my *separateness* from everything else. In fact, the unique character of this experience anchors within me the ontological core, or "being," of my human nature as an individual different from all other individuals and all other things. Moreover, the individuation of my self, the process by which I become a fully competent person, begins in and continuously depends upon this existential reality.

The fact that I am separate from everything else imposes fundamental limitations on any ideas that I might entertain about being merged with, continuous with, fused with, or in any other way combined with other persons or things in some collectivist conception of the world. The biological basis for autonomy lies in a simple reality: the body and self of each person remain forever discontinuous from the bodies and selves of all other persons and from the substance of all other things. This reality remains true regardless of how strongly we may yearn for magical fusion with others, and how determined we may be to achieve that fusion through religious, mystical, sexual or political rituals. Denial of these limitations, either for political purposes or for psychological defensive purposes, has been the cause of much wishful thinking and profound political mischief among liberal intellectuals of the last two centuries. More specifically, in its denial of the separateness, agency, autonomy and sovereignty of the individual, the liberal agenda can also deny that the individual, and only the individual, must be regarded as the ultimate economic, social and political unit, not some arbitrary group or collective. The importance of the point cannot be overstated. It is only by means of such denial that the liberties and lives of millions of individuals have been sacrificed on collectivist altars. *It is the sovereignty of the individual, grounded in the ultimate separateness of the individual, that is deeply honored by the philosophy of individualism. It is precisely the sovereignty of the individual that is scorned by the liberal's creed of collectivism. In denying the physical, biological and psychological nature of human beings, the liberal mind denies the basis of human freedom.*

The Separate and Vulnerable Body

The delivery of the fetus from the mother's womb is, of course, the birth of the human being as a separate physical entity. That event brings about changes in the conditions of existence, both at the moment of its occurrence and ever after, that are surely profound by any measure. Most important among these changes is the fact that cutting the umbilical cord severs the infant's osmotic connection between his circulation and his mother's: his intake of nutrients and elimination of waste are no longer accomplished automatically through his and her conjoined bodies. *In terminating the infant's parasitism in his mother's womb, birth permanently removes all guarantees of material security for the remainder of his life. It is a politically momentous fact that the infant is now a separate and highly vulnerable entity that has been transported from the limited but guaranteed environment of the womb to the unlimited and contingent environment of the outside world. This most basic existential condition, one that lasts life-long for everyone, generates much of modern political conflict.*

The infant's boundary of skin and its various orifices is remarkable for more than its topology. It not only demarcates his existence as an organism separate from his environment. Its physical integrity also enables him to live by assisting in the regulation of body temperature, the intake of nutrients, and the elimination of waste. The body's container is its primary protective barrier. If too much of its skin breaks down, then so do the processes that sustain life. The boundary of the body delimits the living thing, encloses it, keeps it from merging with other things living and nonliving, protects the metabolism that keeps it alive, and provides the physical and biological basis for whatever degree of individuality it may achieve.

But the individual's need for *separateness* from his environment is paralleled, as it is in all living things, by his need for certain kinds of *connection* with it. In the case of humans and most other animals, that connection must be both psychological and physical. Having observed that the body's boundary of skin *separates* us from the environment, we note with equal emphasis that our special organs of intake, digestion, metabolism and elimination *connect* us physically to our environment to ensure survival. (Wiggins & Schwartz 1999).

Similarly, in respect to our psychological existence, the body's boundary of skin grounds the experience of each of us as *separate* entities, but our cognitive, emotive and communicative systems *connect* us to the world, enabling us to relate to the environment and to other actors. These and other realities of human existence, together with certain constraints imposed by early conditioning, define limitations on human freedom. We cannot, for example, be freed from the boundaries of our bodies, nor can we be free of our life-preserving connections to the environment. In these and other respects, freedom is always limited, never absolute.

Beyond such limitations, however, there are certain fears that may arise in anyone who is not well defended against the reality of separateness. In fact, as will be seen later, the doctrine of collectivism itself is, among other things, a massive and irrational defense against separation anxieties inherent in the human condition: fears of isolation, loneliness, rejection, abandonment, feelings of insignificance, and the existential angst that fills the void of spiritual emptiness. In these states, human beings may seek attachments not only to other persons and things but to political doctrines that promise relief from the fear of separateness.

20

Autonomy and the Self

There will never be a really free and enlightened state until the state comes to recognize the individual as a higher and independent power, from which all its own power and authority are derived, and treats him accordingly.

Henry David Thoreau

Self and Agency

The physical separateness of our bodies is as obvious as it is unalterable. The individual mind is necessarily grounded in this fact, but it is also grounded from birth onward in its relatedness to others. These realities are simultaneously limiting and empowering in all human action. Human beings can act separately from others, but also with, for, and against others. The individuated adult is both an autonomous agent and a participant immersed in the interpersonal fabric of his world. His self and the selves of others always remain distinct from each other, yet related to each other in varying degrees by the countless interdependencies of the human condition. Indeed, for his continued mental and physical health in a free society, an adult must maintain a sovereign self with a clear sense of his own identity while at the same time maintaining a dynamic connection with other selves. This relationship between the self and society is reciprocal: while it is true that there is no society without the individuals that constitute it, it is also true that there are no individuals who can live fully without a society to relate to.

The Nature of the Self

What psychologists call the self is the conscious, unconscious and self-conscious organ of the mind. It is also the functional, integrative and executive organ of the mind. The self is functional in so far as it perceives the environment, assesses relevant conditions, sets goals and plans action. The self is integrative in that it organizes and coordinates various mental processes under the control of a unified personality and largely unified consciousness. The self is executive in that it initiates, sustains and terminates willed action while monitoring its effects and altering its direction for further action.

As a psychobiological phenomenon generated by the brain, the self controls itself and the body it lives in by means of the brain's neurophysiological and neurohumoral connections to itself and to other parts of the body. Most notably, it is a fact of my existence that no other brain than the one that resides in my body generates or controls anything that I think, feel, or do. This very simple but fundamental observation has led cognitive psychologists since Magda Arnold and Albert Ellis in the 1950's to emphasize the biologically based fact that each of us must take individual responsibility for his own thoughts, emotions and actions. The cognitive psychiatrist, Maxie Maultsby, put the matter most succinctly when he wrote: "my brain, and my brain alone, creates, maintains and eliminates all of my thoughts, emotions, and behavior." (Maultsby 1984)

This insight into human nature implies that efforts to understand the causes of any given instance of thought, emotion or behavior must take into account the manner in which the individual's biological brain and psychological self process information. The information processed may consist in virtually anything that is registered in the psyche: a change in the weather, a casual remark, an accidental event, someone's compliments or insults, one's own failures or successes, one's own thoughts or physical sensations, another person's financial gain or loss, the death of a loved one, ad infinitum. To manage his life, every person must take into account the meaning which his own mind/ brain attributes to whatever information he receives about his environment since it is precisely on that attributed meaning that he will create, maintain and eliminate all of his feelings, thoughts and actions. In the final analysis of any response he makes, be it action, emotion or thought, it is his own perceptions of events, the value judgments he makes about them, the personal significance he gives them–in short, their meanings for him–that generate all of those actions, emotions or thoughts. Thus, the ultimate locus of control of all that I do lies within myself, in my own mind/brain, as it processes whatever information impinges upon it and responds with whatever behavior it generates.

This fact alone has clear implications for the question of autonomy and for the contest between individualism and collectivism: in the final analysis, it is only the brain/mind—the self—that resides in my own body, not in someone else's body, that brings about what I do. Whatever the contributions of outside stimuli, external events or environmental circumstances—be they physical, economic, social, political, racial, ethnic or whatever—the most proximate of all the causal factors in the genesis of my behavior reside within me.

The Ideal of Individuation

In the case of any given action, of course, there is always a question as to whether or not I have knowing, willful, volitional or rational *command* of the causal factors within me: those needs, drives, impulses, emotions, attitudes, appetites, motives, goals and longings that operate in the production of my behavior. The extent to which I act knowingly, or rationally, or "of my own free will," will vary with the action and the situation, and with the degree to which I am even conscious of the factors that influence my behavior. In any case, however, if I do act, it is because I have chosen to do so, either rationally or irrationally, or because I have reacted to some stimulus impulsively or compulsively, or simply by reflex. In any instance in which it is I who does the acting, it is always my brain and only my brain that chooses among perceived alternatives, either freely or under some impulse or compulsion or transference, and it is always my brain that initiates, sustains and terminates my acts. In these respects, I am always the person *most causally* responsible for my actions since all other factors, notably those external to me, are filtered first through the mechanisms of my brain regardless of how compelling they may appear to be independently of me. The principle of individual responsibility that lies at the foundation of ordered liberty is based on this reality of human nature.

Whether a given person is in fact responding autonomously to his world has always been, as it should be, of great concern in the field of psychotherapy. It is no accident that Maultsby's maxim is the basis for the most modern, widely practiced and best validated of the psychotherapies, the so-called cognitive-behavioral therapies, all of which attempt to install or restore rational thinking, emotional control and functional efficacy to troubled persons. Indeed, the primary goal of all psychotherapy, not just the cognitive-behavioral variety, is to maximize the patient's autonomy: his capacity for reasoned volitional control over thinking, emoting, behaving and relating. But this same goal is also central to any rational conception of child rearing: it is the hope of all reasonable parents that their children become authentically self-governing, self-actualizing and self-reliant adults who are at the same time able to cooperate with others. Thus the goals of psychotherapy and the goals of child rearing share the western ideal of individuated man: the autonomous, self-directed and freely choosing but ethical and moral individual, an agent both sovereign and social, who cooperates with others by mutual consent, not by coercion, in a society ruled by law. Here, in language more behavioral than philosophical, is the psycho-biologically based ideal of individualism. The critical question to be asked, then, is whether and to what extent the arrangements for living in a given society are consistent with that ideal. More particularly, we ask whether and to what extent the *liberal agenda* is consistent with that ideal.

Initiative, Self, and Connection

Human needs for interaction with the environment and with other persons are not met passively; they require intentional acts initiated by individuals acting alone or jointly. A later section will explore more fully the concept of initiative as a developmental achievement. For now, a brief exploration of the nature of initiative and its emergence in the very young child is relevant.

Mere physical survival requires all higher organisms to initiate certain types of action on the environment. For this purpose the potential for initiative is wired into the human brain as it is in the brains of all animals. As already noted, inklings of initiative appear very early in the child's response to an environment he engages with relish. Once activated, his increasing capacity for intentional action is modified by environmental influences, the most important of which are those emanating from his caregivers. When those influences are favorable enough, his capacity for such action is gradually brought under the control of rational choice. The helpless, totally dependent infant is then transformed over a period of some twenty years into an adult source of independent and hopefully prudent initiative. This transformation is obviously essential for adult autonomy. In its eventual contribution to adult competence, it helps to justify the political ideal of personal sovereignty.

It is routine to locate the source of initiative in the commonly understood term, "self," an idea already visited at some length. The self can be thought of as having an envelope or boundary that sustains psychological existence in a manner similar to the physical envelope that sustains the body's biological existence. The body's envelope, on the one hand, is manifestly physical and chemical, consisting of the skin, hair and nails that enclose it. The psychological envelope of the self, on the other hand, is not physical, except for its basis in the brain's physiological processes. Instead, this envelope is a function of the mind's capacity to perceive reality by means of mental representations, especially those that register the real differences or boundaries between self and not-self. More precisely, the envelope of the self consists, first, in representations of the self as a unique physical and psychological entity; second, in representations of the self *in relation to* other persons and things; and third, in representations of the self's *separateness from* other persons and things, all acquired in the course of adequate development.

All representations serve as mappings of one's experience into the memory reservoirs of the mind. All are routinely accessed by associative processes in order to identify and cope adaptively with events in the real world. Interpersonal events are of special interest. Realistic representations facilitate distinctions made between the self and other selves in economic, social and political processes, and even in such mundane matters as using the pronouns I and we, you and they, he and she, and when specifying possession with the words mine and yours, his and hers, ours and theirs. These mappings of interpersonal experience operate in both conscious and unconscious regions of the mind. How well they serve as boundaries depends on how clearly representations of the self are differentiated from representations of others, and to what extent representations of both separateness and connection properly limit the mind's tendency to confuse disparate images of any kind.

Of special importance is the effectiveness of these mappings in helping the individual to assess the realities of the interpersonal world. Those realities include economic, social and political processes initiated by individuals and groups. They include the worldviews of the culture in which the individual lives as a separate entity that is also immersed in collective action. A given individual's ability to assess the reasonableness of those processes and worldviews depends, in part, on how and to what extent he construes both his separateness from and relatedness to other persons. Mental representations that blur the boundaries between self and others foster the illusions of collectivism and its denial of the agency, autonomy and sovereignty of the individual. Mental representations that recognize the separateness and especially the autonomy of individuals support the principles of individualism.

The Body-Self, Agency and Autonomy

The bipolar configuration of the self has early developmental origins. Gabbard has summarized Stearn's research on the five domains of the self-experience in infants and small children. (Gabbard 2000) The infant's first sense of himself is that of his *emergent or body self,* which is primarily concerned with physiological needs. it appears during the first two months of life. A second sense of the self emerges between two and six months of age, the *core self.* It is a primitive self-with-other, which evolves out of the child's deepening attachment to its mother. A third sense, the *subjective self*, appears between seven and nine months. This self is characterized by an increasing capacity for emotional resonance or matching of affective states with the mother. The fourth sense, the *verbal or categorical self,* "emerges between fifteen and eighteen months and is associated with the child's growing ability to think symbolically and communicate verbally." A fifth sense of the self arises between three and five years of age and is called the *narrative self.* With this achievement the child begins what is to become a lifelong historical perspective on himself, as his memory enables him to know the continuity of his existence, and his enduring self-representations allow him to see himself as the protagonist of his own history.

Of particular interest for present purposes is the fact that the function known as *agency* is among four essential features that Stearn identifies with the child's emerging sense of himself; the other three are coherence, affectivity, and continuity. Agency, as noted earlier, refers to the child's emerging sense of himself as an instigator of events, a being with causal efficacy. The additional feature of *coherence* in this scheme of self-development refers to the fact that the child begins to see himself as a distinct and enduring being with boundaries that delineate him from others. Of course, as his self emerges from the relatedness in which it forms, he also deepens his attachments to others, true to his bipolar nature. The affects which energize and deepen these attachments define the emotional core of the self. Thus the human self is born in a self-with-other relatedness to the mother, develops its emotional core in that relatedness, differentiates itself into an entity that is coherent and distinct from her, and achieves agency and continuity as individuation proceeds. It is in part this progression, or failure in progression, that prepares or fails to prepare the child for later relatedness to the world.

21

Autonomy, Individuation and Individualism

What the research on mother-infant interaction has uncovered about early reciprocity and mutual influence is best conceptualized as the development of the capacity for mutual recognition
Jessica Benjamin

Individuals have rights, and there are things no person or group may do to them (without violating their rights). So strong and far-reaching are these rights that they raise the question of what, if anything, the state and its officials may do.
Robert Nozick

The Elements of Individualism

The idea that a human being is entitled to direct his own life arises from the philosophy of individualism, a more or less coherent set of beliefs, attitudes and value judgments that recommends how individuals would best relate to themselves, to others, and to the institutions of society. This philosophy asserts that the individual is the primary economic, social and political unit of society, in contrast to collectivism, which gives that distinction to one or another group of persons, a [1]"collective." Moreover, individualism holds that the *causes* of human behavior at every level are to be found primarily in the motives, values and actions of individual persons, not in collective forces such as a "national will."

These assertions have special importance for the dynamics of human liberty. Individualism insists that an individual's freedom to live as he chooses may not be subordinated to any collective-based rules beyond those essential to ensure social order and equal liberty for all individuals. It insists further that in order to preserve the agency, autonomy and sovereignty of the individual, official policy decisions must give first importance to the individual, not to a group and especially not to a government. The only legitimate function of government is to foster the lives of citizens by protecting their rights *as individuals,* not as members of a class or group; no collective cause should be allowed to override those rights. Individualism opposes any conception of the state or other collective as primary in value over the individual. In particular, it opposes any notion that the individual exists for the good of the state.

These principles are consistent with the bipolar nature of man, with his innate capacity for autonomy understood as self-government and his innate capacity for mutuality understood as respect for the rights and sensibilities of other persons. No rational individualism would endorse the idea that one should be able to do or have anything that one wants without regard for others, nor claim that others have a duty to admire one's person, indulge one's wishes or submit to one's will. As contemplated by individualism, the genuinely autonomous individual assumes, until proven otherwise, that every other person is also an autonomous agent in his own right, not a mere object to be exploited. Stated in intersubjective terms, he recognizes the other as a subject, not as a mere object, as a person, not a thing.

Rules and Rights Under Individualism

It is an especially important consequence of this conception that the individual, and not a group or collective, must be regarded as the ultimate *political* unit. That is, since any rule of government prescribes what *individuals* must do or not do, and since any rule of this type necessarily determines how the lives of *individuals* are benefited or harmed, it is the *individual* that must be the primary subject and object of policy decisions, whether they are made in economic, social or political realms. Without this emphasis, the individual may be denied his most fundamental right to life, liberty, property and the pursuit of happiness. Without these rights he may become, as one writer put it, "absorbed into the social mass."

To guard against this outcome, individualism holds that certain legal rights must be guaranteed by law. These rights are, or should be, rules for human conduct designed to protect all individuals equally in their persons, property and contracts, and in their freedom to live their lives as they choose. In particular, rights of this type are necessary to protect individuals from being harmed by other persons acting alone or in groups and especially from harms arising from the actions of governments. As entitlements to individuals and not to classes or groups, liberty rights have evolved in keeping with the nature of man and the conditions of his living. They have proven to be essential to peace, order, safety and happiness. A critical characteristic of these rights is that they are relatively gratifying to all when obeyed but painful to at least some when violated. The right not to be enslaved, for example, is relatively gratifying to everyone, while enslavement may be highly gratifying to slave holders but intensely painful to the enslaved.

For the protection of individuals against any and all collective intrusions, it is necessary that rights be attributable *only to individuals*, not to groups. If this is not the case, then a right held by a *group* of persons may violate rights essential to the liberty of individuals, whether members of the group or not. To see this, assume that a certain group is given a legal right to force one of its members to have a tranquilizing drug injected into his body. Assume also that the member will not consent to the injection. If the group's legal right to inject the member overrides his objection, then he no longer has control of what is done to his body. As a result, he has lost a basic property right in his body that is necessary to life and safety; his freedom to live his life as he chooses has been drastically compromised. As another example, assume that a certain group of persons is given a legal right to free housing paid for by a ten percent tax on the annual income of all individuals earning more than 100,000 dollars a year. Whether these individuals object to the tax or not, they will have lost a basic property right in their material assets. Their freedom to use those assets as they choose has been drastically curtailed.

These arguments can be repeated as needed for any other pair of individual and group rights. They prove that any legal system that puts collective rights ahead of individual rights cannot be acceptable to persons who value individual freedom as a primary political ideal. For that reason, collective rights, regardless of their superficial appeal, cannot be the basis for rational social policy. Accordingly, there can be no legitimate group rights beyond the simple aggregate of individual citizens' rights. [2]

The Biopsychological Bases of Individualism

Much of the preceding discussion has been concerned with the manner in which individualism relates to the economic, social and political lives of human beings and with certain rules and rights needed to ensure ordered liberty. For the sake of coherence as a political philosophy, however, it is clear that the principles of individualism must be consistent with those biological, psychological and social traits basic to human nature. To demonstrate that consistency, it will be useful to list again several traits that define that nature. All human beings are characterized by:

- The body's need for a bounded container to separate it from its environment (Wiggins and Schwartz)
- The body's vulnerability to biological death in the event of breakdown of the boundary
- The body's need for connection to the environment in order to maintain normal temperature, ingest and metabolize nutrients and expel waste
- The presence of a brain and associated neurological mechanisms that generate the individual's self and its conscious, unconscious and self-conscious faculties
- A self that develops only in relation to others and needs ongoing connection with others to maintain its structural and functional integrity
- The self's need for intact boundaries to maintain functional coherence and emotional equilibrium, in analogy to the body's need for an intact container
- The self's needs for separation from and connection with the interpersonal world of other selves, in analogy to the body's needs for separation from and connection with the physical world
- Faculties of perception, cognition, affective response and motor control that confer upon the self the power of volitional choice, causal efficacy and self-directedness

- Vulnerability to breakdown of the functional boundaries between the self, other selves, and the physical world under the effects of illness, injury, isolation, excessive stimuli, etc., resulting in loss of emotional equilibrium, functional coherence, volitional control and adaptive efficacy
- An innate developmental thrust toward self-directedness, cooperation, and self-transcendence (Cloninger and Svrakac 2000)
- An innate potential for the achievement of intersubjectivity (Stolorow, et al 1994, Benjamin 1995): i.e., the perception of and respect for the other as an autonomous self with needs, values, agency and purposes of his own.

These defining characteristics of human beings provide the physical and mental foundations on which the process of individuation gradually constructs a competent person, one capable of autonomous action and voluntary cooperation. In the course of this process, the individual develops a sense of himself that goes beyond the mere fact of his physical separateness from all other persons and things: he also develops an enduring sense of his own *importance.* This sense of the self's significance is central to human nature, to the dignity of the individual, and to the conduct of human affairs. It is the individual's normal *narcissistic investment in himself,* a value which he places on himself as against others, that arises from multiple sources, biological, psychological and social. The investment process begins in earliest childhood. It is integral to the larger process of individuation. Among the influences giving rise to the individual's sense of self-importance are the following:

- The biological instinct for self-preservation
- The mother's and others' early loving investment
- Satisfaction in the exercise of will and initiative for one's own ends
- An increasing sense of control over one's thoughts, goals, desires, motives, sentiments and actions
- Emerging feelings of pride in one's own effectiveness
- The ongoing validation of one's worth that derives from the care and admiration of others

- The unique value one acquires in the eyes of others by reason of his instrumental importance to them
- The value he has by reason of the other's attachment to him
- The value that grows out of shared sentiments, empathy and identification in a relationship
- The fact that in any given any particular individual, it is his brain and his brain alone that creates, maintains and eliminates all of his thoughts and emotions; and it is his brain and his brain alone that initiates, sustains and terminates all of his actions.

Beginning in his earliest years, the child's sense of who he is and what he is worth derives importantly from his mother's perception of him as a very special being who belongs to her. In later years, his sense of unique personal worth is supported by the esteem of others for his particular identity, for his specific personal traits, and for the meanings he evokes in the minds of those who care for him.

The Relational Basis of Individualism

Ironically, these observations indicate an important relational basis for the philosophy of individualism. This basis arises out of the nature of man, the conditions of his life, and the manner in which human beings interact with each other. A particular expression of this phenomenon is the tendency to relate to individuals more intensely than to groups. Although it is common for us to care about certain groups of persons, there is nevertheless a universal tendency for humans to bond to and care strongly about particular individuals as opposed to generic ones. This type of caring confers value on a specific person not because he is a *generic* human being or a member of some collective, but because he possesses certain traits that belong specifically to him and because he has a unique significance to those who value him. This type of caring is among the defining characteristics of the human species. The experience of being cared for because of one's particular traits is normally present from birth onward in cultures where individualism is not suppressed.

Individualism is also consistent with the volitional nature of human beings. The source of human action always begins in the mind of a distinct individual even if he is acting in concert with others. Casual observation easily verifies the fact that it is the mind of an individual, and not some illusory group mind, that causes human events. It is the individual that makes plans; chooses and decides among alternatives; creates intentions; and initiates, sustains and terminates actions which affect others. And it is another individual mind, acting alone or in a group, that responds to such actions with choices, plans, decisions, intentions and actions of his own that counter or compliment those that affect him. Human events begin in the minds of individuals on either side of such transactions. They may, at any time, result in consequences ranging from trivial to tragic: great benefits, great disasters, great joy and great pain have arisen from the actions of individuals. World War I was precipitated by the action of an individual. The atomic age began with the actions of another individual.

These observations give rise to more general prescriptions for human relating, rules that have proven themselves in the course of history. If one respects the rights of others and treats them fairly, and if one keeps promises, meets just obligations, and takes care that he not injure others carelessly, then those others will be more disposed to return the favors, as the Golden Rule prescribes. This is the principle of reciprocal altruism. If, on the other hand, one violates another individual's rights, treats him unfairly, offends or humiliates him, fails to keep promises to him, or injures him through negligence, then one runs a strong risk of retaliation at the hands of the injured party. All of this may strike the reader as a firm grasp of the obvious, and so it is. But homely examples illustrate the point: the rights and strongly felt sensibilities of individuals must not be ignored at any level of human action. When they are ignored, one form or another of social disorder ensues: domestic violence, gang wars, racial discord, post office massacres, to note a few. The principle at issue bears repeating once more: it is always the individual, not the collective, who feels joy, suffers pain, generates ideas, pursues happiness, initiates action, seeks vengeance, consents to cooperation. It is ultimately the individual who effects and is affected by human action, and it is thus the individual whose actions must be permitted or constrained by social policy. Accordingly, it is the individual that must be the subject and object of any rational system of rules. There should be no surprise in this. Recognition that individuals are ultimately important in the events that affect them has evolved in keeping with the nature of man and the nature of his relationships with other men and in keeping with the conditions of human existence. The always intense and often vulnerable relatedness of man defines the human condition. For this reason, the illusions of collectivism never withstand the test of experience.

Ethics and Individualism

The *ethical* core of individualism assumes the right as well as the duty of the individual to make himself and his pursuit of happiness the top priority in his life, subject to any commitments, loving, charitable or otherwise, that he may freely make to persons other than himself. But if he is an ethical person in his own right, his pursuit of happiness will, as Adam Smith observed, almost always benefit others, though his efforts be expended for his own gain. The Wright brothers' passionate quest for human flight, for example, was surely motivated by the pursuit of personal happiness, not by devotion to others. But the benefits to the world of their passion have long been incalculable. In a rational society of rational persons, the individual's pursuit of his own satisfaction regularly produces goods, services and relationships that are beneficial to many others. The innate compatibility of long-term individual interests and long-term societal interests is evident in everyday life. It rests on the twin ideals of personal liberty and social cooperation, both of which are integral to the ethics of individualism.

Individualism and History

Historically, of course, it has been the possibility of realizing these ideals that has brought millions of immigrants to America and continues to bring them in the present. Their quest is a testament to the fact that every sane person flees, if he can, any government policies that bury the individual and his rights in some grandly conceived but always irrational common good. Indeed, persons escaping to America have always sought to live under the most basic of individualist doctrines: that the individual is sovereign under a system of laws protecting his right to relate to himself and to others by choice, not force. [3] In its insistence on the primacy of the individual over the group, individualism represents an ideal that specifies the types of societal arrangements in which human beings are best able to flourish. It validates the essential role of freedom in the life of man as it validates the essential role of cooperation in the life of man. There can be no rational compromise between the virtues of individualism and the destructiveness inherent in all forms of collectivism: in socialism, communism and fascism, in the madness of all cults, and in the persecutions of infidels by radical religions.

[1] *The following definition of collectivism from Theodorson and Theodorson,* Modern Dictionary of Sociology *is typical: collectivism is "The doctrine that economic activity should be controlled through collective action and not left to the unregulated actions of individuals in pursuit of their self-interests. It is the opposite of the philosophy of* laissez-faire. *The term is usually defined in a broad sense to include both systems of collective ownership of the means of production and distribution and systems of private ownership with strong state or other collective regulation. However, the term is sometimes used as the equivalent of socialism or communism."*

[2] *Consider the case where a lone man is near death from starvation and steals food from another person who has plenty. In strict terms the former has violated the property rights of the latter, although an ethic of compassion may trump the immorality of the crime. Furthermore, this type of theft will typically be excused under the doctrine of privilege for cases of necessity. Suppose, however, that the theft is committed by a large group of starving men against a large group of other men with plenty. We may then ask whether the numbers matter, and if so, how many starving men may steal from others who have plenty before this becomes an unacceptable violation of property rights. These examples illustrate the inevitable ambiguity of rules for human conduct in what the law terms "hard cases."*

[3] *As a matter of law, moreover, individualism precludes any person from even giving consent to being dominated or enslaved by someone else since any such consent is deemed irrational on its face and therefore invalid. This is the basis for the claim that the right to liberty is an inalienable right.*

22

Cause, Effect and Will

Where you are is where you are. Where you're going is up to you.
Charles Givens

If there is one word that describes our form of society in America, it is the word—voluntary.
Lyndon Baines Johnson

Intention and Will

As the growing child develops an increasing awareness of his own self-and-body as something distinctly different from all other things, he learns to act first on impulse and then by intention. By first willing something and then doing it, he finds that he can make things happen all by himself, entirely independently of anyone else. Foremost among these discoveries are the intentional movements he makes with his own body. His repeated experience of willed control over his body gives him his most immediate understanding of cause and effect in the world of instrumental acts. In addition, as he communicates to others using words, tone of voice, facial expressions, gestures and posture, and as others affect him by similar communications, he learns still another category of cause and effect, those actions that mediate relatedness to others. The experience of acting by independent initiative and being acted upon by others is the basis for the child's sense of agency in himself and in them.

The concept of will has obvious importance to the nature and significance of human choice, autonomy, agency and action, with special implications for the psychology of freedom. As a *noun,* the word "will" typically denotes some type of volitional process: an intent, inclination, commitment or disposition to do something, as in "he said he would go to the doctor but lacks the will to do it," or a command, as in referring to the will of God. Will may emphasize strength of purpose (where there's a will there's a way), denote energy or enthusiasm (he has a will to succeed) or denote a request, wish, or desire (her will that you come home). We emphasize the power of self-direction or self-control when we say that a person has a strong will, and the power of conscious and deliberate choice when we speak of freedom of the will. To make a will is to formalize one's specific desire concerning the disposition of certain matters.

The *verb* "to will" has obviously related meanings: to will something is to form a distinct volition to do something, i.e., to choose, prefer, select, decree, ordain, direct or order something; or to decide on some particular choice; or to convey or express a command. It is also relevant at this point to note the definition of the term *intention* as a closely related idea. A common meaning of intention refers to a mind-set or mental disposition, or determination to do a specified thing, act in a particular manner, or adhere to some line of action with a fixed purpose. To intend to do something is to have a resolve or resolution to do it. In a less common meaning, the term intention denotes the mind's capacity to refer to or think about something.

The emergence of will in the toddler age child either incorporates or foreshadows virtually all of these senses of will and intention. As noted earlier, the exercise of choice emerges naturally as the brain's most fundamental capacity, that of responding selectively to input from the environment. As this capacity matures and is integrated more broadly into the developing personality, both perception and response are influenced ("modulated") by increasingly complex brain processes. Multiple interrelated meanings may then be attributed to the simplest perceptions. Newly acquired, more elaborate responses constantly enlarge the repertoire of possible actions in any given situation. The mind becomes increasingly more complicated as the child grows.

The Emergence of Human Action

As he relates to himself and others, the child desires, prefers, chooses and initiates action, and thus becomes a source of willed action, wholly within himself. Unless suppressed by developmental trauma, this emergence of human agency invariably leads to the adult conviction that one can indeed live in a world of freedom simply by the unimpeded exercise of one's will. On this consideration alone, the concept of agency has far reaching social and political implications. Some additional observations regarding the origins of willed action in a free society may be useful at this point:

- To the extent that the child is allowed to exercise his will in a manner appropriate to his abilities, he develops a proper sense of himself as an *effective* actor. He acquires an early confidence in his own efficacy.

- To the extent that he learns to limit his willed action within the moral and ethical constraints of his immediate family, he develops a proper sense of himself as a *legitimate* actor. In an atmosphere of "family law and order," he learns the early rudiments of conscientious action, the later basis of cooperation.

- To the extent that he is allowed to act on a variety of desires and to gratify them as he wishes, he enjoys an introduction to individual liberty. He develops a proper sense of himself as a *free* actor, whenever and wherever such freedom is legitimate.

- To the extent that his willed actions are responded to in a cooperative manner, as opposed to exploitation, rejection or abuse, the child develops a proper sense of himself as a *cooperative* actor, as a willing participant in collaborative endeavors.

- To the extent that the child's interaction with caregivers requires him to recognize and respect them as autonomous persons in their own right, the child becomes a *mutual* actor. He honors others as sovereign agents with independent purposes, not as depersonalized objects to be exploited for his own purposes.

Human action is healthy when it is *effective* in the pursuit of happiness, *legitimate* in its respect for the rule of law, *free* because coercion is prohibited, *cooperative* when consent is voluntary and rewards are earned or given freely, and *mutual* in honoring the universality of rights to liberty and justly acquired property. The economic, social and political arrangements inherent in all collectivist societies invariably render individual action less effective because it is disempowered by the state, illegitimate because it is condemned by the state, unfree because it is oppressed by the state, less cooperative because it is coerced by the state, and less mutual because it is dehumanized by the state.

Erikson on the Nature of Will

In his 1964 book, *Insight and Responsibility*, Erikson continued the evolution of his thought on the child's early growth toward autonomy. It is appropriate now to review some of his ideas on the emergence of will as an inherent expression of that growth and to consider its relevance for individual liberty. Erikson understood will to be one of the fundamental character strengths of the human psyche and thus deemed it a virtue. It is an obvious expression of the innate capacity for volition, appearing spontaneously in the child's development if cognitive maturation is adequate, if the foundations of basic trust have been acquired, and if the self, in its early vulnerability, is not overwhelmed by anxiety, fear or shame. *Erikson's definition of will is relevant to a philosophy of liberty: will, he said "is the unbroken determination to exercise free choice as well as self-restraint in spite of the unavoidable experience of shame and doubt in infancy." This idea can be extended a bit: if the child's inevitable conflicts with the wills of his parents and others do not strangle his own emerging ability to respond to the world as he chooses, then he will be well-positioned, assuming other circumstances are adequate, to grow into an autonomous adult, an individual empowered to direct his own life as he accommodates others directing theirs.*

If matters go well enough during the first fifteen months of life, the child's capacity for volitional choice appears spontaneously. Then, with basic trust in place, his repeated experience of choosing and intending some purpose and making things happen by an act of will validates his role as a causal agent in the world of events. His exercise of will becomes the most observable manifestation of his growing autonomy and a primary expression of his developing self.

Unfortunately, no part of this process is inevitable. Erikson knew that the development of authentic autonomy and virtuous will is too often derailed when the self is excessively shamed into deep-seated self doubt, when the child's fundamental right to develop a mind of his own is challenged by threats of rejection, abandonment, injury or scorn. Under these circumstances, the foundations of self-direction, self-responsibility and cooperation are undermined. Not uncommonly, the damage is irreparable.

Will as a Virtue

As Erikson understood it, the concept of *virtue* intends those "basic human strengths which have evolved with man's prolonged childhood and with his institutions and traditions." He used the term, essentially, in two ordinary senses. First, to the extent that virtue limits disruptive behavior in the population at large, it denotes the *voluntary* exercise of restraint in the interest of social harmony. In this respect, virtue relates self-control at the individual level to social process in the aggregate. In a second meaning more specific to the individual's pursuit of happiness, the term virtue is understood as a "principle of human interaction that enables one to live a fully human life." Here Erikson recognizes virtue as an indispensable ingredient of character, one that plays a critical role in the individual's search for personal fulfillment. In this more personal meaning, the virtue of will as "will power" is the determination to persevere in the face of difficulty and energize what we commonly call courage. It is an element of resilience and the ability to tolerate frustration. Will and will power are part of man's moral dimension, as in the will to resist temptation and to delay or deny gratification in favor of higher moral values. *Erikson was quite explicit about the moral dimension of virtue, noting that it reflects those types of human pursuits that are "somehow right." The importance of this dimension cannot be overstated. It concerns, in particular, the question of what is necessarily right or virtuous in order for man to be free, given the peculiarities of his nature and the conditions of human existence.*

In accordance with customary distinctions, Erikson wrote that, "to will does not mean to be willful, but rather to gain gradually the power of increased judgment and decision in the application of drive." In this context, the use of will power refers to both an enduring refusal to indulge impulse, drive, appetite or temptation for maladaptive ends, and to the capacity for willed persistence in pursuit of rational goals, the virtue of determination. His definition explicitly rejects the perversion of will into childish demandingness or opposition. It notes as well the importance of increasing realism in the child's efforts to assess his world and respond to it. Erikson affirms the function of the will on behalf of purposes that protect and enhance human flourishing, those "applications of drive" that advance human mastery in the service of well-being. This lesson is critical in the child's early years, when his emerging will must yield to the realities of his physical and interpersonal worlds, lest he sacrifice well-being to illusions of omnipotence, or relatedness to self-centeredness. In Erikson's words: "man must learn to will what can be, to renounce as not worth willing what cannot be, and to believe he willed what is inevitable." The serenity prayer recalls this principle.

Will and the Foundations of Law

Society demands that each individual exercise will power in restraining those behaviors that might encroach on the persons and property of others. It creates rules, both formal and informal, that define the boundaries of acceptable and unacceptable behavior in our interactions with each other. The law assumes that we can choose to do right or wrong in these situations. Erikson understood that the rules created to govern human behavior are logically grounded in the concept of volition and in the child's early experience. In his words, "will is the basis for the acceptance of law and necessity, and it is rooted in the judiciousness of parents guided by the spirit of law." Judiciousness, here, is that soundness of judgment informed by the law's spirit of right conduct. The training of the child's will under this guidance must begin early in his development to ensure that his powers of self-direction do not become destructive to himself and society. As Erikson put it:

> Will, in turn, matures to be the ego's disposition over the strength of controlled drive. Such will power, however, must join the will of others in such a way that drive remains powerful and resourceful in all, even as it is restrained by voluntary self-abnegation and ready obedience. The institution which gives "eternal" form to such judiciousness is the law. The judiciousness which governs the training of the small individual's willfulness in its infantile beginnings is thus carried on by the individual (in his personal conduct) and, as a social demand, carried into institutions which guard the

> traditional and support a balance of leadership
> and followership, of privilege and obligation,
> of voluntary action and coercion. To its majesty
> organized man surrenders the disposition over the
> leftovers of willfulness in himself and in others,
> half hoping and half fearing that he himself may
> get away with small transgressions once in a while,
> even while watching his neighbors with coercive
> righteousness." (Erikson, 1964)

The law assumes that the individual has the capacity, or "ready obedience," to conform his conduct to the requirements of right action by a willed rejection of wrong action. This is the principled "self-abnegation" of the citizen who is both free and law-abiding. The law formalizes in statutes what reason tells us we must do in joining the will of others to live in harmony, or just to live at all. To deter wrong action, to validate our principles of right action, and to satisfy our desire to punish the wrongdoer, we legislate penalties to be imposed on those who violate the law. And we do this on the assumption that each of us is individually responsible for our wrongdoing; in a given instance, each of us could have willed to do other than we did.

Underlying this principle of law, as observed earlier, is the western individualist tradition, which implies the sovereignty of the individual and his natural right to direct his own life. But this tradition also entails individual responsibility and individual assumption of risk. Without these obligations we have only an apparent adult who, in fact, behaves like a child eager to direct his own actions but unwilling or unable to respect the rights and privileges of others, and unwilling or unable to tolerate the unhappy consequences he brings upon himself. If an adult directs his own life, after all, then it is he and he alone who must take responsibility for what he does, for who else can assume such responsibility without infantilizing him? If an adult directs his own life, then it is he and he alone who must anticipate and accept the adverse effects, not just the benefits, of all that he does, for again, who can do this for him without infantilizing him? All of this is comprehended in the legal concept of guardianship, where precisely those capacities for self-direction, responsibility and assumption of risk may, in fact, be found defective in a particular person. Then and only then, can some other individual who is truly competent be authorized by law to direct the incapacitated person's life, take responsibility for it, and assume its risks on his behalf.

23

Rules and the Child

By the just we mean that which is lawful and that which is fair and equitable.

Aristotle

Additional Meanings of Will

The child's eventual capacity to live in a lawfully ordered society depends heavily on his perceptions of family members who obey, or don't obey, certain rules in the conduct of their affairs. Erikson observed the education of the child in "domestic law and order" through rules communicated by parents and others. He noted that a certain balance must characterize the judiciousness that governs the rearing of offspring. Ordinary experience reveals that if parents assume an overly permissive posture regarding rules in the home, their children are more likely to become self-centered, presumptuous and self-indulgent. If parents are too restrictive, on the other hand, their children are more likely to become compulsive, self-suppressed and over-controlled. Thus the rearing of the child's will must encourage self-direction that is limited by appropriate self-restraint.

In this regard it is obvious that parents as models of prudent action are critical to the child's development. Children learn by trial and error, certainly, and by percept and precept as well, but they also learn a great deal by imitation and identification. They will observe sound judgment, or the lack of it, in the actions of their parents and others and will imitate it until it becomes habitual.

The child's early experience in the law and order of the home and in the economic, social and political logic that governs relatedness there becomes foundational for his later understanding of the privileges, obligations and prohibitions that order human action in society at large.

Erikson observed that the social problem of will is contained in the words "good will," a concept more complex than it might at first appear. As already noted, the good will expressed in courteous behavior contributes to social order by avoiding needless insult. *A more important concept of good will embodies a mutual limitation of all wills that prohibits any one individual from imposing his demands on others by force.* To achieve this most basic requirement for the mutuality essential to social order, some limitation must be imposed on the will of the child early in the course of his development. Otherwise his innate tendency toward imperiousness will override his ability to respect the sovereignty of others. Of course, at the ages of two and three years, his obvious physical and mental frailty, in itself, requires that he submit to the wills of others who are far more powerful than he is, even as his own will is emerging with great energy. This fact alone sets limits on what he can actually do, although not on what he can imagine doing. But we are ultimately interested in the child's development of rational self-restraint, not his submission to force; hence, the imperative that his will be recruited early in consideration of others.

Within a household of conflicting wills, Erikson asserts, a judicious parent "will gradually grant a measure of self-control to the child who learns to control willfulness, to offer willingness, and to exchange good will." The early development of the child's will is thus, ideally, a conditional process; it demands the beginnings of mutuality in both his attitudes and behavior by giving up willfulness, and it sets limits on his early illusions of omnipotence and inherent grandiosity. It demands that he show willingness to cooperate within the limits of his abilities. And it demands that he show good will, not ill will, toward others as he is instructed to respect others. All of this is consistent with our earlier observations on the emergence of intersubjectivity. In her efforts to train her child, the good mother requires that he recognize her as a subject in her own right, a person with purposes of her own to be understood and respected. For his benefit and as a matter of right conduct in her eyes, she will not allow him, after his infancy has passed, to treat her as just an object, a mere resource to be willfully exploited for whatever satisfaction he can extract from her at the moment.

Mutuality and Power

Setting limits on the child's will has both real benefits and perceived losses for him. Erikson recognized the disappointment the toddler age child feels in giving up his willful demandingness, his imagined grandiosity and his illusions of infantile omnipotence. In fortunate children, parental love and empathy in support of increasing self-control and mutuality minimize the pain of this passage. In these cases, parental affection and judicious limit setting eventually dissolve the willfulness of the toddler into realistic self-direction and willing cooperation with others. *For less fortunate children, by contrast, this turning point in the autonomy phase of development is a crisis never resolved but only defended against by a relentless drive to make the imagined omnipotence of childhood come true in adult life. In these cases, early failures in affection, empathy and limit setting on the part of parents result in children who grow up feeling deprived of love, impaired in self-direction and self-restraint, unable to be mutual and determined to dominate. As adults they seek power over others in order to get by force what was not given to them in childhood.* As noted elsewhere in this book, the drive for power in such persons seeks to quiet the primitive fear and rage associated with early deprivation and the shame of helplessness. The original trauma leaves such children with life-long ambivalence toward the caretakers who alternately gratified them, deprived them and dominated them. This original ambivalence is easily transferred to others in later life, complicating relatedness with oscillations between love and hate, dominance and submission. Less well known is the ambivalence felt by the child toward himself. He easily imagines himself grand and powerful when gratified, but unlovable, inferior and weak when frustrated. As Erikson observed: "In the end, the self-image of the child will prove to have been split in the way in which man is apt to remain split for the rest of his life. From here on, the able and the impotent, the loving and the angry, the unified and the self-contradictory selves will be part of man's equipment: truly a psychic fall from grace."

The Just Social Order

At the same time, Erikson recognized the possibilities for healing the child's anger, disillusionment and humiliation in discovering that the world is not his to command. These possibilities reside in the values of the culture generally, and in the ability of parents more specifically, to convince the child that giving up his infantile grandiosity and omnipotence is not a deprivation or injustice or humiliation, but instead a major achievement on the road to maturity, something about which to feel proud and pleased, not ashamed. When this effort is successful, pride in self-reliance and pleasure in mutuality eventually replace the small child's insistence that he ought to run the universe. The ability of parents to convey this message of consolation depends, Erikson understood, on their own grounding in "a reasonably just civic and world order that offers a healing sense of justice." In western cultures, the reasonably just social order he speaks of is one that must be based on those principles that reflect the bipolar nature of man:

- The just social order must honor the sovereignty of the individual by recognizing his right to direct his own life, as it honors the relatedness of all individuals in the community through an ethic of voluntary cooperation.
- The just social order respects the liberty of the individual as it requires him to take responsibility for himself and to assume the risks that inhere in his actions; it does not intrude on his natural freedoms, nor try to protect him from himself, nor compensate him for his mistakes by giving him something taken from others.
- The just social order respects the ownership of property justly acquired and the integrity of contracts fairly made; it does not violate property rights nor invalidate properly binding agreements.
- The just social order respects the principle of equality under the law as a barrier to political manipulation; it does not exempt some from the requirements of the law nor grant political favor to others.

- The just social order requires constitutional limits at all levels of government to prevent it from violating man's natural rights; it does not deprive an individual of the ownership of his life, liberty or property through the politics of coercion.

Needless to say, such abstract matters cannot be explicitly taught to the child by his parents or anyone else, at least not at an early age. But the child can be taught how to live in a just social order by observing the everyday actions of competent parents and others. To be empowered by principle in such teachings, parents must be grounded in those moral and ethical traditions that tell them what is fair, just, morally right and equitable. To guard against erosion of these values, parents must also realize that a just social order cannot endure when fundamental freedoms are violated by organizations that coerce others, especially those organizations called governments. The child does not grow in, and parenting does not occur in, a vacuum of societal values.

24

Attachment Revisited

Anxiety is the dizziness of freedom.

Soren Kierkegaard

Attachment and its Vulnerabilities

As an extension of the infant's need to achieve basic trust, the toddler-age child's most primitive need in the service of survival is a secure attachment to those who care for him, typically his mother or her surrogates. This attachment is inherently vulnerable to disruption from both sides. The toddler's perception of disconnection or disturbance in this attachment may be real or imagined. When the disturbance is real, as when the mother's behavior is affected by symptomatic illness or personality disorder, the child's experience is invariably one of intense anxiety, and it may well progress to disorganized fear and rage, the so-called "catastrophic reaction." His alarm may be so intense under these circumstances as to precipitate a tantrum of violence against his caretaker, or against an inanimate object, or even against himself. The child's growth is adversely affected if these experiences are repeated often enough, because he is then forced to construct defense mechanisms to reduce the pain of overwhelming dysphoria.

In addition, evolution has so sensitized the child to separation from his caretakers that he may also *imagine* or misconstrue threats to his attachment, especially in respect to his mother, and believe that she is not available to him when in fact she is. Typically, these perceptions will be countered by the reality of what is in fact a secure attachment, with the happy consequence that no adverse effects develop over the long term. Still, this pervasive hypersensitivity in the toddler-age child's experience of relatedness reaffirms the critical role of attachment in human development. Sustained disturbance in the bond between mother and child has predictably dire consequences for his growth to competence. Especially notable is the fact that the experience of repeated real threats to secure attachment in infancy and childhood undermines the individual's expectation in later life that he can achieve an enduring sense of security through voluntary cooperation.

Insecurity and Tyranny

The child's enduring perception of insecurity typically generates a compensatory urge to control others by one means or another. The psychology of attachment has helped to understand the dynamics of persons who use power for such purposes, especially the tyrant's use of the power of government. Modern attachment theory confirms what has long been understood intuitively: that any serious threat to the child's earliest attachment to the mother, when repeated often enough, produces a lust for power over others that is acted out later on in one or another of life's arenas. In political arenas, as in economic, social and personal ones, the tyrant's motive is not derived primarily from his instinct for aggression *per se* nor from some real or imagined need for sexual satisfaction. Nor are his pretenses to grandeur or divinity or his obsession with material wealth understandable as primary expressions of sexual, aggressive or acquisitive instincts. Instead, these perversions of human relatedness are better understood as consequences of traumatic early attachment and their distortions in the development of the self. Of course, no infant is born with such perversions. Rather, the adult drive toward omnipotent control of others, in any arena whatever, is rooted in fears of separation, abandonment, loss or abuse—the residual effects of early attachment gone wrong. The need to dominate others arises from the tyrant's need for absolute assurance that the catastrophic loss of dependency or the pain of abuse so devastating to him in his earliest years will not be repeated. In his determination to control the world, he constantly defends himself against what Karen Horney aptly described as the most basic of human fears: being alone and helpless in a dangerous, indifferent world, the nightmare of the abandoned, terrified child. Persons plagued with such fears easily conclude that it is in their greatest interest to dominate others, or to imagine that they can, and to set about achieving that goal through the manipulation of government power.

When attachment is secure over most of the child's early years, on the other hand, a foundation is laid for the development of healthy mental representations of the self and others and for relationships grounded in cooperation, not coercion. Under these circumstances, and where parental and cultural values support the child's growth to maturity in the tradition of western individualism, the emergence of increasing degrees of autonomy proceeds apace. In this tradition the child increasingly defines himself as a unique, sovereign individual who seeks to actualize himself through cooperation with others, while rejecting on principle any opportunity to dominate them.

Personality Structure, the Self and Others

It has already been noted that the development of the very young child is colored by certain inherited temperamental traits which affect both his general tendency to persist in whatever he is doing and his more specific reactions to harm, novelty and reward. On this infrastructure of temperament, the child internalizes representations of himself and others as he acquires patterns of behaving toward himself and others. These patterns result in the "structuring" of the psyche. We say that a given individual's psyche or personality is structured, and uniquely so, to the extent that certain patterns of thinking, emoting, behaving and relating have become firmly entrenched in and characteristic of his personality over time. These structures constitute, in the reigning metaphor of the day, a personalized operating system and database on which the events of routine existence are processed and routine responses generated. As growth proceeds, these structures give rise to the executive functions of the self and establish its competence to meet the challenges of living.

The most important of the child's enduring dispositions are those that involve his attitudes and behaviors toward himself and others. It is intuitively understood that the child reared in an atmosphere of love, affection, protection, empathy, stability and limit setting is likely to experience his life as largely satisfying. Under these conditions he will not often feel negatively aroused in any enduring way about himself or about the persons he relates to. Instead, the emotions that he associates to himself, to his caretakers, and to his relations with his caretakers will be positive for the most part; he will feel generally good about himself, about them, and about relating to them and to others. If he is appropriately satisfied over the first three or four years of his life but not unduly indulged, he is likely to find that giving up his infantile demandingness and reducing his toddler-age self-centeredness cause him no great distress. He can willingly leave those eras behind as he enjoys growing beyond them.

In fact, the very atmosphere of love, affection, protection and empathy that is so desirable for child rearing is a reciprocal process in which the child *gives* love and affection as he receives them. In this earliest experience of reciprocal caring, the child learns to be aware of, to identify with, and to accommodate to his caregiver's mental and emotional states, not just his own, and he learns to do all of this joyfully and with pride. Repeated experiences of *reciprocal* caring encourage and reinforce the child's capacity for mutuality within the limits of his abilities. They also lay the groundwork for self-esteem based to a significant degree on his ability to cooperate and to empathize with the inner world of the other. On this foundation, the preschool age child quite willingly renounces his infantile need to control others by coercive means. His embrace of the ideals of voluntary cooperation and his growing ability to take pleasure in the happiness of others proceed naturally as he leaves the tyranny of infantile narcissism behind.

25

An Overview of Early Development

We learn about empathy and compassion not from what we're told but from how we're treated.

Stanley Greenspan

The Complexity of Development

Much of this work so far has described early developmental influences that affect the individual's ability to cope with the expectable challenges of adult life. Emphasis has been placed on the child's attachments to his mother and others who take care of him during the first few years of his life as critical influences in his development. Common observation verifies the claim that the child who is raised in a reasonably stable atmosphere of safety, affection and love will be empowered later on in his efforts to meet the challenges of adult life effectively. In addition, certain developmental processes have been described that are central to the construction of the child's personality. Primary among these is the process of individuation, which builds on the achievement of basic trust in the first year of life and continues during the second and third years with rapid advances in cognitive abilities and instrumental skills. Individuation proceeds further with the emergence of agency, the acquisition of stable mental representations of self and others, and the beginnings of early relational patterns that strongly influence later capacities for mutuality and cooperation.

A first encounter with this array of processes can easily become confusing to the uninitiated. To minimize such confusion, it may be useful at this point to review in outline certain developmental phenomena that are intrinsic to human growth and that favorably affect an individual's ability to cope with adult life in a free society. The following are among the more important physical, cognitive, instrumental, and relational changes that characterize the first three years of life. Implications for later development are noted where relevant.

Biological and Early Psychological Foundations

1. A given human being is a physically separate entity whose integrity as a biological organism depends upon an intact, bounded container for protection. Despite its separateness, and also because of it, the body must maintain certain connections with its environment. The combination of separation from and connection to the physical environment protects the processes needed to sustain life. The physical separateness of human beings is the biological basis for individualism.

2. A normally endowed human being has a brain and associated neurological mechanisms that generate all of his mental processes, including his self-system and its conscious, unconscious and self-conscious faculties. The self develops only in relatedness to other selves and seeks enduring connections with others. In analogy to the body's need for an intact container, the self needs intact boundaries to maintain functional coherence and emotional equilibrium. In analogy to the body's needs for separation from and connection with the physical world, the self needs separation from and connection with the interpersonal world of other selves. Breakdown of the mental boundaries between the self and other selves disrupts the ability to function rationally, control impulses, regulate emotions and cope effectively. The self's separateness from other human beings is the psychological basis for autonomous action. The self's connectedness to other human beings is the psychological basis for cooperative action.

3. Physical maturation in the first three years of life results in major increases in physical strength and coordination, together with increased control over eating and eliminative functions. These advances are paralleled by rapidly expanding cognitive and communicative capacities. Emotional states and their expression are increasingly differentiated and elaborated in this period, and they are to an increasing degree regulated by cognitive processes. The child's greater tolerance for physical separation from the mother parallels his rising interest in the world around him.

4. The maturing faculties of perception, cognition, emotional response and motor control confer upon the self the faculty of agency: the power to make things happen by an act of will. When combined with increasing capacities for choice, preference, self-assertion and opposition in the context of expanding instrumental skills, agency permits an increasingly complex self to express its intentions through willed action. With this development, the child becomes a cause in the world of human events.

5. Good enough attachment to and largely satisfying experiences with the mother and her surrogates during the first fifteen months of life lay the foundation for basic trust, a kind of preverbal visceral optimism about existence. In a continuing atmosphere of positive emotion, the child further internalizes, solidifies and differentiates earlier benign representations of the self and others.

6. Rapidly developing cognitive abilities, expanding instrumental skills, and enhanced control over emotion and body functions permit greater interaction with the physical and interpersonal world. These experiences enrich the toddler's representations of himself and others; they reinforce his realistic sense of control, autonomy, will and agency as his interactions with others become more elaborate. Increasingly stable self-representations and other-representations in the second and third years parallel the child's increasing control over mood and emotional response. These integrative developments contribute to

what has been called "self-cohesion," "self-constancy" and "object constancy." These terms refer to the enhanced mental, emotional, behavioral and relational stability that characterizes the child's experience of himself and others, even as that experience becomes more complex.

7. Under good enough parental care, the structuring of the self proceeds by integrating its innate capacities to perceive, think, emote, choose, act and relate into adaptive patterns of behavior. With good enough parenting, these patterns incorporate Erikson's virtues of hope, will, purpose and competence, and Cloninger's character traits of self-direction, cooperation and conscientiousness, together with certain additional capacities noted below. The child's ability to accomplish these developmental tasks depends upon continuing parental care, which must support his growth on the foundations laid down in the first three years of life. Listed below are certain developmental achievements which have their origins in those years and which affect the child's eventual growth to maturity:

    • Increasing depth and complexity of attachment to others
    • Expanding cognitive, communicative and executive functions
    • Differentiation, elaboration and control of mood and emotion
    • Regulation of aggressive, sexual, dependent and acquisitive impulses
    • Tolerance for frustration, delay, disappointment and loss
    • Limit setting, compromise and substitution of satisfaction
    • Demarcation of personal and interpersonal boundaries
    • Understanding of cause and effect in the physical world
    • Choice, will, preference, intention and agency
    • Reduction in infantile dependency, early interdependency
    • Affection, intimacy and loving sentiments

- Identification, empathy and recognition of the other
- Mutuality, generosity and accommodation with others
- Separations, reunions and substitutions with caretakers
- Self- esteem and other-esteem, idealized self and idealized other
- Personal identity, personal space and parameters of relatedness
- Acquisition, possession, ownership and property
- Understanding of cause and effect in interpersonal transactions
- Efficacy, legitimacy, freedom, cooperation and mutuality in action
- Understanding of approval, disapproval, acceptance and rejection
- Value judgment and the rules of engagement with others
- Mitigation of infantile omnipotence, dominance and submission
- Mutuality, right conduct and constraints in the formation of conscience
- Elementary ideas of rights, fairness, merit, reward, penalty and punishment
- Realism, reason and rationality as governing ideals
- Elementary negotiation, compromise and accommodation in conflict

8. These massive changes occurring in the child's cognitive, affective, behavioral and relational abilities in the second and third years of life enable him to assume more and more of the functions for which he was totally dependent on his mother and surrogates during the first year. During the toddler era he displays abilities to think in ways forecasting later intellectual competence; he learns the rudiments of cause and effect, the fundamentals of speech in grammar, syntax and vocabulary; he learns to identify and communicate about his body and its various states such as hunger, thirst and malaise; he responds

emotionally to his world in increasingly complex ways; he develops choice and will and the ability to pursue a goal; he transports himself from one place to another; and his rapidly expanding abilities to think, feel, imagine and play enrich his life and structure his self. He is, in short, capable of action on his own behalf, however primitive, imprudent and often foolish it may be. This early capacity for self-directed action is the basis for later autonomy.

9.   The rapid expansion of the toddler's instrumental skills, his burgeoning power to choose, his growing ability to communicate, and his voracious appetite for exploring the world all fuel his individuation. This era marks the early flowering of the self, the first element in the concept of self-governing. The child's experience with the physical world, as with his interpersonal world, lays the foundation for his personhood. Perceptions of the world which are endlessly intriguing seduce him each day and move him to explore to the point of exhaustion. He plunges eagerly into this world, playing with it, grappling with it and reveling in it joyfully as he discovers a universe beyond his mother. In no small measure, it is this passionate romance with new things and events that helps the toddler to differentiate himself from his caretakers, who are now no longer his *only* world, however critically important they remain for him. To be sure, if all is well between mother and child, his deepening attachment to her and his budding attachments to others proceed apace. But his growing immersion in the world at large during the first three years of life feeds his blossoming self by broadening and deepening his experience with every new facet of life presented to him.

The small child's increasing mastery in these years gives rise to the beginnings of that later self-competence from which the core meaning of autonomy derives substance. To appreciate the extent of the transformation during this period, one need only recall that just two years earlier, in the first year of life, the infant was totally dependent upon his mother. At that time he was little more than a bundle of physiological functions, unable to feed himself, put on his clothes, take care of toilet functions, transport himself anywhere, or communicate his wants in any but the most rudimentary ways. Moreover, and notwithstanding its particular temperamental endowment and the parents' projections of special characteristics into its primitive behavior, there is not much in the infant's presentation that can be described as "personality." But this picture soon changes dramatically. With another two years of life under its developmental belt, the largely physiological infant has fleshed out the contours of a future self. He has now become a small but dynamic source of human action, with a budding identity all his own.

The Emergence of Mutuality

The discussion so far has reviewed the concept of autonomy in rather conventional terms, emphasizing the child's beginning individuation as a process involving his emerging self and his increasing assumption of functions formerly under the control of his parents. It has been observed that although his mental processes are still very limited in the second and third years, he is nevertheless able to perceive and think for himself in ways that he could not begin to do as an infant. He can better regulate his mood and emotions. He can behave in more complex and even symbolic ways in relating to himself and others. He can participate in more elaborate communications with others. Empowered by his expanding skills within the protective embrace of his family, the child's pleasure in his increasing competence leads eventually to an enduring sense of self-ownership and a core of self-esteem, if all else goes well enough.

But setting the foundations of true autonomy in the first three years of life should establish not just greater independence of action and an enduring sense of efficacy. These years should also install firm representations of the caretaking other—not just the self—as good, lovable, and deserving of consideration. Under adequate care, a core of loving esteem for the mother develops in the child concurrently with his developing esteem for himself. Of course, her tender attentions to him in themselves generate loving sentiments at the core of his attachment to her. But her awareness of his growing cognitive and emotional competence will suggest a growing relational competence as well and should lead her to ask more of him as a condition of her approval. For this purpose she will make her wants known to him more often while always taking into account his actual limitations. Her own levels of fatigue, frustration, anxiety and anger will affect her empathy for the child's needs and her estimate of what he can do for her and not just for himself. Whether to indulge or limit him, permit or prohibit him, may not be an easy line for a mother to draw. Her projections of her own unconscious thoughts and emotions, her own unresolved needs and longings, all constitute potential distortions in her assessment of what is best for his growth, and for herself, at any given moment and may easily affect her response to him, often negatively.

But when her care taking is good enough, and when she teaches her child to be as considerate of her as his limited abilities allow, she lays the foundation for mutuality in his future. She teaches him how to cooperate. She sets firm limits on any residual tendency he may have to manipulate others as a mode of relating to them. She avoids the development of pathological narcissism and ensures against the malignancy of sociopathy. *A mother who is thus able to require of her child that he treat her to an ever increasing extent as a sovereign individual instead of a mere instrument for his ends has profound significance, not just for the child's growth but also for the broader social order. In the family that facilitates his growth to competence rather than to character disorder, a framework of family "law and order" obligates the child to reciprocate the loving embrace from which he consistently benefits. Among other things, this framework demands of the child that he play by the rules: that he respect the persons, property and sensibilities of others and do what he agrees to do. The family communicates and enforces this obligation as both an expression of their love and a condition of it.*

The Deprivation of Indulgence

As should be apparent by now, any enduring over-indulgence of the child will deprive him of the foundations of conscience and the achievement of individuation. The "spoiled" child who grows up dependent upon overly-indulgent parents is deprived of the virtues of self-reliance and self-control and the attitudes needed for cooperation with others. Though he may present a façade of autonomy, he remains pathologically dependent on persons who accommodate him uncritically and thus fails to develop the capacity for self-regulation that is the essence of individuation. And because he has not been taught to be considerate of others, the indulged child is also deprived of the capacity for thoughtfulness toward others that is the essence of mutuality. The individuated person, by contrast, is able to regulate himself responsibly in a world of free choice and cooperates voluntarily in a world of shared goals. In particular, his autonomy immunizes him to that most pernicious residue of failed development, the need to manipulate others. Unlike the self-indulgent adult-child, the individuated man actively rejects, as a moral imperative, any opportunity to dominate, coerce, manipulate or defraud others. He rejects any such opportunity because his standards of fairness strictly prohibit it, and because any such maneuvers would immediately signify a character weakness of which he would be deeply ashamed.

26

Initiative

There is in every child at every stage a new miracle of vigorous unfolding, which constitutes a new hope and a new responsibility for all. Such is the sense of and the pervading quality of initiative.
                                                                    Eric Erikson

The Concept of Initiative

If a child's development has proceeded well enough over the first four years of his life, roughly speaking, he will in all likelihood have acquired a sense of basic trust that permits him to engage the world without undue fear. In addition, if he has not been too traumatized, he will have acquired capacities for desiring, choosing and willing as fundamental dispositions essential to anything approximating a normal life. As physical maturation proceeds rapidly during these early years, the child acquires still another fundamental disposition: the ability to initiate purposeful action designed to reach an imagined goal, however childish the goal must be at a tender age. The capacity to initiate action develops naturally along with his ever increasing physical dexterity, his intense curiosity about a world that he feels compelled to explore, and his expanding ability to understand what he encounters. Blessed with boundless energy, he is forever doing something, even though the extent of his initiative may be limited by the effects of certain temperamental factors, especially those of novelty seeking, harm avoidance and reward dependence (Cloninger). Whatever these limits may be in a given child, he is otherwise disposed by nature to engage the world with persistence, subject only to his parents' prohibitions and to what will later become the constraints of conscience.

In these respects the concept of initiative is quite intuitive: to initiate is to begin, to commence, to take a first step or make a first move, to act or to think without being urged to. I make something happen in the real world if I imagine some action, choose to do it, plan its execution, intend its realization, and finally initiate it. Initiative is, above all, a biologically wired-in potential in all normal brains. It has primitive roots in survival and reproductive functions and is altogether essential to them. To live, after all, is to initiate something—anything—unless one is seriously disabled for some reason. The question in the case of the child is not whether he will act and continue to act as he grows through adolescence. Acting—and "acting out"—are what children and adolescents do every day until fatigue sets in. The question, developmentally speaking, is whether the child's innate ability to make something happen will evolve toward adult competence guided by standards of right conduct and good purpose and constrained by good conscience. The question, in other words, is whether a given child's trivial capacity to start something, including trouble, can be transformed into a grownup's ability to pursue goals that are personally self-actualizing but also socially useful and respectful of the rights of others.

Purpose and Initiative

The concept of purpose as a developmental achievement in the Eriksonian sense is clearly different from the usual meaning of the word purpose, which is often used as a synonym for motive or goal. The difference is especially evident where the development of mature initiative has failed. Defects in the achievement of purpose as a virtue that guides adult initiative leave the individual with literally childish purposes: motives or goals that are neither self-actualizing nor socially useful. The immature adult's childish purposes may be quite benign, especially if they narrowly restrict his interaction with the world as a defense against feeling overwhelmed. But it is not uncommon that such purposes in adults are not benign at all and may instead entail some form of aggression against others: attempts to control or dominate through manipulation or intimidation, for example, along with attitudes such as arrogance, belligerence or conceit typically arise as a consequence of distortions in early development. In the sexual domain as well, persons not guided by good purpose may engage in compulsive seduction and manipulation of others for acquisitive, vindictive, dependency and self-esteem purposes.

In these modes of perverse initiative the actors are on the make and on the take. Their purposes do not contribute to self-determination, do not transcend the self, and are not subordinated to mature ideals or to mutuality and respect for others. Their purposes are not limited by the constraints of mature conscience but instead serve the satisfaction of primitive drives. Excessively self-directed endeavors in such persons are geared to exploitative ends, not benign or socially useful ends. They are not directed to the joy of learning, nor to a pursuit for its own sake, nor to a wish to contribute to a community with which one identifies, nor to the pleasure of cooperation for mutual benefit. Contrast, for example, the concert artist whose self-fulfillment derives from his success in realizing musical ideals, his respect for a composer's intentions, and his wish to please the audience, with the ego-driven performer who is indifferent to musical ideals and who seeks instead to overwhelm his audience in an exhibitionistic display of virtuosity. Consider as another example the statesman committed to bettering the human condition by realizing ideals of individual liberty, the rule of law, equality before the law, religious freedom, property rights and the integrity of contracts. Contrast this person with the political predator who seeks elected office for personal aggrandizement, power, wealth, celebrity, and the opportunity to manipulate and dominate others instead of cooperating with them.

From a developmental point of view, it is quite clear that constructive ideals and good purpose are derived initially from the child's idealized perceptions of his parents, his imitation of them, identification with them and incorporation of their values. In the absence of appropriate values transmitted "judiciously" by parents, to use Erikson's term, the child's immature initiative will too often be used for maladaptive purpose, not constructive ones: his innate ability to make things happen will be recruited for impulse satisfaction and for defense against whatever wounds he has suffered in his formative years.

Normal and Pathological Guilt

Building on good enough development in the first two or three years of life, the capacity to feel guilty, and to restrain behavior to avoid guilt, arises in the third or fourth year. Among other prohibitions—those against undue self-indulgence, for example— the early emergence of guilt serves importantly to suppress the child's primitive erotic and aggressive fantasies toward his parents. If all goes well enough in subsequent years, that capacity eventually expands into a fully functional adult conscience with broadly based standards of right conduct. The affective or emotional component of the well developed adult conscience can be called "normal guilt" on the understanding that it acts adaptively when it regularly prohibits bad actions from occurring or punishes the actor appropriately when he yields to temptation. Arising in the course of healthy development, normal guilt is a fundamental component of the mature psyche, integral to the functions of normal conscience, that is, to its primary task of conforming one's actions to rules of right conduct.

The *pathological* guilt that opposes initiative in Erikson's developmental scheme is a related but qualitatively and quantitatively different concept. In his conception of guilt as a barrier to healthy initiative, Erikson had in mind the immobilizing effects of pathological guilt, not the properly constraining effects of normal guilt. He understood pathological guilt as an irrational, self-condemning force that could severely inhibit normal initiative in the adult, crippling his capacity for self-assertion and undermining constructive engagement with the world. Guilt of this type may be understood, in addition, as an extension of pathological shame acquired in earlier development. Together, these highly maladaptive emotions lead to serious impairments in all dimensions of adult life, especially those involving intimacy with others.

The Biology of Initiative

As observed earlier, the brains of lizards, like the brains of animals more or less primitive than lizards, routinely initiate those fundamental actions necessary for survival and reproduction. All animals initiate movement toward or away from environmental stimuli in order to satisfy an instinctual impulse or escape a noxious event. Particular regions of animal brains have evolved to initiate action that flows first from a plan and then from an intention to act. It is also well known that these regions must be neurologically intact in order for action to occur. The Greek word for acting or doing is "praxis;" the word apraxia is the term used by neurologists to designate an inability of the brain to initiate action because of some injury to the neural circuits that mediate action.

While the basic biological capacity for initiative requires only a healthy brain, the psychological capacity for initiative requires a minimally healthy mind, one that is not blocked from certain types of action by pathological shame, guilt or fear. In parallel with these observations, the neuropsychiatrist distinguishes between two types of impaired initiative, those due to a neurological disorder—a stroke, for example—that disrupts the biological mechanisms of initiating action; and those due to an emotional conflict–a fear or guilt syndrome, for example—that inhibits the individual from initiating action.

In problems of the first type, an injury to the brain due to stroke may prevent a patient from initiating speech or moving his hand; the cause of the problem resides in a disease of the physical and chemical machinery of the brain. In problems of the second type, sometimes called "neurotic" or "functional" disorders, an emotional conflict, as distinct from a disease of brain tissue, may cause an inhibition or even a "paralysis" that also prevents the patient from initiating speech or moving his hand, but not for the same reason. In cases of this type, the impaired initiative is caused by unconscious mental mechanisms, not physical or chemical injury to the brain. Mechanisms of this type are almost always associated with underlying personality defects that have their origins in early childhood.

Impairments in initiative inevitably have profound effects on one's adult life. They may impair one's ability to "get a life" in the broadest sense: to initiate sustained effort in seeking the conditions of a good life. Deep seated feelings of guilt, humiliation or failure, or fears of retaliation or loss, in such persons prevent the pursuit of relationships, work and leisure interests. For those so afflicted, to initiate action for self-interested reasons is to risk unacceptable danger. In cases of this type, the brain is healthy but the mind is not, and neither life nor liberty can be fully enjoyed or appreciated. Creativity and ingenuity are stifled, and zest for life is short lived, if it emerges at all, as energies are dissipated in activities that protect against expected threats.

27

The Failure of Initiative

Nothing is so intolerable to man as being fully at rest, without passion, without business, without entertainment, without care. It is then that he recognizes that he is empty, insufficient, dependent, ineffectual. From the depths of his soul now comes at once boredom, gloom, sorrow, chagrin, resentment and despair.

Blaise Pascal

Initiative, Industry and Virtue

Although he surely acknowledged its deep biological roots in the human psyche, Erikson thought of initiative as a developmental achievement in a psychosocial sense, not primarily as a biological function. The fundamental challenge in this phase of development turns on whether the child's capacity for initiative can emerge freely in a manner that leaves him civilized but not disabled, and on whether he can acquire a normal conscience that appropriately limits his impulses without destroying his ability to think and act for himself. The extremes of failure in this phase are well known in legal and clinical settings: persons who have either no conscience at all, at one end of the continuum, or an overly restrictive one at the other end. In the first case, where initiative is allowed free reign in his formative years, a child is likely to become, at best, an adult narcissist who readily exploits others. At worst, he becomes a felon who commits heinous crimes with no guilt whatever. In the second case, where the child is made to feel guilty just for existing and to fear that having purposes of his own will trigger dangerous retaliation, the eventual result is an adult whose inhibitions render him unable to have a life of his own.

It is a truism that few good things happen in a person's life if he does not initiate them himself. And it is equally true that initiative must be guided by good purpose, by the pursuit of goals that are congruent with the principles of human happiness, and that do not bring the individual into conflict with his community. Obviously, the presence or absence of good purpose strongly affects whether what is initiated in a given instance brings benefit or harm to oneself and others. For most good purposes, initiative will be coupled with industry: the sustained, competent application of knowledge to the achievement of good ends. With the addition of innovation as a third element, initiative and industry lead to new ways to enhance the life of man. Inventions in modern technology are obvious examples.

The joint benefits of initiative and industry are especially evident in the economic arena, where one's pursuit of personal goals is achieved to a large extent by providing goods and services that please others. In this arena, the marketplace of goods and services communicates one's desires through buying or refusing to buy another's offerings, thus seeing to it that a particular individual's initiative, industry and innovation benefit the community as it benefits him. This extraordinary dynamic, the well known invisible hand of Adam Smith, is the mechanism through which individual initiative, expressed through self-interested pursuits, becomes the basis for the community's material security. Evolution has hard-wired the potentials for these dispositions into the human brain. They strongly define our nature as social animals who, when civilized, initiate and sustain cooperation with each other for the economic, social and political good of all.

Initiative and the Good

Much hangs on the term "civilized" here. It is clear, of course, that initiative can be used for destructive, even barbaric, ends. The concept of initiative that counts as a developmental achievement, however, envisions ends that are constructive for the individual and congruent with his community's good values. A normal capacity for initiative is obviously essential to the production of economic goods and services, but social and political processes essential to orderly community life also depend on initiative. The legal enforcement of lawful behavior and the protective functions of the military, for example, require the initiative of individuals acting alone or in concert.

With these observations in mind, the question arises as to what influences are likely to move human initiative in civilized directions: those that promote human wellbeing and not human suffering. What forces direct human initiative away from actions that merely discharge tensions or gratify impulses, often with destructive consequences? What forces direct initiative toward actions that enhance life, liberty and the pursuit of happiness? Erikson answered these questions with his definition of purpose as a virtue. His concept is explicitly a moral one, consistent with the fact that the developmental phase in which initiative emerges (Freud's oedipal phase) is also a phase of emerging morality in the child. Erikson wrote:

> "Purpose, then, is the courage to envisage and pursue valued goals, uninhibited by the defeat of infantile fantasies by guilt, and by the fear of punishment."

The definition says much in a few words. It observes that the development of initiative must overcome the potentially immobilizing fears and fantasies of life's earliest years. This is no mean developmental feat, since the fears of the first few years can easily be traumatic to the child's development, even to the point of crippling his capacity for initiative. Clinical experience reveals that fears arising in early childhood cause many persons to retreat from the challenges of adult life for reasons of imagined safety rather than "pursuing valued goals with courage" in the service of self-fulfillment. Avoiding this kind of impairment is critically important. The achievement of normal initiative and good purpose in the formative years of childhood empowers a person not only to act without undue fear, but to act effectively and to do so in harmony with others. It is worth noting in particular that the term "valued goals" –i.e., good purposes—entails a moral standard consistent with the idea of virtue. For Erikson, good purpose implies initiative that is undertaken both individually and cooperatively in the service of constructive endeavors: those that affect the human condition in a manner consistent with the values of one's culture and which enhance community life. Erikson's concept of good purpose is also consistent with his closely related conception of individual maturity: the ability and willingness to take responsibility for one's self and not blame others for life's difficulties without cause.

Further Reflections on Initiative

The present inquiry into the biopsychological foundations of liberty has been concerned with whether or not a given individual feels free enough in his own thought processes to know what he wants in life and to initiate the pursuit of self-fulfillment based on his own desires. Since all rational conceptions of freedom imply freedom to *act,* the concept of initiative has particular importance. In its most elemental form, the term initiative denotes the human mind's ability to implement internal commands through action, to move and control the body in the performance of instrumental acts. Initiative is what first enables the child and later the man to operate on his physical and interpersonal environment for some non-trivial purpose. The four and five year old child, earnestly immersed in the theater of his mind, exercises initiative as he pursues his playful goals for hours at a time. He takes this play seriously, absorbing himself in some literally fantastic pursuit. In his fantasy world he is actor, producer and director; he is the initiator of everything that happens. But a few decades later, the child who once played with such intensity in his tender years will resolve a business dilemma, or a family's logistical problem, or create a new theory of how the universe works. The initiative of the five-year-old child absorbed in play becomes the initiative of the adult in pursuit of the day's chores, or the dream of a lifetime.

As a social scientist, Erikson recognized initiative as a species-wide developmental achievement that spanned all cultures, and he concerned himself with those early influences that could impair the emergence of initiative as an essential human disposition. As a psychoanalyst, he recognized inhibitions of initiative in his patients, especially those arising from excessive guilt acquired in the early years of childhood. As an analyst in the Freudian tradition, he understood the special power of the oedipal drama and its origins in the small child's increasingly intense, erotically tinged, and possessive attachments to his parents. It is now common knowledge that in the third and fourth years of life the child's ever deepening attachment to his parents leads him quite naturally to imagine himself as the boyfriend or girlfriend, or husband or wife or lover, of either parent in turn, and to imagine that this romantic melodrama will become real and endure. Sometimes conscious of his wish to do something sensual with one or another of his parents, and sometimes less than conscious of such ideas, the four year old child imagines a fantasy romance with his nuclear family, replete with erotic excitement, angry competition, jealous rivalry, fearful retaliation and injury, humiliating rejection, guilty possession, and shame over inadequacy. This remarkable and literally fantastic drama, known to many as the Oedipus complex of ancient Greek theater, English literature, French philosophy and Freudian psychology evolves innocently and naturally from the child's elemental attachment to his caretakers. How this drama plays out in the long run has fateful implications for the child's future life and for his capacity for initiative.

Initiative, Virtue, and Freedom

As all psychoanalysts do, Erikson understood that for the child to become a member of society at large and not remain forever the child of his parents, he must sooner or later leave the drama of his family behind and invest his energies in the opportunities, relationships and rules that constitute the world outside of his home. He must feel free enough from his early ties to make a life for himself, and construct his own drama, beyond his family of origin. Part of that task involves the exercise of initiative, fueled by energies that would otherwise have remained confined to the family home. In fact, by the end of the fifth or sixth year of his life, typically, the child has largely given up his Oedipal fantasies, hiding them from himself and others in the darker recesses of his unconscious. Henceforth, residual elements of that drama may appear in dreams, or may be acted out indirectly in conflicts with spouses and coworkers, or perhaps explored later on in therapy. But its original scope and astonishing power will not ordinarily be readmitted to consciousness unless provoked by some extraordinary development—an emerging neurosis, perhaps, or the turmoil of a psychotic breakdown.

These observations on early development indicate that budding capacities for trust, hope, autonomy, will, initiative and purpose, together with their related dispositions, emerge in the course of normal human development. Ordered liberty thrives when individuals are able to trust in each other, cooperate through informed consent, make choices among alternatives, initiate action for their own benefit, and act in accordance with standards of right conduct in mutual relations with others. These capacities constitute the psychobiological grounding of human freedom. When properly evolved into their adult versions, they lie at the heart of all theoretical justifications for individual liberty in the pursuit of happiness and for the freedom to relate to others by mutual consent.

Additional Remarks on the Pathology of Initiative

Obviously the manner in which initiative emerges in the very young child depends strongly on what has gone before in his brief life, and on his genetic endowment. The first four or five years have already occasioned massive alterations in his budding psyche, transformations that are greatly facilitated in a positive direction by parental love, affection, empathy and engagement, and by what Erikson called the judicious guidance of parental caretaking. But these transformations are highly vulnerable to the effects of deprivation, neglect, abuse and indulgence, since under these influences serious distortions in personality development are likely to occur. The following patterns of pathological behavior are strongly associated with developmental distortions that emerge during the first four years of life. They are divided for convenience into two categories: those that represent *exaggerations* of normal dispositions acquired during these years, and those understood better as *inhibitions* of normal dispositions. The reader will easily identify persons who embody one or the other of these types.

In the first category are dispositions characterized by excessive aggression toward or manipulation of others in the exercise of initiative. Behavior arising from dispositions of this type is typically thought of as neurotic or character disordered, but may in some cases be part of a psychotic process. Persons who act in this manner are often seen as arrogant, haughty, hostile, brazen, rude, demanding, intrusive, controlling, overbearing, dominating, condescending, contemptuous, hyper-assertive, intimidating, "castrating," vindictive or sadistic. Additional examples include initiative in the service of spite, defiance, opposition, withholding, stubbornness, soiling and despoiling. In many instances, behavior of this type is criminally exploitative and destructive. Such persons are often described as being on the make or on the take and are not uncommonly engaged in conning or hustling others for material gain. Excessive initiative in the service of pathological greed is especially common.

A second category consists in those dispositions where initiative is seriously inhibited. Inhibition of this type leads to behavior that is fearful, unassertive, over repressed, over restrained, "castrated," guilt-based, shame-based, overly compliant, submissive, meek, dependent, defeated, passive, selfless and self-effacing. Such persons are typically lacking in self-direction, will and purpose and may be easily manipulated and humiliated. They are also disposed to seek childlike relationships with others, yielding their rights to self-determination in return for another's real or imagined protection from the responsibilities of adult life. Persons with this type of personality will often assume a childlike role in relation to government, voting for those who promise material security through collective obligation rather than for those committed to the protection of individual liberty. For such persons, freedom entails a degree of personal responsibility, including the exercise of initiative, that is too burdensome or too threatening to tolerate.

In some cases these modes may alternate in a given individual, with exaggerated initiative on some occasions and inhibited initiative on others. Behind these pathological dispositions is an abnormal personality organization that renders the individual vulnerable to intense anxiety, depression, rage and emptiness. Abnormalities typically present in these personalities include defects in basic self-representations and object-representations, excessive dependency and pathological self-centeredness. As already noted, these and other maladaptive characteristics are the enduring effects of early trauma of one kind or another. Serious defects in intersubjectivity, the capacity for mutuality and recognition of the other's personal parity, figure prominently among the deficits in these personality types. Associated impairments in self-restraint, frustration tolerance and the functions of conscience are obvious to the trained clinician.

Psychoanalytic self-psychology has also described the classical narcissist whose capacity for initiative typically serves exploitative motives. With behavior that is often aggressive and intrusive, and with characteristically entitled, grandiose and self-indulgent patterns of relating, persons with this type of pathology use their capacity for initiative to control others and manipulate them for personal gain. Narcissists typically feel exempt from the constraints that limit others. They are not above breaking rules, including formal laws that seek to protect the unwary. With initiative augmented by grandiose expectations, many narcissists ascend to leadership roles in major corporations or seek public office in order to further personal agendas for admiration, wealth and power while remaining indifferent to the obligations to others that are inherent in the offices they hold. The underlying pathology in these persons includes a defective self that is unable to regulate its own emotional state without manipulation of others, and unable or unwilling to respect the other's agency, basic rights, personal parity or equality under the law. Typically in denial of these patterns, the narcissist views others as mere objects to be used for selfish purposes and not good purpose, and certainly not as other selves to be respected within the meaning of the Golden Rule. In these dispositions and in his conviction that he is exempt from the constraints that others must respect, the narcissist presents potentially serious problems for the community dedicated to individual liberty, mutuality and the rule of law.

28

The Foundations of Industry

We can further recognize that the trait of industry is encompassed on the one hand by the danger of habitual compulsive striving to excel in competition, and on the other, by defeatist trends seen in an unwillingness to accept and face meaningful challenges.

Theodore Lidz

The Juvenile Era

If the foundations of trust, autonomy and initiative have been acquired in the first five or six years of life, and if the beginnings of their associated virtues of hope, will and purpose have been installed, the now school-age child is ready to take the next step on the way to his eventual adult identity. Erikson denoted this step by still another dichotomy: industry versus inferiority. In this stage, the juvenile era, the child learns much about society's arrangements for living, especially those that foster material security and govern social relationships and political process.

Freud characterized the juvenile phase, roughly the years from six to twelve, as a period of latency in which infantile sexual impulses fade into the recesses of the psyche, to remain largely dormant there until puberty reawakens them. Despite a reduction in overt sexual interest in this period, however, the child is very busy with other matters: his intellectual abilities advance rapidly as he acquires new instrumental skills and new social skills in further preparation for adulthood. His use of language becomes more elaborate, more richly communicative, and more useful as a tool of conceptual understanding. His emotional states and associated thought processes become more elaborate, more differentiated, and more expressive, and his sense of gender identification and role more consolidated. In the industry era the child learns to make things and do things and to relate in more complex ways to persons outside of his nuclear family.

The achievements and failures of this era have important implications for eventual participation in a free society. In preparation for later adult life, the child's relationships become more elaborate in their economic, social and political dimensions. In this period children observe others:

- Buying, selling and trading goods and services
- Sharing and dividing labor in joint endeavors
- Honoring and breaching agreements
- Acquiring, disposing of, borrowing and returning property
- Paying and defaulting on debts
- Earning and deserving material rewards
- Arguing the merits of a purchase
- Estimating the costs, risks and benefits of actions contemplated

Sooner or later the child learns to trade things on the playground, works in odd jobs, earns a fee or allowance, saves or spends money, makes decisions about what he can afford, considers competing alternatives, and learns that in most cases to choose A is to forego B. The era of industry is an era of elementary economic education.

In this period children also observe others:

- Doing the interpersonal activities of everyday life
- Socializing, cooperating, caring, care taking, opposing, thwarting, blaming, forgiving, apologizing and reconciling
- Feeling envious, jealous and competitive
- Setting and changing goals with others
- Keeping and breaking promises with others
- Making, breaking, repairing and rejecting friendships

- Being courteous to enhance the security and comfort of relating

Sooner or later the child learns to be friendly or not, to cooperate and accommodate or not, to forgive and forget or not, to treat others with respect or disrespect, to care for others or ignore them, to have fun and enjoy others, or create turmoil and frustrate others. In doing all of this the child begins a long series of experiments in roles, styles, personas and mannerisms in the search for and construction of an identity for life. The era of industry is also an era of socialization; the child discovers the world within himself as he discovers the world beyond himself.

In this period children also observe others:
- Engaging in the politics of the neighborhood and town
- Leading, following, negotiating, persuading, influencing, manipulating
- Coaxing, coercing, forming coalitions and managing opinion

Sooner or later the child encounters the politics of the schoolyard and the playground; the dynamics of clubs, cliques and gangs; favoritism and the seeking of favor; the hierarchies, maneuvers and delegations of authority; and ways of leading, following, conceding, compromising, dominating, controlling, yielding and submitting. The era of industry is an era of elementary politics in which the child learns the dynamics of influence. In the age of industry the child intensifies his rehearsal for life to come.

The Technologies of Everyday Living

The capacity for sustained, rational goal-directed effort is, of course, fundamental to adult identity. The ability to pursue a useful goal and to persist in the face of difficulty is not only essential to making a living but is also required for the achievement of anything else that is worthwhile in adult life. In the industry phase the child learns how to set goals, especially in his lessons at school, but also in chores at home and in projects in church, and how to sustain effort in the pursuit of goals. In countless daily encounters, the child's budding capacity for useful effort is rewarded conditionally by parents, teachers, and neighbors.

The child who learns to be industrious makes a critical contribution to his future for at least two reasons. First, what is learned in this phase involves various types of instrumental skills eventually needed for material security. The juvenile era introduces the child to the business of living, those activities that address the body's demands for food, clothing, shelter, medical care, transportation and other goods and services that sustain our lives. A second major acquisition in this phase is the "technology" of relatedness: the myriad interpersonal skills essential to the pursuit of joint effort for any purpose. Ideally the child learns in this phase of his development his culture's rules, conventions and social skills for interacting with others, especially those needed for cooperating in multiple venues.

The normal grade school child is eager to learn about the world; the rational society must be ready to accommodate him. In school he continues in a differently structured setting the preparation for adult life that began in the home. If all goes well in these years, he learns much about his culture's means of producing the goods and services needed for everyday life. Impelled by his innate curiosity, his introduction to the world teaches him to make things, do things and use things for useful ends and to do some things just for pleasure. He learns, in particular, the importance of voluntary choice in these pursuits. As he observes adults in the unending transactions of everyday life, he acquires an operational understanding of mutual consent: the routine voluntary buying, selling and trading that defines an economically free and socially well ordered society.

In the typical sequence of development, the foundations of industry laid down in the child's elementary school years emerge soon after the achievement of initiative in the toddler era. The child's increasing capacity for sustained purposeful effort channels his energies and gives direction to his initiative. In his growing interests in some school subjects and not others, in some sports and hobbies and not others, and in some persons and not others, he makes countless choices in what becomes a life long process of defining and differentiating himself as a unique individual. Of great importance in this individuation process is the growing self-confidence that mastery of instrumental skills builds over time. Under ideal circumstances this sense of mastery gained in the juvenile era reinforces an already healthy core of self-esteem grounded in earlier experience of parental love.

Equally important is the expansion of social skills beyond those acquired in the nuclear family. In the juvenile era, skills that are first learned in the preschool phase are expanded in associations with persons and groups outside of the family. New relationships with peers in school, church and temple validate the child's sense of belonging and advance his understanding of an interpersonal universe that he will one day inhabit as an adult.

The Juvenile Era: Play, Magic and Mystery

Selma Fraiberg wrote about the magic years of childhood, those of the toddler who lives in a fantasy world more than he does in the real world, and whose thought processes are not bound by facts and logic. But as every clinician knows, the capacity for magical thinking remains intact lifelong and is surely prominent, or should be, in the grade school years. The child who is overly serious, who lacks a capacity for what might be called benign impulsivity, not only misses the joy of play but also neglects the development of his innate capacity for creative thought and its power to help him solve life's problems. "Thinking outside of the box" should be child's play for the child. For proper development, such thought should be a routine experience, not just an occasional diversion from an otherwise sober practicality. Indeed, clinical experience in this regard suggests that the prematurely sober child is most likely depressed.

Acquaintance with things mysterious, magical or ineffable is not, of course, confined to play or to artistic pursuits but is instead integral to the human experience unless it is actively suppressed. The capacity for religious experience, for example, appears to have evolved in the human brain and to have survival value. A community whose members are united by shared religious faith may be more likely to withstand threats to its existence, regardless of their nature. Religious faith aids human endurance in the face of catastrophe, be it war, famine, disease or natural disaster. The rituals of worship count among the skills that facilitate such faith, bolstering courage in times of hardship and solidifying the bonds of relatedness in solemn ceremony.

Impairment in the industry Era

The observation that much behavioral pathology becomes evident during the juvenile era is consistent with the fact that the child's developmental task in this period is daunting. Success is by no means guaranteed though the process may go very well in some cases. When what is learned in this phase falls largely within accepted codes of conduct, the child's growing acquaintance with his culture's possibilities helps to channel his interests toward pursuits that enhance cooperation. When things do not go well enough, he may drift toward behavioral disorders, drug abuse or delinquency and the aimless discharge of tensions antithetical to cooperation. Especially ominous are those pursuits that involve the satisfaction of primitive impulses in antisocial, reckless or self-destructive acts. The twelve-year-old who has become immersed in a subculture of sex, drugs, delinquency and aggression in order to lessen inner torment is an all too common casualty of developmental deficits accumulated in the juvenile era and years preceding. Behind facades of breezy unconcern, children with these problems are typically tormented by anxiety, shame, depression, envy and rage. Their underlying sense of inferiority, which may be only dimly perceived, is paralleled by actual deficits in education, social skills and constructive identifications that may in the aggregate preclude the later achievement of adult competence. Aside from their manifest emotional pain, children who attempt to become adults with such deficits are unable to find a niche in the community of productive and cooperative citizens. Rather than contributing to the community, they are likely to burden it socially as well as economically. Developmental outcomes of this type have important effects on social policy and constitute an underlying dynamic in the liberal agenda. This point is developed further in a later section.

Failures in the grade school and adolescent eras usually do not occur without preceding developmental injury. Too often, deficits in earlier phases undermine the achievement of basic trust, autonomy and initiative and generate enough pathology to derail subsequent development. Children who have suffered such early injury have not acquired basic trust in the goodness of themselves and the goodness of life, nor the foundations of autonomy, nor the initiative needed for useful achievement. In these cases, residual anxiety, fear, depression, emptiness, anger, guilt, shame and self-doubt interfere with the child's ability to benefit normally from later phases. Attitudes arising in association with these pathological emotions may lead to passive-dependent behavior as a defense against fears of abandonment, shame or retaliation, or to oppositional, defiant or antisocial behavior as a defense against dysphoria and rage. For children already in serious conflict with their parents, the subcultures of gangs, delinquency and drugs may offer alternative affiliations that further undermine industry and competence. What is too often learned under these influences are the social skills of the delinquent subculture and the technologies of crime. The acquisition of useful knowledge about the world of good purpose and the constructive socialization of a normal industry phase are lost on these children, who then go on to suffer additional impairment in adolescence.

A potentially crippling outcome of the juvenile era emerges in those cases where a combination of parental deprivation and indulgence results in a "spoiled child" syndrome, a personality configuration characterized by demanding self-centeredness, low frustration tolerance, underlying depression, self-pity and chronic resentment. All of these traits impair the ability to meet life's challenges. The adult who has acquired them typically complains excessively as he seeks sympathy and indulgence from others. Behind an often whiny persona lies a needy inner child who is angry about not receiving what he believes to be his due as compensation for past and present deprivation. Attitudes of entitlement are prominent in these persons when they reach adulthood. Examples may be seen in political advertisements that feature elderly persons or other ostensibly disadvantaged groups. In the typical ad, an elderly person is outraged that someone, usually the government, is not providing something she needs: some form of health care, for example, or perhaps housing or transportation. Self-pity is prominent; so is envy. The origins of these attitudes lie in the formative years, not in the hardships of the present.

Healing in the Juvenile Era

For children who have not been too seriously derailed in their earlier development, however, the industry phase offers opportunities for adaptations that are less than optimal but still allow for some accommodation to adult life. Erikson alluded to the child who becomes too industrious by totally immersing himself in instrumental tasks as the "good little helper" or "good little worker." Children of this type may later define themselves primarily by what they can do, not who they understand themselves to be, or what dreams they pursue, or how they relate to others emotionally. They are likely to live primarily in the world of work. In that realm they may well perform dependably and productively, and often compulsively, but are likely to relate only superficially to others.

For some children, the industry phase becomes an opportunity for intense competitive striving in an effort to overcome feelings of inferiority and to discharge aggressive impulses. These children create an interpersonal world where triumphant victories, humiliating defeats and hated rivals are a daily drama. Heated contests become one's reason for being; life is a succession of competitive challenges, replete with bluster and intimidation where needed. The arenas for this drama are anywhere and everywhere: at the neighborhood playground and sports field, in the classroom, beauty pageant, talent contest or school politics. Later the drama shifts to battles in the business or professional or political world, or wherever a rival, real or imagined, is there to be defeated. As adults these persons describe "a fire in the belly" that drives them to the achievement they need for inner peace. But the peace is usually short lived, and soon the battle is joined again.

A related defense against feelings of inadequacy, doubts about being lovable, and fears of rejection seeks compensation in attitudes of elitism, conceit, pretense, special privilege and flaunting of material wealth, among other maneuvers. These attitudes often become evident in the juvenile era. In the world of adult striving, various combinations of such states and their defenses constitute the neuroses of everyday life. They are easily observed in economic, social and political arenas at every level. They are especially prominent in the halls of political power where the control of persons and policy can become an addictive fix against inner torment. The holding of government office provides an opportunity to act out a personal agenda disguised as a principled campaign for a noble cause. But all too often the noble cause, if it ever existed, is lost in the office holder's self-serving maneuvers for personal gain.

29

Achievement in the Juvenile Era

The morally responsible person whom conservatives admire can only grow out of the affectionate and secure family that liberals demand.

Stanley Greenspan

The Well Developed Juvenile

If the school age child's involvement in persons and pursuits outside of his nuclear family is healthy, the expansion of his world furthers his individuation into an increasingly unique personality, one that is now determined significantly by his interests and abilities. He gradually learns to define himself by trying out various roles and by participating in activities that he finds rewarding or frustrating. If he can explore the opportunities open to him in a reasonably safe manner, and if his choices are supervised by competent parents, the juvenile-era child learns an important fact about individual liberty: the pursuit of personal fulfillment through doing what he *wants* to do, when and where appropriate, is compatible with doing what he *has* to do in order to cooperate with others.

Assuming a juvenile has arrived at age twelve with average genetic endowment and without significant developmental deficits, what might he look like? An alternative question asks what a reasonable parent would hope for in her child at this age, given good enough nature and nurture. The following profile of a well-developed twelve-year-old of either gender illustrates a healthy growth track, one likely to satisfy most parents.

First, a reasonable parent would probably hope that her child is happy in the conventional sense of that term: free of depression, undue irritability or troublesome fears; generally enthusiastic about life; usually cheerful; actively engaged with the world; and blessed with the energy typical for the age. A genuine zest for life is not too much to expect in a healthy twelve-year-old. Second, a reasonable parent would probably hope that her child has at least enough intelligence to learn the usual school lessons and to acquire by intuition and instruction those minimal social skills needed to get along with most other persons, be they adults or children. A willingness to talk about his progress in school and about any significant problems in social interactions would certainly be useful in a twelve-year-old. For that matter, most reasonable parents would hope that their child of that age would be willing and able to talk about anything with them, for the usual reasons.

Third, most parents would hope for spontaneity in their child, since playfulness is inherent in the nature of children and important for their growth. Someone once remarked that play is the child's work. Johan Huizinga's writings suggest that play is the child's earliest expression of human freedom. (Huizinga 1955} It is true, of course, that an age-appropriate capacity for serious engagement in some tasks is desirable but not to the exclusion of whimsy, fantasy or imagination. Interest in fiction, in tales of the supernatural and mysterious, in drawing and pretending and playing with models of things, all stir the child's ability to imagine a world different than it is. Creativity of all types, like freedom itself, has its roots in childhood feeling and fantasy. Imagination gives rise not just to artistic works but to the ability to solve problems in every dimension of life. In this respect, creativity is integral to our adaptive nature. In persons in whom it has not been stifled, creativity remains active well into old age.

Fourth, it would be desirable if our hypothetical twelve-year-old has learned most of the rules that make for fairness in human relating, not just fairness in games. The reasonable parent would hope further that her child knows at least dimly that human relating requires a balance of legitimate rights, permissible actions, and associated obligations that promote order in the community. She would see to it that her twelve-year-old has acquired a healthy respect for law and order.

Fifth, one would hope that a twelve-year-old is known by most people as a "good kid" or a "nice kid:" that he or she is reasonably courteous, appropriately friendly and willing to cooperate. Most reasonable parents would not want their child to be surly, presumptuous, rebellious, hostile, spiteful, defiant, oppositional, insolent, aggressive, destructive or arrogant. It would also be helpful if this good kid would respect property rights and understand the importance of keeping a promise. It would be desirable if he were able to consider the sensibilities of others in order to avoid needless offense. We would be pleased if he would only rarely act in a loud, unduly disruptive or otherwise obnoxious manner. Ideally, the well-developed twelve-year-old would exercise such control on the understanding that living rationally with other persons imposes some constraints on one's conduct. While allowing for the average juvenile's inclination to break at least a few rules, the child that most reasonable parents would like to call their own would only rarely be profane in public and would not engage in sexually suggestive behavior in front of others.

In addition to these traits, reasonable parents would probably want their child to understand that one has to earn the enduring respect, loyalty and consideration of others and that those blessings are not one's due just by being alive. More specifically, reasonable parents would hope that by age twelve their child would have acquired substantial capacities for personal responsibility, dependability, obligation and accountability. Pride in doing what one is supposed to do or has agreed to do should be a part of a twelve-year-old's emerging standards of conduct. The connections between actions and consequences and the logic of reward and punishment should be firmly understood by this age. Most of us will not wish for a child who feels entitled to everything he wants. We will not hope for a child who tries to talk his way out of problems that he has caused, blames others for his difficulties, or acts as if he is exempt from the rules that apply to all. In this regard, the early sociopathic syndrome, like the spoiled child syndrome, counts among the worst of the potentially bad outcomes of the juvenile era. In these very troubled children, nearly all of the hoped for virtues are missing or poorly developed; and they are notoriously difficult to install at a later age.

Finally, most parents would prefer that a hypothetical twelve-year-old has learned the meaning of altruism and the satisfaction of service to others. If he has been the lucky recipient of good enough parenting, he will know directly what it means to be helped in a time of difficulty: to be understood, supported and encouraged when overwhelmed, cared for when sick, or rescued from a state of helplessness. The juvenile who baby-sits learns the elements of caring for someone much smaller, weaker, and more dependent than he. The school age child who cares for his younger siblings learns an attitude integral to Erikson's generative adult, the mature individual able to parent his own children and more broadly to nurture a good cause for his community.

The Virtue of Competence

Under good enough circumstances, the twelve-year-old child has learned much over the preceding six years. Most notably, his ability to think has advanced well beyond Piaget's sensory-motor and preoperational levels of the first six years. By the end of the juvenile era the child is able to think effectively in concrete operational terms and has begun to think abstractly. He has, remarkably enough, acquired most of the practical reasoning ability that he will need for daily living in the adult world. One theorist summarized the child's evolving cognitive capacities in this way:

> As a child develops cognitively, she or he can move beyond the observed to the inferred, beyond percept to concept, beyond concrete to abstract, and beyond intuitive knowing to conscious reflection. She or he becomes aware that events can have internal and symbolic meaning beyond their external and literal significance. As she or he invests events with meaning, the child can go beyond content to appreciate formal similarities, patterns and processes. As the child reflects on patterns and processes, she or he can reflect on systems, including social systems. Older children can reflect on their own patterns and processes and how they relate to those of others and the larger social world. (Yates 2002)

With vastly increased intelligence as compared with only a few years prior, and with several years of grade school under his belt, the normal twelve-year-old child has learned a great deal about the physical world and most of the rules governing the social world. He knows how to make things, do things and use things. He is thoroughly acquainted with physical cause and effect, and he understands the basics of psychological cause and effect. He knows a great deal about right and wrong. He understands the elementary economics of everyday life. He has enough social skills to get along. He has at least a crude grasp of the politics of the schoolyard and neighborhood. If he has been fortunate enough to be nurtured by authentic parental love and empathy and has acquired commonsense ideas of good conduct along with age-appropriate constraints of conscience, then he is as prepared as he can be for the coming challenges of adolescence. He has achieved the foundations of competence.

Competence and Healing

The events of the first six years of life establish the most basic structures of the personality and are therefore the most profoundly formative in the course of human development. It is nevertheless clear that the juvenile era is deeply influential in its own right, involving as it does complex processes by which the child is further defined and actively begins to define himself. The juvenile era is multi-modal in the most literal sense. Any review of the changes taking place in these years reveals important acquisitions in all areas of development: intellectual, physical, emotional, behavioral and relational. These acquisitions seem to occur most readily in this era as compared with others, as if there is some biological readiness for them once the psyche has acquired its initial structuring in the first six years. The contributions of the juvenile era build on those earlier acquisitions. All of them can deeply affect the child's eventual ability to live in the economic, social and political arenas of adult life.

Acquisitions specific to the industry phase are not the only benefits to be enjoyed in this period of the child's growth. Of particular interest is the fact that this period often serves to repair or at least mitigate the effects of earlier trauma. If a child's experience of neglect, deprivation or abuse has not been too severe, the industry phase of his development may offer opportunities for healing early wounds, especially through mentor relationships but also through his discovery of some interest around which he can build an identity, gain self-esteem, apply initiative and learn persistence. Teachers, coaches or counselors, for example, or perhaps an uncle or grandparent, may offer the child the kind of instruction, guidance, encouragement, empathy, affection and modeling of adult competence that he or she needs in order to overcome deficits in basic trust, autonomy or initiative. The restoration of hope and confidence in oneself that flows from a supportive adult may inspire the child to succeed in efforts he would not otherwise make. In fact, anecdotal evidence for such growth is strong, even in later eras. Stories of individuals who have found inner strength from mentors are legion, and the potential for such growth seems to remain active over the entire life cycle in most of us. For this and other reasons, social policy must appeal to the latent strengths of those persons who may yet reach competence, not offer a reward for disability that would foreclose that achievement.

30

Morality in the Juvenile Era

Holding people to account for their actions while raising children capable of accountability is the central task both of parents and society.

Stanley Greenspan

In the loving embrace of the family, the rules of the preschool home begin to socialize the toddler by setting limits on his impulses to do or have whatever he wants, whenever he wants it. Earlier discussions noted that the child's loving attachments to his caretakers are used as leverage to curb his narcissism, increase his capacity for mutuality, and reward his recognition of others as persons deserving of respect, not servants at his disposal. The industry phase then furthers these developments through attachments to persons, things and institutions beyond the family home. Mutuality is enhanced in cooperative efforts as the child enjoys the companionship of others in shared tasks. Enduring impulses toward dependency, aggression, acquisition, rivalry and self-aggrandizement, among others, are muted through discharge in approved activities such as games, sports and after-school "lessons." The child's daily encounters with the standards of morality and the conventions and traditions of acceptable conduct deepen his understanding of the behavioral requirements for civilized life. His caretakers grade his good and bad conduct just as his teachers grade his homework.

What the child does as a juvenile is likely to come under someone's close scrutiny. Approval of what he does is and should be increasingly conditional. Hopefully he learns the negative consequences of lying and cheating. He learns the elements of integrity and the dynamics of blaming, excusing, and disciplining. He learns the morality of social presentation: the goodness of humility and modesty versus the tedium of bragging and pretense. In the juvenile era the child learns about varieties of crime and proportions of punishment, about fairness and justice, and about the role of religion in the education of a moral life.

Children in this era continue to learn what it means to be good or bad, to be "nice" or "mean," and to do good acts and bad acts. Ideally the child is introduced to the technology of reconciliation as well. If his early narcissism has been tempered with increasing mutuality, he will learn how to repair or attempt to repair broken relationships. The process is straight-forward and intuitive. It begins with a personal acknowledgment of what wrongful act led to the problem in question, followed by an expression of understanding as to the nature of the injury imposed on the other. Then, a sincere apology expresses remorse for the bad act and regret for the injury. If appropriate, an offer of reparation or restitution attempts to compensate the wronged party and redeem the wrongdoer, who resolves to learn his moral lesson.

A homely example will suffice to illustrate the process. A little boy takes a toy belonging to a little girl and accidentally breaks the toy. His mother discovers what has happened and guides her son through the moral lesson. She tells him first what he probably already knows: that he acted badly by taking something that didn't belong to him. If appropriate, she may also tell him that he broke the toy through carelessness. She then tells him to confess to the little girl and to at least one of her parents that he took the toy and broke it. Where needed, his mother can instruct him to say to the girl something along these lines: "I know I hurt you by taking your toy, and I'm sorry. It was a bad thing to do and I should not have done it. I won't do it again." To achieve restitution, the boy and his mother get the toy repaired or buy a replacement. All of this is carried out by the adults with an emotional tone that conveys the solemnity of the matter. No exaggeration of the wrong is needed, but the matter must not be dismissed by the parents either if they are properly committed to the moral instruction of their children in this elementary morality play. Some form of punishment may or may not be indicated. Often the embarrassment of the reparative process is enough.

Why go to all of this trouble? Because the blessings of freedom can be secured only in a moral society whose members repeatedly reaffirm their good will by actions, not just words. Those who would be free must be willing to be held accountable for their obligations to each other, whether implied or contractual. Clearly, a breach of trust between children over a stolen toy will not convulse the community, let alone the world. But in the adult world, a breach of trust must be followed rapidly by bona fide efforts to restore trust. Proactive effort of this type is necessary in order to protect against serious and sometimes catastrophic consequences that follow betrayal of trust. In recent years, to cite a well-known example, high level corporate executives have betrayed the trust of shareholders and pensioners with disastrous consequences, financial and otherwise. The child who learns to admit his wrongful acts, acknowledge the damage he has done, apologize in earnest, and undo the injury if possible can later become an adult who institutes a similar process in order to mitigate the doubt, fear and rage of those betrayed at his hands, even if only out of carelessness and not malice.

The capacity to restore trust through humble apology and restitution serves to reestablish relationships characterized by confidence, not suspicion. Indeed, the example just noted illustrates a little recognized but critical insight about the human condition: that nearly all transactions among human beings are either directly ethical or moral in some respect, or have significant ethical or moral implications. A corollary insight is that no society can function for long if its members cannot maintain trust or restore it when the inevitable breach occurs. This capacity is essential to all rational societies and inherent in their laws and judicial proceedings. The protection of trust through integrity and the restoration of trust through humility are among the most important lessons to be learned by the child on the road to adulthood.

Altruism in the Juvenile Era

If raised in a free and lawful society of mature adults, a child in the juvenile era will witness charitable acts toward others and will understand that such behavior is a moral good. Ideally, much of the charity he sees will have begun in the home, as the saying goes, but it will also be apparent in the missions of religious and civic organizations. It should be no news to anyone except radical libertarians that taking care of persons in need is basic to social order. That idea is not usually in dispute. What *is* in dispute are the motives and mechanics of charity and the choice of who administers and delivers it. Modern liberals endorse a welfare system run by a large government apparatus funded by compulsory taxation. The proceeds of this essentially confiscatory process are then distributed to persons chosen by the government, not the taxpayer.

The question arises as to what a twelve-year-old child might think about this arrangement if it is called to his attention. He may well understand that a genuinely charitable act is a voluntary one done in a spirit of compassion for the recipient. If he witnesses such acts performed by his parents, among others, he will probably conclude that giving generously to others, especially those in need, is a morally good thing to do. On the other hand, a juvenile who sees his parents paying taxes to the welfare state is observing an act of lawful compliance, at best, and a surrender to government coercion at worst. The payment he sees his parents make to avoid being charged with tax evasion is quite different in nature from a contribution he sees them make voluntarily to a charity of their choice. Sooner or later, though perhaps not as a juvenile, a child may notice that taking someone's money by force is called a crime unless it is done by a government, in which case it is called a duty and is understood to be mandatory on threat of prosecution. At some point, a thoughtful youth may feel puzzled by this paradox. If, in addition, he also observes his parents evading taxes illegally, he learns a different lesson entirely, one that is not likely to be explained to him in detail. Given that the juvenile era is the child's introduction to the community life of man, and given the prominent role that welfare programs play in modern life, it would seem reasonable that the welfare concept and its implications should be a part of the child's education as soon as he can understand it. The differences between genuine altruism and government theft must be part of that understanding.

31

Adolescence and Identity

Although adolescence is the epoch par excellence of individuation and autonomy striving, it is similarly impossible to have a full understanding of adolescent development apart from its specific biological, family, community, cultural and historical contexts.

Robert King

Introduction

If any phase of the life cycle embodies the innate human urge to be free, it is surely that of adolescence. In this phase, the individuation process begun in the second year of life is sharply accelerated by major advances in self-direction and self-reliance, energized and reconfigured by the hormonal changes of puberty (Pfeffer 2000). Healthy growth in adolescence is marked by increasing physical strength and coordination, by rapidly expanding intellectual and instrumental competence, and by continued gains in autonomy. Unless barred by earlier deficits, these transformations awaken in the child a growing realization that an eventual life of freedom is both desirable and possible. Increasing emancipation from the family and greater identification with society at large proceed apace. By the end of the era, the anticipated result of these changes is a competent adult who will establish himself within a few years as an economically productive, self-responsible, cooperative and generative member of the human community. At the core of this complex process is the achievement of a coherent sense of identity. In recognition of this achievement and the struggles that attend it, Erikson called this phase of the life cycle the age of identity versus identity confusion. (Erikson 1950).

Adolescence: Concept and Course

Following standard textbook definitions, (Pfeffer 2000, Cotton 2000), adolescence may be viewed as both a period and a process. It is, first, a prolonged developmental era occurring between the juvenile period of childhood and the earliest phase of adulthood. It is a phase of growth that continuously revisits and reorganizes earlier dynamisms of basic trust, autonomy, initiative and industry while adding major new transformations of its own. The new transformations include physical, cognitive, emotional and relational changes. They are shaped not only by family and community influences but also by cultural, socioeconomic and historical forces, and by racial, ethnic, national and religious factors.

The *cognitive* changes of adolescence are notable in their own right. As compared to the juvenile age child they include (modified from Pfeffer):

- Increased linguistic and executive functions
- Increased capacity for abstract thought, better information processing skills and greater knowledge base
- Increased capacities for realistic, adaptive inference in concrete and social experience
- Increased capacities for hypothetical thought (ideal case and "what if" scenarios, etc.)
- More differentiated, multilevel, and multidimensional thinking
- Higher order ethical and moral assessments
- Increased capacities for choice, will, preference, intention and agency
- Views of the self, others and society, including ethical and moral views that are more subtle, complex, and related to context
- Increased capacity for empathy and mutuality

- Increased scope and complexity of personal/social roles.

Concurrent *emotional* changes in adolescence give rise to more intense and varied emotions in response to a greater range of activating events than a juvenile child can experience or communicate. The adolescent is capable of greater differentiation, elaboration and control of mood and emotion. The adolescent experiences:

- More intense erotic arousal
- More intense aggressive impulses
- Improved regulation of aggressive, dependent and acquisitive impulses
- More intense feelings of affection, tenderness and love
- More intense sadness, sorrow and grief
- More intense feelings of envy, jealousy, hurt and anger
- Increased tolerance for frustration, delay, disappointment and loss

Interpersonal/relational changes in adolescence lead to a major reorganization of social functioning. The adolescent is involved in:

- Increasing depth and complexity of attachments
- Increased potential for conflict with parents
- Increased self-reflection and self-awareness
- Increased need for peer validation
- Increased testing of social skills
- Increased capacities for mutuality, accommodation and compromise
- Greater empathy for, recognition of, and identification with others
- Enhanced compassion and altruism
- Continued need for guidance from parents, peers and teachers
- Intense urges for independence oscillating with heightened dependency
- More intense rivalry and competition
- The politics of cliques, cults and cabals
- Preoccupation with future possibilities and plans

- Increased appreciation of acquisition, possession and ownership
- Decreased dependency on parents in middle and late adolescence

The Risks of Adolescence

The integrative task in this mental and physical restructuring of the self is clearly substantial. The adolescent's sense of identity is altered as he explores multiple, often contradictory personas on the way to constructing a new self. He must meet new challenges to already established balances between trust and mistrust, autonomy and shame, initiative and guilt, industry and inferiority. He must come to terms with a rapidly changing body and new impulses and assimilate them into his already familiar sense of himself. An increase in self-consciousness is common in this phase, accompanied by concerns about how one appears to others and how an imaginary audience will respond. Taken as a whole, this phase tests the child's:

- Optimism, frustration tolerance, and mood stability
- Capacity for rational choice over impulsive discharge
- Sense of himself as physically adequate and socially acceptable
- Capacity for sustained useful effort despite obstacles
- Ability to relate to others in greater depth using skills and roles acquired in earlier phases.

In the course of all this, the adolescent must reinvent himself as he acquires a new body, new drives, new powers and new expectations. The task is not a cake walk. The budding adolescent risks new levels of shame and doubt as he tries to become more autonomous. He risks intensified guilt as he initiates new ways of relating and grapples with sexual, aggressive and acquisitive impulses. He risks repeated failure, competitive defeat and feelings of inferiority as he tries to achieve new levels of competence. Of greatest interest to the present work is the risk he takes in trusting his society's institutions. Though he may not be conscious of it, the adolescent wants a worldview he can believe in, one broader than the conventions of his family and neighborhood. He must somehow orient himself in his culture's rules for living. In his everyday actions and in actions that sometimes defy the rules, he tests the substance, coherence and integrity of society's values. A more detailed discussion of this process is set out below.

Any of these developmental efforts may cause some degree of emotional distress. Periods of confusion, anxiety or moodiness are not uncommon. In some cases the integrative task can be overwhelming and may precipitate a symptomatic illness. The physical changes that compel sexual behavior and the emotional drives that seek intimacy, for example, may reactivate old dynamisms in the vulnerable teenager that compromise his hold on reality. Distress in these children may induce a state of intense dysphoria and even an acute disorganization of the psyche. In severe cases integration fails altogether and a psychotic state ensues. In some cases reintegration requires treatment in a hospital.

When the self-reconstruction process of adolescence goes well enough, however, personality dispositions acquired in earlier phases of development are effectively reorganized without undue distress. A new level of integration is achieved together with a greatly increased capacity for self-observation. The late adolescent is able to describe his enlarged and more complex personality with a new awareness of his psychological makeup: a composite of beliefs, emotions, motives, wishes, values and attitudes rather than a mere physical description of himself or list of superficial personal traits (Cotton). His increasing consciousness of who he is facilitates an integration of past and present selves with imagined future selves, paving the way for further advances toward adult competence.

The Transition to Adulthood

In his tour of the teenage years the adolescent must reconcile the countless influences that impinge upon him from family, culture, race, ethnicity and socioeconomic sources, among others, with personas and dispositions acquired in earlier years. If his efforts succeed, major advances in development emerge toward the end of the era, with progression toward a healthy balance of autonomy and relatedness to others (Cotton). These advances include expanded instrumental and social skills, increased self-reliance and dependability, enhanced capacities for cooperation with others, a deeper understanding of personal assets and limitations, a more accurate sense of one's overall identity, and greater confidence in one's gender identity. On the whole and in the absence of major psychopathology, the massive reorganization of adolescence generates a more complex and differentiated personality, but one that is also better integrated. Under favorable circumstances, the close of the adolescent era sends the individual into his twenties ready, willing and able to meet the challenges of adult life. Those challenges include the opportunity to live as one chooses in a free society while at the same time accepting the responsibilities of liberty, the consequences of free choice, and the imperative to cooperate with others rather than manipulate them.

32

Adolescence and Freedom

Where large numbers of people have been prepared in childhood to expect from life a high degree of personal autonomy, pride and opportunity, and then later in life find themselves ruled by superhuman organizations and machinery too intricate to understand, the result may be deep chronic disappointment not conducive to healthy personalities willing to grant each other a measure of autonomy.
Erik Erikson

Adolescence and the Elements of Freedom

So far, our review of the first twenty years of life has identified various dispositions that prepare the child for an eventual life of liberty. Following Erikson's conceptions, the adult person's ability to engage the world with hope and optimism was linked to the emergence of basic trust in infancy. The foundations of autonomy appearing in the second and third years of life then promote the child's early moves away from total dependency. The evolution of will into initiative in the late preschool years enables the child to expand his world with good purpose instead of arbitrary opposition, while at the same time learning the rudiments of cooperation. In the grade school years these early acquisitions of trust, autonomy and initiative together with their associated virtues of hope, will and purpose lay the foundations of industry and the beginnings of competence. The close of the juvenile era at about age twelve finds the child with greater instrumental and social skills and an increasing ability to direct his own actions while cooperating with others.

If the first twelve years of life gradually establish the basis for an eventual life of liberty, the transformations of adolescence dramatically accelerate the process. Biological, psychological and social forces compel a major overhaul of the self and its modes of relating to the world. Increasing self-determination is of the essence in this process; the adolescent's growing efforts to direct his own actions reflect the drive toward freedom that is innate in the human soul. Just as the individuation stage of the second and third years of life constitutes a second birth, the redefinition of the self in the transformations of adolescence is a second individuation, (Blos 1967) characterized now by increasingly autonomous action and enlarged capacities for responsibility and accountability. Among myriad other effects, the individuation process continues to emancipate the individual from his family of origin, fortify him for the challenges of adult life, further his efforts to become his own sovereign person, and ensure that he does not remain his parents' dependent child or become an adoptee of the state. By the end of adolescence, the individual has acquired new attitudes about himself as a unique, substantial and free person who is fit to run his own life. As Jane Loevenger put it so succinctly, "personality develops by acquiring successive freedoms."

Individuation and the Consolidation of Identity

The individuation process of adolescence lays the groundwork for a core identity function basic to western individualism: the young person's growing perception of himself as the owner of his mind and body and the corollary conviction that he is entitled to a life of his own. He understands that this life is to be lived in voluntary cooperation with others of his choice, not in servitude to unknown masses through the offices of government. In large part, this perception grows out of the adolescent's exercise of free choice in ever widening domains, energetically choosing as he wishes among persons, things and values. He realizes that he is increasingly autonomous, an agent willing and able to act independently of others. To an ever greater extent he constructs his own views of the world, generates his own goals, and creates and implements his own plans. The adolescent has a growing sense of the ownership of his mind's doings and of his own significance. He realizes more than ever that he can make things happen for good or bad in a manner and to an extent that he could not imagine as a younger child. And because his growing strength of will and body make him a force that must be considered, he cannot be brushed aside with impunity.

At a more personal level, the growing adolescent is intensely aware of his own emotions, impulses, longings and desires. He feels increasingly identified with them as expressions of who he is. He feels similarly identified with his most personal beliefs, fantasies, perspectives and value judgments. They are his alone if he chooses to keep them so, and many of them remain his secret for a lifetime. This intense sense of literal self-possession is a first-person introduction to the political ideal of self-ownership. It grounds the adolescent's conviction that he is entitled for the duration of his life to an elemental property right in himself.

The Enlarged and Private Self

In concert with this enhanced sense of self-ownership, an increasing concern with privacy emerges in adolescence, strongly determined by the physical changes of puberty, especially those involving the genitals and secondary sex characteristics, and also by changes in the content of thought and the nature and intensity of emotions that may be difficult to share with others. The adolescent is typically more self-conscious—given to both private introspection and to concerns about how he is perceived in the eyes of others, including imagined others. He is acutely aware that he is mirrored by his peers, and he may seek validation through conformity, stereotypes and group ideals, including some that are antagonistic to the prevailing culture's norms. Along the way he explores and experiments with multiple and often contradictory personas, a process which anticipates the eventual integration of past, present and future selves. All of these developments generate an increased potential for shame, humiliation and embarrassment in early and mid-adolescence especially. They typically activate an increased demand for privacy: a greater insistence on being let alone when solitude is desired for any reason. These innately determined needs to exclude others from certain domains inform the larger demand for personal sovereignty. They are reflected in Justice Brandeis' oft quoted remark that "the most basic of all rights and the one most revered by civilized men is the right to be let alone." The transformations of adolescence highlight the bio-psychological origins of this most natural of human rights.

Strongly driven by physiological changes, and stimulated by opportunities increasingly available to him, the adolescent expands his world into more varied and intensified erotic, aggressive, acquisitive and relational domains. He turns to others for companionship from same sex chums and opposite sex friends and for infatuation and sexual experimentation. He explores the possibilities for self-actualization through new intellectual and recreational activities. In the aggregate, these additions to the adolescent's experiential life constantly redefine his growing uniqueness, his distinct identity apart from all other persons and to an important degree apart from all other externalities such as birth place, nationality, ethnic origins, race, skin color and religion. A growing awareness of his personal boundaries develops as well, along with a feeling of greater authority over his personal affairs and a demand that others not intrude without permission. These late-childhood transformations expand the self while consolidating it; they differentiate the self more uniquely while reintegrating it into a more organized, cohesive identity, capable of setting its own course. When the process has gone well enough, this newly consolidated identity feels like the "real me" to the budding young adult, although this self, too, will undergo still more change in adult years. Hopefully, what emerges by late adolescence is what Cotton has described as a "clear, integrated, realistic, internalized sense of an acceptable self," a sense of one's person that has now become comfortable enough to take into adulthood.

A Mind of One's Own

While the ultimate biological basis of mind in the generic sense of the term remains mysterious, we can nevertheless understand any particular mind as a complex synthesis of a nature that is genetically given and nurture conditioned by its environment. If healthy enough, the mind of the late adolescent has largely integrated his innate biological and psychological drives—those concerned with sex, aggression, dependency, narcissism, nurturing, acquisitiveness and relatedness—into a personality that is at least reasonably functional and more or less acceptable to others. *By the twentieth year of life, at the latest, this synthesis has generated a person who is well acquainted with his own desires and clearly aware of his freedom to initiate action in a world of cause and effect.*

He feels increasingly entitled to make deliberate choices intended to achieve particular goals. In these efforts he typically assumes without question his right to life, liberty and the pursuit of happiness—and he is not alone in this assumption. Others validate his emerging role as an active agent in his own life. Having watched him acquire a mind of his own, they expect him to construct a life of his own and to do it within a few years. Reflecting his bipolar nature, they expect him to seek personal fulfillment and at the same time become useful to others in a manner of his and their agreed choosing. No one reasonably expects him to subordinate himself to another person or to an institution unless he makes such a choice voluntarily. No one will reasonably argue that he can somehow give away his right to liberty. His freedom is both innate and inalienable.

In keeping with these perspectives, it is now possible to observe that the developmental achievements of late adolescence establish for the first time in the life cycle both the existential and ontological bases for individual liberty in an ordered society (as opposed, for example, to individual liberty in a lawless ghetto). The well developed late adolescent has achieved enough basic trust, autonomy, initiative, industry, competence and understanding of who he is and what he can do to make a life for himself. He has the ability to live as he chooses while voluntarily cooperating with others in pursuit of those biological, psychological and social purposes intrinsic to human life.

Brief Adolescent Regressions

Whether this positive outcome will be realized in a given case is, of course, uncertain. The question then arises as to what can go wrong in the course of adolescent development and whether, in particular, one or another form of psychopathology may turn a developing adolescent away from a life of self-fulfillment, self-responsibility and cooperation and toward a life subordinated to collectivist control. Before answering this question, it is worth taking yet another look at the course of adolescence, this time revisiting the ideals of individual action that contribute most usefully to realization of the self in a free society.

First to be noted is the fact that the developmental path in adolescence is not simple or linear, an observation valid for all phases of human growth, but especially so for this one. Even casual observation reveals repeated shifts between more mature and less mature modes of behaving and relating as the overall trend of a normal growth path proceeds toward adult competence. One author observed the shifts in adolescent behavior "between continuity and metamorphosis, moving forward toward maturity and backward for familiarity and grounding." (Cotton). Such regressions to earlier, more childlike modes of relating to the world are typically brief in the course of adolescence. They serve growth over the longer trend, providing occasional respite from the hard work of growing up. But they may also serve more protective purposes by fortifying a still vulnerable self against psychotic disintegration or suicidal depression. Regressions to more childlike states may help to heal a temporarily broken psyche, one that has fragmented under the challenges of development.

Contrary to popular myth, however, adolescence is not usually a time of great emotional turmoil despite the major realignments that characterize it. But it is certainly not free of tensions either. Even in normal adolescence, the process of self-discovery involves some degree of discontent, confusion and anxiety as the self undergoes major reorganizations. The process involves, after all, the emergence of a new body, new intellectual powers, new sexual and aggressive impulses, new personas and new modes of relating. Accepting and rejecting different aspects of the self, reconciling contradictory self-images, and exploring occupational, religious, political and gender roles are all part of the reorganization process. This observation echoes Erikson's original description of identity consolidation through selection, repudiation and resolution of various elements of the self acquired in earlier phases. This is no mean task; it is a major, labor-intensive construction and reconstruction project that must be measured in years.

33

Adolescence, Healthy and Unhealthy

The integration now taking place in the form of the ego identity is more than the sum of the childhood identifications. It is the inner capital accrued from all those experiences of each successive stage, when successful identification led to a successful alignment of the individual's basic drives with his endowment and his opportunities.
                                                                    Erik Erikson

Healthy Action Revisited

Given the accelerated reorganization of the self in adolescence, it is natural to ask what a healthy outcome of these transformations might look like. An answer to this question begins by revisiting an already familiar perspective, one that was first considered in the toddler phase. In Chapter 22 it was observed that the small child's development was on a healthy track if he could experience his actions as effective, legitimate, free, cooperative and mutual, assuming certain adjustments for his very young age. With a few minor alterations these same criteria can now assist in judging whether or not an adolescent is on a reasonably good developmental track.

First, to the extent that the adolescent is allowed to exercise his will in a manner appropriate to his abilities, he is likely to acquire a secure sense of himself as an *effective* actor. With adequate teaching and supervision he can, in fact, make good things happen and for the most part avoid making catastrophic mistakes. If he is given tasks suitable to his skills, he can gain increasing confidence in his ability to act effectively, follow a task through to completion, and expand his sense of instrumental competence. Repeated experience of this type reinforces his self-esteem and aids him in defining himself as competent among his peers.

Second, to the extent that he learns to accommodate his actions to society's moral and ethical conventions, he develops a conviction that he is a *legitimate* actor. In an atmosphere of community law and order and in a society that values individual responsibility and accountability he learns the principles of conscientious action, the foundation of ordered liberty. In the process of validating his actions, the approval of others validates his person as well, affirming his identity as someone with the "right stuff" and helping him to put old self-doubts to rest.

Third, to the extent that he is allowed to pursue his own desires and to gratify them as he wishes, he enjoys an introduction to individual liberty. He develops a proper sense of himself as a *free* actor, whenever and wherever such freedom is legitimate and does not encroach on the freedoms of others. As his opportunities expand to act as he chooses, he identifies with the western world's honored tradition of individual liberty and makes it part of himself.

Fourth, to the extent that he is appropriately rewarded or penalized in joint efforts with others and is neither demeaned nor overestimated in his contributions to shared causes, the adolescent develops a proper sense of himself as a *cooperative* actor, one who collaborates with others by common consent and who can be held to account for his contribution.

Finally, to the extent that the adolescent's interactions with others require him to recognize and respect them as autonomous persons in their own right, he becomes a *mutual* actor. He learns that the most satisfying transactions are those in which all parties gain. He learns to be considerate of others, to honor them as sovereign agents with independent purposes, and to avoid treating them as depersonalized objects to be exploited for his own purposes.

The capacity for such healthy action in adolescence can be achieved when the child's overall development has been nurtured well enough by his parents, and when society's reigning values offer ways of living that are compatible with individual liberty and voluntary cooperation. Such a happy outcome is, of course, not assured. The capacity for healthy action may be undermined from within by physical disability or personal psychopathology, or from without by the social pathologies of the culture, especially by the tyranny of collectivism. To these concerns the discussion now turns.

The Personal Pathologies of Adolescent Competence

As a first approach in this discussion it will be useful to review once again the personal pathologies of adolescence, especially in its late phase: those types of physical and mental illness that may undermine the emergence of adult competence and abort the young person's transition to a life of adult liberty. Various social pathologies that have the same effect can then be examined.

In the matter of physical disability, it is of course clear that certain disorders—paralysis for example—may render a young person seriously disabled both occupationally and socially. In these unfortunate cases ordinary compassion easily motivates financial and other forms of support to compensate for the disability or fund rehabilitation efforts. All but the most radical egoists will voluntarily contribute to the material welfare of those so handicapped—and both sides will feel the better for it. In such charitable efforts, clearly, there is no decrement to the cause of freedom in the community at large, and the freedom of the beneficiaries of such largesse is enhanced to the extent that their fears of helplessness are allayed.

But it is equally obvious that certain mental disorders can also destroy the adolescent's emerging capacities for self-determination and self-responsibility. Three categories of disorders capable of derailing normal development in this era are nearly identical to those found in adults. The first category, usually referred to as disorders of mood and emotion, can generate intense anxiety, depression, excitement, irritability and anger. Bipolar or manic-depressive illness is a prime example. A second category, often called thought disorders, causes major distortions of perception, reasoning and judgment that grossly impair one's ability to understand and cope with reality. Schizophrenia is the primary example in this category. When severe enough, illnesses in either category can seriously disable the sufferer's ability to work and relate to others and as a consequence render him unable to enjoy the blessings of freedom.

A third category of disabling illness, organic brain disorders, arises from physical or chemical brain damage that impairs ordinary cognitive functions, especially those involving attention, concentration, comprehension, memory, reasoning, judgment, planning and problem solving; these disorders often disrupt emotional and relational capacities, as well. They too can cause severe occupational disability and preclude growth to competence. They include certain post-concussion states and some cases of brain damage from alcohol or drug abuse.

Thus, if a young person is unlucky enough to have developed a serious disorder of mood regulation, thought processing or cognition, and if his condition is strongly resistant to treatment, then he may be unable to achieve the occupational and social competence needed for self-reliance and may instead need a guardian for his care and protection. The outcome depends to an important extent on what kind of personality traits persist despite his illness. A person's ability to live in freedom even though handicapped with a major disorder of mood, thought or cognition turns largely on whether he has acquired certain skills, habits and values that fortify self-reliance and oppose dependency. More on this topic follows below.

Personality Disorders and Freedom

In addition to the major symptomatic disorders just described there is another category of mental disturbance which may cripple a young person's ability to thrive in a community of freedom. Personality disorders, as defined earlier, are those enduring patterns of thinking, emoting, behaving and relating that undermine the individual's efforts to cope with the challenges of adult life. Depending on their severity, the impairments associated with these disorders may diminish one's prospects for living a life of liberty as he enters the adult world. A brief description of personality pathology will aid in understanding this difficulty. Additional observations on the personality characteristics essential to liberty follow this review.

Personality Disorder Clusters

Disorders of personality are currently classified in three rather loosely defined clusters and ten more tightly defined types. (DSM IV 1994) Persons suffering from Cluster A disorders, the schizoid, schizotypal and paranoid personality types, tend to exhibit odd or eccentric behavior. Persons with Cluster B disorders, those currently known as borderline, narcissistic, histrionic, or antisocial personality types, can be identified by their more erratic, dramatic and emotional behavior patterns, which are nevertheless more conventional and much less odd than those of Cluster A disorders. Persons with Cluster C disorders, those commonly known as avoidant, dependent or obsessive-compulsive types, tend to be more overtly anxious and fearful in their efforts to cope with life. An additional category of personality disorders is called "personality disorder not otherwise specified." It is essentially a waste basket category that allows the clinician wide discretion in describing a person with a mixture of traits from two or more types.

By definition, all of these personality disorders are characterized by maladaptive ways of relating to oneself and the world, and all have potentially negative effects on the ability to direct one's life, make a living and cooperate with others. In many cases the maladaptive patterns are obvious on casual observation. All are typically characterized by a combination of major developmental failures. Deficits in basic trust, autonomy, initiative, industry, identity and intimacy are always present, even if subtle, and late-life deficits in the development of generativity and integrity can be expected as a matter of course.

Cluster A Disorders

Among the Cluster A disorders, persons with *schizoid personalities* are notably reclusive. They strongly prefer solitude and are emotionally distant and detached on those few occasions when they relate to others. More likely to be noticed are individuals afflicted with a *schizotypal personality*. They are typically less withdrawn but more obviously odd, eccentric or peculiar in behavior, speech or manner of dress. Their overt actions reflect an equally unusual inner world of bizarre beliefs, mystical or magical thoughts and fantasies, or suspiciousness to the point of paranoia. A third type, called *paranoid personality* disorder, is characterized by frankly persecutory beliefs. A person with this disorder is delusionally convinced that malevolent others are actively harming him or conspiring to harm him. All of these types suffer from impairments in basic trust, autonomy, identity and intimacy, and all are likely to be occupationally and socially impaired to significant degrees.

Nevertheless, some persons with paranoid, schizoid or schizotypal personality disorders may be able to live in a free society if, despite their handicaps, they still retain a skill with which to make at least a minimal living, still have the ability to cooperate with others well enough to use that skill, and still refuse to demand through government that others take care of them. Choices open to such persons are often severely limited by the disabilities of their illness, yet they may retain a substantial degree of self-determination when they take certain jobs, such as night watchman or janitor, that are compatible with social withdrawal and that tolerate strange ideas or odd mannerisms. It is true that such persons tend to live only marginal social lives, but that is an unfortunate consequence of their pathology. Their peculiar and limited lifestyles are not caused by any type of societal arrangement and are not remediable by social or political means. For the most part, persons with Cluster A disorders make few if any demands on others for anything, including financial support. They tend to remain on the periphery of social relatedness and will not usually intrude on the liberty of others. Even a frankly paranoid individual may be able to keep his delusions of persecution largely to himself and not alienate an employer to the point of getting fired or interfering with his own business if he is self-employed.

If his illness escalates, however, the paranoid person may then become a genuine threat to the community by acting on his delusional beliefs. He may, for example, initiate abusive litigation or in some cases become violent as a means of defending himself against imagined persecution. More generally, in their tendency to distort interpersonal reality, persons with severe personality disorders may indeed disrupt the peace and order of the community and the freedom with which others can go about their business. The outcome in any given case is determined by the nature and severity of the disturbance. Depending on his particular abilities and disabilities, a person with a schizoid, schizotypal or paranoid personality may or may not be able to sustain himself in a community of free persons. His effort to do so will depend to a significant extent on whether his disorder spares him the ability to make at least a marginal living, enables him to respect the property rights of others, and allows him to maintain a moral conviction that he should not become an adoptee of the state.

Cluster B Disorders

A second and more complex group of personality disorders includes those labeled narcissistic, sociopathic, histrionic, and borderline types. These types are characterized by abnormal degrees of self-centeredness, by attitudes of entitlement, and by marked impairment in mutuality. All lack genuine empathy for and recognition of others. Persons with frankly sociopathic personalities are essentially criminal in their motives, always ruthless at some point and callously indifferent to the rights of others to life, liberty and property. Some are cunning and highly skilled in their ability to con their victims. Many are sadistic. Some are brutally destructive and count among the mass murderers and serial killers of history. As a person who is literally unconscionable, the sociopath is obviously a direct and serious threat to the freedom, peace and order of any community in which he acts out his pathology.

The other three disorders in Cluster B are generally not as threatening as sociopaths, but narcissistic personalities in positions of political power can cause enormous conflict, including conflict on a global scale. In their overestimation of their own importance and in their preoccupations with grandiose goals, they are likely to exploit others for admiration, political power, social status, business or professional advancement, or accumulation of wealth. Central to their make-up is a striking disregard for the legitimate interests of others; their immense self-centeredness allows them to use people without guilt or shame. They are strongly predisposed to bend any rules that might interfere with their search for self-gratification. Desire for both status and control lead some narcissists to seek elected office, where the powers of government enable large scale exploitation. In these venues presumptions to exceptional political insights and a sense of entitlement to run the lives of others are common. In any situation, public or private, the narcissist's self-centeredness eventually becomes oppressive as his marked indifference to the sensibilities of others becomes apparent.

Borderline personalities, by contrast, tend to cause problems in more limited domains. They do not usually seek positions of power over the masses, but will be obsessively demanding on those close to them in order to satisfy intense dependency needs and avoid feeling abandoned. Excessively angry and punitive in intimate relationships, they too can easily become oppressive to others and may even violate their rights. Relentless demands for connection may escalate to stalking. In some cases, real or imagined rejection may motivate revenge through violence, an outcome not at all rare in the world of domestic conflict. These and other actions clearly violate the sovereignty of the persons whose attention they seek, and the intrusions may on occasion reach the level of criminal offense. Persons with a related condition, histrionic personality disorder, are typically attention-seeking, emotionally shallow and even theatrical. They are usually more annoying or even amusing rather than threatening to the freedom of others.

Overall, it is a common observation that persons with diagnosable borderline, narcissistic and histrionic pathology cause serious difficulties in relationships, especially where respect for others is needed to complete joint efforts. Intimate relationships, marriage in particular, are especially vulnerable to these disorders. The need for collaboration in the rearing of children, managing a household, and coordinating schedules, for example, will seriously stress the highly self-centered or easily angered spouse who feels entitled to special treatment, who demands exemption from the usual requirements for compromise, or who imposes irrational demands for attention on his partner.

Cluster C Disorders

In Cluster C disorders, those known as avoidant, dependent and obsessive-compulsive types, anxiety, insecurity and dependency are the most prominent symptoms. Difficulties in making a living or relating to others, or both, are typically present. The dependent personality is especially likely to find the liberal agenda's invitation to the welfare state appealing. These persons lack the capacity for self-determination; they avoid responsibility for themselves, fear they will become helpless, and constantly seek caretaking from others. They are willing to forego much of their freedom when given real or illusory promises of security.

Persons suffering from an avoidant personality disorder, another diagnosis in Cluster C, are strongly inclined to perceive themselves as inadequate or inferior and to avoid situations in which they might feel criticized, shamed or rejected. To the extent that such tendencies diminish the ability or willingness to provide for themselves materially, persons with this disorder may also accept the collectivists' invitation to government welfare programs. By contrast, persons with obsessive-compulsive personality disorders, the third diagnosis in Cluster C, are likely to be hard working, productive and conscientious about managing money. The majority of such persons are willing and able to support themselves, and they are much more likely to contribute to the overall material wealth of the community than deplete it. In addition, they seek strict control over most aspects of their lives and tend to hoard material possessions. For these and other reasons, obsessive-compulsive persons tend to be suspicious of any governing body that seeks to take what they have through taxation or regulate what they can or cannot do through legislation. Intense opposition to government intrusion and regulation is not unusual in such persons. In some cases, however, an obsessive-compulsive individual may decide to join the government rather than fight it. When he does so, his innate preoccupation with order, details, organization, rules, lists and schedules is likely to qualify him for a happy position in the government bureaucracy. Indeed, so vast have the offices of modern government become that virtually any personality type or combination of types may find employment there provided the disorder is not too severe. A schizoid person, for example, may be hired to clean government buildings. A paranoid individual may find a place in the defense department or in counter-espionage. The narcissist will seek the grandiosity that attaches to public office, the borderline will seek its intrigue, and the sociopath will use the levers of government to exploit others under the guise of serving them. In the world of modern liberalism, government has become every man's employer.

34

Adolescence and Social Pathology

In our day, ideologies take over where religion leaves off, presenting themselves (in addition to other, more practical claims) as historical perspectives on which to fasten individual faith and collective confidence. As religions do, they counteract a threatening sense of alienation with positive ritual and affirmative dogma, and with a rigorous and cruel ban on alienisms in their own ranks or in foreign enemies.

Erik Erikson

The Personal Requirements for Liberty

So, what are the psychological requirements for liberty? What particular mental and emotional characteristics, if any, distinguish persons who are fit for freedom from persons who are not? Evidently, given the observations of the last chapter, the presence or absence of a diagnosable mental disorder is not decisive. It is possible, at least for some individuals, to be quite disturbed in certain respects and still thrive in a community where the primary political goods are liberty and cooperation. And it is equally clear from both casual and clinical observations that some persons who are "normal"—that is, who do not have any of the usual signs or symptoms of mental disorder—are unable or unwilling to participate in such a community. These persons are willing to diminish their personal freedom greatly by inviting more governmental control into their lives. Apparently, the traits that facilitate a life of liberty may be present in both normal and disturbed persons.

In fact, from the discussion so far, it appears that the key to whether an individual, even one with a mental illness, can thrive in freedom has to do with whether he has acquired at least one occupational skill sufficient to command a living wage, together with a moral conviction that his life remains his own responsibility, not the duty of other persons. Common observation as well as clinical experience reveals that even a chronically psychotic individual, one who is quietly delusional or hallucinated, may still hold a modest job, pay his bills and not interfere in the lives of others if, despite his handicap, he remains empowered by a sturdy belief that he should support himself materially while respecting the persons and property of others. Even though burdened by distorted perceptions in many areas, such an individual will continue to value his right to run his own life, he will elect to live only at a material level he can afford, and he will not feel entitled to the material support of others, nor to particular social or political concessions for real or imagined disadvantages. He will not make direct or indirect demands on others through the use of political power.

At least some persons with serious disorders of mood or thought, and even some persons with limited brain damage or severe personality disorders, can lead lives that are economically independent and socially self-directing. Those who are able to do so illustrate an observation made earlier in this work, namely, that the ability to live in a free society does not for the most part require a high level of personality development or exceptional skills. What is required instead is a minimum level of occupational and social skill, combined with a belief in self-responsibility and a robust respect for the rights of others to relate to whom they choose, or to relate to no one in particular. This combination of instrumental skill and moral conviction can enable an otherwise handicapped person to achieve at least minimal competence, that is, to have a life of his own. Able to participate effectively enough in the general market of goods, services and relationships, he will refuse as a matter of moral principle to exploit the power of government. Unless genuinely disabled he will not become a child of the state or dependent for his livelihood on the charity of others.

Moreover, he will be able to contribute, however modestly, to the aggregate of his community's goods and services, thus bolstering his self-esteem by being useful to others as well as himself. If not too handicapped socially he may also be able to engage others in a manner that both he and they find satisfying.

Society and Freedom

Having inquired at length whether one or another form of *psychopathology* might be a deciding factor in turning an adolescent away from a life of individual liberty and toward a life under a collectivist agenda, the question can now be asked as to whether one or another form of *sociopathology* could account for that preference. Of course the answer is yes in the trivial case where a strict socialist dictatorship indoctrinates the citizen from his earliest years into a conviction that collectivism is the only way to live, and where that choice is the only one allowed on penalty of imprisonment or worse. In these cases, physical coercion is the primary mechanism underlying economic and social order, and authoritarian government is the necessary form of political organization. The dictatorships of Iraq and North Korea are extreme examples of this genre.

At the other extreme is an equally trivial but infinitely more desirable situation in which a child's natural dispositions to both individual liberty and voluntary relatedness are nurtured over the course of his growth to adulthood in a society whose moral traditions support those ideals. In these cases, free choice and voluntary consent are the primary mechanisms underlying economic and social order, and constitutionally limited government is the principle form of political organization.

The respective outcomes in each of these cases are built into the preceding conditions: the child indoctrinated into collectivism is made to acquire a form of developmental psychopathology which suppresses his innate longing for autonomy and thereby denies a fundamental aspect of his human nature. The indoctrination process determines his preference for a central government to control society's dynamics and then conditions him to live with it. He will know no other choice. Rather than desiring personal sovereignty he will have been trained to reject it. If he is allowed to learn about self-determination and self-responsibility as theoretical concepts, he will conclude that the ideal of living by such values is either a fiction or illegitimate and even immoral both for himself and others. He will agree that such manifestations of individualism should be suppressed by law if necessary. Voluntary cooperation will be permitted in very limited domains but will not be an organizing principle that coordinates human action.

By contrast, the child whose natural longings for freedom are nurtured by parents and by traditions that idealize self-determination and cooperation will choose to live in a society where individual liberty and the freedom to relate by choice are constitutional guarantees, and where the use of coercion for any purpose other than the protection of such freedoms is considered an evil. A child raised under these circumstances will find that both aspects of his bipolar nature are validated by his society's rules for living. He will learn eventually about coercion under collectivism and will be appalled by it. He will view the suppression of individual liberty as profoundly immoral.

Societies that are neither strongly collectivist nor ideally free offer a mixed menu to the adolescent as he wonders how he might make a good life for himself. The mixed society typically offers some domains of individual freedom, responsibility and cooperation, but these are seriously limited by collectivist policies enforced under authoritarian government. It is commonly understood that contemporary western democracies lie somewhere between collectivism at one pole and individualism at the other. But it is also apparent that their modal position is not at or near the midpoint between those poles. Instead, these societies, whether on continental Europe or in the Americas, are strongly socialist in character and have been so for many decades. All of them embody variations on collectivist ideals: major economic, social and political processes are heavily regulated, massively bureaucratized, and in many cases owned or controlled outright by governmental or quasi-governmental bodies. In societies of this type, an implicit moral imperative is given to the newly minted adult: his first duty through various tax and regulatory systems is to support the offices of government and all of its collective purposes. He is not to spend too much of his energies in directing his own life–in pursuit of self-actualization, for example—as that would be too selfish. From a political perspective his primary identity is not one of individual sovereignty under an ideal of individual liberty. The primary political good in such a society is not personal freedom. Rather, the importance of the individual lies in his economic and to a lesser extent social contribution to the well being of the collective, however that entity is defined by the state's rulers. The ostensible primary political good in these arrangements is the well being of all of the state's subjects. In actuality, however, the primary beneficiaries in such societies are those who run the governments.

35

Adolescence and the Liberal Agenda

Adolescence is thus a vital regenerator in the process of social evolution; for youth selectively offers its loyalties and energies to the conservation of that which feels true to them and to the correction or destruction of that which has lost its regenerative significance.

Eric Erikson

Benign Collectivism

Before proceeding further in this analysis, a brief comment will avoid confusing two different meanings of the term collectivism. As it is used in the present work, the term has referred to those collectivist economic, social and political institutions whose basic principles subordinate the individual to one or more groups of persons and, as a consequence, diminish individual freedom and impair personal development. Aside from this meaning, however, there is another meaning that should be noted and then largely set aside. In discussions of the behavior of teenagers, collectivism sometimes refers to those conformist tendencies that make a temporary appearance on the adolescent developmental stage and then typically fade away. These tendencies, which seem almost intrinsic to the early and middle stages of adolescence, commonly find their expression in the teenager's compulsive conformity with fashionable affectations of speech, manner and dress and in nearly unanimous overestimation of certain group-approved cultural icons—rock music stars, for example. For a time, the adolescent who is caught up in this process submerges his uniqueness in favor of whatever social clichés are dominant, trying his best to look, act and be like the popular figures of the day. This sort of collectivism, a kind of homogenized group identity, is typically benign. As long as it does not escalate into destructive behavior or a "negative identity" outcome, it will more than likely contribute positively to the long-term individuation process and to a healthy transition to adulthood. As noted earlier, an adolescent's group affiliations, including his conformities with stereotypes, provide mirrors for his emerging self as he experiments with roles outside of those learned in his nuclear family. Typically, the process helps him to validate roles that work for him socially and repudiate those that don't, assisting him in the gradual consolidation of an identity that he can carry into adult life. Well before adulthood, as a rule, this temporary immersion in hyper-conformity resolves itself spontaneously. It does not compromise the adolescent's later ability to live a life of liberty.

The Liberal Agenda's Offer to the Adolescent

In contrast to this benign adolescent process, however, the collectivism of the liberal agenda is an entirely different matter. It is not a benign phenomenon nor a passing phase en route to an emerging culture of freedom. It does not consist in mere mannerisms but is instead a permanent and defining social architecture, dangerous to ordered liberty precisely because its principles are in direct opposition to it. Given modern liberalism's dominance in the contemporary world scene and its growing presence in western culture over the past century, it will be useful to ask again what collectivism has to offer to the adolescent, whose further development requires a worldview that both inspires his allegiance and resonates with his emerging identity. Partitioned into more Eriksonian terms, the question asks:

- What does the collectivist society offer to the adolescent that will inspire his fidelity? What values will elicit his idealism, his trust and his loyalty? To which societal values can he commit himself and which institutions, if any, can he revere?

- In what available adult roles in a collectivist culture can he continue to define himself, given what he has become in the first twenty years of his life?
- Will the values and ideals of this culture assist him or hamper him in the lifelong process of individuation? In what coordinates of his culture, if any, can he be autonomous yet affiliated?
- Does the collectivist society prepare the adolescent for a life of freedom and voluntary cooperation?
- How can the trust, energy, initiative, industry and purpose of his first twenty years be channeled to create a life that is self-actualizing and at the same time useful and respectful toward others? To what can he pledge his allegiance? In defense of what ideals might he call upon himself to fight or die?

In addressing these questions further, it will be useful to list those collectivist principles that have already been noted in this book. From this review, the underlying ideals of the agenda will become readily apparent.

The Liberal Manifesto: Major Principles

The liberal agenda offers a large collection of attitudes, beliefs, values and philosophies that prescribe for individuals and groups certain ways of thinking, feeling, behaving and relating. Government plays a powerful role in this prescription, and the agenda therefore offers a particular kind of relationship between government and the governed. For the late adolescent seeking a better sense of what it means to be an adult and a more explicit understanding of the world he is about to enter, modern liberalism offers the following principles for living.

1. The citizens of a modern nation state are, in effect, the children of a parental government; they are the members of a very large family with enforceable obligations to each other. These obligations are not defined by traditional, largely individualist western social and religious conventions, nor by mutual consent among individuals based on moral imperatives, but are instead prescribed by liberal intellectuals and politicians through legislation, judicial decisions and the canons of political correctness.

2. The individual's relationship to government should resemble his original relationship to his parents, or the fiduciary relationship between guardian and ward, or a combination of the two. The state is a proper source from which to gratify the longings of the people for various forms of surrogate parental care. This care should encompass the entire life span from cradle to grave. It should consist of various forms of economic, social and political assistance, protection and indulgence in every major sector of life. Self-reliance and the role of individual responsibility should be diminished in this society in favor of collective caretaking administered by the state.

3. This relationship between government and the governed properly diminishes the sovereignty of the individual in favor of the state. As a political entity, the state is superior to the individual and is prior to the individual. Moreover, the individual cannot exist without the state. For these reasons the individual must be subordinate to the state. Any contest between an individual's claim of authority over himself and his property, on the one hand, and the state's claim of authority over him and his property, on the other hand, is to be settled in favor of the latter, barring exceptional circumstances.

4. The people will be better off under the direction of government programs than if they take care of themselves through cooperative arrangements of their own. Because most citizens are not competent to run their own lives effectively they need government guidance to do what is good for them. In the most important sectors of life, government direction by an elite core of social philosophers and engineers is superior to directions the people choose for themselves. Collective remedies coordinated by the state are nearly always preferable to those initiated by individuals on a voluntary basis.

5. Socialism and its variants with far reaching power vested in centralized government is the proper political foundation for an ordered society. Collectivism is the proper political philosophy for an ordered society. Government coercion is needed to ensure that the activities of the people achieve politically appropriate ends. Extensive use of that power through central planning and regulation will permit the greatest happiness for the greatest

number of citizens. Traditional property and contract rights and other protections of individual liberty against encroachment by the state must be subordinated to this collective process. Major economic, social and political functions are to be socialized through programs conceived by government planners and administered by government offices.

6. It is not necessary that a good life be earned through diligent individual effort, voluntary cooperation with others, or conduct consistent with traditional moral values. Instead, a good life is a government entitlement owed to each citizen regardless of the nature and quality of his acts and their usefulness to others. Material assets under the control of the government are to be distributed to those deemed in need of them. Few if any qualifications are required beyond claimed or perceived need, inequality or suffering, and the benefits given away should not have to be repaid. The beneficiaries of government handouts are entitled to them and owe no debt of gratitude to the persons who fund them. They are, however, indebted to government officials for receipt of these benefits and should support their terms in office.

7. Voluntary cooperation based on the consent of the parties in a transaction is not an especially important ideal and may be overridden by the coercive apparatus of the government. Consent of all parties is not morally or legally necessary to complete a transfer of material assets for welfare purposes or to alter an individual or group's circumstances in the name of social justice. In fact, collectivist concepts of justice require that redistributions of power and social status as well as material assets should be effected regardless of the objections of those who possessed these goods prior to their transfer to others. In the social arena, no one who desires membership in a social group should be excluded, and those deemed socially disadvantaged should be given preferential legal or political assistance to remedy their plight. In respect to both economic and social situations, prior binding contracts or long held agreements based on tradition may be invalidated by the authority of government. In these cases collectivist definitions of distributive and social justice should override older considerations of earned benefits, just title, freedom of exchange, due process, rights of association and historical precedent.

8. The natural and acquired inclinations of moral persons to cooperate with each other in a framework of laws governing property rights and contracts are not the primary basis for an orderly society. Rather, a large government regulatory apparatus, analogous to the authority of parents in a family, is needed to exercise control over the citizenry and to ensure that social justice is achieved. Certain economic, social and political goals must be prescribed by enlightened government officials in view of the fact that citizens are not competent to decide such matters for themselves. Judicial activism is a proper mechanism for ensuring that legal disputes over economic, social and political matters are decided in favor of politically approved outcomes. Judicial decisions should not be bound by precedent, by established principles of procedural law, or by strict interpretation of the Constitution. Where legal disputes emerge, court decisions should be determined in accordance with collectivist ideals. Outcomes in social matters should be judged by whether or not they promote material and social equality, aid the disadvantaged, enhance diversity, reduce envy, protect self-esteem and mitigate disparities in social status, among other considerations.

9. Altruism may be found in some persons and may represent nurturing instincts toward others, a benevolent identification with others, or compassion and empathy for others. But altruism is better understood as a virtue of the state, a socialized function or collective expression of the General Will embodied in government programs. Voluntary acts of compassion and charity by private individuals or groups are always inferior to the welfare activities of the state, cannot be substituted for the state's welfare machinery, and cannot meet the welfare needs of the people. Massive welfare programs administered by the state at taxpayer expense are necessary to meet the needs of the disadvantaged.

10. An individual's destructive actions against himself or others are not primarily the consequence of his personal choices, values, goals or other mental and emotional processes occurring in his own mind, but are instead caused by negative influences impinging upon him from his culture. He should therefore not be held responsible for his bad actions. Rather, he and others should be encouraged to view his actions as the collective fault of a society

that has in some way oppressed, neglected, deprived or exploited him.

11. Traditional ideas about the separateness and sovereignty of the individual are invalid. Although he is a physically separate entity, an individual's political significance derives from his membership in a collective; the collective is the primary economic, social and political unit, not the individual. Rights formerly held to reside in the individual, such as property rights in his person and possessions, are no longer primary but are to be subordinated to the rights of the parental state and its family of citizens. The will of the people as understood by government officials takes precedence over the rights of the individual and may properly displace older ideals of liberty and procedural justice whenever necessary. Claims to personal sovereignty and the right to have a life of one's own are selfish and therefore morally wrong. Personal sacrifice for the sake of others, mandated by the state and channeled through its collective institutions, is a higher ideal than older individualistic ideals of self-reliance and benefit to others through cooperation or the pursuit of personal goals.

12. Material subsidies are to be paid to persons designated by the state and based on need, suffering or inequality, not on merit or desert. Reparations to persons deemed by the state to have been wronged may be made by forcible transfers of property from other persons who are assigned responsibility for injuries or disadvantage even though they have personally done no wrong. In general, rights to life, liberty and property enshrined in the U.S. Declaration of Independence and the U.S. Constitution's Bill of Rights should be set aside in favor of whatever collective rights are asserted by the state.

13. Human nature is highly malleable. Not only can it be molded to accommodate collectivist ideals without contradicting that nature and without adverse consequences, but adherence to collective ideals will improve human nature. Government programs based on social science research can and should alter behavior toward politically approved ends. Liberal insights are superior to traditional conservative beliefs, in part because liberal policy makers are intellectually superior to conservatives and other opponents.

14. Prescriptions for how to act and how not to act should not be based on the distilled ethical and moral wisdom of the centuries but should instead be decided by liberal intellectuals and promulgated through canons of political correctness or evolved through the creation of alternative life styles in a spirit of cultural diversity. Many behaviors traditionally counted as offensive, immoral or illegal should now be deemed acceptable, including various sexual and aggressive behaviors that are strongly condemned by conservative standards. Behaviors of this type are not to be judged in regard to their moral or ethical implications or by their tendency to disrupt social order, but should instead be explained by the motivations behind them and understood as expressions of human freedom, healthy absence of inhibition, progressive morality, or defensive reactions to adverse social influences. Sexual freedom, in particular, should be given wide latitude among consenting adolescents and adults even if its exercise results in extramarital pregnancies and single parent families, increases the incidence of sexually transmitted disease, violates traditional marriage vows, invades stable unions or destroys family integrity.

15. Similar considerations apply to the prominence of sexual and aggressive imagery in the media. The possibilities that such imagery might adversely affect social order or indicate a disorder of cultural values should be denied in favor of the idea that its display is an expression of freedom from excessive inhibition. Pornography is not harmful to children; under First Amendment protection, exposure to it should not be restricted. Similarly, established traditions of decency and courtesy are unduly restrictive given modern liberal insights. Traditional courtesies may also be rejected because they support class distinctions that oppose the liberal ideal of social equality.

16. In general, traditional social ideals, ethical standards and prohibitions of conscience are to be regarded as outmoded, opposed to the evolution of progressive social codes, and not applicable to modern social systems. In fact, there are no objective grounds on which to favor one set of societal arrangements over another. Rules governing human interactions that have evolved over thousands of years and have come to define what is fair and just in human dealings deserve no special respect. Traditional Judeo-Christian moral and ethical codes such as the Golden

Rule may be rewritten *ad libitum* in view of insights gained from contemporary relativistic and multicultural constructs. Likewise, traditionally noble sentiments or heroic actions should be regarded as archaic and socially naïve in part because such actions are largely determined by cultural influences.

17. Traditional moral, ethical and legal codes have not been promulgated for such reasonable purposes as ensuring social order or promoting good will or human happiness, nor have they been based on a rational understanding of human nature and the conditions of human existence. Instead, they are essentially political constructs created for manipulative purposes by persons who seek power over others. Equality before the law, for example, is a fiction even as an ideal and represents an apparently ethical cover for what is in fact the exploitation of certain subgroups such as women and ethnic or racial minorities.

18. Good character as an embodiment of certain virtues is not an important ideal. Individual dispositions to behave with honesty, integrity, responsibility, self-direction, mutuality and dependability in interactions with others are not to be especially valued or praised. More generally, one should avoid judging the actions of another person based on standards of ethics, morals or virtue. Condemning the behavior of another person on grounds of right and wrong or good and evil is harsh, mean-spirited and judgmental and may diminish self-esteem, but this criticism of others by liberals should not itself be subjected to disapproval because it is needed to achieve social justice. Economic, social or political disadvantages should be sought for as explanations for bad behavior by any definition, and such explanations are to be understood as excuses for that behavior. An individual who commits a bad act should not be held personally responsible for what he does even if he does it with malicious intent. Malicious intent, if present, cannot properly be attributed to the perpetrator himself. An obviously criminal motive, for example, should not be seen as a fault in the offender but as an unfortunate consequence of hardship inflicted upon him in the past or disadvantages suffered in the present. Because such hardship and disadvantage are caused by other persons and other factors, the individual committing the bad act should receive sympathy, not blame. Society's primary response to such actions should be to treat or rehabilitate the

offender, not punish him or require him to make restitution for his wrongdoing. Persons who have been disadvantaged should not be held to ordinary legal duties or obligations if such responsibilities would be burdensome to them.

19. These considerations also apply to alleged good and evil behavior between nations and among religious and ethnic groups, including various types of terrorist acts that inflict devastating injury and death on apparently innocent persons. Moral and ethical judgments about what individuals or groups do on the international scene should be withheld pending further analysis of their motives and the economic, social and political context in which the acts occur. Retaliation, especially of a military type, should not be initiated against terrorists as that will only compound the problem and cause greater destructiveness. Empathy, understanding, negotiation, compromise, concession and appeasement are far more effective in resolving those cultural and other conflicts that are the root causes of the problem. In general, U.S. foreign policy makers should assume that American imperialism and capitalist exploitation of other peoples have been major factors in provoking aggressive acts by other nations or by religious or ethnic groups.

20. In the interest of social justice, it is the duty of the state to determine which groups or classes of persons suffer from deficits in material security and in social and political status and to cure these deficits through government initiatives. The state should provide benefits to persons of its choosing based on perceived need, or on certain types of inequality, or on past, present or ancestral hardship. Except for considerations of need, inequality and suffering, there are no valid criteria for deciding which benefits a recipient deserves. Neither he nor his actions should be judged on any traditional scale of merit or desert, because moral and cultural relativism properly deconstructs all arguments based on these scales but not arguments based on the state's perception of need, inequality and suffering. Traditional concepts of merit and desert are themselves unjust, fraudulent and injurious to the sensibilities of those who are unfairly blamed for wrong doing, self-neglect, laziness or other self-defeating tendencies. These tendencies, if present, should not be condemned as weakness, immaturity, irresponsibility or moral turpitude.

21. More generally, time-honored conceptions of justice as reflected in common sense, ethical philosophy, judicial practice and the history of political thought are invalid (Kekes 1997). It is not true, for example, that a person should be rewarded or punished in proportion to the good or evil he causes. It is also not true that the outcome of a transaction is fair just because the processes that lead to its completion are fair and the decisions made by the parties to the transaction are informed, voluntary and competent. Justice should no longer depend on concepts of desert, earned reward or punishment, moral merit or procedural fairness. Instead, justice must be based on considerations of need, inequality, disadvantage and suffering. An outcome that leaves one or more parties to a transaction in a disadvantaged, unequal, or needy state is unjust by definition. To satisfy need, remove inequality and eliminate and compensate for suffering, it is proper to take economic goods from persons who own them according to older standards of just title and give them to persons or groups now deemed deserving by government officials. It is also proper to lower the social and/ or political status of certain persons and elevate the social and political status of certain other persons based on considerations of need, inequality, disadvantage and suffering. Adjustments of this type are proper even if those demoted in their status have not committed any social or political wrongs. The ideal of equalizing disparities in status justifies the realignment.

22. Traditional ideals of self-determination, self-responsibility and self-reliance are invalid. These concepts are illusory anyway, since the manner in which any one person conducts himself cannot be attributed to particular characteristics that differentiate him from others. What appears to be virtuous effort or moral integrity, for example, is merely a complex result of societal influences expressed through the individual. His own effort, talent, ingenuity, risk taking, persistence, courage or other apparent personal contributions to his success, including those he sustains in the face of hardship, are illusory or derivative. Furthermore, the fruits of an individual's labors should be shared with others without compensation, because his talents, virtues and abilities are actually collective assets belonging to the population as a whole, and his achievements are more reasonably attributed to the collective process from which he benefits.

23. Economic activity should to a great extent be carefully controlled by government. Where the means of production are not owned outright by the state, they should be closely regulated despite burdensome administrative costs, interference with prior ownership and contractual agreements, or negative effects on allocation of resources and incentives to economic activity. Adverse effects on the freedom with which individuals can run their economic lives, even when severe, are appropriate concessions to the ideals of government regulation, especially where redistribution of material wealth is concerned. Likewise, the distribution of what is produced should be strongly influenced by government, as should the nature of what is produced, the persons who do the producing, the sale price at which products are offered, and the margins of profit enjoyed at each stage between production and consumption. Consumer goods should also be carefully regulated by the state, and patterns of consumption should be influenced by tax policy. Profits that appear to be earned through free market mechanisms are probably the result of manipulation of the consumer, and high profits should be condemned as obscene. What appears to be voluntary consent by persons employed in manufacturing and other businesses is often illusory and masks exploitation of workers, women, the poor, certain minorities and other disadvantaged classes. Competition at all levels of economic activity, including that arising from innovation, is unduly harsh, demands excessively hard work, and may cause financial and other hardships through job loss, business failure and career change. Comprehensive government protections are needed to mitigate these dangers. It is well known that capitalists and the rich rise to wealth and power on the backs of the poor. The policy that wealth should be passed on to the heirs of one's choice wrongfully deprives others of material goods to which they are entitled by collectivist principles.

24. Every individual is born into the world with a legally enforceable obligation to take care of an indefinite number of persons whom he will never meet and with whom he will establish no voluntary association or agreement. He will be entitled to only a portion of the fruits of his own labor, and that percentage will be determined by government policy. Citizenship in a collectivist society properly implies that as soon as an adolescent makes the transition to adulthood, a substantial portion of his time,

effort and ability becomes rightfully indentured to others. The persons to whom he is obligated will be identified for him by the state according to their membership in a group or class deemed deserving. The more economically productive one is, the greater his liability to others. This system is designed to combat the greed that causes productive persons to want to keep what they earn.

25. The primary purpose of politics is the creation of an ideal collective society run by a liberal elite committed to a just redistribution of economic, social and political goods. This redistribution is to be achieved along egalitarian lines using the coercive power of the state. Traditional negative rights that protect individual liberty through guarantees of freedom from encroachment by others should not limit the state's actions and must instead yield to positive rights that guarantee freedom from material need and from disadvantages in social status and political power. Government enforced entitlements are to be the primary means to these ends.

26. The traditional social institutions of marriage and family are not very important in the dynamics of social process and should yield to progressive alternative lifestyles that emphasize the satisfaction of sexual and relational needs. The traditional bond of marriage is too restrictive and does not allow for more diverse social and sexual experience, including the self-discovery that comes from relating to a variety of partners. An enduring and exclusive sexual relationship with one other person for a lifetime is not an especially valid ideal, nor does it serve to deepen one's experience of himself and what it means to love another person. Similarly, children do not need parents who are deeply committed to each other or to an intact traditional family consisting of a mother, father and siblings, nor are grandparents, cousins and other extended family members important in the rearing of children. If a child needs attention, love, affection, guidance, protection, training, education, medical care, socialization and acculturation, these needs can be met by daycare facilities, village programs, summer camps, neighbors, sitters, teachers, social workers and other staff in public schools. Moral and ethical values and the family's racial, ethnic and cultural traditions can be acquired from these and other sources and do not have to be taught by parents or extended family. Finally, traditional religious training instills a

narrow, prejudicial and judgmental view of morality and culture and should be replaced by more enlightened secular philosophies, especially those that promote cultural diversity. Morality and ethics should be seen as evolving value systems subject to progressive insights. There are no moral absolutes for human relating, nor is it possible to make a valid argument for the superiority of one moral code over another.

Collectivism over Freedom

Based on these considerations, the question of whether modern liberalism prepares the emerging adult to live in freedom must be answered in the negative. Far from an interest in preparing its children for lives of genuine liberty based on personal autonomy, self-reliance and cooperation by consent, the liberal agenda promotes an uncritical childlike accommodation to the rules, regulations and expropriations essential to the collectivist state and an equally childlike dependency on a society that likens itself to an all embracing family. Mature competence is achieved only with difficulty, if at all, under these conditions. By the very nature of its operations, every government program comes with an increase in the state's power and a decrease in the domain of individual freedom: the will of government officials is substituted for that of the individual citizen whenever and wherever a government program tells him what he may or may not do. *With directives for nearly every conceivable situation, the programs of modern parental government constantly interfere with the individual's most immediate experience of personal freedom: that of making his own decisions at the countless choice points of daily living. These intrusions undermine his growth to competence by extending the dependency of childhood well into his adult years and even for the duration of his life. More specifically, the collectivist society diminishes the young adult's opportunities for continued development of autonomy, initiative and industry; subordinates his personal sovereignty to the authority of the collective; and defines him politically by his obligations to the state.* In addition, the directives of the modern liberal state dramatically weaken the social, ethical, moral and legal foundations on which stable civil societies are constructed and promote instead varieties of class conflict, ethical relativism, moral laxity and judicial activism. All of these effects undermine both poles of the individual's bipolar nature and destabilize the social systems in which he must try to orient himself. The ideals of the liberal agenda encroach upon his right to live largely as he chooses, intrude by force into transactions that would otherwise proceed by mutual consent, and subvert the rules for living that are critical to social cooperation.

Illusory Freedom

Of course proponents of the liberal agenda routinely deny these realities and their significance for the lives of the people. Of particular interest in this denial is the liberal claim that the state's welfare programs not only do not undermine freedom but instead increase it by liberating the individual from the oppressive burdens of his own well being—obtaining adequate food, housing, medical care, child care, retirement security, etc.,—and from certain injustices of political and social inequality. With these burdens lifted from his shoulders by appropriate government programs, it is argued, the citizen of the collectivist society has greater freedom to make a good life for himself.

But this cannot be an authentic freedom. The person liberated from the burdens of adult life is also liberated from the opportunity to grow up. Only by leaving behind the dependency of childhood is it possible to acquire the instrumental and moral competence that provides for one's material security, grounds adult identity, solidifies adult self-esteem, and generates the strength needed to cope with life's challenges. Strongly collectivist societies do not permit such growth. Because he is supported, sheltered and supervised by the state, the collectivized citizen can enjoy only the pseudo-freedom of a child at the playground, one whose material well-being, identity and social status are provided to him by his parents whether he acts responsibly or not, usefully or not, cooperatively or not. The well-socialized man cannot construct a life of his own or a self of his own through the limited choices he makes or the limited consequences he takes. He receives passively from government what he need not seek actively by his own industry and cooperation with others. It is this surrender of autonomy, initiative, industry and adult identity that ultimately ties the socialized man-child to the skirts of the maternal state. It is intrinsic to the human condition that genuine competence is achieved only through active struggle with real world difficulties, not passive dependency on the nanny state. Under collectivism, the "autonomy" given to the citizen through government subsidy is a pseudo-autonomy. It is a childlike existence that demeans the recipient as it aggrandizes the state. In a world so managed by government, the individual cannot write his life's story through free choice and consequence because the state's rulers write its main plot for him. To play an assigned role is not to live in freedom.

This situation has profound implications for the young person as he graduates from adolescence and enters an adult world. Under the creed of modern liberalism, he is not called to maturity but is instead invited to begin a second childhood. Like the child at play, he is given, or at least promised, ultimate economic, social and political security without having to assume responsibility for himself. The liberal agenda requires him to remain in an artificial environment—the daycare program of the grandiose state—where he need not become an adult, take responsibility for his own welfare, or cooperate with others to achieve what the state will give him for nothing. But this regressive relationship is a Faustian bargain between citizen and government, one that invalidates the newly minted adult's right to live as he chooses, to accept and learn from the consequences of his actions, to decide the nature of his relatedness to the world according to his ambitions and abilities, and to respect the time-honored rules essential to social order. The state's rightful duty to create the political conditions essential to ordered liberty is breached in this bargain. The architecture of responsible liberty is sacrificed in modern liberalism's determination to conscript all persons into a grand socialist collective, a great corps of mutual servants, subjects and surrogate parents under the rule of liberal government.

36

Young and Mature
Adulthood

Whatever his preparation, the time has come for the young adult to make his own way in the world; he can delay and linger in the protection of his home, or in the halls of his alma mater where the storms of the world are filtered and refined, but he cannot tarry too long without commitment and the direction it provides. The choice of an occupation and the choice of a mate are the decisions that start him on his way.

Theodore Lidz

The Nature and Purpose of Adulthood

This chapter and the next will inquire into a few matters important to early and middle adulthood and explore their relevance for living in a society of ordered freedom. The discussion here will be relatively brief, as earlier sections have already reviewed a number of topics from an implicitly adult perspective. Before proceeding further, however, it will be useful to recall once again the overall purpose of human development through the first twenty years of life. That purpose arises inevitably from the biological nature of man: the transformations of childhood have as their goal the achievement of those physical and mental capacities needed to survive as an adult individual and reproduce as a species. At the very least, the physically competent adult must acquire the instrumental skills essential to daily living, together with the parental skills needed to rear children. These endeavors typically require both individual and cooperative efforts, reflecting as always the bipolar character of man.

Given these observations, a reasonable *definition* of adulthood assumes, first, that the normal processes of physical maturation to adult levels of height, weight, strength, sexual capacity, etc., and to one's biologically determined level of intelligence are essentially complete; and second, that capacities for both autonomous action and social cooperation at effective levels have been acquired. Stated in these terms, competent adulthood implies a willingness and ability to:

- Terminate childhood dependencies on parents and achieve economic and social self-sufficiency in the adult world

- Develop a relationship of mutuality and equality with parents

- Achieve an adult conception of self and other

- Experience sexual and emotional intimacy in a committed relationship

- Become a parent (or contribute to rearing others' children)

- Find or continue stable friendships outside of the natal family

- Learn to play in a manner consistent with the obligations of adulthood

- Achieve a viable and gratifying adult work identity by choosing freely among opportunities in a free market of occupations

- Establish economic and social interdependence with others by mutual consent in a free market of goods, services and relationships (footnote: modified from Lidz 1968 and Colarusso 2000).

These capacities apply to both men and women. Housewives and/or mothers who are not directly self-supporting through gainful employment but who otherwise contribute substantially to the division of labor in a committed marriage, family or partnership would also qualify as adults under these criteria. Adults who live a single life may achieve the status of adulthood minus the achievement of intimacy through responsible self-support, mutually gratifying friendships, or contributions through work or other activities to their community's economic and procreative resources—as a childless teacher or playground supervisor might do.

Note that the last two items in this list refer to economic and social self-sufficiency and interdependence with others through the exercise of free choice and mutual consent. These achievements emphasize, in turn, a set of *ideals* which support both individual freedom and social cooperation. As noted in earlier sections, they can be listed as capacities for:

- Respecting the sovereignty of other individuals and the value of individual lives

- Valuing freedom to choose and cooperate as defining elements of the human condition

- Honoring the non-relativity of core ethical and moral values as essential for safety and happiness in community living

- Recognizing the right to be let alone as a foundation of individual liberty

- Honoring the obligations of promises, contracts, ownership and property rights

- Relating to others with honesty and integrity

- Relating to others with decency, courtesy, civility and thoughtfulness

- Caretaking and nurturing behavior including tenderness toward children and sympathy for the chronically ill or disadvantaged

The Adult Society

These are, of course, *individual* character virtues. Their importance to a free and peaceful society has already been argued and will be further argued below. But the character of the *society* itself matters as well; it is not sufficient that citizens try to achieve these adult virtues in a culture that cannot validate them. For competent people to realize a life of ordered freedom, the society in which they live must itself have achieved a degree of "adulthood:" its major institutions must be founded on a rational appreciation of the human condition and the bipolar nature of man. The adult society must foster among other things self-reliance, not government dependency; lawful self-direction, not government direction; moral realism, not moral indulgence; and cooperative individualism, not coercive collectivism. To qualify as a validating environment for the individual who has achieved authentic adulthood, an "adult state" will support the evolution of free markets, install the legal protections needed to sustain them, and establish the infrastructure of moral values and legal protections that allows economic, social and political processes to be conducted by valid consent instead of force. The adult individual's capacities for a life of ordered liberty must compliment, and be complimented by, the institutions that secure the conditions needed for that liberty.

Redefinition of the Self

These ideals, values and virtues have implications for ongoing identity development. In early adulthood the self is rapidly expanded through educational and occupational endeavors and through deeper and more enduring sexual and emotional relationships. This redefinition gives a major boost to the individuation process begun in the second and third years of life and accelerated dramatically in the transformations of adolescence. In early adulthood, marriage connects sexuality and sensuality to emotional intimacy; meets needs for attachment, dependency and companionship; deepens the experience of relatedness by mutual self-disclosure; and challenges one's ability to cooperate in close encounters of the marital kind. Marriage requires a specific variation on the human capacity to love: the ability to deeply value another person in an enduring sexual union while committing to her safety, well-being and personal fulfillment. Marriage is a clear-cut example of the mutuality of social cooperation as it voluntarily divides and combines such daily labors as making a living, keeping house and relating to others.

Getting married and having children fill an emotional and relational void left by one's separation from the family of origin, but there is a price to pay: the togetherness of marriage challenges all who try it in the mental, emotional, physical, sexual, intellectual and relational dimensions of their human nature, and in the economic, social, political and spiritual realms of their lives. If the capacity for marriage represents a high level of personal development, it is only because marriage is also the most challenging of all social institutions.

Both marriage and work reexamine earlier achievements of trust, hope, agency, autonomy, will, initiative, purpose, industry, competence, identity and fidelity. Enhanced capacities for resolving conflict over occupational and relational goals, muting aggressive impulses arising from disputes in the home and workplace, and coordinating the use of jointly owned or used property are essential to everyday living. Working out mutually acceptable divisions and combinations of labor in work, marriage and social relating challenges the young adult's ability to compromise. Assuming financial responsibility for oneself becomes a major challenge in its own right, and a still bigger challenge when a spouse and children are added to the burden. Restated in more Eriksonian terms, adulthood reactivates earlier developments of the self in respect to:

- Basic trust as expressed in the ability to maintain optimism, security and satisfaction in the worlds of work, marriage, child rearing and friendship, as opposed to persistent distrust, pessimism, envy and depression

- Autonomy as expressed in the ability to direct one's life by choosing freely among real alternatives that include overarching commitments to a mate, children and work; self-interest pursued through rational self-assertion and without undue stubbornness or defiance or immobilizing shame or doubt; reasonable compromise without resentment or humiliation

- An attitude of good will reflected in accommodation, cooperation, mutuality and coordination of interests as opposed to an attitude of ill will reflected in demandingness, manipulation, entitlement or indifference

- Recognition of and respect for the sovereignty of others as opposed to self-centeredness, exploitation and dominance over others

- Initiative directed toward good purpose in the workplace, marital home and community: the ability to handle competition and rivalry without undue hostility, envy, jealousy or guilt

- Industrious effort through social and instrumental skills applied to tasks of work, marriage and community vs. apathy, detachment, social withdrawal or inferiority in one's self or skills

- A sense of identity as a basically valuable and lovable person; as a free, legitimate, effective, mutual, cooperative and purposeful actor with pride in one's self and zest for life, as opposed to confusion about one's nature, worth, lovability, goals, skills, gender and sexual appetite, or confusion as to the realities of one's racial, ethnic, economic, social and political status

- Emotionally intimate and sexual love for an exclusive partner, and increasing self-reliance and occupational identity through commitment to productive work; establishing adult friendships that connect one's personal values to those of society through shared experience.

Identity and Commitment

In the loving commitment of marriage, a partial merging of selves occurs that alters each partner's psychological boundaries, challenges self-centeredness, and uniquely modifies the sovereignty of each self. The boundaries of the self are expanded to include the spouse and his or her assets, liabilities and ambitions. In the embrace of marriage a new part-self is acquired in the person of the other. The self is redefined in terms of an overarching "we," in addition to and well beyond the familiar "I." The arrival of children extends this redefinition process further, turning spouses into parents and marriage into family (Lidz 1968). The "we" is enlarged to enfold offspring into a new and more complex entity, and the "what and whom" that one is willing to live and die for grow as well. But this expansion of the self and its new world also requires a complementary alteration of the premarital self's interests: a viable marriage requires that at least some of one's former activities be limited or renounced altogether in order to provide time and energy for new interests compatible with a shared life. Some of these new interests properly engage the community: the newly arrived adult is now an adult neighbor, citizen, consumer, taxpayer and voter, and he automatically becomes a member of a socioeconomic class, however ill-defined that category may be. He may also be a member of a religious organization, spend time in charitable activities, or become active in local government.

Adult and Government

With graduation into the world of work, marriage and community, the newly minted adult begins a much more direct encounter with society than he has had previously. Having left behind the buffers provided by parents, school, neighborhood and home town, he will now relate to the economic, social and political realities of life in a manner that is more direct, more personal, and more telling for the future than has been the case in earlier years. If he is living away from his family for the first time, a young person's awakening to the adult world is likely to be exciting, given his freedom to relate to new persons and new values and to explore new lifestyles without the usual scrutiny of parents. Going away to college or holding a job is an opportunity of this kind.

But holding a job, or more precisely, earning an income is a special event in a young person's life in at least two other respects. In the first place, in achieving gainful employment, the previously dependent child now becomes his own self-supporting person, and this change strongly solidifies his adult status. In the second place, the mere fact of earning an income quickly brings the hitherto anonymous citizen to the attention of the government, whose interest in him signals a new, distinct and uniquely permanent relationship in his life, one that also has major implications for his identity. In his earlier, mostly unemployed years, as a student for example, a young person is likely to understand government only vaguely and from a distance—as something studied in class or mentioned in the news. Even with the right to vote at eighteen, the average adolescent does not take seriously the reality of government and does not feel much affected by it unless drafted into military service. Moreover, the child's concept of authority typically attributes power to parents or teachers or to local police and courts, and not to the offices of government per se.

Once employed and the recipient of income, however, a young adult becomes directly acquainted with the power and reach of government at all levels, most notably its power to tax, regulate and license, and less directly its power to imprison and do violence at home and abroad. The young citizen learns that he can do certain things only with a government license, that he must do and not do certain things on the job according to federal and state law, that he can be arrested and fined or jailed if he fails to comply with government regulations, and that a substantial portion of what he earns or inherits can be taken from him permanently. The now employed adult is thus confronted with a new relationship. The new relationship is a forced and permanent marriage to the state. And the new spouse is demanding, imperious, usually unreasonable and very expensive.

Mature Adulthood

In the aggregate, the commitments of adulthood to work, marriage, family and community redefine the individual as they test the preceding twenty years of preparation for maturity. If preparation has been adequate, this redefinition constitutes a third individuation in the life cycle: the transition into adulthood forever alters one's identity, first with work and a spouse, and again with children, and yet again in a lifelong affiliation with the society of man. If the transition goes well enough, these years also offer opportunities for self-transcendence—for commitment to persons, principles or causes beyond one's self-centered concerns—and a further step in growth to maturity. But failure to complete the most basic of these transformations, those involving intimacy and work, threatens the individual with long-term social disconnection: the potentially tragic outcomes of isolation, self-absorption, and stagnation that Erikson described so poignantly.

These unfortunate states preclude not only the achievement of intimacy but also the emergence by middle age of generativity, a parent-like commitment to community well being, and especially to the current generation of parents and their children for the next generation. As a developmental achievement grounded in the human instinct for nurturing, generativity is an expression of middle-aged altruism—a form of social interest, to use Alfred Adler's term—that attempts to make the world a better place for present and future generations. At its core, for Erikson, is a critical virtue: a capacity for caring that further defines the individual, now as a member of the community in which he is both benefactor and beneficiary. In the context of the present work, the achievement of generativity completes the individual's growth to mature adulthood if it is not blocked by earlier pathology.

To meet the challenges of this stage the newly arrived adult must engage the world on several fronts. If he wishes to become as fully human as his nature allows, then he will establish an occupational identity grounded in productive work, commit himself to another person in a sexual and emotionally intimate relationship, fulfill his biological destiny by having and rearing children, and contribute positively to the life of his community. With success in these efforts come at least four new individual virtues: the abilities to take care of oneself responsibly, to love another person intimately, to devote oneself to children, and to care about one's community enough to try to make it better—however modest that effort may be. In these endeavors the self is further individuated, redefined in its relatedness to itself and the world, and more focused on good purposes: preserving and enhancing life already here and creating and helping to create new life.

The relevance of each of these developments to freedom and social order should be clear. The tasks by which a young adult comes to define himself also turn out to be those which sustain the economic, social and political worlds in which he lives. Productive work in a chosen occupation adds to society's material wealth. Commitment to another person in marriage of one's choice creates the foundation for a family, the most important of society's social institutions and the only one proven effective in the rearing of children. Devotion to the care of children increases the likelihood that they will grow to competent adulthood. Generative activities that are freely chosen reinforce attitudes of good will, charitable concern and healthy morality essential to ordered freedom. But the achievements that signify maturity in the individual and contribute so critically to the health of his community must be reinforced by the overall character of the society in which he lives. The long term rational interests of both are clearly congruent, which is to observe once again that citizen and society are constantly interactive and mutually influential. The actions of each reflect the values that guide them. If the citizen insists on a life of liberty through self-reliance and cooperation, he will resist the state's invitation to become its child. If he longs to regress in his fear of freedom and on the illusory promises of collectivism, the liberal agenda will accommodate him. In the end, the nature of government reflects the will of the people, its sanity or its madness.

37

Freedom and Family

The family is a society limited in numbers, but nevertheless a true society, anterior to every state or nation, with rights and duties of its own, wholly independent of the commonwealth.

Pope Leo XIII

A Definition of Family

Beyond its everyday meaning, the idea of family as a social institution can be defined by its functions. A typical definition of this type, modified from a sociology dictionary, holds that a nuclear family consisting of parents and their biological or adopted children is expected to:

- Reproduce, protect and socialize the young
- Regulate sexual, aggressive, dependent and acquisitive behavior
- Act as a major focus of productive work
- Provide emotional comfort, support and refuge for its members
- Serve as a reference source for certain types of status, such as ethnicity, culture and race

These functions appear to be nearly universal across cultures, societies and historical periods.

A major psychiatric text on children describes the family from a slightly different vantage point:

"Families render humans human. Genetic

endowment and maturational factors strongly predispose to the relationships and intimacies that draw the infant into the human race, one interaction at a time. But it is the family in all its permutations that ultimately embraces that child's maturational promise, and through powerful, reciprocal interactive forces, converts tissue, synapse and instinct into human development." (Pruett 2002)

Yet another perspective on family functions can be found in legal standards for evaluations in child custody litigation. The controlling standard in these cases is the Best Interests of the Child doctrine. Statutory guidelines for the assessment of these interests typically assume that a competent parent will provide her child with love, affection, guidance, empathy and moral and religious instruction in a physically safe and emotionally stable home environment, and also provide broader physical protection, health care, education, material wellbeing and opportunities for peer relationships. The special importance of the child's attachment to each of its caretakers is also emphasized in these guidelines, which require each of the competing parents in a custody dispute to foster the child's bond to the other parent, not degrade or obstruct it.

Each of these conceptions emphasizes the direct impact of the family on the child's personal development, with fully functional adulthood as the desired end product. As already noted, however, an examination of the family and its functions in a larger context reveals its pivotal importance to society's economic, social and political institutions including its role in transmitting the values that sustain those institutions. Common observation confirms that it is the child's experience with his caretakers that prepares him or fails to prepare him for life as a free and responsible adult, one who is genuinely autonomous and self-reliant at one pole of his bipolar self, and able to cooperate voluntarily and with integrity at the other pole. Growth of this type is most likely to occur in a family that is strongly functional in certain respects. Some of these respects have already been noted. A more comprehensive list follows in the paragraphs below. Each numbered paragraph describes functions performed by a highly capable family committed to rearing children who are both self-directing and mutual by the time they reach early adulthood. A family of this type will perform at least the following functions:

1. Supervise the child's and other family members' basic instinctual drives to ensure that behaviors driven by sexual and aggressive impulses, dependency and security needs, narcissistic strivings, acquisitive desires, nurturing instincts, and needs for relatedness fall within legally, morally and socially acceptable limits.

2. Teach and model standards of right conduct and the prohibitions of conscience as the foundation for character virtues such as self-reliance, self-determination, mutuality and cooperation.

3. Serve as the primary regenerative unit of society by transmitting cultural values essential to economic, social and political stability.

4. Facilitate the achievement of basic trust, hope, autonomy, will, initiative, purpose, industry, competence, dependability, cooperation, fidelity, intimacy, recognition, love, caring, sympathy, mutuality, friendship, tolerance, loyalty and forgiveness.

5. Familiarize the child with the nature of economic processes in a free society and with a common sense understanding of first possession, ownership and transfer of property; the nature and obligations of contracts; the basic mechanisms of production and exchange of goods and services; the need for restitution and compensation; and the elementary facts of scarcity, supply, demand and price.

6. Teach and model ideals of fairness (e.g., honesty, impartiality) and justice (as defined by certain rights) in relating to others, honoring agreements, and administering rewards and punishment based on merit or desert.

7. Teach coping mechanisms to deal with physical suffering and the emotional pain of fear, insecurity, deprivation, loss, loneliness, neglect, injustice, inequity, competition, envy, jealousy and cruelty.

8. Teach and model how to live in a free society while discharging obligations and responsibilities attached to freedom, including the avoidance of negligent harm to others; how to deal with authorities such as police and government offices; how to manage conflict within and outside of the family; how to negotiate and compromise; and how to respond to reasonable and unreasonable demands of others.

9. Teach and model how to think rationally: to comprehend objective reality; protect one's life, safety and wellbeing; facilitate the achievement of reasonable goals; comply with the standards of good conscience; and avoid conflict with society's reasonable rules for living. (Maultsby)

10. Teach and model respect for privacy, confidentiality and the keeping of confidences, and the right to be let alone.

11. Establish an enduringly intimate faithful marriage as the foundation of the family and support the ideal of the family as a relatively autonomous and rational economic, social and political decision-making system based on loving attachments and on dynamics of authority, rights, power and obligation, all administered for the safety, wellbeing and growth of its members.

12. Establish clear leadership in parents, clear boundaries between generations within the family and between family and community, a generally positive emotional climate in the home, adequately communicative language and behavior, and a spirit of devotion to the nurturing and rearing of children. [1]

13. Serve as a microcosm of society at large, in which the family constitutes a miniature social institution engaged in useful economic, social and political endeavors, and governed through the family's executive, legislative and judicial decisions.

14. Establish itself as a primary reference point for each member's sense of personal identity, significance and worth through belonging to the family, first in the primal attachment to the mother, then to father and siblings, and to others in the extended family, with additional elements of identity arising from attachments to the family home, neighborhood, school,

community and nation, and from racial, cultural, ethnic and religious affiliations.

15. Provide a repository of love, affection, concern, companionship and refuge from life's stresses, and caretaking for all family members and especially aged, sick and disabled family members.

16. Teach care and preservation of the physical environment of the home and extend that attitude to environments of neighborhood, town, nation and planet, with recognition of "mother Earth" as the ultimate source of human life and a generative attitude toward her wellbeing.

17. Provide for continuity of the family name and a sense of personal immortality through the continuation of family memories and bloodlines in successor generations and for the transfer of real property and other assets by inheritance for the material security of members.

18. Validate the child's innate spirituality and intrigue with the mysteries of life, death and existence; introduce the role of spirituality in coping with the challenges of life and death; and provide religious/spiritual education that bolsters the character virtues essential to ordered liberty.

The Competent Family

Reflecting its interaction with the larger society in which it is embedded, these functions define the family as a complex social institution whose primary purpose is to rear children to competence. Although they make demands on all family members, these functions can be achieved by parents who are free of serious psychopathology, who revere the ideals of ordered liberty, and who live in a culture that validates their efforts. Such families contribute positively to the community by acting in accordance with high ideals and by rearing children who relate to others by mutual consent, assume responsibility for themselves, and hold themselves accountable

When this level of function is present and mature adulthood has been achieved, it is reasonable to speak of the *competent family* as a compliment to the ideal of a competent adult. When embedded in a society committed to liberty and cooperation, a competent family functions at or near the levels just listed by rearing its children to self-direction, self-responsibility, cooperation and altruism. Note that the competent adult and the competent family have an obvious reciprocity between them: competent families are best equipped to produce competent adults while competent adults are best equipped to create yet another generation of competent families.

But this argument can take still another logical step: given earlier observations on the reciprocal influences between individuals and families, on the one hand, and the society in which they are embedded, on the other hand, it also makes sense to speak of a *competent society,* one which supports the efforts of competent families to rear competent adults and validates the virtues of both. In this conception, the competent individual remains the primary economic, social, and political unit, the competent family continues to be the primary civilizing and socializing institution, and the competent society provides the overarching structure of ordered liberty. The tradition of western individualism, it will be noted, is clearly alive and well in this conception and lies at its core.

[1] Modified from Pruett in Lewis text.

38

Family Functions and the Liberal Agenda

The family is the American fascism.

Paul Goodman

The Liberal Assault on the Family

The philosophy of collectivism at the core of the liberal agenda downgrades not only the individual as the central actor in human relating but also the nuclear family as society's primary socializing institution. The following remarks will describe some of the agenda's contemporary assault on the family, using the preceding chapter's list of mature family functions as a baseline. The numbered paragraphs below correspond to the numbered paragraphs in that list. Each paragraph below begins with a summary sentence in standard text; selected liberal arguments follow in italicized and bracketed text. Recall that the preceding chapter's list asserts that the highly capable family:

1. Ensures that the child's behaviors fall within morally and socially acceptable limits by curbing his instinctual drives. *[Guidelines for morally and socially acceptable behavior are arbitrary constructs and should be revised by enlightened social science. Judeo Christian traditions, for example, are the product of historical accident*

and have no particular validity. There is no objective basis on which to decide which rules for behaving should govern a society except that they should be based on modern liberal insights and should respect cultural relativity and diversity. Guidelines for interpersonal relating should be taught in public schools, which should assume many of the child rearing functions formerly assigned to the family. Furthermore, traditional curbs on instinctual drives, such as sexual repression, have been excessive and have had deleterious effects. Traditional families have been sexually repressive. The sexual revolution properly liberated people, especially women, from excessive inhibition in sexual expression. Moreover, basic strivings for dependency and material security that are often problematic in the family need not be a problem when managed by the state, because the state can harness human nurturing instincts and ensure material security for the good of all. Giving free reign to narcissistic strivings is also healthy in allowing for self-expression, self-fulfillment and creativity. Needs for relating to others in constructive pursuits are best facilitated through state programs based on the universal brotherhood and sisterhood of humankind, not on fundamental patterns learned in the family.]

2. Ensures that its children learn standards of right conduct and good conscience as foundations for self-reliance and cooperation. *[Teaching self-reliance promotes selfishness, greed, mean spiritedness and indifference to the plights of the poor, ignorant, sick and oppressed. The private charitable activities of traditional families and related institutions such as the church are woefully inadequate to society's needs. Cooperation taught by families in capitalist societies has been based on economic motives such as exchange or profit rather than true sympathy for the needy. Authentic mutuality comes from a feeling of belonging, not to the traditional family but to the brotherhood of man, to the collective for which the state is the chief representative.]*

3. Serves as the primary regenerative unit of society by transmitting cultural values to its children. *[Traditional cultural values taught by tradition-oriented parents result in exploitation of the masses by the rich and powerful and should not be transmitted from generation to generation through the family. Instead, culture should be reinvented according to the insights of contemporary social scientists and other members of the liberal intellectual elite. By rejecting individualistic notions of the person, family and society, and by using modern social concepts, these thinkers are able to create*

plans through which government policy can overcome society's discontents for the good of all.]

4. Helps the child to achieve certain values and virtues in the service of ordered liberty. *[The family should educate the child in values and virtues that serve collectivist goals. Thus it is good to be sympathetic, empathetic, compassionate, caring, pitying, lenient, non-judgmental, tolerant of deviancy and faithful toward the state, but it is not good to be morally strict, insistent on integrity and competence, and committed to holding adults accountable for their actions. Initiative and industry are also virtues if they contribute to collectivist goals and not to the pursuit of self-interest.]*

5. Familiarizes the child with the nature of economic processes in a free society and with a common sense understanding of property and contract rights and the basic mechanisms of production, exchange and consumption. *[The family should leave the teaching of these matters to schools and the media, which will educate the citizen in government ownership or regulation of property, labor and capital; government management of resources, production and distribution; government control over supply, demand and price; and the socialization of education, transportation, communication, housing and health care.]*

6. Teaches fairness and justice. *[The traditional family fails to teach the principles of social justice and fairness as applied to the poor, sick, ignorant and downtrodden persons in the population. Traditional ideas of fairness omit egalitarian principles which call for a redistribution of economic goods, social status and political power. Public schools and other government-influenced social institutions, rather than families, should assume primary responsibility for teaching children the principles of what is fair and just.]*

7. Teaches coping mechanisms to deal with life's inevitable suffering. *[Like most aspects of life, coping with individual suffering should be socialized as much as possible and should not depend on teaching in the family. Government policies can and should remedy certain economic, social and political conditions that are the root causes of suffering. Enlightened liberal policies can eradicate poverty, ignorance, ill health and other forms of social injustice that lead to mental and physical pain. Policies based on egalitarian distributive*

*justice and a philosophy of brotherhood, for example, can eliminate
the conditions that cause fear, insecurity, envy, jealousy, hopelessness,
ignorance and isolation. Enlightened understanding of this type
cannot be taught by the family.]*

8. Teaches children that freedom entails certain responsibilities
as well as certain skills for relating to others and managing life's
difficulties. *[Children should be taught in school and through
other public channels that the welfare of all citizens entails certain
responsibilities that are best discharged through government
programs. A citizen's primary responsibility is to the state and to
those designated to be in need. Most difficulties should be resolved by
appeal to collectivist principles, not to principles based on individual
decision-making, property rights, contract rights or procedural
fairness. Managing life's difficulties is a collective enterprise.]*

9. Teaches children how to think rationally and realistically
about objective reality. *[What most people call objective reality is
a social construct based on capitalistic power hierarchies and on
dominant-race hegemony. One's personal safety and well being are
largely the result of societal conditions that are external to the individual
and the family and beyond their comprehension or responsibility. True
rational thinking honors the universal brotherhood of human relating,
the obligation of all to all, and the need for extensive government
oversight to ensure social justice.]*

10. Teaches children respect for privacy, confidentiality and
the right to be let alone. *[Although there are rights to privacy that
make abortion legal, families should understand that certain rights to
privacy and confidentiality are overly concerned with the individual
and therefore may be overridden by the state for the collective good.
Older claims to a right to be let alone in one's person and property,
for example, should yield to the state's duty to provide for the general
welfare. The welfare of the population as a whole also justifies the
state's intrusion into the family, as when it authorizes a teenage girl to
have an abortion without notice to her parents.]*

11. Establishes a stable marriage as the foundation of the
family and the family as a relatively autonomous and rational
decision-making system dedicated to the well being of its members.
[There is nothing sacred about marriage or the traditional family,

and neither entity is necessary for raising children. Approximately half of all marriages fail, and those that don't fail create unhappy children and families. Alternative arrangements for adults and children living together, including single parent households, are as effective as the traditional family, if not more so, in the rearing of children. Educating and socializing children, including instructing them in morality, are best left to public education teachers, daycare workers, and social commentators who espouse liberal social thought. Furthermore, the traditional family as a decision-making system is grounded in an authority hierarchy contrary to liberal principles of equality among all persons.]

12. Establishes clear leadership in parents, clear boundaries within the family and between family and community, and a spirit of devotion to the rearing of children. *[Parental leadership in families is likely to be excessively authoritarian rather than egalitarian and therefore oppressive to children. As compared with traditional guidelines for conduct, children should have fewer boundaries and greater discretion in their activities including sexual activities, homework, sleep schedules, manner of dress, substance use, whom they relate to and use of language. Furthermore, the burdens of child rearing should not be allowed to stifle the parents' pursuit of personal fulfillment. Much of the care of children can be properly handed off to sitters, neighbors and daycare centers without adverse effects on their development.]*

13. Serves as a microcosm of society at large. *[In its equal concerns for all of its members, the family should serve as a microcosm of collective society, which should in turn be modeled on the family. Society should embody in its laws the common family ethic that each member shall be provided with the means to a good life according to his need and each member will contribute to that purpose according to his ability. Children should be taught by families and schools to extend this ethic to the global human family in order to foster greater collective sentiment. Just as all members of the natal family are equally important, all human beings in the global family should be seen as equally important, and all are therefore equally entitled to whatever is required for a good life. Those necessities, especially a minimum income and material goods such as food, clothing and shelter, are best provided by a parental government, just as real parents who govern their household provide necessities for*

their children. Considerations of merit or desert should not intrude into this ethic, as the need for such goods is sufficient for entitlement to them. Similarly, self-defeating behavior in recipients, including lack of effort to improve their lots, should not determine whether they receive such goods. Finally, it is not the duty of a family to foster a child's individuation, as that process encourages selfishness that is antithetical to collective feeling.]

14. Establishes itself as a primary reference point for each family member's sense of personal identity, significance and worth through belonging to the family and through affiliation with other groups in society. *[One's personal and family identities are less important than one's identity as a member of the global human family, which is achieved through identification with the collective at all levels. Membership in the natal family is only the beginning of one's ultimate identity.]*

15. Provides a repository of love, a refuge from life's stresses, and caretaking for aged, sick and disabled family members. *[Families are too often repositories of "acute personal tensions and conflicts" that lead to "severe mental illness and other forms of dysfunctional identity."* [1] *It is a myth that the family is a source of love, refuge and caretaking; in fact, the family is often broken by divorce, financial hardship or illness. Care of the aged, sick and disabled cannot be left to the unpredictable efforts of families but is instead the proper responsibility of the custodial welfare state.]*

16. Teaches care and preservation of the physical environment of the home, extends that care to environments beyond the home, and develops a generative attitude toward Mother Earth as the ultimate source of life. *[Citizens whose political orientation is conservative and/or libertarian will not protect the environment from the ravages of materialism, capitalism, imperialism and greed. The only hope for preservation of the environment lies in government programs that drastically curb economic activity and lower our excessive standard of living. Left to their own choices, the people will not cooperate voluntarily to preserve the environment but will instead destroy it. To save the earth, principles of enlightened liberal environmentalism must be enacted into laws enforced under world government.]*

17. Provides for continuity of the family name and a sense of personal immortality through successor generations, and for the transfer of property by inheritance for the security of members. *[Immortality by any means is a dubious notion at best. But any sense of immortality through the family should yield to a greater sense of identity as part of the grand collective, whose importance vastly exceeds that of the family. Further, all transfers of property through inheritance should be terminated. Assets acquired by anyone prior to his death are obtained either by virtue of conditions provided by society or at the expense of other members of society or both. Accordingly, those assets properly belong to society as a whole, not to one's heirs. Assets in a private estate at the time of death should be appropriated by the government for uses that will benefit all citizens, not a select few.]*

18. Validates the child's spirituality while fostering its role in coping with life's challenges, and provides religious values consistent with ordered liberty. *[True spirituality is secular, not religious, emerges in the communion of the collective, and is consistent with the intellectual insights of modern liberalism. Traditional religion is the opiate of the masses. Modern liberalism's scientific analysis of social process has revealed the State as the proper object of human reverence. Historical religion may be mined for moral principles opposed to individualism but should otherwise be discarded.]*

The Fruits of Modern Liberalism

Consistent with the broadly destructive effects of its social philosophy, modern liberalism has had significant success in undermining the foundations of the traditional family despite the fact that its concept of society is modeled on the family. These effects have resulted from the agenda's legislative initiatives and from its persistent invitations to relax the constraints of conscience. The middle and later years of the twentieth century, in particular, witnessed the agenda's advocacy of alternative life styles, sexual permissiveness, drug abuse, easy divorce and dissolution of the family; its promotion of personal gratification at the expense of personal responsibility; its contempt for religion and traditional moral codes; its support for tax codes favoring single parent families and penalizing marriage; and the institution of welfare programs fostering wide spread economic, social and political dependency. These policies seriously undermined the foundations of American society. They were especially devastating to the family, and most notably to black families, which had managed to remain largely intact through the first half of the century despite the effects of continuing prejudice. These efforts to redesign the terms of human relatedness at individual, family and society levels continue in the late 1990's and early 2000's, although a succession of defeats in federal and state elections in these years have led liberal politicians to mute their customary socialist message. This tactical change has not altered the basic liberal strategy, however, which remains that of infantilizing the population, collectivizing the major dimensions of social intercourse, and bringing them under the ever increasing control of the state.

[1] *Norton Dictionary of Modern Thought p 308.*

39

The Competent Society

Where there is no law, there is no liberty; and nothing deserves the name of law but that which is certain and universal in its operation upon all members of the community.
Benjamin Rush

Introduction

A given *individual's* personality and character, as noted throughout this work, are reflected in his enduring patterns of thinking, emoting, behaving and relating. Comparable patterns describe a given *society's* overall "personality" or character: its dominant rules for living and modes of relating expressed in laws, traditions and customs; its political principles and modes of government; its morals, ethics and religions. A society's character is reflected in whether its people are governed by justice and the rule of law grounded in individual liberty rights or by a socialist state's entitlement to the lives and labors of its citizens. A society's character is distinguished by its science and technology, by its spirit of inquiry and respect for truth. It is distinguished by whether it intends freedom, safety and prosperity for its citizens or exploits them on threat of violence; by whether its rules provide checks and balances on the abuse of ownership and the depletion of resources; and by how its laws deal with problems of personal and local knowledge, interest and power. (Barnett 1998) A society is characterized by its passions for justice and fairness; its dispositions to caring, thoughtfulness, generosity, good will and courtesy; its commitment to the well-being of children; its preference for cooperation over coercion. Indeed, a society's *competence* may be defined and measured by the entirety of its arrangements for living and, in particular, by whether it provides a *set of rules* that are rational enough, stable enough and predictable enough that its citizens are able to seek good lives for themselves and know that the rules will not be changed in the middle of the game.

Preceding chapters have introduced the idea of a competent society, one which compliments the competent individual's ideals of self-reliance rather than government dependency, lawful self-direction rather than government regulation, moral realism rather than moral relativism, informed altruism rather than welfare statism, and cooperative individualism rather than coercive collectivism. In pursuit of this idea, the next two chapters will reaffirm certain dispositions that characterize the competent individual and will then inquire as to what *societal* rules are needed to support his efforts to live a life that is both free and cooperative. It should be clear by now that such a life cannot be realized unless a society's basic institutions do in fact protect ordered liberty. At its most fundamental level the competent society must acknowledge the bipolar nature of man when adequately nurtured: his *individual* nature as expressed in dispositions toward autonomy and his *relational* nature as expressed in dispositions to cooperate by consent. The following discussion will elaborate further on the idea of the competent person embedded in a competent society.

Competence Revisited

The most basic requirement, by far, for the development of competence in human beings is the curbing of innate sexual, aggressive and acquisitive instincts. These instincts are wired into human biology. They can be civilized by adequate nurturing, but they cannot be eliminated altogether. Their expressions in destructive acts are not caused by poverty, ignorance, physical disease, discrimination or capitalist oppression. The manner in which they are expressed in a given *individual* depends upon the extent to which they have been brought under the control of appropriate moral and ethical standards enforced by the prohibitions of conscience. *The manner in which they are expressed in a given situation and culture depends upon how the actor perceives the consequences of his actions, what incentives and constraints the situation offers to him, and what overarching values define the culture in which his action occurs. Human instincts can be controlled only where the constraints of individual conscience are adequate, cultural morality supports their control, and society's laws deter their criminal expression.*

It is, of course, a commonplace observation that unrestrained impulses arising from *aggression* lead to murder, torture, war and genocide, to brutally violent revolutions, to mayhem in riots, and to mutilation by sadists. Unrestrained impulses arising from *sexual* instincts lead to illegitimacy, infidelity and the disruption of stable unions and families. When joined with aggression and pathological narcissism, unrestrained sexual impulses lead to rape, lust murder, child molestation, criminal exhibitionism and compulsive exploitation of each sex by the other for erotic pleasure, power and egotism. Unrestrained impulses from the acquisitive instinct to *take things from others* lead to the countless acquisitive crimes endemic in all cultures: robbery of individuals and groups; theft, fraud and embezzlement in corporate, commercial and private arenas; and the inevitable criminal confiscations of government.

But additional instincts beyond sex, aggression and acquisition also disrupt social order, and these must also be curbed. When pathological in its expression, the instinct for *narcissistic satisfaction* disrupts effective cooperation at all levels of society by exploiting others in the selfish pursuit of grandiose goals instead of respecting the sovereignty of others in the pursuit of reasonable self-interest. If unrestrained, the instinct for *dependency* undermines self-reliance, autonomy and mutuality by attempting to extract from others certain types of material and relational security that should be earned through productive effort, not demanded through government welfare or solicited through fraudulent charity schemes and political pork barrel. If unrestrained and misdirected, impulses arising from the instinct for *nurturing* lead to infantilizing and indulgence of individuals and groups and abort the citizen's growth to competence. As observed earlier, the competent adult's capacities for inhibition, restraint and delay of these basic instinctual impulses become, in the aggregate, the indispensable self-regulatory infrastructure of the well ordered community.

The community must in turn adopt a system of rules that compliments the individual's ability to regulate himself. A society's recognized ideals—its morals, ethics, laws and conventions, and even its rules of deportment, manners, dress and etiquette—will, in the ideal case, support its citizen's inner restraints against all forms of antisocial conduct. As Hart observed, all viable societies adopt, at a minimum, certain primary rules of obligation that prohibit acts of violence, theft and fraud. Citing a few "elementary truths concerning human beings, their natural environment, and aims," he asserts that certain universally recognized rules of conduct constitute "the minimum content of natural law" required for "the protection of persons, property and promises." In both moral commandments and legal statutes these rules become society's overarching code of conduct. Their intent is to prohibit as much as possible any criminal expression of sexual aggressive, acquisitive and other instincts in acts of violence, theft and deception. (Hart 1994)

A System of Rules

Based on these considerations, a system of mutual obligations and duties designed to curb destructive acts is clearly essential to ordered liberty. The most important rules in this system consist in criminal laws that define deliberately wrongful acts and the punishments that attach to them. Less critical but still essential are tort laws which define negligent, as opposed to deliberate, harms and which specify what kinds of compensations are available to victims. Additional principles of behavior not formalized in statutes but understood as morals and conventions essential to a rational society serve to lubricate social intercourse at all levels. These are the countless moral, ethical, social and religious principles that tell us how to behave toward ourselves and others and toward our social institutions. Society's rules prescribe how to relate to our spouses or other intimates, to our parents and siblings and extended family, to our neighbors and fellow citizens, and to our governments and their officers. Some rules are cast as virtues such as integrity, temperance, patience, conscientiousness and bravery. These rules describe standards of excellence. They stem from what Lon Fuller has deemed the *morality of aspiration*: certain ideals of conduct tell us what we should aspire to in order to make a good life still better for ourselves or more beneficial to others. To complement society's rules for civilized freedom, the competent citizen obeys the rules that temper human destructiveness, deter human negligence and aspire to human excellence. (Fuller 1969)

These efforts on the part of the individual assist society's broader efforts to limit human destructiveness and sustain the structure of liberty. They require the good citizen to consider the impact of his behavior on others: to strive as he may for whatever goals will enhance his life but do so without offending others or violating their rights. Given the nature of man and what it takes for human beings to cooperate with each other, the rational citizen will strive to:

- Obey laws that protect against criminal and negligent acts
- Honor obligations essential to promises, contracts, ownership and property rights
- Relate with honesty and integrity to other persons who act similarly
- Reject all opportunities to dominate, control or exploit others
- Honor the non-relativity of core ethical and moral values essential for security, happiness and social cooperation
- Recognize the right to be let alone as a foundation for individual liberty
- Achieve an adult conception of self and other through respect for the sovereignty, agency, autonomy and freedom of all individuals
- Achieve economic self-sufficiency and a viable and gratifying adult work identity by choosing among opportunities in a free market of occupations
- Establish economic and social interdependence with others by mutual consent in a free market of goods, services and relationships
- Solve social problems through voluntary cooperation
- Understand that one must please others to be rewarded for his behavior
- Treat others with decency, courtesy, civility and thoughtfulness
- Relate sympathetically toward others where appropriate
- Become a married parent, or take care of and nurture children or the chronically ill or disadvantaged
- Terminate childhood dependencies on parents
- Reject childish feelings of entitlement

- Reject the state's attempts to take over altruistic functions
- Find or continue stable friendships outside of the natal family
- Learn to play in a manner consistent with the obligations of adulthood. (Lidz 1968 and Colarusso 2000).

All of these rules are important to the construction of good lives in a free and civilized society. Some are rules of aspiration. All accommodate the bipolar nature of man. All contribute to the character and competence of the individual and his society. Despite their proven worth, however, adherence to these rules is not easily achieved by large portions of the population. The knowledge about human nature needed to value the rules, and the character needed to comply with them, are learned readily in the formative years but only with difficulty in later years. Teaching the child how to live and relate according to the rules is the central task of the nuclear family's socializing and civilizing efforts. But the character of the society in which all of this takes place is just as critical. As Black observes, whole nations die when the basic rules for social life are ignored or overthrown for false gods. (Black 1994). The citizen embedded in a life of relationships is equally embedded in the rules that govern them.

The Relevance of Character

As already noted at several points in this work, the list of capacities that define the personal *character* needed for life in a free society overlaps the list that defines competence. The citizen of good character is able to act in accordance with certain virtues, those of honesty, integrity, responsibility, self-direction and dependability, among others. The citizen of good character chooses to act in these ways out of personal pride and satisfaction, and because he feels a responsibility to do so, not because he is compelled by government authority. The citizen of good character provides for his own needs and the needs of those to whom he has assumed a voluntary obligation. He respects the time honored rules essential to social order. Citizens of good character keep promises and honor contracts. They do not make legally enforceable but unjust claims on the time, effort or material assets of other persons. They do not feel entitled to be subsidized by others. The individual with the character to live in freedom believes he has the right to decide the manner of his relatedness to the world within the constraints of mutuality and social order. Within those constraints he holds himself accountable; he takes responsibility for his actions and accepts their risks and consequences.

The Competent Society

These are, of course, *individual* capacities and character virtues. Their importance to a free and peaceful society cannot be disputed, but the *character of the society itself* is also critically important. It is not sufficient for the making of a good life that citizens achieve a long list of adult virtues in a culture that cannot validate them. For competent people to realize a life of ordered freedom, the society in which they live must itself have achieved a degree of "adulthood." It must be a society of good character. It must be a competent society. Its major institutions must be founded on an adequate appreciation of the human condition and the bipolar nature of man. The adult individual's capacities for a life of ordered liberty must compliment, and be complimented by, the institutions that secure the conditions needed for that liberty. *To qualify as a validating environment for the citizen who has achieved adult competence, a society must establish a basic set of rules that permit freedom; it must establish the infrastructure of moral values and legal protections that allow economic, social and political processes to be conducted by mutual agreement.*

The family has a central role in this system because of its profound effects on individual development. In fact, competent families are best equipped to produce competent adults, who are in turn best equipped to create another generation of competent families. The additional observation that the family is indeed society's primary socializing and civilizing institution, yields a triad of entities—individual, family and society—each of which deeply affects the other. Of course each entity retains a degree of autonomy in this conception: the competent individual remains the primary economic, social and political unit of the free society, the competent family continues to be the primary socializing and civilizing institution, and the competent society itself provides the overarching structure of ordered liberty. But it is also clear that each social entity influences the other in a constant interactive dynamic. Each is dependent upon the other for its identity and stability. Each entity can be injured, and ultimately destroyed, by serious defects in the other two.

With these perspectives in mind, the question then arises as to what properly characterizes a truly civilized society, one that is competent enough to serve as the overarching structure needed for freedom and order. From what has been observed so far concerning the competent individual, it follows that a competent society's ideals, values, rules, conventions and traditions ought to:

- Accommodate the bipolar nature of man and the human condition
- Honor ideals of individual liberty, self-reliance, voluntary cooperation, moral realism and informed altruism
- Accommodate and regulate human instincts for self-preservation, sexuality, aggression, narcissism, acquisition, dependency, attachment and nurturing
- Validate Erikson's developmental achievements and virtues
- Secure economic, social, political, moral and legal institutions that validate the capacities of competent individuals
- Secure economic, social, political, moral and legal institutions necessary for ordered freedom by defending basic liberty rights and resolving problems of knowledge, interest and power
- Accommodate the realities of human vulnerability and human limitations in knowledge, altruism, resources, strength of will, frustration tolerance and morality (Hart 1994)
- Create the means to defend the state from foreign invasion
- Inspire children to become effective, legitimate, free, mutual and cooperative citizens
- Accommodate economic realities of scarcity, uncertainty, supply, demand, price and imperfect knowledge, as well as uses of land, labor and capital. [1]
- Address the trade-offs and side effects of laws and institutions such as incentive and allocation effects, administrative costs, and unintended consequences of human laws and institutions

- Teach and reward the morality of aspiration, the virtues of cooperation, and the evils of coercion unless it is necessary for defense.

Which rules will serve these purposes? Relevant studies have been done in recent years by scholars interested in the effects of social rules on human behavior in economic, social and political realms. Examples include the writings of Richard Epstein and Randy Barnett in legal philosophy, Thomas Sowell in economics and social philosophy, and John Kekes in political philosophy. These scholars have made important contributions to theories of social organization. Their contributions are characterized by a particular virtue in common: they are rigorous thinkers who base their conclusions on verifiable facts and careful reasoning. All are university scholars, but none are mere armchair theorists. They do not indulge in deductive exercises based on unproven assumptions. They do not argue that utopian illusions are realizable. All are well-grounded in history's lessons on what kind of societal arrangements create or destroy civilized freedom. All have studied the dynamics of social process extensively. All base their conclusions on the moral and practical consequences of particular social policies.

Epstein and Barnett, in particular, have each articulated a set of rules that are foundational for a society of ordered liberty. Because a systematic statement of their ideas is far too lengthy for the purposes of this book, limited elements of their work will be mentioned in summary form only. Including their ideas here serves the present author's efforts to ground a theory of ordered liberty in verifiable facts about human nature and in the real world conditions in which human beings live. The next few sections will describe certain rules essential to the structure of liberty, briefly explain their relevance, and then relate them to the capacities and virtues of the competent man. A discussion of the grounds on which the rules themselves are justified will follow.

Rights That Structure Liberty

The rules most important to a society of ordered liberty are those that translate into what have been variously called natural rights, liberty rights, negative rights, or basic or background rights. [2] Each right specifies a certain domain or sphere of liberty in which the right-holder, the ordinary citizen, is entitled to be free of interference from others including the state. (Epstein 1995, Barnett 1998). A set of four basic rights has been called the libertarian quartet:

- The right to self-ownership or autonomy
- The right of first possession
- The right to own and exchange or transfer property
- The right of self-defense or protection against aggression

Additional rights for a more complete set include:

- The right to just compensation for legitimate taking of property
- The right to limited access to another's property in emergency
- The right to restitution for injury or use or illegitimate taking of property

A few obvious questions immediately come to mind: Why should these rights be regarded as basic to freedom and social order? Why should they be obligatory? Why should they be binding in conscience? Do these rules support and even inspire the common man to live competently? An appeal to common sense morality and a look at the practical consequences of each right are the first steps in answering these questions.

The Right of Self-Ownership

First, and most obvious, the *right to self-ownership or autonomy* simply reflects the *moral* prohibition against human slavery. If Friday is not entitled to own himself entirely, if he is not the *sole* owner of his person, then one or more other persons, Crusoe or a gang of strangers, for example, may own all or a portion of him. If all of Friday is owned by another person or group, then he is fully enslaved. If only part of Friday is owned by another person or group, then he is partially enslaved, and his authority over himself is limited to what his other owners permit. On this argument alone, anything short of full ownership of one's self is morally repugnant and must be rejected. But the *practical consequences* of slavery are surely absurd if not as repugnant. Any society allowing slavery creates not only an immediately destabilizing class conflict but also insoluble administrative problems, such as deciding who will be slaves and who will be owners, who will own how much of whom, how will the allocation of slaves be decided, how will owners' jurisdiction over slaves be monitored, etc. Thus, on both moral and consequentialist analysis, anything other than full self-ownership is social madness. The competent man's defining characteristics—his instinct for self-preservation and his autonomy evident in capacities for self-reliance, self-direction, choice, agency, initiative, industry, identity, intimacy and sovereignty—all assume his entitlement to self-ownership. An even earlier developmental achievement, that of basic trust, also assumes a rule of self-ownership: the individual who knows that his society's most basic values support his dominion over himself can trust that his right to run his own life will be protected from those who will try to run it for him or simply dominate him. Absent self-ownership, basic *mistrust* is the only possibility.

The Right of First Possession

Assuming that Friday is entitled to full ownership of himself, his first responsibility according to the human instinct for self-preservation is to acquire the means to survive: he will have to find food and shelter, among other things, just to stay alive. If he is still on a desert island with few or no other persons around, he is likely to encounter land and other physical resources that are not already claimed by others. To achieve some degree of safety and comfort, he will exercise a natural inclination to use whatever resources are available on his island. He will eat what he is able to gather or catch, and he will fashion some kind of shelter out of whatever works for that purpose. The second of Friday's basic rights, then, is the *right of first possession*. This right entitles him to take control over previously unowned or abandoned resources and use them as he must to survive and prosper. The *moral* basis of this entitlement is simply the right to life: given the fact that Friday, like any other human being, must somehow provide food, shelter and other goods for himself in order to survive, and given the fact that survival must be a moral good if anything is, then some method of establishing original ownership of resources becomes a moral imperative. If he finds an unoccupied cave, for example, then a common sense understanding of right and wrong asserts that he is entitled to take possession of it for his own use. The same moral principle asserts further that it would be wrong for someone to displace him from the cave by force or fraud. Friday's first claim on previously unowned property makes him the first rightful owner of it. Moreover, the right of first possession, like the right to self-ownership, reinforces the competent man's autonomy, his capacity to direct his own life.

The Right of Ownership and Exchange

But Friday's right of first possession makes little sense if his initial ownership of something cannot be continued beyond staking a claim to it. A right to *continuing ownership* emerges naturally from a right to first possession, based on the same moral justification: if Friday is entitled to use a resource in order to survive when he first takes possession of it, then common sense argues that he is entitled to continue to use it indefinitely. And a logical extension of that argument makes it wrong for anyone else to take his resource away from him. If, for example, Friday gathers unowned wood and makes a cabin out of it with his own labor, then common sense argues that it would be wrong for Crusoe or anyone else to evict him from it. In addition, the moral argument that allows Friday to own his cabin also allows him to *abandon* it if he decides that he could live better elsewhere. The same argument also allows him to *trade or exchange* his right to use the cabin for something he wants more than the cabin—a boat perhaps, if Crusoe or somebody else is accessible and happens to have a boat to trade. As Adam Smith observed, human beings have a strong propensity to "truck, barter, and trade," and persons who come to own things by first possession or some other means often choose to exchange what they already have for something they would like to get. The fact that each party feels that he has bettered his lot by the exchange—or he wouldn't do it in the first place—makes it a win-win transaction. The third basic right, then, is the *right to own property and exchange it by agreement or "contract:"* that is, to acquire, control and use a physical object or resource, and to dispose of it by selling, trading or giving it away. The competent society's support of this right guarantees one of the most fundamental of human capacities: that of choosing how to use and dispose of things rightfully owned in order to better one's situation. Exercise of the right to own and exchange property reinforces the sense of basic trust in one's control over material possessions, which in turn fosters the virtues of self-reliance and self-determination.

A *consequentialist* argument for the right to own and exchange property compliments the moral argument. Any society which does not have legally enforceable property and contract rights descends into a state of social chaos where control over physical property is achieved only by the violence of thugs, not by rule of law. Where laws protecting property ownership and the right of contract are absent or not enforced, turf wars among urban gangs and warlord control over lawless territories decide who has dominion over physical resources and usually over local human populations as well. Indeed, history has taught an enduring lesson on the relationship between property and liberty: *the enforceable right of the individual citizen to own physical property is the greatest single protector of individual freedom. The historical record of political experiments documents the fact that state ownership of property in the name of the "people," as seen under communist regimes, has always been a prescription for tyranny, not liberation of the masses as advertised. Similarly, state control over what is done with private property under socialist regimes always trades away individual liberties for the illusions of collectivism.*

In fact, property rights permit control over material objects and resources needed to achieve personal autonomy, initiative and industry. The same rights permit ownership of a safe and materially comfortable home in which to achieve intimacy and rear children. The *ordinary* individual cannot develop normally or make a good life for himself without the ability to acquire and control what he needs and desires. The *creative* individual is not free to improve or replace what belongs to someone else. Products that make an entire society's living standards better will not be invented, created, produced or purchased in the absence of rights to private ownership. Schumpeter's dynamic of "creative destruction" at the core of capitalist innovation requires ownership by individuals working alone or in concert. The collapse of the Soviet Union illustrates the fact that without individual rights to own and exchange property, only the second term in Schumpeter's phrase prevails: no significant creativity is possible, only the eventual destruction of an entire society. Similarly, the liberal agenda's gradual erosion of property rights in favor of regulatory control over the citizen and his material assets threatens the viability of modern economies. Contemporary Europe's economic stagnation is a case in point.

The Right of Self-Defense

With rights to self-ownership, first possession and ownership of property under his belt, Friday has acquired three critical rights in support of life, liberty and the pursuit of happiness. But these rights are meaningful only if he and the things he owns can be protected from aggression by others. A fourth critical right, the *right of self-defense*, entitles Friday to do whatever it takes to protect himself and his property from the predations of his fellows, and especially from the claws of the state. Its justification in common sense morality lies in the most basic instincts for self-preservation and safety, and in the rights to ownership and property as essential to those ends. Similarly, its justification in terms of consequences is obvious, since without the right of self-defense both life and property are easy prey for the lawless. Basic trust then becomes impossible. Absent a right to self-defense, personal sovereignty may be violated at any moment, and one's possessions are constantly at risk.

The right to self-defense, added to the first three rights, completes the libertarian quartet of simple rules for a complex world. (Epstein, Barnett). Taken together they go a long way toward establishing the foundations for a society that is both free and orderly, as Epstein points out. They create the first barricades against a Hobbesian war of all against all, a war inevitable in a world where there are no rules at all, only lives that are "solitary, poor, nasty, brutish and short." As necessary as they are, however, they are not sufficient in themselves for a sane society. Three additional rules, already listed above, help with a few matters not yet addressed. Two of these rules illustrate the fact that individual ownership of property cannot reasonably be absolute; some property must be compromised at times for the collective good, albeit only for sharply limited reasons.

The Right to Just Compensation for Takings

The first of the three additional rules involves an owner's right to be compensated if his property is taken from him by the state. The government's power of eminent domain, its power to take control of property for a well-defined *public* benefit, makes sense only if the taking serves an important public good, and only if the private individual or group from whom property is taken receives adequate compensation for the loss. If Friday has unwittingly built his cabin over a water well, for example, and the lives of the rest of the island depend upon access to the well, then the island's government (assuming it has one) may "condemn" the cabin and the well for the greater public good. Friday will then have to move his cabin or dismantle it but not without compensation. Both moral and consequentialist reasons for this rule become apparent with a little reflection.

The Right to Limited Access

A second exception to absolute ownership occurs under a rule of limited access to another person's property in an emergency. Under this rule, Crusoe has a right to seek refuge in Friday's cabin from a life-threatening storm, even though Friday has not given him permission to do so. Of course, Crusoe does not have a right to stay in the cabin after the storm passes, but from a moral perspective, his right to seek life-saving shelter in an emergency takes precedence over Friday's property right to exclusive use of his cabin. Beyond this moral perspective, however, is a good argument based on consequences: the rule that permits Crusoe's action in a storm also permits Friday and every other citizen to seek shelter in comparable circumstances. The net result of the rule is that many lives are saved that might otherwise be lost, even if property owners are briefly inconvenienced.

The Right to Restitution

Closely related to this argument is a third rule that allows any citizen to seek restitution for damages. If Crusoe has to break a window in Friday's cabin to use it for safety, or if he simply breaks it by accident, then Crusoe has a moral obligation to repair the damage himself, or pay to have it done, or offer Friday some monetary or other compensation for the damage. This argument provides a moral backbone to Friday's right of restitution (or compensation) for injury. But this rule, like the others, passes muster on consequentialist analysis, too, because the net consequences for the population as a whole are favorable: payment for damages to a victim tends to mitigate the injury, conveys a concrete expression of gratitude for use or regret for injury, and creates at least a modest deterrent to an attitude of careless disregard for other people's property.

Reflections on Rights and Rules

The seven rights just outlined are basic rules for life, liberty and the pursuit of happiness. They provide a relatively simple but solid foundation for a peaceful and orderly society of citizens willing and able to obey them. They impose duties on what human beings must do for themselves and not do to others if they hope to make good lives for themselves. They apply in principle to all persons equally and without exception or prejudice. Despite their importance, however, these rules are not the whole story. Without pretending to exhaust the subject, several additional reflections on the rights and rules of liberty are relevant at this point. [3]

As a first observation, it is clear that the basic rights provide the foundation for, and indeed the necessity for, a minimal state to prevent their violation. No rights, especially the seven just described, can have any meaning without some kind of organized authority to enforce them. To embody such authority in a government, the basic rights of liberty and the standards of justice they imply must be enshrined in a *constitution* endorsed by the people it governs. With that authority established, a *legislature* must be formed and empowered to enact and revise or repeal the *substantive laws and procedural rules* that constitute the *rule of law*, taking care that all statutes are consistent with constitutional principles. *Law enforcement organizations* must be developed to ensure compliance with the law. A system of *courts* and a *judiciary* must be constructed to decide whether a statute qualifies as law, interpret laws that stand, ensure due process, and adjudicate disputes that cannot be settled by agreement of the parties. At a more concrete level, government offices must be created to record titles to property, and liens against property, and addresses of property owners to legitimize ownership and protect the integrity of contracts. In the world of business, laws deterring collusive monopolies must be developed, and some regulation may be needed for natural monopolies. A *military force* must be created for national defense. Some means by which the people can *elect* representatives to public office and remove them from office must be devised. Overall protection of the environment, supervision of waterways, construction of roads, and regulation of transactions between jurisdictions, among other functions, are usually best coordinated by government bodies rather than private parties. Like it or not, funding mechanisms, taxing bodies, provisions for collection of taxes, and myriad other administration and coordination functions must be handled by governments to enable citizens to conduct the complicated affairs of modern life.

Although this list is by no means exhaustive, it suggests at least the *kinds* of institutions needed for social order and gives some hint as to their number. But government activities of these or any other type cannot be allowed to multiply without limit. Real world experiments in the nature and scope of government, and especially the original American experiment in limited government, argue that the institutions needed for ordered liberty require a strong enough but still limited state, one with limited control over limited resources, dedicated to the protection of relatively few basic rights. What cannot be allowed to develop is a monster state dedicated to micromanaging the lives of its citizens. Note, however, that the *limited* state described here to compliment the competent man is not the idealized *minimal* state of radical libertarianism, and certainly not the anarcho-capitalist ideal argued by Rothbard. [4]

The latter ideal has no historical precedent on which to pass the test of experience, and even in theory this conception of human society leaves more to the individual than he can manage by private agreement. The libertarian minimal state, as Epstein notes, is simply not equipped to solve the complicated coordination problems of modern life.

At the opposite end of the spectrum of government lies the modern socialist state: a bloated and always bankrupt Leviathan which makes dependent children and slaves of its citizens and has the historical precedent to prove it. Between the defects of the minimal state and the excesses of the socialist state is an ideal of social order implied in the works of Barnett, Epstein, Hayek, Sowell and others. These scholars readily comprehend human needs for autonomy and mutuality. A society grounded in the rules they articulate allows individuals the broadest possible liberty for human endeavors while permitting a state with enough power to manage those critical functions that the private sphere cannot or will not manage.

The Evolution of Rules

This discussion leads to a second observation about rules. Those that have proved essential to a free society have not emerged simply from methodical reasoning about moral principles and practical consequences, as the preceding remarks might suggest. Instead, as Hayek, Barnett and others observe, the common law's gradual *evolution* over centuries has played a critical role in deciding what will work and what will not in the conduct of human affairs. In fact, the principles of liberty have evolved over long periods of time, as common law trials of countless cases have sorted out competing claims to both substantive and procedural rights. Of course, this process first involves trying to determine how laws already in place apply to the disputes in question. But ultimately the laws themselves, not just the cases at hand, are likely to become the focus of such questions as: What is morally right and wrong in this or that law? What will be the consequences of applying a particular law in this or any similar instance? What have been the consequences of applying it in particular ways in the past? Lon Fuller considers certain factors that make for a good law: whether it does in fact state a rule that can be understood and obeyed; whether it has been published to the people it is supposed to govern or is imposed retroactively; whether it is consistent with other laws; and whether it is capable of reasonable enforcement. In the final analysis, whether a given law is a good one depends on whether it incorporates or violates acceptable moral principles, whether it respects the basic rights of ordered liberty, and whether its application to the problems it is intended to solve results in reasonable or unreasonable social effects. At some point any law will be, or should be, the focus of such questions as whether its behavioral effects are feasible and compatible with each other, whether the effects lead to useful incentives and constraints on conduct, whether the law's administrative and allocative costs are acceptable, and whether it has unintended effects that are tolerable. Among its other functions, the evolving common law serves as a natural laboratory in which the moral implications and practical consequences of given laws and court rulings are examined and reexamined for their effects on real human beings seeking answers to real world conflicts. In the work of that laboratory, moral principles, practical consequences, and the empirically observable results of common law trials and errors blend together in the evolution of legal principles.

A third observation is in order: even when inhibition, restraint and delay over primitive instincts are firmly implanted in the individual's psyche, and even when capacities for self-reliance and mutuality have been well developed through adequate nurturing, it is still true that human beings need certain basic rules, many of them legally enforceable, by which to live together in peace and freedom. These basic rules are needed to compensate for the innate limitations of human nature. Beyond the problems posed by our instincts, we are inevitably limited in our concerns for others, in our understanding of situations, in the resources available to us, and in our strength of will, as Hart has observed. Even at our best, we are motivated primarily by self-interest; we easily become selfish or worse. No matter how mature we might be, we tolerate only so much frustration and we have only limited energy. Most important, we are all approximately equal in our vulnerabilities to predation and to the harmful negligence of others, hence every citizen, not just some, needs the protection of rules. In view of these realities, some form of government is essential. The seven basic rules are needed to protect people, property and promises: to limit violence, establish and preserve ownership, enforce contracts, make restitution and provide compensation for takings.

[1] *The competent society embraces the dynamics of free markets: e.g., the coordinating functions of relative prices in free markets to [1] signal what is scarce [2] reflect supply and demand [3] indicate how much to produce [4] ration how much to consume.*

[2] *In modern usage the term 'human right' labels almost any claim that one person decides to make against another or against society as a whole. The use of this term will be limited in this discussion.*

[3] *Far more systematic expositions of these rules and their implications for liberty can be found in the works of Epstein, Barnett, and Hayek. See also H.L. A. Hart's* The Concept of Law, *and Lon Fuller's* The Morality of Law.

[4] *See Murray Rothbard,* The Ethics of Liberty

40

The Force of Rules

Men may but women cannot see morality as essentially a matter of keeping to the minimal moral traffic rules, designed to restrict close encounters between autonomous persons to self-chosen ones.

Annette Baier

Hypothetical Imperative

The last chapter emphasized the moral and practical consequences of certain basic rules for living grounded in the nature of man and the human condition. Historical experience in the evolution of common law was cited for its role in sorting out which rules have worked and which have not in regulating human conduct. The question of why any rule should be obeyed or a particular right honored was answered with an appeal to its moral content and behavioral effects: a given rule should be obeyed or a particular right honored because it makes sound moral sense to do so, and because if humans obey the rule or honor the right, the result is more good social consequences than bad ones. If, in addition, the rule has been tried in the past and found to support freedom and social order, so much the better.

Still another perspective on why a rule should be obeyed involves what Randy Barnett calls a natural rights analysis. This perspective states that a rule should be obeyed when the behavior it commands or forbids follows logically from certain assumed facts. The argument follows a given-if-then format. A few examples will illustrate the idea:

- *Given* the biological facts of human nature, *if* a human being wishes to avoid starving to death, *then* he must eat food.

- *Given* the psychological facts of human nature, *if* a small child wishes to feel good about himself, *then* he must please his parents.

- *Given* the social/relational facts of human nature, *if* a child wishes to play in peace with others, *then* he must not steal their toys.

Each of these propositions asserts a practical necessity. Each is cast in the form of a hypothetical imperative. Propositions of this type declare a truth about the way things work under certain assumptions: *given* certain conditions in the real world of human and natural events, *if* you want to achieve a particular goal, *then* you must do or not do a specific act. A hypothetical imperative does not assert that anyone has a duty to pursue a particular goal based on a moral or religious commandment or government edict. It merely states that given certain facts about the world of human action (the first hypothetical fact), if an individual wants to achieve a particular goal, be it moral or practical (a second hypothetical fact), then, because of the nature of the goal itself, he *must* perform certain actions essential to realizing the goal (the imperative that follows from the assumed facts). The word hypothetical refers to conditions that are assumed to be true of the world. The word imperative implies that there is a necessary relationship between the given conditions and the prerequisites that must be put in place to reach the desired goal. If the conditions are not met and the prerequisites are not achieved, then the goal cannot be realized.

This line of reasoning was implicit in an earlier discussion concerning how Crusoe and Friday might arrive at rules to govern their actions with each other. In essence, they would, if they were wise, agree to the following hypothetical imperative: *given* the fact that their human nature renders each of them vulnerable to physical injury at the hands of the other, *if* they wish to live cooperatively and without physical pain or injury at the hands of the other, *then* each must not attack the other physically. Here, because of the nature of the goal, the prohibition against such an attack becomes a rule or a right whose *moral* force follows logically from the assumed givens. The hypothetical imperative bridges the gap between the way things are in the world and the way human beings ought to behave if they wish to achieve certain goals.

Similar use of this argument gives moral and practical force to the seven basic rights of ordered liberty, and also argues that a government is needed to enforce them. In the last chapter, the moral and consequentialist arguments for these rights were set out. Assuming the validity of those arguments, here are the seven rights stated as hypothetical imperatives:

1. Given the immorality and negative social consequences of *slavery*, if human beings wish to pursue happiness and prosperity while living together in peace and freedom, then each human being must have a *right to self-ownership*.

2. Given the immorality and negative social consequences of depriving a human being of *property acquired by first possession,* if human beings wish to pursue happiness and prosperity while living together in peace and freedom, then each human being must have the *right to first possession*.

3. Given the immorality and negative social consequences of depriving a human being of property he has acquired by first possession, mutual consent, or gift, and given the additional immorality and negative social consequences of depriving him of the *ability to sell, trade, or give such property away,* if human beings wish to pursue happiness and prosperity while living together in peace and freedom, then each human being must have a *right to ownership of property and the freedom to exchange it by mutual consent.*

4. Given the immorality and negative social consequences of depriving a human being of the ability to *defend himself and his property from aggression*, if human beings wish to pursue happiness and prosperity while living together in peace and freedom, then each human being must have a *right to self-defense.*

5. Given the immorality and negative social consequences of depriving a human being of *compensation for property taken from him by the state for public use,* if human beings wish to pursue happiness and prosperity while living together in peace and freedom, then each human being must have a *right to just compensation for takings.*

6. Given the immorality and negative social consequences of depriving a human being of *restitution for injury to himself or his property*, if human beings wish to pursue happiness and prosperity

while living together in peace and freedom, then each human being must have a *right to seek restitution for such injury.*

7. Given the immorality and negative social consequences of depriving a human being of *limited access to another's property in emergencies*, if human beings wish to pursue happiness and prosperity while living together in peace and freedom, then each human being must have a *right to limited access to another's property in emergencies.*

The additional proviso for a government on which these rights depend can also be stated as a hypothetical imperative:

8. Given the fact that to be effective the first seven rights require the administrative, legislative, judicial and law-enforcement capabilities of governments, if human beings wish to pursue happiness and prosperity while living together in peace and freedom, then they must form a government with the authority, offices and power to protect those rights. A corollary proposition asserts that given the dangers of government power, any such government must have only limited control over limited common property.

Obligation and the Hypothetical Imperative

The word imperative comes from a Latin verb, *imperare,* meaning to command. The commanding force of a hypothetical imperative lies in the cause-effect meaning implicit in it. The imperative force of the proposition, "*Given* the biology of human nature, *if* a human being wishes to avoid starving to death, *then* he *must* eat food," arises from the obvious cause-effect relationship between lack of food and death by starvation. The fact of human nature, that lack of food causes death by starvation, guarantees the truth of the commandment to eat food if survival is the goal. But a similar certainty attaches to the proposition declaring a right of self-ownership: given the immorality and negative social consequences of *slavery*, if human beings wish to pursue happiness and prosperity while living together in peace and freedom, then each human being must have a right to self-ownership. The cause-effect relationship here is just as clear: the biological, psychological and social nature of human beings prevents them from pursuing happiness and prosperity in peace and freedom while they are enslaved. With human happiness, prosperity, peace and freedom as assumed primary moral goods, there cannot be any doubt about the immorality of slavery or the badness of its social consequences. Once that doubt is removed, the imperative of self-ownership follows logically and with moral force. Moreover, the truth and obligatory force of this proposition have been validated by experience in the real world of political arrangements: every experience of slavery attests to the fact that it is evil in relation to human nature and the human condition, while self-ownership always contributes positively to the pursuit of a good life.

The logic of the hypothetical imperative can be further understood if the imperative result is assumed false. If a sculptor digs up clay from previously unowned ground and makes a statue with it, and if he does *not* have a right to keep the statue, then he has no grounds on which to object if a thief steals it from him. But the moral wrong of such a theft is obvious, and so are the social consequences: a culture of thievery where no one has a right to property he has acquired justly. The realities of material objects and the fact that widespread taking of objects from their first owners causes social chaos guarantee the truth of what should be an enforceable commandment: thou shall not take what another person owns. Historical attempts to undermine this truth with collective "ownership" of property by "the people" under communism have failed because they violate the cause-effect relationships that make individual ownership of material objects essential.

As forceful as this line of reasoning may be, however, it is also vulnerable to disputes over what is "given," as Barnett points out. When what is assumed as a fact of human nature is well established, for example, and when what is desired is reasonable in view of those facts, then the imperative follows with confidence. As already noted, there can be no doubt about the relationship between eating and death by starvation: any attempt to dispute this proposition is absurd given the facts of biology. It is also difficult to dispute either the assumed facts or the imperative conclusion in the statement noted earlier: given the psychology of human nature, if a small child wishes to feel good about himself, he must please his parents. Both the given facts and the resulting commandment are well established and causally connected.

What is not yet established in the world of intellectual discourse, but is nevertheless true in the present author's opinion, is the major thesis of this book: *given* the biological, psychological and social characteristics of human nature and their implications for economic, social and political processes, *if* human beings wish to pursue happiness and prosperity while living together in peace and freedom, *then* they must obey certain rules essential to ordered liberty, including the seven basic rights already described. Of course, the biological, psychological and social "givens" of human nature can be and have been vigorously disputed by the modern liberal mind. Liberals deny, for example, that capacities for autonomy and mutuality are fundamental to human nature, that most citizens are competent to run their own lives, and that voluntary cooperation can solve most problems better than government coercion. Liberals also deny the reality of certain economic givens (such as the law of supply and demand), the essential role of self-interest in production and exchange, and the disincentives to a healthy economy that follow from collectivist regulations. Even when such givens are granted, however, liberals will deny their critical roles in the pursuit of happiness, prosperity, peace and freedom. Widespread denial of reality is one of the defining characteristics of the liberal mind.

Hence the burden of this book in overcoming liberalism's denial: to establish by observation and argument that certain behavioral dispositions do indeed characterize the nature of man and that they do, in fact, bear directly on the economic, social and political conditions needed for ordered liberty. More precisely, I argue that it is only within the bipolar conception of human nature that particular rules and rights are able to provide a legal and moral foundation for the structure of ordered liberty. These rules can achieve this goal only if they accommodate the nature of man: the property rights of the libertarian quartet, for example, accommodate the nature of man while the "positive rights" of modern collectivism violate the nature of man. The social architecture that permits civilized freedom must be grounded in certain behavioral dispositions that do in fact characterize human conduct.

Based on the behavioral dispositions described so far, an argument based on the hypothetical imperative format asserts that if a society's rules for living are to be consistent with the analysis of adult competence set out in this book, then it must promote, among other things, the development of self-directing, self-responsible and cooperative citizens who revere ordered liberty and are committed to certain standards of morality and ethics. Its guiding ideals must be those of self-reliance, not government dependency; lawful self-direction, not government regulation;

moral rectitude, not moral license; informed altruism, not welfare statism; and cooperative individualism, not coercive collectivism. *Given* the nature of man and the human condition, *if* a society's citizens wish to pursue happiness and prosperity while living together in peace and freedom, *then* the rules that govern their conduct must *not* promote a population of dependent, demanding, manipulative and envious citizens who deny the principles on which peace and freedom depend. Human nature imposes certain unequivocal constraints on the rules that support ordered liberty. They determine what kinds of social policies are reasonable and what kinds are unreasonable. Societies that ignore the difference enjoy neither order nor liberty.

The Importance of Rules

The basic rights exercise their function in the protection of people, property, and promises by imposing certain *duties* on competent citizens. The connection between rights and duties has been mentioned only in passing so far. Here is a more explicit statement of duties implied by basic rights when considered one at a time:

- When the right to *self-ownership* is enforced, a duty is imposed on all others to refrain from doing something to the right holder's body without his permission.

- When the rights of *first possession* and ownership of justly acquired property are enforced, duties are imposed on all other persons to refrain from damaging that property or seizing it from its rightful owners.

- When the right of competent persons to *exchange or transfer property* by voluntary and informed consent is enforced, a duty is imposed on all others to refrain from interfering with that transaction or forcibly altering its outcome.

- When the right to *self-defense* is enforced, a duty is imposed on all others to refrain from interfering with any individual or group's freedom to protect themselves and their properties from assault or theft.

- The rights to just compensation for just takings, limited access in emergency, and restitution for injury each create analogous duties.

The limitations on human conduct imposed by these duties make freedom and cooperation possible; without these limitations, freedom and cooperation are not possible. *Consistent as they are from both moral and consequentialist perspectives, and tested as they have been by historical experiment, the basic rules of liberty, when expressed as rights, validate the nature of man instead of contradicting it. And because these rules are moral, right and just, they also establish the foundations of legal justice and the rule of law. Actions in accord with the basic rules are just actions. Actions in violation of the basic rules are unjust actions. The basic rules constitute the bedrock principles on which any society of cooperative freedom must be built. They form the minimum content of natural law. They are, as Hart puts it, a natural necessity.*

At the level of everyday interactions, the rules offer protection from violence, theft and fraud perpetrated against individuals, groups and families. The rules help to create an orderly environment in which human beings can do what they are made to do: generate ideas, set goals, make plans, create strategies, explore alternatives, recruit resources, build relationships, initiate actions and better their lives. These and virtually all other human actions require stable, predictable and free conditions in which interactions occur largely by mutual consent and coerced interactions are rare. But the rules have broader implications. *Because they provide for a large sphere of individual and small group ownership of property and imply only limited control over limited property by limited government, these rules eliminate socialism, communism, fascism and theocracies as political systems for a society of competent citizens. For the same reasons, the rules not only permit capitalism but also imply it, since they institutionalize self-ownership, private ownership of property, and freedom of contract, among other economic conditions that define capitalism.* The rules require, for example, that all or nearly all economic transactions must occur by consent, not by coercion. Buyers buy only what they choose to buy based on their needs and desires. Producers choose to produce, and sellers choose to sell, only what they believe will yield a profit when buyers choose to buy. Under capitalism but not under any form of collectivism, individual freedom of choice, not a government edict, is the dominant mode of human relating. By their contributions to Smith's Invisible Hand, the basic rules help to channel normal self-interest and even rampant selfishness into actions that benefit others in both economic and social realms. Moreover, the fact that the rules apply equally and universally to all legally competent citizens promotes social order. No one is given special treatment because of race, color, gender or other arbitrary criteria. The basic rules treat Crusoe and Friday and Smith and Jones alike.

Rules and Human Development

As it happens, however, the basic rules, and the rights and duties associated with them, provide more than the moral and legal foundations of ordered liberty. They also create the social conditions in which individual development can proceed to mature competence. Absent foreign invasion or natural disaster, a society organized on individual liberty and property rights creates an environment of peace, freedom and material security in which families can rear their children without fear of sudden and traumatic social upheaval. From reasonably functional parents who are thus confident in the future and who also honor ideals of freedom and cooperation, and from a community of law and order that enforces rights against violence, theft and fraud, children are able to acquire a sense of basic trust grounded not only on what good things routinely occur in the family but also on what good things routinely occur in the culture at large. Of course, the foundations of basic trust remain grounded in the child's earliest and most intimate experience with his caretakers, and that trust is hopefully fortified in later relationships in the neighborhood and schools. But trust begun in the home is also affirmed or not by the character of the larger culture in which the child is raised. Basic trust acquired early in life is best validated over the remainder of one's life in a benign society whose rules ensure personal safety and whose economic, social, and political processes are conducted by consent and not by force or fraud.

In addition to their favorable effects on the achievement of trust, the basic rules also maximize opportunities for the development of autonomy, initiative and industry. The rules that guarantee rights to self-ownership and the right to own and exchange property validate the child's growing capacity to choose, to initiate, to act on good purpose and to sustain productive effort. In a society governed by the basic rules, the child learns that he can keep what he makes with his hands or trade it for something else. He can earn money by doing chores as a juvenile or working after school as a teenager. He learns that he can buy what he wants with what he earns and that he has a right to keep, give away or trade what he has earned or bought for something else. He learns that the more productive he becomes through his own initiative and industry, the more he benefits himself and others. He learns, in addition, that he has to negotiate with others to get what he wants from them, because the rules forbid him from taking what others will not willingly give him.

All of these relational principles are secured by the basic rules and the rights derived from them, and all help to prepare the child to cooperate as an adult. By creating powerful incentives to become productive for one's own benefit, and by forbidding dependency on others without their consent, the rules not only support but demand self-reliance. By prohibiting one person from taking what he wants from another by force or fraud, the rules not only support but demand voluntary cooperation. Moreover, from the fact that the rules of exchange require both sides to agree to a transaction, the child learns that to better his own life he must offer to others something that they believe will better theirs. The mutuality that grows out of this mode of relating extends the mutuality learned in one's family of origin; the rules thus help to merge individual self-interest with the common good. In effect, the rules provide not only a system of prohibitions against certain harms, but also promote those traits that foster mutual consent.

Additional benefits accrue from the basic rules. As Hart observes, the rules specify those personal interests and inclinations that must be given up in order to achieve social order. By the powerful threat of arrest, prosecution, conviction and punishment, the rules enacted as laws exert a compelling pressure for all citizens to renounce certain freedoms for the sake of securing others. Even beyond this benefit by threat, however, the rules provide a positive reinforcement for personal identity. By complying with clear legal guidelines on what one must and must not do to be a good citizen, the well-motivated individual will feel enhanced self-esteem when he can rightly declare himself to be a good person in harmony with the good rules of a good society: obeying the rules identifies the law abiding individual positively with his lawful culture, to the enhancement of both. Disobeying the rules, on the other hand, risks the shame of public scorn and social ostracism and the penalties of the law where they apply. *In a larger sense, in fact, the rules are implicit declarations of what is morally, not just legally, right and wrong. Because they prescribe how one must and must not treat others, society's formal laws echo the moral lessons taught to the growing child in his early years and thereby constitute standing moral lessons for the adult population. In a rational society, the rules and rights that govern our most important economic, social and political transactions ensure that what parents teach their children about right and wrong is backed up by institutions at all levels of society: our criminal and tort laws, our religious and secular commandments, our traditions, taboos and ethical standards. When the rules at all levels of society are consistent among themselves, as they should be, a prescriptive integrity characterizes the complex fabric of society.*

Rules and Freedom

A coherent conception of modern western society thus requires a set of rules that guarantee both liberty and order in the economic, social and political life of man. This conception begins with the bipolar nature of human beings and the human condition, acknowledges the power of human instincts and attachments, stipulates to the realities of human vulnerability and material scarcity, and observes with special emphasis the inherent limitations in human goodness, patience, altruism, empathy and knowledge that make the rules necessary in the first place. The rules required to ensure both liberty and order are the moral imperatives of western individualism, especially those prohibiting violence, theft and fraud. *Out of those rules a set of rights is generated that define certain domains of freedom and certain corollary duties that limit what human beings can do to each other. Institutions created to protect these rights and enforce these duties give rise to an organized system of justice under the rule of law. Then, and only then, can the human drive for self-fulfillment coordinate with the human need for cooperation. A society so conceived permits the innate disposition to autonomy to be reconciled with the innate disposition to mutuality.* Validated by the historical record of experiments in social arrangements, this conception of human society stipulates to the genius of the original American experiment in libertarian government. It specifies, among other things, that men have certain liberty rights and certain duties under those rights; that all such rights and the rules of law that arise from them must apply equally and universally; that all laws, like all rules, entail trade-offs that include incentive effects, administrative and allocative costs, and the inevitable unintended but tolerable consequences; and that any system of justice will always be imperfect for marginal cases.

PART III

Preface to Part III

Organized around the first seven of Erikson's developmental phases, Part II elaborated extensively on the individual's growth to adult competence and then reviewed certain institutions critical to ordered liberty. Part III turns to a psychodynamic analysis of the liberal mind itself. *Benign* liberalism's erroneous urgings for a welfare state are seen as a reflection of human nurturing instincts and the natural inclinations toward altruism that make human beings social creatures. This form of liberalism naively assumes that individual freedoms can be preserved as society is made more "caring," even under the heavy hand of government.

Radical liberalism, by contrast, intends far more than this: an authoritarian state organized on socialist principles and ruled by liberal elites. This utopian ideal sacrifices the tangible blessings of ordered liberty for the illusory benefits of the welfare state. The psychodynamics that drive the liberal mind to his irrational goals are then set out in a first-person-singular confession: expressed in his own words, as it were, developmental insights articulated in earlier chapters provide a clear, in-depth look into the madness of the liberal mind.

Part III continues with a review of the last of Erikson's developmental phases, then reminds the reader once again of the abuses with which modern liberalism violates the principles of ordered liberty. A description of the liberal neurosis observes the signs and symptoms which qualify it as a personality disorder. The book closes with brief discussions of how modern liberalism can be eradicated, first in the afflicted individual, then in society.

41

The Benign Liberal Mind

Thou shalt love thy neighbor as thyself.
Leviticus 19:18

The Assault of Modern Liberalism

This book has argued that with good enough childrearing in a culture committed to ordered liberty, the natural thrust of human development produces an individual who is at once autonomous and mutual, a self-reliant source of initiative and voluntary collaboration in the activities of everyday life. This book has also argued that the modern liberal agenda's collective causes have undermined the rights of the individual and his growth to adult competence; undermined the integrity of the family as the primary civilizing and socializing entity in society; and undermined the proper function of a modern society, that of providing an overarching social structure for lives to be lived in peace and freedom. Modern liberalism has achieved these destructive results through relentless rhetorical, legislative and judicial attacks on the autonomy and sovereignty of the individual; on the natural human tendencies toward cooperation, mutuality and altruism; and on the principles of moral realism distilled over centuries of western civilization. The liberal agenda has fostered government dependency instead of self-reliance; government direction instead of self-determination; moral indulgence and relativism instead of moral rectitude; coercive collectivism instead of cooperative individualism; indentured servitude instead of genuine altruism. In favor of various collective causes, modern liberalism has succeeded in displacing the individual from his rightful position as the primary economic, social and political unit of society. It has undermined the sanctity of marriage and the cohesiveness of the family. It has undermined the natural harmony that exists between individual, family and community. It has weakened the obligations of promises, contracts, ownership and property rights. It has disconnected rewards from merit and desert. It has corrupted the moral and ethical basis for civilized living. It has polarized the population into warring classes with false claims of victimization and villainy and contrived needs for political rescue. With enormous growth beyond the definition of government and its functions set forth in the U.S. Constitution, modern American liberalism has created the idealized parental and administrative state and endowed it with vast managerial, caretaking and regulatory powers. History records the inevitable result of such expansions of government power: individual liberty and the peaceful coordination of human action are severely compromised or lost altogether.

The Appeal of America

This book has asserted, among other things, that certain characteristics of human nature are critically relevant to the manner in which individuals relate to each other in community life and that certain conditions, especially obedience to fundamental rules governing human conduct, must occur if people wish to pursue self-fulfillment and security while living in peace and freedom. These conditions and especially certain rights and duties detailed in the last two chapters are not optional as Epstein, Barnett and others point out but are instead essential to the making of good lives. The conclusion that these conditions are essential does not come from armchair theorizing but from careful observation of human action, both historical and contemporary. Many such observations have been summarized in this book.

One of the most relevant among them is the persistent historical migration of vast numbers of people to the United States since the time of its founding. There has never been any mystery about why millions have risked so much to come here; all have made their reasons clear. The prospect of living a life of economic, social and religious freedom in a reasonably predictable environment of law and order has overwhelming appeal to the human spirit. This appeal is a function of the inherently bipolar nature of man, a nature that seeks to live according to the individual's own choices, not someone else's choices, and to cooperate by mutual consent, not by fear of imprisonment. History has, of course, validated the immigrant's choice. People who have come to the United States have typically stayed here because they believe that the quality of life to be sought here is superior to anything available elsewhere, even when it means accepting full responsibility for one's self and one's dependents. Indeed, the requirements for individual responsibility and assumption of risk have been happily embraced by all who understand that the freedom to be lived by the competent adult is not the pseudo-freedom of the welfare recipient. It is true, of course, that the increasing collectivism of American social policy has begun to attract a new breed of immigrant, one who is intrigued by opportunities for entitlement and dependency instead of self-determination and cooperation. The degradation of American social policy has affected the intentions with which immigrants seek refuge here. The noble structure of liberty that defined America's first two hundred years attracted people with courage and determination. The increasingly ignoble seductions of the welfare state are now attracting immigrants with different intentions. The virus of collectivism has now firmly entrenched itself.

But these reflections invite an obvious question: why is the virus here in the first place? If the liberal agenda does, in fact, undermine the life of the citizen who reveres individual liberty, recognizes the sovereignty of the other, takes full responsibility for his own life, assumes the inherent risks of freedom, and commits himself to collaborating with others for mutual gain, then why would anyone commit to the principles of modern liberalism and proclaim its superiority in coordinating human conduct? What is it that tempts human beings to overthrow the historically validated blessings of the greatest political achievement in history for the regressive promises of the liberal agenda? Why trade the freedom to live responsibly as one chooses for the indulgence and oppression of the managerial/regulatory/welfare/nanny state? What appears so valuable to liberals about this type of arrangement that justifies giving up one's personal sovereignty to adoption by government?

Caretaking Sentiments

The short and inadequate answer to these questions is that liberals, like many others, feel compassion for the suffering of the disadvantaged, wish to alleviate it, and think that governments can help. Elihu Root observed that human beings "see how much misery there is in the world and instinctively cry out against it." Compassion for the suffering of others emerges in human beings from tending, nurturing, caring and rescuing instincts. Erikson viewed the mature expression of these urges as an adult developmental achievement: he used the term generativity to denote not only the rearing of children but also caring behavior that benefits the community as a whole. Of course, overt expressions of such instincts can be found long before adulthood. They emerge in early childhood and are easily observed in all later years. If reared well enough, the average child will respond with tender concern to parents and siblings who are sad or hurt or ill. A toddler age child, even if not well loved, will often feel sorry for injured or crippled animals and for sick friends and for weak and fragile elders. Preschool children will assume obvious caretaking roles when they play house. Juveniles and adolescents take on nurturing roles toward ill or injured siblings or parents. The juvenile or adolescent babysitter prepares herself for later childrearing. In part because they care, children of all ages may take on an undeserved burden of guilt toward a family member who is suffering. The child in the juvenile and adolescent phases of development is likely to feel sympathy for the poor, the enslaved, the oppressed or the helpless, or for any human being who suffers. A typical response will include a wish to help or rescue, to comfort or heal or alleviate pain. For the most part, and despite our pervasive tendencies toward self-centeredness, the compassionate wish to help others still burns eternal in the human spirit.

The work of any free society testifies to this point. Numerous professions including those of medicine, nursing, psychology, social work, ministry, teaching, law and law enforcement, firefighting, surrogate parenting and running a nursery involve caring for or protecting others. Tending instincts are obvious in farming, ranching, animal husbandry, wildlife preservation and environmental protection. Holding political office and other forms of public service, along with religious and various types of charitable and philanthropic work obviously count as caretaking behavior, as do military and coastguard duty and various rescue missions such as the American Red Cross.

In a broader sense, in fact, a great deal of ordinary economic and social activity contains elements that are directly or indirectly motivated by the wish to assist, care for or please others. A merchant's "taking care of business" typically involves his personal satisfaction in meeting the needs and desires of his customers, not just making a profit. In the absence of pathological narcissism, most human beings wish to help their fellows even if their efforts are modest. Recall, in addition, that the normal course of growth to adulthood results in acquired capacities for empathy, identification and recognition. These capacities clearly contribute to altruistic attitudes and are fortified by sentiments of tenderness, sympathy and pity. An instinctive tendency to assist others is part of the general human urge to cooperate for mutual benefit. This urge overlaps with innate tendencies toward reciprocal altruism, another disposition with survival value that extends caretaking desires beyond the relatively narrow boundaries of family and kin. All of these attitudes are part of the biological, psychological and social equipment of human nature. All motivate powerful urges to help others, care for others, and even suffer and die for others. "Doing well by doing good" is not an empty cliché. In the genius of social cooperation, as Hazlitt asserts so clearly, the long term self-interest of the individual is reconciled with the common good.

Options for Helping

Once the urge to help asserts itself, however, the question arises as to how to implement it. There are only two basic methods by which human beings can aid each other: voluntarily through individual and joint efforts, sometimes on a large and even international scale (the American Red Cross, for example), or coercively through the power of government. Because they operate only by the consent of those who organize them, voluntary methods preserve all of the basic rights that ensure individual liberty and social order. And because an operation of this type remains under private control, it also channels charitable motives at every level of society, from local to international, through persons who can be held accountable for their actions. Laws that properly regulate the activities of charitable groups, those concerning asset ownership, obligation and transfer, are routinely applied to financial transactions of all types, so legal recourse is available if what appears at first to be a beneficent program turns out to be something else. In addition, if donors to charitable organizations so desire, they can require that their contributions to recipients be conditioned on some type of rehabilitation program designed to restore self-reliance whenever possible.

The second method, the government-run welfare program, attacks all of the basic rights that protect individual liberty and social order while it disconnects the charitable motives of the citizen from the kinds of distributions the program makes and from the identities of its beneficiaries. The state's welfare offices cannot be held accountable for wasteful decisions, malfeasance, misdirection of benefits, or simple incompetence in its operations except by an occasional journalist's investigation or indirectly through the ballot box, and neither of these methods allows for terminating the operation altogether. Additional disadvantages inhere in government welfare programs: destructive effects on individuals, families and the culture as a whole; inevitable distortions of incentives and asset allocations; and endless bureaucracy, patronage and corruption that invariably infect their operations.

The Benign Liberal Mind and Its Illusions

Given the record of modern liberalism's failed "wars" on poverty and drugs, the ineffectiveness and bankruptcy of its collectivized educational, health care, retirement, transportation and housing programs, to name a few, and given the corrupting effects of its social programs on the character of the people, we may ask yet again: why has western society created the idealized parental and administrative state and endowed it with vast managerial, caretaking and regulatory powers over the people? The answer to this question can be found in the statement of the question itself and in its implied goals. The modern liberal mind believes in the following propositions:

- An idealized liberal state or its close approximation can, in fact, be created in the real world.
- The idealized *parental* state can and will act as a benign and loving parent.
- The idealized *managerial* state can and will manage the people's lives for their great benefit just as loving parents manage their children's lives.

- The idealized *caretaking* state can and will ensure the health, economic security, and social status of the people.
- The idealized *regulatory* state can and will control the lives of the people to eliminate economic adversity, social strife and political conflict.
- The idealized liberal state can and will meet all or nearly all of the people's needs and desires, including their desire to be indulged.

As this book has been at pains to prove, however, the promises in these propositions *cannot* be realized because of the realities of human nature. Moreover, they *should not* be realized because they violate the basic human rights essential to ordered liberty. Nevertheless, the naïve liberal citizen chooses to believe in them for many reasons. Here are some of them:

- These promises represent him and his best intentions toward the wellbeing of everyone, and they declare his support for those most in need.
- These promises make him feel that he is doing something good for others, thus allowing him to feel altruistic and generous and avoid feeling guilty.
- These promises assign charitable tasks to government agencies so the citizen himself need not do the actual work of charity or cope with difficult recipients.
- These promises reassure the citizen against his own fears of helplessness, neediness, inferiority and envy.
- These promises reassure the citizen against his own fears of economic adversity, political impotence and social conflict.
- The naïve liberal can maintain his ignorance and denial of the programs' failures in its primary objectives.
- The naïve liberal can maintain his ignorance and denial of the programs' unintended destructive effects.
- The naïve liberal can maintain his ignorance and denial of the financial and political exploitation of the programs by government officials.

In contrast to the Radical Liberal Mind to be discussed in later chapters, this well-intentioned but naïve citizen is the Benign Liberal Mind. He feels compassion for those who are poor, needy, diseased, desperate, downtrodden, ignorant, hopeless and helpless. He seeks a power greater than himself and his fellows, and greater than religious and volunteer organizations, to help all of those in dire straights. He has some conservative values but is ambivalent about conservative institutions, especially economic institutions. He suspects that conservatives are fundamentally selfish, and he is unaware that this belief is, in part, a projection of his own unconscious selfishness. He believes to a considerable extent in the idea of individual liberty under the rule of law but is unsure about how much individual responsibility anyone including himself should have to assume. He believes in market-based economies but thinks that they must be closely regulated by government officials, not just by laws protecting property and contract rights. He believes in the principle of self-ownership, in the right to own property, in the right to exchange property by mutual consent, and in the right to self-defense, but he is quite often willing to yield these rights to a collective cause, and he is strikingly unaware of the extent to which they have already been compromised by the liberal agenda. He believes in greatly expanded rights to restitution and is ambivalent about compensation for takings. He believes in a right of access to private facilities in emergencies. In the conduct of most adult interactions, he believes that it is better to be honest than dishonest, better to be courteous than rude, to be self-reliant than dependent, to be mutual than selfish, to be generous than stingy. With this more or less positive but ambivalent support for the ideals and aspirations of liberty, it does not occur to the Benign Liberal Mind that the effects of government welfare programs have already seriously undermined the foundations of his freedom and will eventually destroy it. On the contrary, he believes that the free and orderly society established by America's founders has already been enhanced, not degraded, by having the unarguable virtue of the welfare state grafted onto it, and that it can be enhanced still further with more of the same. He believes this in ignorance of the manner in which the dynamics of government welfare policy attack the underpinnings of ordered liberty and corrupt the people. Details of that attack have been listed at length in Chapter 35 and elsewhere in this book

42

The Fallacies of Positive Rights

The passion for equality penetrates on every side into men's hearts, expands there, and fills them entirely. Tell them not that by this blind surrender of themselves to an exclusive passion they risk their dearest interests; they are deaf. Show them not freedom escaping from their grasp while they are looking another way; they are blind, or rather they can discern but one object to be desired in the universe.

Alexis de.Toqueville

Positive Rights and the Injustice of Suffering

Direct perceptions and indirect reports of suffering, hardship and need are powerful messages in the liberal agenda's efforts to create a welfare- driven collectivist society. But an equally powerful force derives from the agenda's success in portraying *most* human suffering, not just some of it, as unjust instead of seeing it as an inevitable part of the human experience. In fact, the view that all or nearly all suffering is unjust is the flip side of the liberal mind's argument for positive rights or entitlements: *if human beings have positive rights to food, clothes, houses, jobs, education, medical care, child care, abortion, a clean and safe environment, adequate social status, leisure time or any other good, service or condition, and if those entitlements are deemed enforceable, then persons who don't have them are being neglected and deprived and are therefore victims of injustice.* On this understanding of the human condition, the liberal mind views the minimal libertarian state as profoundly unjust because it zealously protects only the basic rights essential to life, liberty and the pursuit of happiness in a peaceful and orderly environment, and explicitly refuses to guarantee all of those goods and services which only individuals and groups can provide through their own initiative. In fact, however, it is the liberal agenda's collectivist state that is profoundly unjust precisely because any attempt to enforce its platform of positive rights immediately violates the negative rights essential to ordered liberty. Examples of this type of injustice are noted below.

Varieties and Causes of Human Suffering

The biological, psychological and social nature of man renders him vulnerable to privation and hardship of all kinds. In the first place, the laws of nature cause him to suffer death, illness, injury, pain and loss whenever they lead to earthquakes, tornadoes, floods, droughts, volcano eruptions and other natural disasters in which he happens to be present. Because they cause great suffering these events might reasonably be called *evils.* But they are at the same time integral to the natural world we live in and for that reason cannot be called *injustices.* There is no *cosmic* law that states that such naturally caused suffering should not and must not occur. On the contrary, there are numerous laws of physics, chemistry and biology that *guarantee* that such suffering must and will occur whenever the prerequisites for it have been met. Thus any claims by the liberal mind that the suffering of victims of natural disasters is unjust cannot be reasonable. Of course there is no basis on which to assert that victims of such disasters *deserve* what befalls them, and in this sense their injuries are unfair. But this insight doesn't change the argument. The effects on human beings of events in the natural universe are not subject to considerations of fairness, merit or desert: an earthquake may inflict the most painful suffering on the most innocent child while the worst scoundrel escapes harm completely. Although laws made by *human beings* regularly connect fairness, merit and desert to human action and its consequences, there is no law of the universe that selectively protects the worthy from floods or punishes sinners with earthquakes. In natural disasters there is no villain to be blamed or sued for wrongful injury.

Like natural disasters, unavoidable accidents, human fallibility and bad luck also cause death, injury, pain and loss. The best intentions and most conscientious efforts sometimes fail to prevent misfortune. But again, since there is no cosmic justice to prevent such events from happening, they cannot reasonably be called unjust no matter how terrible the suffering that ensues. Unavoidable accidents and bad luck may kill and maim the innocent while the devil is spared; in the world of chance, too, no natural laws protect the innocent or punish the guilty. Hence, suffering that follows bad luck, though undeserved, is not unjust. It is instead an unfortunate and often tragic but inevitable element of the human condition, and there is no one who can be reasonably held at fault or deemed liable for compensation.

Furthermore, beyond suffering due to natural disasters and unavoidable accidents lie death, illness, injury, pain and loss from self-neglect, self-abuse, or reckless, impulsive and otherwise irresponsible actions. Are these consequences unjust? If so, then who has perpetrated what injustice upon whom? It might well be argued that the person injured by his own reckless behavior or self-neglect has failed in his duty to himself and has therefore done *himself* an injustice. On the other hand it might be argued that the harm he suffers is in some sense a just punishment for his carelessness. Whatever position one takes on that argument, all competent adults know that actions have consequences and that some actions have harmful consequences. *For the competent man to act freely is to assume risk and accept responsibility; only young children or adults with childish ideas expect to act otherwise. In fact, the competent man as a matter of pride blames no one but himself for his self-inflicted harm and holds no one but himself responsible for whatever recovery he may achieve.* In the event that he is too disabled by his injury to help himself, then he must hope for charitable aid. Of course, anyone who so desires can help him, and many will believe that coming to his aid is a moral duty. In a free society, however, self-caused injuries cannot justify a legally enforceable claim on other persons who are not parents or guardians. More precisely, the self-injured victim is not legally entitled to the time, effort, money or life of another human being who has done him no wrong. Any meaningful conception of freedom demands responsibility and assumption of risk by all competent citizens, not a childlike insistence that arbitrary others make one whole. If freedom is in fact disconnected from responsibility, as it is in the liberal agenda, then we have a society of literally care-free persons, each of whom is falsely held to be responsible for everyone else, and none of whom is properly held to be responsible for himself. By the very definition of self-inflicted harm, the competent man who injures himself through carelessness or self-neglect cannot claim that he is the victim of injustice by someone else, nor can he rightfully demand that "society" compensate him. Thus, whenever the modern liberal expands his conception of injustice to include suffering of all types, he is bidding, at best, for a fantasy world free of risk and unsatisfied need. In the course of these efforts the agenda's advocates will increase the collective burden on the individual; diminish his freedom; tax his time, effort and material assets; and ignore his sovereignty. This kind of burden is bad enough and unjust in its own right. But the agenda's ideal of a world governed by positive rights is not merely burdensome. The entire concept is hopelessly grandiose: the prospect of any power on earth, governmental or otherwise, providing millions if not billions of human beings with food, clothing, housing, medical care, retirement security and all the rest of liberalism's promises is absurdly utopian and literally fantastic.

Authentic Injustice

Although the idea of justice does not apply to natural disasters, unavoidable accidents, bad luck and self-inflicted harm, it does apply to the rules men make to govern their own conduct. In that world, the idea of justice becomes immediately relevant and integral to the structure of liberty. Among other sources, statutory laws based on *negative rights* create entitlements and duties which define justice. When these are breached, the harms that result are properly called unjust. For example:

- Breaking a *criminal* law is unjust because the victim's property rights are violated.
- A breach of *contract* law is unjust because it violates the victim's right to own and exchange property.
- Violating a *civil* law is unjust because the victim's right against negligent injury is breached.
- Analogous claims of injustice arise from violations of *procedural* laws that ensure due process, especially those that govern the conditions of arrest, detention, interrogation, trial, representation and sentencing, and rules related to pleading, proof, notice and evidence.

- Similar claims of injustice properly arise from violations of laws that protect rights to restitution, just compensation for takings and access in emergency.

The question then arises: are these civil, criminal and procedural laws themselves just? As this analysis and others have argued, the answer is yes if they honor the basic rights and duties that ground ordered liberty, as they do in the modern *libertarian* conception of the state. The answer is no in the case of the modern *liberal* conception of the state, because each *positive right* to some good or service violates at least one *negative right* essential to ordered liberty. Smith's positive right to a house, for example, can be realized only when a liberal government gives it to him. But the government first has to buy or build a house before it can be given to anyone. To achieve either of those ends the government must forcefully take labor and/or materials and/or money from some citizens other than Smith. But taking anything by force from anyone violates the negative rights that are supposed to protect the most basic liberties of every citizen: his rights in himself and his labor, his rights to acquire and own money and property, and his right to sell, trade, keep or give away what he owns. Hence, the realization of Smith's positive right to a house must violate the liberty rights of his fellow citizens, and the liberal mind's entitlement agenda is revealed for what it is: a full-fledged injustice in itself. This argument holds regardless of whether the positive right being enforced provides housing, food, medical care, retirement security or whatever to Smith or anyone else. *The enforcement of any positive right means that somebody's time, energy, money, intelligence, labor and property must be confiscated in the process, a clear violation of rights basic to liberty and therefore a clear case of injustice.*

The Just State

As noted at length in earlier chapters, the libertarian rule of law emerges from the following basic argument: *given* the nature of man as both autonomous actor and voluntary cooperator, *if* human beings wish to pursue happiness and prosperity while living in peace and freedom, *then* they must live by certain fundamental rules protecting property and contracts and must permit only a limited government's limited control over limited common goods. The historically unprecedented success in terms of human freedom, happiness, order, safety and wellbeing that grew out of the original American experiment in government has validated the fact that its system of government is just. The system is just because the rules that ground it are consistent with the nature of man, protecting as they do his bipolar need for freedom to act independently and to cooperate by mutual consent. As noted in an earlier chapter, in the libertarian conception of the state the reasonably just social order is one based on the following principles:

- The just order honors the sovereignty of the individual by recognizing his right to direct his own life as it honors the embeddedness of all individuals in the community through an ethic of voluntary cooperation.
- The just social order respects the liberty of the individual as it requires him to take responsibility for himself and to assume the risks that inhere in his actions; it does not intrude on his natural freedoms, nor try to protect him from himself, nor compensate him for his own mistakes by giving him something taken from others.
- The just social order respects the ownership of property justly acquired and the integrity of contracts fairly made; it does not violate property rights nor invalidate properly binding agreements.
- The just social order respects the rights of the individual to restitution, just compensation and access in emergency.
- The just social order respects the principle of equality under the law as a barrier to political manipulation; it does not exempt some from the requirements of the law nor grant political favor to others.
- The just social order requires constitutional limits at all levels of government to prevent it from violating man's natural rights; it does not deprive an individual of the ownership of his life, liberty or property through the politics of coercion.

For all of these and other reasons, and because the liberal agenda also corrupts the character of the people it dominates, the just libertarian social order rejects the liberal fantasy that a society grounded in positive rights and free of risk and unmet need can be created by any government, including a very large, powerful or even worldwide government.

The Vagueness of Liberal Principles

One of the most striking characteristics of modern liberalism, whether benign or radical, is the actual vagueness of its social policies despite their apparent nobility of purpose. A typical "progressive" liberal platform, for example, will announce its goals to be the eradication of hunger, poverty, ignorance, disease, faulty child care, material inequality and political oppression. The platform will dedicate itself to the provision of adequate jobs, housing, nutrition, education, social harmony and medical care. But in the real world, attempting to reach even one of these goals is a colossal undertaking, whose difficulties the liberal agenda never adequately spells out for review. Consider, for example, the announcement of a program whose intent is to end starvation in a single third world country. Questions of the following type must be answered with verifiable facts and proven or at least plausible strategies if the program is to succeed:

- What is the history of the problem? When and for what reasons did the starvation begin?
- Has the country ever been able to feed itself? How?
- How do weather factors affect the problem?
- What has made the problem better or worse?
- What are the economic, social, political, religious, legal and ethnic factors affecting the problem and any realistic attempts at solving it?
- What are the logistical problems in providing food to the population?
- Who will provide the food? Who will grow it, collect it, preserve it, record its type and amount, ship it?
- Who will ensure that the food is preserved and edible when it arrives for consumption?
- How and by whom and at what cost will it be received and distributed to those in need?
- Who will administer the program? How will corruption and graft be prevented?
- How and by whom will all phases of the program be funded and how much will it cost?
- How will providing food to the target population affect them socially, psychologically, politically?

- What are the attitudes of the people toward the program?
- Will anyone, especially politically positioned persons, object to the program?
- Will anyone attempt to thwart it? Assist with it?
- Who will benefit financially and politically from the program? How much?
- Who will be harmed by the program?
- How long is the program to continue?
- Does the program incorporate a plan to make the population self-sufficient? What is it?
- What are the medical consequences of the starvation to date?
- What are the developmental consequences of the starvation?
- What will be the incentive and disincentive effects of the program?
- Toward what better uses, if any, could the funds, efforts and resources for the program be allocated?
- What exit strategy will terminate the program?

Verifiable facts and proven or plausible strategies to answer most of these questions will not be offered by anyone proposing a program of this type, and any such proposal is therefore meaningless for practical purposes. If the program is only one among many comparable programs to guarantee other positive rights, then the entire platform is even more meaningless since no amount of planning can hope to bring such a grand scheme to life. In that case, the announcement of the platform's goals serves only rhetorical purposes—feeling good about one's intentions, for example, or rallying support against a political opponent.

This list of questions illustrates the kinds of essential inquiries that are routinely omitted from any liberal politician's campaign to impress voters with his good intentions and with reasons why he should be given more power and money. By tacit agreement, the liberal voter will not challenge the liberal politician with these questions, and the politician will not have answers to them if the questions are asked. Both will content themselves with an implicit trade-off: the voter will feel that he is a good humanitarian doing something truly charitable for others in need, the politician will get more power and money, and the liberal agenda will be validated in its noble intentions (but defective substance). Equally important, if any attempt is made to implement the program, it will fail in its primary objectives for practical reasons, suffer from massive cost overruns and losses to fraud, and result in severe unintended consequences. No one will be held accountable for these outcomes, but blame will be placed on irrelevant persons, organizations and events.

The dedicated liberal will argue that these and other objections are merely a cynical cover for persons who are essentially selfish and don't care if starvation persists. But history records the failed objectives and destructive consequences of nearly all programs of these types. African dictators, for example, have gotten very rich on programs to end their country's poverty while the people continue to starve and live or die in squalor. In Chicago the effort to enforce a right to adequate housing for the poor has had such disastrous economic and social effects that the projects had to be torn down. Despite history's negative report card on programs of this type, the true believer in the liberal agenda nevertheless presses ahead with "progressive" programs, ignoring their repeated failures. Meanwhile, the character of all the people, those to whom the state gives and those from whom it takes, is profoundly demeaned. The dignity and sovereignty of the individual are lost in the state's perverse ministrations to the collective social mass.

43

The Radical Liberal Mind

Crisscrossed by invisible tripwires of emotional, racial, sexual, and psychological grievance, American life is increasingly characterized by the plaintive insistence, I am a victim.

Charles Sykes

The Liberal Mind's Perception of Reality

Earlier chapters have dwelled repeatedly on the obvious: that a human being is both an *independent actor* in his own right and an *interdependent collaborator* in joint efforts. In this case, the obvious has great importance for matters of governance: any system that claims to regulate human conduct effectively must enforce certain rules that protect the individual's freedom to act alone and with others of his choice. General obedience to these rules is essential for success in the human enterprise; any widespread breach of them leads to social breakdown. The principles involved are important enough to be stated again in a hypothetical imperative: *Given the biological, psychological and social nature of man, if human beings wish to pursue happiness and prosperity while living in peace and freedom, then they must honor certain property and contract rights that protect the individual's ability to act on his own or in concert.* A corollary to this imperative declares that those rights must be protected by a limited government with limited control over limited common goods. The fact that these propositions assert fundamental truths about the human condition justifies a libertarian political order. Viewed more broadly, they also constitute a test of the suitability of any political system for the regulation of human affairs.

The liberal agenda fails this test because its deeply flawed conceptions and the rules implied by them fail to protect the rights essential to the overall structure of liberty. Modern liberalism misconceives the nature of man, the nature of human relating, the nature of human development, the conditions in which relating and development must occur, and the ideals and institutions needed to promote and protect ordered liberty. These misconceptions foster economic irresponsibility, social conflict and political incoherence. By undermining capacities for self-reliance, voluntary cooperation, moral realism and informed altruism, they degrade the character of the people. When implemented in social policy they interfere with the acquisition of essential developmental achievements including basic trust, autonomy, initiative, industry, identity and competence. The liberal agenda upsets the balance of reciprocal influences between individual, family, community and government. The modern liberal mind generates these misconceptions because it suffers from systematic distortions in its perceptions of the world. It is a mind afflicted with madness.

The Values of the Radical Liberal Mind

Like all other human beings, the modern liberal reveals his true character, including his madness, in what he values and devalues, in what he articulates with passion. Of special interest, however, are the many values about which the modern liberal mind is *not* passionate: his agenda does *not* insist that the individual is the ultimate economic, social and political unit; it does not idealize individual liberty and the structure of law and order essential to it; it does not defend the basic rights of property and contract; it does not aspire to ideals of authentic autonomy and mutuality; it does not preach an ethic of self-reliance and self-determination; it does not praise courage, forbearance or resilience; it does not celebrate the ethics of consent or the blessings of voluntary cooperation. It does not advocate moral rectitude or understand the critical role of morality in human relating. The liberal agenda does not comprehend an identity of competence, appreciate its importance, or analyze the developmental conditions and social institutions that promote its achievement. The liberal agenda does not understand or recognize personal sovereignty or impose strict limits on coercion by the state. It does not celebrate the genuine altruism of private charity. It does not learn history's lessons on the evils of collectivism.

What the liberal mind *is* passionate about is a world filled with pity, sorrow, neediness, misfortune, poverty, suspicion, mistrust, anger, exploitation, discrimination, victimization, alienation and injustice. Those who occupy this world are "workers," "minorities," "the little guy," "women," and the "unemployed." They are poor, weak, sick, wronged, cheated, oppressed, disenfranchised, exploited and victimized. They bear no responsibility for their problems. None of their agonies are attributable to faults or failings of their own: not to poor choices, bad habits, faulty judgment, wishful thinking, lack of ambition, low frustration tolerance, mental illness or defects in character. None of the victims' plight is caused by failure to plan for the future or learn from experience. Instead, the "root causes" of all this pain lie in faulty social conditions: poverty, disease, war, ignorance, unemployment, racial prejudice, ethnic and gender discrimination, modern technology, capitalism, globalization and imperialism. In the radical liberal mind, this suffering is inflicted on the innocent by various predators and persecutors: "Big Business," "Big Corporations," "greedy capitalists," U.S. Imperialists," "the oppressors," "the rich," "the wealthy," "the powerful" and "the selfish."

The liberal cure for this endless malaise is a very large authoritarian government that regulates and manages society through a cradle to grave agenda of redistributive caretaking. It is a government everywhere doing everything for everyone. The liberal motto is "In Government We Trust." To rescue the people from their troubled lives, the agenda recommends denial of personal responsibility, encourages self-pity and other-pity, fosters government dependency, promotes sexual indulgence, rationalizes violence, excuses financial obligation, justifies theft, ignores rudeness, prescribes complaining and blaming, denigrates marriage and the family, legalizes all abortion, defies religious and social tradition, declares inequality unjust, and rebels against the duties of citizenship. Through multiple entitlements to unearned goods, services and social status, the liberal politician promises to ensure everyone's material welfare, provide for everyone's healthcare, protect everyone's self-esteem, correct everyone's social and political disadvantage, educate every citizen, and eliminate all class distinctions. With liberal intellectuals sharing the glory, the liberal politician is the hero in this melodrama. He takes credit for providing his constituents with whatever they want or need even though he has not produced by his own effort any of the goods, services or status transferred to them but has instead taken them from others by force.

It should be apparent by now that these social policies and the passions that drive them contradict all that is rational in human relating, and they are therefore irrational in themselves. *But the faulty conceptions that lie behind these passions cannot be viewed as mere cognitive slippage. The degree of modern liberalism's irrationality far exceeds any misunderstanding that can be attributed to faulty fact gathering or logical error. Indeed, under careful scrutiny, liberalism's distortions of the normal ability to reason can only be understood as the product of psychopathology. So extravagant are the patterns of thinking, emoting, behaving and relating that characterize the liberal mind that its relentless protests and demands become understandable only as disorders of the psyche. The modern liberal mind, its distorted perceptions and its destructive agenda are the product of disturbed personalities.*

As is the case in all personality disturbance, defects of this type represent serious failures in development processes. The nature of these failures is detailed below. Among their consequences are the liberal mind's relentless efforts to misrepresent human nature and to deny certain indispensable requirements for human relating. In his efforts to construct a grand collectivist utopia—to live what Jacques Barzun has called "the unconditioned life" in which "everybody should be safe and at ease in a hundred ways"—the radical liberal attempts to actualize in the real world an idealized fiction that will mitigate all hardship and heal all wounds. (Barzun 2000). He acts out this fiction, essentially a Marxist morality play, in various theaters of human relatedness, most often on the world's economic, social and political stages. But the play repeatedly folds. Over the course of the Twentieth Century, the radical liberal's attempts to create a brave new socialist world have invariably failed. At the dawn of the Twenty-first Century his attempts continue to fail in the stagnant economies, moral decay and social turmoil now widespread in Europe. An increasingly bankrupt welfare society is putting the U.S. on track for the same fate if liberalism is not cured there. Because the liberal agenda's principles violate the rules of ordered liberty, his most determined efforts to realize its visionary fantasies must inevitably fall short. Yet, despite all the evidence against it, the modern liberal mind believes his agenda is good social science. It is, in fact, bad science fiction. He persists in this agenda despite its madness.

The Psychodynamics of the Radical Liberal Mind

The first step toward an in-depth understanding of adult behavior is to comprehend its origins in childhood. Whether adaptive or maladaptive, the enduring patterns of thinking, emoting, behaving and relating that define adult personality begin in the early years of life. In fact, our earliest experiences with caretakers and others, acting on inherited temperament factors, strongly determine our later personality traits, including those expressed in political values and beliefs. The dispositions of the liberal mind are no exception: his hopes and fears, beliefs and passions, values and morals are in great measure the legacy of his childhood from birth through adolescence. The traits that define who he is are the traits that lead him to pursue particular *goals* in the political arena and to use particular *methods* to achieve them.

The radical liberal mind's goals are now familiar, of course, but another brief summary will prove useful in highlighting their essentially childlike nature. Just noted were the grandiose goals of providing for everyone's material welfare and healthcare, protecting everyone's self-esteem correcting all social and political disadvantages, educating all citizens, and eliminating all class distinctions. In his pursuit of these goals, he intends to construct a universal human family, one united in bonds of mutual love, concern, caretaking and tolerance. Through drastic government action the radical liberal seeks the following:

- A powerful parental government to provide everyone with a good life and a caring presence
- An elite corps of surrogate parents that will manage the lives of the people through approximately equal distributions of goods and services, just as real parents provide equally for the needs of their children
- A guarantee of material security from the state, similar to that which a child expects from his parents
- A form of parental social justice that cures or mitigates all states of deprivation, inequality, suffering and disadvantage

- A guarantee that negative rights for the protection of individual liberty will yield to positive rights that reduce or eliminate inequalities of wealth, social status and power, just as good parents would balance benefits to their children
- Government laws that will punish the "haves" for their excesses and compensate the "have-nots" for the pangs of envy, just as good parents would do for their children
- Government directives from wise and caring officials that channel the citizen's initiative and industry through social programs and tax incentives, just as wise parents determine the directions of the family's labors
- Government policy that instructs the people in how to relate to each other politically, just as good parents instruct their children in how to conduct themselves properly
- Permissive laws passed by sympathetic legislators that lower the obligations of contracts, ease codes of acceptable conduct, and relax the burdens of established institutions such as marriage and adoption procedures, just as indulgent parents would do
- Government welfare programs that free the citizen-child from the duties of altruism, just as parents do
- An international caring agenda that will enhance the family of nations by understanding everyone's hardships, tolerating destructive actions by others, and empathizing with aggressors to bring them to the negotiating table, just as good parents do in resolving family disputes

These and other goals dear to the modern liberal heart are remarkable for the childhood needs they address and the adult needs they ignore. As noted in more detail below, what the radical liberal mind really longs for, as revealed in his political goals, is a child's relationship to a loving family whose caretaking compensates him for the injuries he suffered in his early years. He seeks all of this in the contemporary political arena. The major problem he faces is that a substantial portion of the population is still competent: it is a population that deeply reveres individual liberty, readily accepts its responsibilities, and passionately opposes its destruction. It is not about to yield to the liberal's mad dream. *Because competent people know that they can direct their own lives and provide for their own security through voluntary cooperation, and because they love a world of freedom in which to live as they choose, they have no need for, and indeed vehemently reject, the oppressive intrusions of liberal government. What the competent citizen wants, in contrast to the modern liberal, is a coherent and dependable structure for ordered liberty, secured by a limited government that respects the autonomy and sovereignty of the individual and protects his property rights against the constant invasions of collectivism.*

The liberal mind rejects this prescription on principle and attempts to overthrow it in government policy. What the liberal seeks in order to feel secure is the modern welfare state with its endless guarantees and endless regulations. This *goal* is literally fantastic in its own right. But equally irrational is the *method* by which he attempts to achieve it. He is willing to use any kind of government power, including power which destroys the foundations of civilized freedom, in order to get what he demands: government insured safety and security over the entire lifespan, along with accommodation to his neurotic demands. He seeks through the state that degree of coercion needed to redress the trauma, injustice, helplessness and humiliation experienced at the hands of his original caretakers. He hopes to do this by passing laws that indulge his impulses and exempt him from the proper obligations of mature adulthood. Considered in its entirety, the liberal's goal of making the state into an ideal parent/family and his method of achieving it by compelling competent people to do his bidding constitute the radical liberal agenda. Above all, the agenda is a blueprint for the use of irresistible government power. Driven by his irrational needs and desires, the radical liberal mind is more than willing to sacrifice the noble structure of liberty that originally defined America for the shabby asylum of the modern welfare state.

Radical Liberal Themes

Certain neurotic themes are dominant in the radical liberal mind's perceptions of the world. All of them portray the citizen as a suffering child who is victimized, helpless and in need of rescue. All are evident in various liberal platforms. They represent the liberal mind's transference of childhood dynamics into the world of adult relationships. As expressed in his most passionate political pronouncements, the radical liberal mind believes that:

- A very large portion of the population is suffering; they are suffering because they are deprived, neglected, exploited or abused.
- They are suffering because of certain injustices inflicted upon them.
- They are helpless to stop their suffering.
- Bad people, such as capitalists and the rich, cause the victims to suffer by depriving, neglecting, exploiting and abusing them.
- These bad people are villains who must be stopped from preying on their victims.
- The villains are ruthless, powerful, selfish, cruel and mean spirited.
- The bad institutions supported by the villains are economic, social and political in nature; they include free market capitalism, basic property rights, strict moral and ethical accountability, reasonable social decorum, personal and financial responsibility, individual sovereignty, and justice based on merit and desert.
- These bad institutions promote economic enslavement, social discrimination, political disenfranchisement, exploitation of minorities, forced pregnancies, and coercive advertising, among other things.
- The people are innocent victims; they have no important role in causing their suffering.
- Modern liberals are heroes whose mission is to rescue the victims from the villains.
- Modern liberals are compassionate, wise, empathetic and nurturing.
- Modern liberals are devoted to saving the victims from the villains just as nurturing parents protect their children from harm by others.
- Like children, most citizens cannot adequately direct or manage their own lives.
- Most citizens need a powerful liberal government to direct and manage their lives.
- Because the villains and their institutions are ruthless and powerful, the people need a powerful liberal

government, The Modern Parental State, to protect them from the villains and the institutions supported by the villains.

- The Modern Parental State is the answer to problems created by the villains.
- The Modern Parental State will rescue the people and protect them from the villains and from other misfortunes.
- The Modern Parental State will nurture the people by providing for all their needs and desires.
- The Modern Parental State will blame and punish the villains for their deprivation, neglect, abuse and exploitation of the victims.
- Much of the suffering of the victims comes from too much freedom in economic markets, which allows the villains to exploit the victims for unjust gain.
- Proper controls instituted by The Modern Parental State to regulate the markets will prevent the villains from economically exploiting the victims.
- The Modern Parental State will cure the deprivation, neglect, exploitation and abuse of the victims by taking the wealth, power and status of the villains away from them and redistributing it to the victims.
- Some of the suffering of the victims comes from too little social freedom and too many restrictions on behavior in social situations.
- The Modern Parental State will lower the standards of social conduct in order to free the victimized citizen from guilt and from adverse legal consequences when he acts criminally, irresponsibly or offensively.
- By remaking the institutions of society, The Modern Parental State will liberate the victims from exploitation and oppression by the villains.
- The libertarian structure of ordered liberty grounded in basic property and contract rights allows the villains to exploit the victims.
- The Modern Parental State will eliminate these individual rights and create a new political architecture for a secure society modeled on the loving nurturing family.

These and related themes of deprivation and neglect, exploitation and abuse, domination and control, blaming and punishing, caring and caretaking, protection and security, rescuing and nurturing—all are the radical liberal mind's unconscious projections of early childhood dynamics transferred into the political arenas of adult life. These projections define the transference neurosis of the radical liberal mind:

- They are the liberal's projections of a painful neurotic disorder; they are the legacy of his childhood.
- They represent his desperate longings for attachment, attention, affection, empathy, significance, esteem, adoration, recognition, indulgence, relatedness, guidance, direction, belonging and love.
- They represent his desperate efforts to heal real emotional wounds that he suffered when he was, in fact, significantly deprived, neglected, exploited or abused.
- They are his efforts to defend against his suffering by constructing an idealized world of loving care and exemption from responsibility; he seeks a world that will compensate him for the traumas of his childhood, relieve his neediness, indulge his impulses and heal the enduring wounds to his soul.
- They are distorted perceptions of the real world of economic, social and political processes; the liberal agenda is based on these transference perceptions.

Unfortunately, all of the radical liberal's efforts based on these perceptions are badly misguided. Because he does not understand the childhood origins of his pain, he projects his neurosis into a contemporary world of imagined villains, victims and heroes. Once he locates himself in this world, he hopes to find in the ministrations of the Modern Parental State what he missed as a child. He may not admit to himself or others that he did, in fact, suffer early wounds. If he does admit this fact, he will not realize that his wounds drive his political views. If he realizes this causal connection, he will not admit it to others.

Additional Dynamics of the Radical Liberal Mind

The madness of the liberal mind is the result of early trauma. The undercurrents of mistrust, fear, anxiety, depression, emptiness, anger, rage, shame, doubt, disgust, guilt, envy and jealousy that plague him arise from the radical liberal's personal history of neglect, deprivation and abuse, including early deficits in attachment, attention, affection, empathy, validation, direction and discipline. These and related traumas lead him to fear freedom itself: the prospect of genuine autonomy arouses primitive fears of aloneness and danger. The challenge of self-reliance reactivates primitive fears of inadequacy. The challenge of self-responsibility reactivates primitive fears of failure and punishment. The challenge of cooperation activates primitive fears of betrayal and exploitation. The challenge of gratifying others for the sake of mutuality arouses primitive anger and envy.

Additional symptoms arise from these early traumas. A sense of entitlement attempts to compensate for fears of helplessness, abandonment and isolation but compounds the liberal's problems because it prevents him from recognizing the sovereignty of others. To defend against his pain, the radical liberal projects his selfishness onto imagined villains, then rages against them for their ruthless neglect and exploitation of victims. In his fear of autonomy and disbelief in mutuality, the radical liberal believes that human relatedness will work only if it is controlled and manipulated. Free and productive people who remind him of his own deficits have to be reigned in: they must be taxed, regulated and penalized through the power of the state. In his fear, envy and rage, and in his bitterness about old wrongs, the radical liberal lacks good will and good purpose. He longs for some means to avenge old injustices, to punish villains past and present, real and imagined. In his paranoid obsession with victimization, he perceives whole communities of free and cooperative people to be warring victims and villains.

Because he has not achieved competence himself, the radical liberal cannot comprehend, let alone empathize with, the autonomous, sovereign and mutual adult who joyfully embraces freedom with all of its risks and responsibilities. The radical liberal empathizes instead with a projected persona from his own unconscious: that of a neglected, deprived, envious, desperately needy, intensely dependent and bitterly angry child. The sentiments that energize this pseudo-empathy are fear, hatred, longing, self-pity and other-pity. The radical liberal's solution to his inner demons is to be rescued by the power of parental government. Striding into the game of life as his own person and playing it for all it is worth is not in his response repertoire. He would rather hide in the skirts of the maternal state. He has been much too traumatized to access the heroic element of human nature; he does not find in himself that core of human courage, persistence and determination that overcomes severe adversity or takes pride in giving one's all, even in defeat. The radical liberal's solution to life's crises, and indeed to the very essence of the human condition, is to control and manipulate the world through the power of the state, not rise to the challenges of life through individual initiative and cooperative effort.

Transference

The concept of transference is essential to understanding the radical liberal's neurosis. His distortions of the present through the traumas of his past are evident in the childlike character of his demands. He seeks a world of unconditional love, status, esteem and comfort. He seeks indulgence of his impulses, exemption from risk, and freedom from responsibility. He seeks the material security of mature adulthood without the initiative and industry essential to it. Because they refuse his infantile demands, America's liberty institutions become the object of primitive emotions always raw from the wounds of childhood. The rules protecting liberty punish poor judgment, carelessness and bad behavior with the pain of rejection, failure, public shame or imprisonment. In these stern consequences, the institutions of liberty represent to the radical liberal the cruel, withholding and indifferent parents of his childhood. He now rages against them for what he perceives to be their unyielding selfishness, the satisfaction of their own appetites to the neglect of his needs and their callous indifference to his pain. He alleges all of this against a structure of liberty that refuses to adopt him, compensate him and pamper him. He rages like a child at a nation that refuses to do for him what only he can do for himself, so he vows to revise the rules that govern it. In this pursuit he demands effects without causes, benefits without costs, and actions without adverse consequences.

Thus the radical agenda is the product of a massive transference neurosis played out in the world's economic, social and political arenas. In the drama of it all, the radical liberal is protesting his original economic, social and political system, his family of origin, because it deprived him, abused him or neglected him. In his bitter rejection of ordered liberty, he hopes to heal the wounds of his childhood with an idealized world created by the modern liberal intellect. Unfortunately, the utopian world he seeks is completely impossible, given the realities of human nature, human relating and the human condition.

In some radical liberals this transference becomes frankly paranoid: mistrust progresses to suspicion, then to a conviction that someone is being victimized, then to fixed delusions of persecution. In other radical liberals the transference is notably grandiose, energized by the confidence that liberal genius can construct a better world than America's founding fathers did. It is a distinctively liberal conceit that by rejecting older conventions, older moralities, and the settled foundations of civilized freedom, the liberal social scientist can create a new world that will redress all of the citizen's grievances and relieve all of his fears, especially those of need, risk, conflict and evil. In disregard of the laws of human development, the laws of economics, the laws of social relating, the laws of rational politics, and the logic of choice, the modern liberal persists in a vain hope that his new world will have all of the advantages of ordered freedom and none of the hardships, burdens, costs, risks and responsibilities that have always attended it. To add to the tragic core of this endeavor, the radical liberal will continue to deny that his efforts will bring terrible destruction to the cause of freedom.

44

The Radical Deficits
of Infancy

It appears indisputable that an understanding of the nature, origin and relations of love and hate is the key not only to the interpretation of psychopathy and of individual character but to the understanding of culture.

Ian Suttie

The Radical Liberal's Developmental Deficits

What are the specific psychodynamic factors that drive the radical liberal mind to create a world that restricts freedom of choice, renounces self-reliance, surrenders personal sovereignty, invites mass dependency, and destroys the foundations of liberty? If he is so preoccupied with suffering or neediness or some other grievance, why doesn't he create voluntary charitable organizations for those purposes and exhort the people to charitable giving? Why does he seek the invasive power of the state to accomplish these tasks for him? Why not, in addition, try to reduce the need for caretaking in the first place by creating private foundations whose purpose is to promote self-reliance and alleviate disability? Answers to these and related questions require a motivational analysis of the liberal mind. The following sections analyze the radical liberal mind's motives from an Eriksonian perspective, supplemented with modern insights from the psychology of individuation and narcissism.

Basic Trust

The developmental processes described in earlier chapters provide a framework in which to analyze the defects that afflict the radical liberal mind. The analysis begins with his earliest developmental failure: his basic mistrust of relationships between persons who act by mutual consent. Put simply, the modern liberal is unable to believe that human beings can make good lives for themselves through individual initiative and voluntary cooperation. He believes that ordinary citizens cannot relate effectively to each other without extensive regulation by the state. Even if the members of a community *appear* to be satisfied while relating by consent, the radical liberal knows that this appearance is largely an illusion. He knows that behind the façade of satisfaction lie neediness, suffering and exploitation. Moreover, he is certain that these agonies cannot be cured or prevented by good will, or by the prohibitions of conscience, or by enforcement of laws based on property rights. He knows in fact that the people simply cannot be trusted to run their own lives effectively; they don't know *what* is truly good for them, they don't know *how* to do what is truly good for them, and they don't have the *will* to do what is truly good for them. Based on his conviction that the people are incompetent, it is obvious to the modern liberal that someone must direct their affairs. The Modern Parental State staffed by an elite core of parent/leaders is what is needed to solve the problem. Guided by liberal insights, these wise and caring leaders will inform the citizens about what is truly good for them and tell them how to run their lives. And because most people have to be made to do what is good for them, the new leaders are prepared to use whatever force is needed for that purpose. By this route the world can be made safe enough for the radical liberal to trust it.

These ideas about human relating, especially his fearful mistrust of relating by mutual consent, are projections of the radical liberal's developmental deficits into the contemporary world of economic, social and political events. The deficits are painful in themselves because they are the residues of traumas he suffered as a child. Projecting them into the outside world rather than feeling them inwardly lessens to some extent the pain he would otherwise suffer: he can reassure himself that the problems that torment him exist outside of him, not inside of him. But his radical view of the human condition still causes him pain; it describes a world of deprivation, neglect, exploitation and victimization, and these perceptions add to his experience of the world as a place of misery. Indeed, the radical liberal now feels driven to create a new world that will eliminate everyone's misery. In this new world the people will be coerced into living lives that are good for them.

The Details of Basic Mistrust

Regardless of where he locates the problem the modern liberal suffers. His developmental deficits generate unconscious beliefs and emotions that continue to torment him. They account for his ideas about why he believes that persons who *appear* to be happy when relating to each other by mutual consent are actually *unhappy* because they are needy, deprived and exploited. His beliefs about their suffering are projections of his own agonies. In the depths of his soul the radical liberal believes that as a small child:

- He was neglected, deprived or abused by his caretakers.
- He suffered unfair and painful separations and losses.
- He never got enough love or attention from his caretakers.
- Others got more love and attention than he did.
- His original caretakers unfairly rejected or abandoned him.
- He was dominated, controlled and exploited by his caretakers.
- He had to endure unfair and excessive frustration.
- His original caretakers shamed and humiliated him.
- His original caretakers made him feel guilty.
- His original caretakers made him feel inadequate.
- He and his original caretakers could not be happy together.
- His conflicts with his original caretakers could not be resolved.

As a result of these early traumas the radical liberal:

- Feels sad, needy, empty, angry, envious and jealous
- Has recurrent feelings of inadequacy, inferiority and failure
- Has anxious doubts that he is lovable or acceptable

- Feels an undercurrent of resentment, bitterness and spitefulness
- Feels an undercurrent of pessimism and cynicism
- Feels an undercurrent of depression and hopelessness
- Has anxious doubts about relating to others
- Has anxious doubts about cooperating with others
- Is unable to soothe or comfort himself without blaming others
- Has an attitude of entitlement to satisfaction from others
- Feels he will never be satisfied without using force or manipulation

As will be seen below, many of these painful states of mind result from failures that emerge in later phases of development, not just the basic trust phase. Essentially, however, the liberal mind's mistrust of freedom and mutuality begins with his conviction that he and others will not be able to make good lives for themselves by working together voluntarily but will need instead to have their relationships supervised by the state. The unconscious fantasy behind this conviction is that The Modern Parental State will enable him and others like him to finally prevail over their early traumas: they will be compensated for the neglect, deprivation and abuse they have suffered at the hands of persons who were unloving, harsh, stingy and cruel.

Failure in Basic Trust

As noted in earlier discussions, the foundations of basic trust begin in the first year of life with an adequate physical environment and a good enough temperament match between mother and infant. They continue to develop when mother is in good enough physical and mental condition to care for her helpless infant, when she and he can achieve good enough emotional attunement to solidify their bond, when she can empathize well enough with her infant's physical and mental distress, and when she is willing and able to protect and comfort him before he is traumatized. Basic trust develops when the mother's capacity to relate lovingly and protectively to her child is not impaired by illness or injury, by the torment of unmanageable mental states, by the disorganizing effects of substance abuse, by the agonies of marital and family conflict, or by chaotic economic, social and political conditions.

When things go well enough in this dyad, the infant's repeated visceral experience that his needs can be met and that intolerable distress can be avoided instills in him an expectation that all is well in his world. And because the emotions he feels in these interactions are generally positive, he looks forward to them, anticipates them eagerly, actively seeks them, and thus "voluntarily consents" to them. A bond that arises from his instinctive tendency to attach to his mother is solidified by the pleasure that each takes in relating to the other.

Thus the infant's emotionally positive interactions with his mother introduce him to a world of relating that is safe, pleasurable, mutually satisfying and "consented to" by both parties. When the relationship with mother and others goes well enough in his formative years, what was once the mere potential for win-win outcomes gradually becomes an assured reality. When repeated often enough over a long enough period of time, this early experience of mutuality becomes a sought-after norm. Primitive and positive relating of this type, occurring at the dawn of the child's life, provides him with the basis for later mutuality with others. It also sets the stage for the beginnings of autonomy in the second and third years of life.

The mother-child dyad that fails to achieve these early milestones, on the other hand, sets a different stage. Various forms of neglect, deprivation or abuse in the first fifteen months of life profoundly undermine the acquisition of basic trust. Most obvious are actual physical neglect and abuse of the infant, yelling and raging at him, or enduring attitudes of disgust or hatred toward him. But attributing false motives and character traits to him, recurrent shaming and ridicule, repeated threats of harm, failing to engage and relate to him, contradicting his accurate perceptions of the world, omitting affection and other physical contact, and discouraging his primitive steps toward independence, to name a few, can also disorganize the foundations of healthy personality development in the child's early years. *Whatever their form, early serious disturbances in the infant's caretaking are likely to instill in him a deep seated expectation that anxiety, frustration and helplessness are the norm; security and satisfaction are not to be had despite one's most intense need for them. Deficits of this type predispose to an increasingly entrenched belief that voluntary cooperation won't work or doesn't exist.* Faced with frequent frustration and the disorganizing effects of early turmoil, the infant resorts to the only power he has to restore equilibrium: he screams and rages in the hope that a good mother will appear and quiet his nightmare. The furious crying of the small child proclaims his fear and rage at a world that cannot or will not accommodate his needs. If this situation obtains over the first year and extends into the second, a basic *mistrust* in the goodness of life becomes his conditioned response. When severe and long lasting, this type of experience eventually leads the child to use force or manipulation to get what he believes he cannot get by other means.

The Cynicism of the Radical Liberal Mind

Based on his early deficits in trust, the radical liberal's skepticism about life is deep seated and cynical. It undermines his ability to be hopeful, leaving him at least pessimistic and often depressive in his outlook on life. Indeed, the radical liberal is not optimistic about himself and the world: he lacks a deep-seated confidence in his and others' abilities to manage life's problems, achieve security and feel contented in a framework of individual freedom. Not only can he not trust that other persons will cooperate with him for his and their benefit, he also believes that they will deliberately ignore him, neglect him, deprive him or exploit him. The radical liberal believes that he has to defend himself against this basic fact about the human condition by getting power over others. He must force other persons to meet his needs or he will remain deprived, frustrated and disadvantaged. When his early trauma has been especially severe, his conviction that he is deprived and abused rises to the level of paranoia. He is then convinced that his suffering is not only painful but intended. He believes that others are conspiring to harm him and keep him down. In adult life this paranoid development finds a home in the politics of victimization

All of this and more will of course be adamantly denied by the radical liberal, who must defend against his deficits by projecting them into the outside world. He will not realize that he misinterprets the present through perceptions from the past. He will not understand that his cynicism flows from the traumas of his childhood. He will insist instead that in a free society under the rule of law, he and many others like him will be deprived, neglected and abused by villains who use freedom to exploit their victims. He will not understand that by projecting his mistrustful perceptions into the world around him he distorts the realities of human relating. But this denial will not withstand scrutiny. The radical liberal's neurosis is evident in his distortions of human nature and human relating. It is evident in what he seeks and what he fears, in what he praises and damns, in what elicits his sympathy and pity, in what stimulates his rage and outrage. It is evident in the values he celebrates and in those he scorns, in the policies he promotes and the principles he opposes, in the responsibilities he rejects and the obligations he shirks, in what makes him envious and jealous, in what agitates him and calms him, in what humiliates him and makes him proud. His neurosis is evident in his ideals and fantasies; in his self-righteousness, arrogance and grandiosity; in his self-pity; in his demands for indulgence and exemption from accountability; in his claims to entitlements; in what he gives and withholds; and in his protests that nothing done voluntarily is enough to satisfy him. Most notably, the radical liberal's neurosis is evident in his extravagant political demands, in his furious protests against economic freedom, in his arrogant contempt for morality, in his angry defiance of civility, in his bitter attacks on freedom of association, in his aggressive assault on individual liberty. And in the final analysis, the irrationality of the radical liberal is most apparent in his ruthless use of force to control the lives of others. As will be noted in more detail below, the radical liberal's obsession with force against others is the child's solution to developmental failures in the first six years of life.

Radical Projection

Because he cannot admit that his fear and mistrust are due to his own distorted perceptions of the world, the radical liberal concludes that his agonies must be caused by events in the world outside of him. His neurosis tells him loudly that he and others like him are being deprived, neglected, exploited and abused by contemporary villains and their institutions. But its strident voice omits a critical insight: these beliefs are the legacy of trauma suffered at the hands of parents and other caretakers when he was little and helpless. He decides that in order to remedy present day injustice and allow persons such as himself to have good lives, he must overthrow the villains who cause him so much pain and destroy the institutions that support them. He decides that what is needed is a new government founded on caring institutions and staffed with concerned leaders. He believes that these new leaders and institutions will provide for him and protect him and other victims in the manner of a loving parent. In pursuit of this goal, he insists that The Modern Parental State will not only give him what he needs, it will also take goods and services from others who have wrongfully acquired them and then redistribute them to him and to other needy persons. The new State will redress his social grievances and punish his political enemies, restructure society's ideals to make it more caring, recast its ethics in a collectivist mode, and loosen society's inhibitions to make life more pleasurable.

The defects in this plan are fatal to any rational social order. The institutions the radical liberal would overthrow are precisely those that protect ordered liberty. In particular, they are the institutions which prevent him from gaining control over the lives of others and taking what he wants from them without their consent. The radical liberal would overthrow the rules that protect self-ownership and property rights and prevent the citizen from being indentured to collectivist programs. The radical liberal would violate the integrity of contracts and overthrow equal protection laws in the name of social justice. The radical liberal would encourage litigation with laws that invite the perception of injustice where there is none. The radical liberal would establish a society of adult children who are incompetent to manage their own lives, dependent on the state's welfare programs, and subservient to its ruling elite. These and other defects inherent in radical liberal goals doom its agenda on the hard realities of the human condition.

Of course, to someone who feels entitled to all that he needs, the rules that structure ordered liberty appear unjust and therefore wicked. In his unconscious, in fact, the persons and institutions that limit him in the present represent the cruel parents and family who deprived, neglected and abused him in the past. The villains of the present keep him from having what he needs now, just as his caretakers withheld from him as a child. At an unconscious level he feels especially deprived of the love, attention, affection and empathy that he needed to feel secure, trusting and hopeful about himself and the world and to trust in the power of cooperation by consent. Through the prism of his infantile transferences he sees the institutions of individual liberty as selfish, harsh, cruelly withholding and even sadistic. Indeed, he is most threatened by liberty itself: by the indifference of citizens who feel free to live their own lives while ignoring him completely. Their indifference is deeply offensive to him and deeply insulting to his sense of importance. The freedom of others to ignore him makes him feel what he felt as a child with indifferent parents: insignificant, inferior, marginal, irrelevant and even nonexistent. When his neurosis is severe enough, the radical liberal sees others' rejection as an active persecution intended to torture him, not just as callous indifference.

45

Radical Deficits in Childhood

On the other hand, students of history continue to ignore the simple fact that all individuals are born by mothers; that everybody was once a child; that people and peoples begin in their nurseries; and that society consists of individuals in the process of developing from children into parents.

Erik Erikson

Radical Deficits; Autonomy, Initiative, Industry

The end of infancy at about fifteen months of age begins the era of autonomy, the second of Erikson's developmental phases. The foundations of self-governing, the literal meaning of autonomy, are laid down in this period along with the foundations of mutuality, an equally important achievement on the road to adult competence. Capacities for autonomy and mutuality form the twin pillars of adult participation in a free society: self-reliance, self-direction, and self-regulation are implicit in the idea of autonomy; capacities for voluntary exchange, sharing and altruism are implicit in the idea of mutuality. Both concepts reflect the bipolar nature of man as independent actor and joint collaborator. The toddler-age child's early interactions with his caretakers determine whether these critical achievements have their proper beginnings in his formative years.

   Similar remarks apply to the third and fourth of Erikson's
eight stages, the eras of initiative and industry, respectively. In
contrast to action driven largely by impulse in the autonomy era,
the child's ability to respond to his environment in the initiative
era is more intentional and goal directed. Increasing demands
are imposed upon him to behave according to social norms and
the effects of his actions on others. In this phase, early sexual,
aggressive, narcissistic, acquisitive, dependency and attachment
drives become better regulated by thought processes and by the
emerging constraints of conscience. Capacities for good will and
willingness acquired in the autonomy phase become capacities for
good purpose and focused efforts to please others in the initiative
phase. Fears of separation and loss are diminished in this phase
as internal images of loving and protective caretakers are more
securely rooted. Jealousy peaks during this phase but typically
quiets down by the grade school years. Competitive impulses are
tempered as the will to negotiate takes precedence over the urge
to dominate. An increasing ability to cooperate replaces earlier
tendencies to oppose. Mutuality is more in evidence as infantile
tendencies toward defiance and entitlement recede. By the close
of the initiative era, more secure feelings of being loved and valued
diminish the torment of primitive envy. Achieving these virtues
continues the child's growing ability to recognize the other as a
separate agent, a person to be respected, not a thing to be used.
   Thus, by the time he begins grade school the child has
acquired substantial control over primitive drives and has largely
made peace with early family dramas. He can direct himself more
effectively, cooperate with greater ease, and conform his conduct
more appropriately. From sources within and outside of his home,
he begins in this juvenile era to learn the myriad instrumental
and social skills and facts about life that eventually lead to adult
competence. He learns how basic economic, social and political
processes work in modern technology-based and communication-
based societies. Throughout this era, the early foundations of
autonomy and mutuality are elaborated into greater capacities for
self-reliance, responsibility and cooperation. When nurtured in a
loving family, early tendencies to be giving and caring are expanded
into a broader ethic of charitable service to others. Of special
importance in this era is the child's increasing appreciation of what
is fair and just in human relating. This advance in understanding,
together with greater abilities to negotiate and compromise, lead

him to reject as a matter of moral principle the use of force in coping with social conflict.

The Radical Liberal's Confession

The individual who has achieved basic trust, hope, autonomy, good will, mutuality, initiative, good purpose, recognition, industry and instrumental competence naturally seeks a life that embodies these virtues: a life of individual liberty and voluntary cooperation. On completing adolescence his identity is that of a competent adult who can provide for himself as he collaborates with others. He takes pride in being his own person while playing by the rules and respecting the rights of others. He also takes pride in his charity to worthy causes. *For this individual, a life of ordered liberty is the logical culmination of all that he has learned in childhood. It is a life that embodies the virtues learned in a competent family. What the competent adult then seeks from a competent government are those protections that ensure his freedom to live by his own choices and relate to others by mutual consent.*

As observed throughout this book, however, that kind of life and that kind of government are not what the radical liberal seeks. What he seeks instead is a dominant government's guaranteed safety, security and dependency over the entire lifespan, along with accommodation to his neurotic demands. He intends through the power of the state to redress the trauma, injustice, helplessness and humiliation experienced at the hands of his original caretakers. He hopes to achieve these goals by passing laws that indulge his impulses and exempt him from the proper obligations of mature adulthood. He seeks a society that is heavily regulated, shaped and administered by The Modern Parental State. The radical liberal's goal of making the state into an ideal parent/family and his method of achieving it by compelling its citizens to do his bidding constitute the radical liberal agenda. This agenda can be stated in a plain-language montage from an adult perspective. When accompanied by insight into its developmental origins, the result is the radical liberal's confession. If he were to declare it with candor and self-scrutiny it would read roughly as follows.

The Radical Confession from Basic Mistrust

At critical periods in my childhood I have been painfully deprived of love, empathy, attention and caretaking. These deprivations cause me to feel hurt, needy, empty, envious and angry, but I have to pretend that I don't have these emotions. When I was little I would beg, demand and cry in order get what I wanted. I still want to act in those ways, but I risk feeling humiliated when I do. No matter what I do, I never feel that I get enough of what I need. This is a terrible injustice, and because of it I believe I am victimized. I am not paranoid for believing this; my basic mistrust is realistic. But feeling needy, envious and deprived also makes me depressed and hopeless. Sometimes I feel panicky and hateful as well. I know that certain people will mistreat me as I was mistreated as a child. I am intensely hurt and angry about the bad treatment I have suffered at the hands of villains, past and present.

To defend against these states I have to blame certain individuals and groups for my problems and try to get them to give me what I want. By hating them for being harsh, cruel and selfish, and by taking what they have away from them, I can vent my anger and feel secure, self-righteous and powerful. *Blaming and hating others helps me to affirm myself as a victim and to see others as villains whom I can punish while I try to get what they have. What they have are certain goods, services and status that I feel entitled to but have not yet received. To end this injustice, I will use the power of the state to get what I want. Then I will stop feeling needy, envious and angry. I won't have to beg, demand, manipulate or intimidate anymore because the state will do all of that for me.*

The fact that the state can take things from others and give them to me is gratifying in itself. I need to have this power over others so I don't feel helpless, as I did when I was a child. The power to take things from others also allows me to get revenge for the wrongs I have endured and to stop suffering. Further, to have things given to me satisfies my greed. I am indeed greedy and envious because of the deprivation I suffered as a child, but I do not admit it to myself or others. I pretend instead that I am not envious, and I firmly deny that I am greedy. I disguise my greedy demands by calling them entitlements. Entitlements are goods that someone should provide for me because I deserve them; I should not be seen as greedy and grasping even though I am. My determination to get what others have is my legitimate need. Their efforts to keep what they have is their selfish greed. (Joe Sobran) Thus they are the greedy ones, not I. Further, they deserve to lose what they have, because they have taken things from others.

These beliefs help me to pretend that I am not envious, greedy or vindictive.

I and others like me who are needy, angry and envious reject any rules that would require us to earn what we get. We should not have to do anything more than we have already done in order to get what is essential to a good life. We have all suffered enough. We deserve to be compensated without additional burdens. The deprivations we have suffered in the past are what make us deserving in the present and the future. The mere fact that we are alive and have endured such hardship is enough to entitle us to free benefits. In fact, we deserve much more than the bare essentials of a good life in order to make up for past hardships. For these reasons, traditional property rights must not be allowed to block the satisfaction of our entitlements. We victims should have unhindered access to the wealth, power and position of others. We do not accept the primacy of property rights in protecting ordered liberty, nor is individual liberty a proper ideal. Our positive rights to have our needs satisfied and our injuries compensated are far more important than basic property rights or individual liberty. Furthermore, we do not recognize the sovereignty of the other person. We do not recognize his right to be let alone. *Our entitlements are more important than the claimed right of others to lives of their own. Because we have suffered certain injustices as children we have certain legitimate claims on other persons for reparations. The fact that the people on whom we make these claims deny any causal role in the injustices we have suffered, either past or present, is not relevant. We are entitled to get what is owed to us from anyone with the resources to provide it. Accordingly, we, the have-nots, are entitled to the time, effort, skills and money of those who have more than we do.*

Seeing myself as an innocent victim of injustice and seeing others as cruel villains who are greedy and withholding gives me a way of relating to the world. I can bond with others who feel as I do, and this kind of relatedness fills some of the emptiness and quiets some of the insecurity that remains from my childhood. It is especially important that in this bond I can feel attached to something and someone. Being attached in this manner makes me feel safe and secure and reduces my anxieties about vulnerability, helplessness, separation and abandonment left over from my childhood. I can also get sympathy and pity for my suffering; that helps to make up for the lack of tenderness that I experienced as a child. Indeed, my bond with other victims against villains creates a family of sufferers, a confederacy of victims, with whom I can identify. *All of us see ourselves as noble martyrs who are united in our sorrow, in our envy and in our pity for ourselves and each other. We are united, as well, in our anger and hatred for the villains in our lives, past and present. This allows me to feel justified when I act angrily and destructively against villains. Moreover, when I see that my problems are caused by others, I can be hateful and vindictive toward them and thus avoid hating and punishing myself.*

My worldview of victims and villains gives me a way to understand the human condition. The world consists of innocent people who suffer and cruel people who cause them to suffer. We who suffer are not in any way responsible for our suffering. Our pain is never caused by our own errors of omission or commission. Our pain is caused by selfish and mean-spirited people and by evil institutions such as capitalism that allow rich and powerful people to exploit poor and weak minorities. With this view of the world I am able to convince myself that my basic mistrust of the world is not a neurotic legacy of my childhood nor a paranoid distortion of reality. It is a perfectly natural and accurate perception of the dire state of human relating. The only bright spots in this unfortunate world are the modern radical liberals. Given the opportunity to do so, these heroic men and women can defeat the villains in our lives, make us all safe and secure, unite us in loving concern for each other, and gratify our needs to depend on powerful leaders.

If they can just get enough political power, our radical liberal leaders will create a great utopian society. In fact, The Modern Parental State is the idealized parent of my dreams, an omnipotent benefactor with magical powers to end human suffering. I view this entity as an infant adores a loving mother, as a teenager idolizes a rock star, as a believer worships the deity. Under The Modern Parental State I fear no evil, for the State abolishes all deprivation, meets all need, cures all injustice. This is the Hegelian World Spirit. It not only creates the context of human relating, it is the ultimate reality of human relating. In a mystical merger with this Spirit, I will experience the oneness of citizen and society, the connection of all to all, the abolition of separation, and the end of alienation in all human being. I will no longer feel alone or abandoned; my existential angst will dissolve in a communion with the collective. I will belong to everyone and everyone will belong to me. I will at last be safe, at last be free of need, at last be free of mistrust. In my fusion with the grandiose state I will achieve not only the security of basic trust; I will feel connected to the very soul of humanity. Moreover, in my collective campaign against individualism I will achieve validation, vindication and significance. My passions will finally be justified in a noble war to defeat selfishness. My life will have meaning and significance in an epochal campaign against evil.

The Radical Confession from Failed Autonomy

In my toddler years I did not feel safe, secure, loved and important because the people who were supposed to take care of me neglected me, deprived me or abused me. They had almost no empathy for my mental states and little understanding of my needs. I often felt overwhelmed, fearful, unprotected, abandoned, ignored and angry in those years, and I was completely unable to relieve my torment through my own efforts. I would try to get what I wanted or needed by crying and whining or by screaming in rage and throwing tantrums. When this behavior succeeded in getting something I wanted, I would feel less helpless. Often I would try to punish the people who denied me by being stubborn, oppositional, spiteful and defiant. Sometimes I felt destructive and even sadistic: I would hit and kick people, break things, and sully things. Sometimes this behavior would make them yield to my demands, and again I would feel less helpless, but when they allowed me to get my way by having tantrums, they deprived me of the discipline I needed to keep from being a spoiled brat. *As I got older I came to believe that life is a game of power, control, manipulation and intimidation. Now as an adult, when I don't get what I want, I try to get power and control over others or find a way to manipulate or intimidate them so I can get what I want.* When I don't succeed in these efforts I get anxious, angry and depressed. Sometimes I still cry or whine or rage at how unfair life is to me, just as I did when is was a toddler, because I still feel neglected, deprived and abused. I envy people who are rich and powerful, but I am also afraid of them because I believe they are somehow exploiting me. I especially hate people who ignore my welfare and act as if I don't exist. They should be made to do right by me because when they don't, I feel insignificant and worthless as well as exploited and angry. I feel their contempt for me and I want to return it by degrading them. Then my manner becomes haughty and arrogant, I show my disgust and contempt for them, and I become imperious in my demands.

To right the terrible wrongs I have suffered I must get control over other people and their resources. That is the only way to feel happy and secure and avoid the painful emotions that plague me. If I can get control of the levers of power, then I will feel safe and gratified instead of fearful and frustrated. I will feel powerful instead of helpless. The power I need is the power of government. The Modern Parental State will force others to do what I need them to do for my welfare and for the welfare of others like me. The power of The State is what is needed to make other people provide for those of us who have been so wronged.

Unfortunately I can't get this kind of power in a free society. People in a free society can live largely as they please. Although *I* want to be able to do as *I* please, I don't want *others* to do as *they* please because then they can refuse my demands for economic goods, social status and political influence. I may benefit from private charities funded by free people, but they offer no guarantee that I will get either the kind or amount of benefits that I need to make me feel good. Crying and whining about how I suffer may get me some results in a free society, but not enough to produce the kind of life I want to lead. If I get angry and blameful, or if my behavior seems oppositional or spiteful, or defiant or hateful, then free people lose interest in me, which I find insulting and threatening. *Accordingly, I reject the kind of freedom that allows others to ignore my demands. I need to know that they can be compelled to provide for me even if they object to it. The fact is that I have certain positive rights, and I demand that they be honored. I am entitled to get what I want and need. My entitlements trump any property rights that protect individual liberty. I adamantly oppose any arrangements in which my welfare is not the legal obligation of others. I therefore oppose any arrangements in which relating is governed by mutual consent.*

For these reasons, I also refuse to recognize the sovereignty of other persons because then I can't control them. Certain people who are selfish and greedy have to be made to do their fair share, which means they have to be made to give up their power and wealth and status for those of us in need. Otherwise, they will ignore us as they go about living their own lives. Their freedom to live without legal obligation to my welfare means that I have to be responsible for my own life, and that is unfair. I do not accept the idea that I should run my own life and get what I need by making it or earning it, or by cooperating voluntarily, or exchanging things by mutual consent, or by persuading others to meet my needs as I meet theirs. In fact, I am not only afraid to live my own life, I am also angry that I should have to be mutual at all. I need the safety and security of knowing that others are forced by law to take care of me, to see me as significant, to know that I matter to them enough to give things to me without me giving anything to them. Because I was deprived, abused and neglected as a child, there are certain goods and services and relationships owed to me as compensation, and I am entitled to all of these benefits without having to offer anything in return. I need to be loved and cared for just for who I am, not for what I do for others. What's more, I want to feel the sense of power and superiority over others that The Modern Parental State gives to me. I want to recapture the toddler age child's sense of omnipotence, the illusion of dominance that a small child has over his mother and other care providers. I want to restore "His Majesty, The Baby" in my life in order to stifle the shame and doubt I feel from being unloved, uncared for, unprotected and unvalued.

I have no interest in good will or willingness, either. Instead I want my will to be done. I want control over others so they can't refuse me or deny me or ignore me. When I have that control, then I have a self that feels good to me: "I control, therefore I am." *When I don't have control I feel weak and inadequate. I find it demeaning, and even humiliating, to have to negotiate with others in order make a transaction agreeable to both of us. I see life as an adversarial process, not a cooperative one. It is a battle of wills, and my will must dominate. "My will be done as I demand," not "our will be done by mutual consent." I don't believe in cooperating by consent, and I don't trust it. In fact, I am so angry about being deprived, neglected and abused in the past that I refuse to cooperate by consent in the present. I don't want to have to work things out to the satisfaction of all parties. I am angry that I have not gotten what I want, so it feels good to thwart others and get control over them. Making the other person do what I want against his will satisfies my angry intent to punish the world for not doing right by me. It makes me feel good to be vindictive, to punish others for their injustices toward me, especially for their failures to yield to my demands.*

To achieve my goals of dominating and punishing other people, I need the power of the state. The power of the state allows me to

do to others what it would be morally wrong and illegal to do on
my own: to coerce them, take wealth from them and regulate them.
That's why I love the philosophy of collectivism; it is inherently
coercive. It is inherently hostile to individual liberty. I hate
individual liberty because if others are autonomous and sovereign
and free to relate only by agreement, then they don't have to do
what I want. I can beg and manipulate and try to intimidate to get
what I want, but they may still refuse me. I realize that I can offer
them something that they want in order to get their cooperation,
but I don't want to do that. I am angry about the fact that they have
not given me what I want. I am also intensely envious of what they
have. For these reasons I refuse to offer them anything that will
increase their satisfaction. Instead, I want to frustrate them and
make them feel deprived, too. This is what The Modern Parental
State can do to selfish people, especially the rich and powerful.

The Radical Confession from Failed Initiative

In the fourth, fifth and sixth years of my childhood, I was
sometimes bold, brash and insistent, sometimes a showoff,
sometimes overconfident, cocky and pushy. I imagined myself
as big and powerful but I often felt weak and frightened in my
littleness. Sometimes I would feel guilty and inhibited and afraid
of being punished, but I also wanted to assert myself by doing
things I wasn't supposed to do. I was not disciplined well enough
to develop a normal conscience, so I acquired a strong tendency
to indulge myself in greedy and spiteful ways. Sometimes I was
competitive and demanding about who or what belonged to me. I
could be jealous and possessive and even combative about having
one of my parents or siblings to myself. I was often afraid that
others would get more love and attention than I would. I wanted to
be dominant, but others who were much bigger and stronger than
I was would dominate me and render me helpless and submissive.
When that happened I felt humiliated and furious. Sometimes I
felt hatred toward those I saw as rivals; I would imagine winning a
fight with them by injuring or killing them. But I also feared being
humiliated in play or games in which I had to perform. I wanted
to be the center of my parents' attention and be admired more
than other children, but the other children were often older and
smarter and stronger, and they could perform better than I could.
On these occasions I felt inadequate and inferior. Sometimes
these feelings led me to give up on initiating anything and become

passive and self-effacing. But then I decided to compete and win by cheating. I decided to break the rules in order to defeat others. I rejected good purpose and became ruthless and vindictive in my childish way. I had to win because losing in a competitive situation was too crushing for my little ego. I also learned to manipulate in order to get my way. I would do whatever it took—charm, cuteness, seduction, promises, lies, anything—to get people to do what I wanted and avoid losing a contest. But cheating and manipulating caused a problem because I was supposed to be learning good behavior. I was supposed to be acquiring a conscience to enforce good behavior, and I didn't want to be limited by the rules. I had to become even more devious in order to cover up my cheating and manipulating and avoid being called spoiled.

I still feel the same way as an adult. I don't want to play by the rules. I'm willing to manipulate and cheat and lie without feeling guilty in order to win life's battles and get what I want. Without a parental government to protect me I feel vulnerable to rich and powerful predators ready to overwhelm me, dominate me and make me subservient to them. In a world of ordered liberty, where competing and performing are everyday fare, I feel insecure and inadequate if I have to suffer defeat and loss of wealth or status. The appearance of inadequacy and the reality of failure threaten me in a world that often requires genuine competence. I feel ashamed for being weak, so I hide my weakness behind an air of superiority, especially intellectual superiority. To get an advantage over rivals I try to impress others by boasting that I'm tough or smart or powerful. I try hustling, bluffing and conning to see if there are any takers, knowing that I can only fake it. I make a display of whatever strength I believe others will buy. I manipulate the politics of the home and office to convince myself that I'm strong. This gives me an advantage over people who play by the rules.

But the biggest advantage I can get is the power of government. With The Modern Parental State on my side I can override the stifling rules of the establishment. I no longer have to feel oppressed, weak or inferior. The State will enable me to compete for power and influence and defeat my rivals. Of course, the most obvious rivals against me and other radical liberals are the establishment villains: the rich and powerful, the capitalists and imperialists. These are the people who threaten me. They are the ones I must defeat. I rebel against them because they deny me, limit me, expose my weakness, reveal my cheating, hold me accountable, and scold me when I break the rules and violate boundaries. I rebel against them because I know that they use force to exploit the poor, the weak and the downtrodden, and they wage wars against the innocent. Less obvious rivals are the people who are simply competent and play by the rules, people with character and integrity. I feel secretly ashamed and guilty in comparison to these people, because I cheat and manipulate and they don't. They accomplish things with real skills through fair dealing. Sometimes I don't want to believe these people are real. I suspect that they are cheating too, because you can't really make it playing straight.

But they will not prevail regardless of how they play the game. With the power of laws passed by The Modern Parental Legislature, I and my liberal comrades will overwhelm Big Business, Big Corporations, Big Military, and all of the Big Men who pull the levers of power. We, the original little guys, will conquer these big adults and regulate everyone else. With the power of the state, other radical liberals and I will be victorious in the classical oedipal drama: as we vanquish the oppressive and dangerous father/king, we will free ourselves and others to enjoy whatever sexual, aggressive and acquisitive satisfactions we please. The strict rules of traditional conscience will no longer bind us like shackles. Acting like snotty spoiled brats will become legitimate. Instead of an authoritarian and punitive father, the new state will be a permissive and indulgent mother who urges us to do whatever feels good to us. A new gratifying morality, that of the radical liberal agenda, will replace the old restrictive morality: under the entitlements of positive rights, the State will ensure everyone's material welfare, provide for everyone's healthcare, protect everyone's self-esteem, resolve everyone's envy and jealousy, excuse everyone's bad behavior, eliminate life's risks and responsibilities, correct everyone's social and political disadvantage, educate every citizen, eliminate all class distinctions, and create a society of universal love. A Modern Parental Judiciary will enforce laws arising from this new morality of obligation. In my and my colleagues' identification with this grand collective architecture, we will feel as noble and superior and powerful as the State. In that affiliation, we will find our true identity.

46

Radical Deficits in the Juvenile and Adolescent Eras

Adolescent man, in all his sensitivity to the ideal, is easily exploited by promises of counterfeit millennia, easily taken in by the promise of a new and arrogantly exclusive identity.

Erik Erikson

Radical Confession from the Industry Era

In my grade school years I learned more about life inside and outside of my family home. I observed how people relate to and influence each other. I saw people buy, sell, trade and borrow things. I learned about earning money and about having it, saving it, spending it and owing it. I learned that I am supposed to respect people's rights and do most things by mutual consent, so both sides of a transaction are satisfied. I learned that I am supposed to acquire certain skills so I can be self-reliant and cooperate effectively with others. I learned that I should be industrious, responsible and reliable and that I should negotiate and compromise when necessary. I learned that hard work is a virtue and that I have to persevere in my efforts and tolerate frustration to be successful. I learned that I should be considerate of others and take care that I don't cause accidental harm to them. I learned that I should be honest and straightforward and that I should follow certain rules and be respectful toward certain authorities and institutions. I learned what is supposed to be right and wrong, fair and unfair, lawful and criminal. I learned that I should be charitable toward people who are disadvantaged. I learned about religion and its role in making us do good things instead of bad things.

I learned all of this by the time I became an adolescent, but given the defects in my development, I could not make these principles my own. I decided instead that getting control over others was still a better way to get what I wanted than relating by mutual consent, cooperating voluntarily, acting virtuously and respecting the rights of others. Of course, I could be fair and do the right thing as long as acting in that manner helped me to get others to do what I wanted. I would cooperate with people and respect their rights, and even be very generous, if it suited my purposes. I would work hard and be honest and act responsibly if doing so eventually allowed me to manipulate people.

I decided on this approach to life for good reason. When I started grade school I was already suffering from the painful events of my first six years. Inwardly I felt mistrustful, fearful and sad. I felt needy and even desperate for something or someone to comfort me. Despite having some abilities, I felt ineffective, ashamed, angry, guilty and inferior. I would try to hide these feelings from myself and others. But I had them anyway because I had never had a secure attachment to my mother or other caretakers. I had never received the love, attention, affection, protection, empathy and discipline that I needed for my soul as much as I needed food and water for my body. I felt angry about this deprivation because it violated my right to be nurtured as a precious child of loving parents. But I also felt guilty about feeling so angry. I felt ashamed and inferior about the deprivation I suffered because it could only mean there was something very wrong with me. I felt ineffective because there was nothing I could do to quiet my torment.

I had to find some way to defend myself against this pain, but I couldn't be honest about the feelings themselves because then I would appear whiny, self-pitying, angry and demanding, and others would then disapprove of me and reject me. Sometime during my grade school years I realized that getting control over other people quieted my anxiety and neediness and lessened my sadness. *I knew that I was supposed to relate to others by mutual agreement, but I didn't trust that kind of relating, and I didn't want to relate in that manner anyway. I was angry about the way things had been in my life. I didn't want to be mutual. In my grade school years I realized more clearly that if I could somehow get control over people, and even intimidate and dominate them, then I could feel effective, confident and superior, not ineffective, desperate and helpless. Getting control became a major ambition, and manipulating others became the means to that end. It was usually easier to manipulate peers, but eventually I learned to manipulate adults too.*

My grade school years, like everyone's, were marked by childish rivalries and competitions over who was most likeable, popular, cute, smart, funny or athletic. I spent a lot of time in these battles. I would side with one or two friends against others or join a clique in a petty rivalry. I would divide people into good guys and bad guys, people I could like and people I could hate, and I would act scornfully toward the ones I hated. I would put on airs and pretend I was superior in order to impress others and make myself feel good. I often felt envious and jealous and afraid of humiliation, but I would hide these feelings by pretending I didn't care or claiming I had more advantages and friends than I really had. To cope with feeling envious and inferior I would denigrate others and ridicule what they had. Sometimes I would try to project an image of perfection, but I knew it was phony. I found that lying was very useful because it helped me get away with things I wasn't supposed to do and maneuver people into doing what I wanted. Lying could make me look good and make others look bad. I would lie to get accepted. I would lie to get exempted from duties. I discovered that friendships can be fleeting and loyalties temporary, and I would change friends and loyalties to gain social advantages. I would get furious when I thought I was put down or snubbed. When I convinced myself that the wrongs against me were severe, I would get revenge by saying or writing bad things about the people who wronged me so I could cause them harm. In the course of this struggle, I came to believe that I was doing what I had to do to feel good. I even created my own morality to support this effort: I decided that whatever got me what I wanted was right and fair and that what others did to oppose me was wrong and unfair. I saw the world as an adversarial place in which you fight to get what you want, compete for status and position, and battle against others who want to put you down and elevate themselves.

By projecting my own hang-ups into this world, I created a theater in which I could act out the dramas of my early childhood: I could feel rejected, neglected, deprived, cheated, abused, fearful, hateful, vindictive and victorious all over again, this time on a larger stage. To expand the players in these dramas, I added peers, teachers and neighbors to my old cast of parents and siblings. I would split the world into victims and villains, and sometimes add a hero to the mix. I usually identified myself as a victim and avoided at all costs looking like a villain. Whenever something went wrong it was always someone else's fault. Sometimes I would imagine myself as a hero rescuing others whom I saw as victims. I could feel hurt and sad and angry over whatever real or imagined wrongs and injustices I could find, and then feel good about getting revenge. I would discover a way to punish people I hated for rejecting or ignoring me or being better off than I was. Sometimes I would hit them or steal from them or try to spoil their relationships with others. I would do these things to even the score that I kept in my head as a victim.

Seeing others as victims and villains helped me to defend against the pain that still tormented me from my early years. Pitying victims with whom I identified gratified my wish to pity myself for all the deprivation I had suffered. I would look for pathetic persons so I could enjoy vicariously the pity they received for their suffering. Because I was selfish, greedy and hateful in my own heart, I looked for villains on whom I could project those traits and then pretend I didn't have them. I could feel offended by others' selfishness and deny my own. With this deception I would convince myself that others were the evil ones, not I, and then I could feel noble and good. Damning others lessened the shame, guilt and self-hate that still haunted me from my earlier years. I could hate them instead of myself and condemn them for being vicious and callous. I could blame others to avoid feeling responsible and accountable. I would misunderstand or misstate the actions and intentions of others so I could collect injustices and feel hurt and victimized. In damning villains for exploiting people I could deny that I was manipulating people. I learned to be ruthless while appearing innocent, devious while appearing truthful, obstructive while appearing helpful. When I felt genuinely sorry for victims I could see myself as caring, understanding and generous. When I felt sympathy for victims I also felt sympathy for myself.

By the end of the juvenile years I had come to the conclusion that life is a pretty grim affair. I decided that the world is a harsh place where villains prey on victims, and victims hope for a hero who will take care of them and vanquish the villains. In my perception of this world I decided that getting power and control over others was the best thing I could do for myself. With power I would turn the tables on the villains and keep them from exploiting and depriving me. I would manipulate and exploit them instead, take what I want from them, and get revenge against them. In retrospect I see that these juvenile dramas were rehearsals for the political battles of adult life. They were early versions of bigger wars to come.

The Radical Confession from the Identity Era

No one really understood the pain of my first twelve years or my efforts to defend against it. My parents didn't pick up on the fact that I was struggling and needed help. Because of my cover-up and their indifference, no one helped me to overcome my basic mistrust of life and relationships. No one helped me to overcome the fear and anger and insecurity left over from those early years. As I became a teenager I still felt like a victim in a world of victims and villains, just as I had in my grade school years. No one helped me to see things otherwise, so learning how to manipulate people continued to look like the best thing I could do for myself.

This choice caused problems for me because traditional American culture has different values. I was now an adolescent, and that meant that more was expected of me. Because I was older, smarter and stronger, I was expected to behave in a more mature manner than I had as a juvenile. I was expected to be more self-directing and more effective in what I did. I was expected to be more responsible, accountable and cooperative and to renounce my childish dependency. I was not supposed to whine and complain. I was supposed to show greater respect for others and to relate by mutual agreement and not by making demands. I was supposed to earn more of what I got, and not think I was entitled to it. I was supposed to follow traditional rules. I was expected to be optimistic, willing to help, and motivated by good will and good purpose when dealing with others. Everyone assumed that as I became more dependable I would be granted greater freedom. It was assumed that I would learn a balance between freedom to do what I wanted for myself and obligations to do what I should for others.

All of this good behavior was supposed to provide me with a certain identity in this phase of my life, one that fits an historic ideal in American culture. I was supposed to become an individuated person: a self-directing initiator of action, a budding adult who takes care of himself and cooperates with others. It was assumed that I would become an effective, responsible and accountable citizen. But I wasn't up to it. I was too insecure to become autonomous and mutual. I didn't want to have to rely on myself or cooperate voluntarily with others. I didn't want to have to be objective about the world; I wanted to think wishfully about how things might be. I didn't want to have to protect myself from harm; I wanted to be reckless. I wanted to indulge myself and deny the consequences. I didn't want to conform to rules; I wanted to break the rules I didn't like. I didn't want to listen to the voice of conscience. I made up excuses for myself. I lied to get what I wanted. I didn't want to earn happiness through pride in good behavior and solid achievement; it was easier to rationalize my failures. To feel happy I did whatever seemed satisfying at the moment. I abused drugs, got drunk, broke curfews, cheated on tests, skipped class, got credit for not attending, got paid for what I didn't do, and kept money and items loaned to me. If I needed something badly enough and couldn't pay for it, I would steal it. If I got somebody pregnant, too bad, it was not my problem. If I got pregnant I got an abortion. As I progressed through the teen years I learned better ways to blame and avoid being blamed. I could always see myself as a victim and the other guy as a villain. When I looked around, I could find other victims like myself to pity, and I could always find villains to blame.

The Epiphany of Politics

In my middle and late teens I had an awakening: I discovered the world of politics. In grade school I had heard about Democrats and Republicans, but I didn't pay much attention. Then, high school politics and the dramas of national elections every few years made the subject relevant. During election campaigns candidates accused and blamed each other and complained that people were suffering unjustly. They argued about who was victimized by whom. Issues of power, control and manipulation were hotly debated. When I became intrigued by these contests, I began to transfer my own feelings about being victimized into political terms. By the time I turned twenty, I held strong opinions on political matters. The politics of victimization had special appeal for me, and I quickly became passionate about liberal positions. I saw that individualism is the philosophy of rich and selfish people, and collectivism is the philosophy of social justice. I learned from political campaigns that conservatives rape the environment for profit and that Big Corporations and the American military conspire against innocent nations to dominate their governments, confiscate their wealth, and leave the people starving in rags while working in capitalist factories for pennies. I learned from my classmates and college professors that such evil deeds would be banished under a compassionate liberal government committed to the poor, the oppressed and the downtrodden.

These messages resonated deeply with the emotional undercurrents of my life. I found that my early traumas were echoed in political rhetoric. I learned that millions of other victims have been and still are neglected, deprived and abused. I learned that powerful interests exploit the disadvantaged in an uncaring world of fear and hopelessness. Heartless businessmen enslave helpless workers in sweat shops. Populations everywhere are kept impoverished and politically impotent under the yoke of profit seeking predators. Yet, in all of this misery hope was still alive. Modern liberal intellectuals dedicated to rescuing the world's victims had been working for decades to overcome these evils and bring truth and justice to the world. They understood that the ills of mankind are due to faulty economic, social and political conditions. If given the opportunity, these brilliant men and women would create a new society based on liberal principles. In this society the conditions of human suffering would disappear.

These and other ideas were part of a new world and a new worldview that I learned in my late teens. They were ideas with which I could deeply identify. Political wars were a part of this world. Each contest was a drama of good and evil in which noble heroes battled wicked villains on behalf of innocent victims. In this world I found a new home for my own dramas. I found a world ready-made for my transferences. I could easily be a victim or hero in this world; my parents and other early caretakers were the cold and unfeeling capitalists or predatory imperialists. The deprivation and exploitation of victims in the world at large recalled what I had suffered as a child. Modern liberals were the knights in shining armor in this drama. They were the new messiahs whose superior intellectual power would vanquish the predators and bring salvation to the masses. I and others like me were entranced by the prospects for a liberal revolution: an ultimate political judgment day would redeem the world from the persecutors and install a true utopia.

In this cosmic drama I had found an ideal that would inspire my fidelity for a lifetime. I saw immediately that this new worldview had substance, coherence, integrity. The world finally made sense to me. The future was clear as well. A time of political reckoning would come soon. Modern collectivism would prove to be the answer to man's quest for justice. Even more, my immersion in this world would give me relief from my neurosis: I could project my personal agonies into a universal morality play. I could believe that I was anxious and depressed because I empathized with the suffering of others, and not because of my own defects or failures or the deprivations I suffered in the first few years of my life. I could attribute all of the bitterness and hatred in my heart to the terrible wrongs inflicted by villains on victims. I could feel my passions without owning their neurotic nature or their origins in my own history. In my newly discovered political world there were evil men to blame and vilify, terrible wrongs to avenge, and despicable rivals to battle and defeat. In the joy of hating I could feel self-righteous. In my contempt for tradition I could feel superior. In the grandeur of liberal insights I could enjoy conceit. These attitudes invigorated my soul and eliminated my feelings of inadequacy. By directing my hostility toward others and away from me, radical liberalism protected me from self-hate. Raging at villains in the present even allowed me to spare the neglectful caretakers of my past.

These weren't the only benefits. Feeling victimized justified my attitude of entitlement; I could act out my impulses without feeling guilty. Being promiscuous meant I was rebelling against the establishment's sexual repression. Having an abortion affirmed my right to privacy. Being violent at political rallies meant I was justly furious with the ruthless capitalists who were dominating the world. Destroying property and yelling profanities in public were not irrational fits; they were acts of civil disobedience and outbursts of revolutionary fervor. I and those who joined me in such orgies were not to be condemned or arrested for battery, trespass, property damage or disorderly conduct. We were to be praised instead, because our tantrums expressed our empathy for the world's victims: we were feeling their pain.

Bonding with others in the spirit of modern liberalism quieted old fears of isolation and loneliness. Belonging to a new political family lifted my mood and calmed my anxiety. I no longer felt abandoned. I united with others in sympathy for the downtrodden and rage at the establishment. We bonded in vows of revenge against political oppressors that stifle freedom, brutal armies that dominate populations, and predatory corporations that rig markets and fix prices. We got high on the grandeur of our vision. Getting aggressive in the political world was a high all its own. Our noble goals expanded our egos. We were no longer insignificant; we were the new liberal elites creating the future of the world. As we dwelled on the intellectual and moral superiority of our beliefs we felt justified in our arrogance. We felt no shame; humiliation was a pain of the past. We became political snobs. Our goals were not just grandiose; they were truly grand. In our many expansive moments we saw a new and benevolent world government whose awesome power would bring peace and justice to all. To rid the world of evil we would bring down the capitalist predators. To make the world happy we would inform the masses as to what was good for them and regulate their lives for their benefit. We knew, of course, that many would resist our plans, but we also knew that the power of government would persuade our opponents to cooperate with us. We would use such force willingly and without guilt because the nobility of our purpose, to remake society, would justify the use of any means available. After all, we were fighting a heroic war against the world's evils. Under the excuse of election campaign zeal we would disrupt our opponents' rallies, lie about their goals and smear their reputations. If we felt especially vicious we would slash their tires, deface their offices, harass their families and falsify election ballots. These efforts alone were empowering. We felt strong, noble, lovable, justified. We were destiny's children— and assured of victory.

Modern Liberalism as Personal Salvation

My discovery of modern collectivism was not just a revelation; it was a personal salvation. In discovering liberalism I acquired an identity and even a life: I was no longer confused about who I was, how I would take care of myself, or what life should mean to me. All of that was resolved. I now belonged to an elite group of enlightened thinkers dedicated to freedom and justice. The rise of The Modern Parental State would provide everyone, including me, with economic security, social status and political significance. I could personally identify with the state's power over selfish villains whose greed and cruel indifference had so deeply hurt me and other victims of the world. Together we, the radical liberal minds, would oppose the villains, frustrate their goals, and deprive them just as they had deprived us. We, the world's new heroes, would be the dominant ones, not the villains. We would seize their authority and render them powerless, then punish them for their bad deeds and destroy their false sovereignty. We would overthrow the strict social taboos that inhibit self-expression. In the permissiveness of sexual liberation and moral relativism we would gratify ourselves without guilt or shame. As newly adopted children of The Modern Parental State we would not have to face the burdens of self-reliance or the risks of self-direction. The need to right old wrongs by violent protest would justify our aggressions against an evil establishment. We would protect the environment from rapacious industry. Distributive justice would gratify our acquisitive impulses. Equal social status and political authority would create a classless, multicultural society. Equality for all would eliminate envy. As society's savior The Modern Parental State would finally guarantee the security that I and others like me had always longed for. The new State's benevolence directed to the noblest ends would abolish the torments that still haunted us. By projecting onto villains all that was bad and defective within us, we would deny our defects: only what was good and right and strong would remain within us. The villains would be the bad and defective ones.

All of these ideas of radical liberalism resonated with my personal history and fortified my understanding of the human condition: it was now more apparent than ever that the world consists of victims, villains and heroes, and that survival in this world depends on seizing the levers of power. I found a home for this understanding in The Modern Parental State. I was not alone in my struggle. Others, too, had been seeking power to manipulate and control in order to fight oppression, vent aggression and overcome deprivation. By continuing a major theme of victimization, self-pity, bitterness and blame from my earliest childhood, I gradually acquired the worldview of a radical liberal. On the threshold of adulthood, my personal development finally found direction.

47

Ideal and Reality in Radical Liberalism

The formation of a world community under world government is needed to eliminate the inequitable distribution of resources and wealth that has allowed the rich nations to dominate and exploit the poor nations.

Mortimer Adler

The Consolidation of Radical Beliefs

The last hundred pages have reviewed the principles of radical liberalism, first as a series of propositions and then as a lengthy first-person confession. The latter is, of course, a composite declaration, parts of which characterize essentially all radical liberals, but the totality of which characterizes no one in particular. Taken individually, the propositions reflect nearly verbatim quotations from various liberal texts, paraphrases of liberal campaign rhetoric, personal pronouncements by avowed liberals, and inferences based on knowledge of what a radical liberal must have experienced in the past, given his behavior in the present. If this shoe or some part of it fits a particular radical's mind, then he is invited to wear it although it can be safely assumed that nearly all will reject the invitation. Benign liberals will find themselves represented only weakly in the radical confession. Most liberals will find themselves at various points on the continuum between benign and radical positions.

The radical liberal has typically consolidated his political beliefs by the time he reaches his mid-twenties. By early adulthood he has expanded the neurosis of his childhood into a personal and political identity. He has become a radical liberal by discovering a present-day universe of victims and villains that echoes his own early traumas. Projecting his developmental deficits into a political arena distracts him from his torments and vents his anger, but his ongoing sympathies for the poor and oppressed and his identification with the abandoned and downtrodden are the legacies of his own childhood injuries. His passions for political reform represent his continuing efforts to heal wounds first inflicted when he was very young and compounded over the remainder of his childhood. *Most of the time, he can ignore the true nature and origins of those wounds. Immersed in the radical goals of the present, he can deny the real causes of his fury and believe that he is a crusader for justice on behalf of victims, not a troubled person defending himself against his own history.* In fact, he can persuade himself that he, too, is a victim of economic, social and political injustice just like the victims he means to protect. With this idea in mind he can feel especially grateful for radical liberalism's solution to everyone's suffering: the imminent coming of a society that guarantees security from cradle to grave by regulating and taxing its citizens from cradle to grave. As a true believer, the radical liberal is convinced that by damning capitalist villains, seizing the reigns of political power, and directing the lives of the people, liberal geniuses will create a monument to human compassion: The Modern Parental State will restore justice to the world and finally bring good lives to all.

The Liberal Agenda as an Evil

Unfortunately the history of radical liberalism's attempts to fulfill this promise has been one of stunning failure. The radical agenda by any other name—communism, socialism, collectivism, progressivism, welfarism—has invariably resulted in large-scale social decline. The reasons are not hard to find. Once translated into social policy, radical liberalism immediately comes into conflict with the defining characteristics of human nature: its capacities for rational choice, will, agency, autonomy, initiative, purpose, recognition, morality, industry, identity and competence.

It then proceeds to undermine the essential virtues of civilized freedom: good will, good purpose, self-reliance, cooperation, mutuality and accountability. Further, the radical agenda violates all of the rights at the core of ordered liberty, presumes to repeal the laws of economics, condemns the traditions essential to civil society, and applauds banality as it snubs excellence. Unearned rewards and unpunished crimes endorsed by the radical agenda corrupt the people's sense of justice. In support of secularism, the agenda attacks the religious foundations of morality and altruism and replaces faith in God with idolatry of government.

Radical liberalism thus assaults the foundations of civilized freedom, and for that reason it is a genuine evil. Further, given its irrational goals, coercive methods and historical failures, and given its perverse effects on human development, there can be no question of the radical agenda's madness. Only an irrational agenda would advocate a systematic destruction of the foundations on which ordered liberty depends. Only an irrational man would want the state to run his life for him rather than create secure conditions in which he can run his own life. Only an irrational agenda would deliberately undermine the citizen's growth to competence by having the state adopt him. Only irrational thinking would trade individual liberty for government coercion, then sacrifice the pride of self-reliance for welfare dependency. Only an irrational man would look at a community of free people cooperating by choice and see a society of victims exploited by villains.

Ideal and Reality in Radical Liberalism

In a competent society the principles of ordered liberty guide the citizen throughout the life cycle. They inform him and his children and the community of the rules by which human beings make good lives for themselves. *Because the rights, laws and duties of the competent society are all of a piece and reflect the bipolar nature of man, the entire ensemble of individual citizen, family, community, society and institutions forms a coherent whole in support of life, liberty, social cooperation and the pursuit of happiness.* Under the rules that govern ordered liberty, the human organism and its physical and social environment are in harmony to the maximum extent possible given the turbulent nature of man.

By contrast, a society organized under radical liberalism comes into immediate conflict with the bipolar nature of man and with the rights, laws and duties needed for human beings to live in peace and freedom. Rather than coordinating the life of the individual citizen with the institutions of his society, radical liberalism sets individuals and institutions into perpetual conflict with each other through its rhetoric of class warfare and victimization, its violations of personal freedom through confiscatory taxation and invasive regulation, its attacks on family integrity, and the endless bungling of government bureaucracy.

To eradicate this madness requires two insights and an educational campaign. The first insight consists in the realization that radical liberalism is in fact a form of madness. That proposition has been argued throughout the present work. The second insight consists in a showing of the myriad ways in which liberal madness manifests itself. That insight, too, has been illustrated in this book with numerous examples. The educational campaign, if implemented, would attempt to disseminate these insights and rebut the madness of liberal policies. To that end, it is important to note the extent to which radical liberalism's avowed purposes diverge from its real world effects. In the following paragraphs, the liberal agenda's stated or implicit goals and claimed virtues are briefly contrasted with their actual consequences.

Rights

The radical agenda argues that positive rights to essential goods and services for all citizens are needed to correct the economic, social and political injustices that plague the disadvantaged. Radical liberalism asserts that entitlements to certain welfare benefits together with rights against various forms of discrimination are needed to remedy "structural poverty" and the social adversities of racial and other minorities. A frequently proposed liberal remedy for the problem of poverty is the right of all citizens to government funded healthcare. The need for medical treatment is said to be so essential to the making of a good life that access to it should not be denied because of limited assets; the state should provide medical care to all who need it. But a similar argument implies that the state should also provide food, clothes, houses and motor vehicles to all who need them, because these goods are at least as essential to the making of a good life as medical care is. Simple iteration of this argument leads to the further conclusion that *all* essential goods and services should be provided by the state. But history has already passed judgment on arrangements of this type: economic and social wellbeing in socialist and communist economies under positive rights is invariably inferior to that found in capitalist economies under negative rights. It is only guaranteed *individual liberty rights,* not collective entitlement rights, that have enabled millions of disadvantaged persons to overcome material hardship, acquire what they need and enhance their social status. The record is also clear on the fact that liberal entitlement rights have damaged the poor by treating them like helpless children, rewarding their dependency and perpetuating their poverty. The devastating effects of welfare programs on the black family in America illustrate the point. The overall result of these policies has been a drastic encroachment on the structure of liberty that destabilizes social order, reduces material wealth, infantilizes the people, makes civil servants out of producers, and pits classes of citizens against each other.

Freedom and Autonomy

Radical liberalism argues that various injustices such as ignorance, poverty, discrimination, political oppression and economic exploitation prevent the exercise of individual freedom and autonomy, even in an apparently free society. The radical agenda recommends major government programs to remedy these injustices:

- Government education to end ignorance
- Government housing, food and healthcare programs along with unemployment, disability and retirement programs to end poverty
- Anti-discrimination and civil rights laws to protect against age, race, gender and job discrimination
- Progressive political and labor movements to counter political and corporate oppression
- Government taxation, regulation, wage, hiring and affirmative action programs to eliminate economic exploitation of racial minorities and the poor
- Government laws permitting abortion to end discrimination against women's right to choose

Changes in societal attitudes on various issues compliment these official programs: the liberal concept of autonomy promotes increasing sexual freedom as an extension of the "sexual revolution." Traditional concepts of marriage and family are broadened and disconnected from their religious and ethnic underpinnings. All of these positions have claimed increased freedom and autonomy to be among their major benefits.

When translated into practical consequences, however, policies based on these concepts have been found to have very harmful effects: all liberal programs against ignorance, poverty, discrimination, political oppression and economic exploitation, when enacted into law, provide only pseudo-freedom and pseudo-autonomy at best, and severely compromise authentic freedom and autonomy at worst. Government schools, for example, are notorious for failing to educate students, for "dumbing down" performance standards, and for governmental barriers against citizen's access to alternative programs, especially those in private schools. Aside from their disastrous economic and social effects, government anti-poverty initiatives, including aid to dependent children, federal housing projects and Great Society programs, have created crippling dependency and drastically undermined the autonomy of recipients. Anti-discrimination laws in particular have generated an entire industry of injustice-collecting that exacerbates class warfare, promotes spurious litigation, buries the businessman in regulations, escalates the cost of producing goods and services, and reinforces liberalism's victim-villain paradigm. Government welfare programs subsidizing food, housing and healthcare benefits increase the burdens of taxation and regulation as they enhance the power of bureaucrats over the people. Progressive political propaganda trumpets the endless entitlements and vanishing responsibilities of the collectivized citizen. Sexual permissiveness erodes public morality. Simplistic abortion rhetoric blurs all valid distinctions between the rights of the mother and the rights of the fetus at various stages of pregnancy and varying degrees of risk to each. Liberal notice-to-parents-policies diminish the authority of parents over pregnant daughters and substitute the state as arbiter of first resort in questions of abortion in minors. Liberal assaults on the family as society's chief socializing and civilizing institution have eroded its structure and increased the incidence of psychopathology in the general population as more and more children are deprived of the early nurturing needed for growth to competence.

Clearly, none of these real-world effects promotes anything that can be rightly called freedom or autonomy. In fact, the liberal agenda first attacks the foundations of ordered freedom and its requirements for self-reliance and mutual consent, and then replaces them with the pseudo-freedom of the welfare state. The citizen inspired by ordered liberty disciplines himself, relies on himself and cooperates by mutual consent. The citizen inspired by radical liberalism indulges himself, depends on the state and demands to be given whatever the state thinks he is owed. The authentic autonomy demanded by ordered liberty is principled self-direction. The pseudo-autonomy of radical liberalism is the playground insouciance of the child. The society of ordered liberty holds all of its citizens accountable for behavior that violates laws and traditional moral standards. The society of radical liberalism holds no one accountable for fear of being judgmental. The few exceptions to this rule include the "rich," the "powerful," "capitalists," and anyone who opposes liberal dogma.

Economic Equality

Radical liberalism promises economic equality, or a best approximation to it, for the general population. The declared goal is to eliminate disparities in wealth by forced transfers of material goods and services from citizens who have more of them to those who have less, but transfers of this type have never improved the long term economic wellbeing of recipients nor corrected economic inequality in the society. Instead, the most prominent effects of such efforts are gross violations of liberty rights and widespread dependency on government. In a *free* society with vigorously enforced property rights, inequalities of wealth are both expectable and large because citizens differ greatly in their motivation to seek wealth, their ability to produce it and their willingness to preserve it. These differences represent normal variations in human ambition and ability. Notwithstanding these natural tendencies, however, and despite the fact that inequalities of this type evolve by mutual consent, radical liberalism regards them as unjust and seeks to "correct" them by confiscating material goods from the "rich" and giving them to the "poor." But these transfers are the equivalent of robbery; they violate constitutional property rights and rights to equal treatment under the law. Such injustices are the inevitable effects of economic policies under modern liberalism. Fundamental rights are always breached in its programs, and so are the traditional standards of morality and just desert on which such rights are based. To add insult to injury, these breaches also corrupt the character of the people by reducing them to wards of the state.

An equally important source of madness in the politics of equality is the idea that inequality is somehow wrong in itself. As Kekes remarks, it is *insufficiency*, not inequality, that causes suffering and is therefore an evil to be remedied. (Kekes 1997) If Jones makes a million dollars per year and Smith makes a tenth of that amount, their incomes are vastly unequal, but no reasonable person would claim that Smith's income is insufficient to make a good life nor that his economic inferiority entitles him to anything from Jones. Inequality *per se* is thus not an injustice, but the liberal mind's pathological envy makes him think it is. Without such envy, the sense of injustice attached to inequality disappears. When envy is so intense as to demand redress by government, however, it can do great damage. It is then a symptom to be cured in treatment or limited in its perverse effects by law, not an evil to be attacked by taking wealth from some and giving it to others. Transfers of this type are in fact a form of legalized theft, and they set a criminal example for the population at large. They create an evil where none existed before.

Ironically, when *economic* welfare programs do get enacted, their subsidies to the poor actually increase disparities in *social* status between self-reliant citizens who produce real wealth and transfer recipients whom the state treats like helpless children. In the real world where social status is reckoned, these programs demean both types of citizens: the productive worker is demoted to an indentured servant while the welfare recipient is reduced to a dependent child nursed by the state. The servants can at least feel noble in their sacrifice, while the recipients are viewed as lazy parasites. The disparity in social status between the two groups widens as the self-esteem of members in both groups falls.

True to form, radical liberalism assumes that the man who actually has insufficient wealth for a good life is in that predicament because he has been victimized. That may, of course, be true if someone has stolen from him or deliberately injured him so he can't work. But insufficiency has many and varied causes, most of which have nothing to do with victimization in the radical liberal sense. Economic insufficiency in the life of an *individual* is most often due to his own bad judgment, or lack of industry, or in some cases to bad luck, but economic insufficiency in a *society* of able citizens is always due to government interference with their freedom to produce as much as they need. Government interference in this process takes many forms—excessive taxation and regulation are prime examples—and the goal of economic equality is high on the list of rationales for taxation. In fact, government takings of wealth for any reason always result in less incentive to produce and less capital to invest. The inevitable consequence of such policies is an overall decline in the nation's wealth: the radical agenda's interference on behalf of economic equality thus causes insufficiency on a national, not just personal, scale.

Distributive Justice

Closely related to the ideal of economic equality is radical liberalism's ideal of distributive justice. This ideal insists that material and social inequalities are evil in themselves and should be eradicated or drastically diminished. This essentially communist goal envisions a classless society of people who have approximately equal amounts of material wealth. The real world fallacies of these ideals have been proven historically and argued for decades. Of greatest importance is the fact that any attempts to distribute economic, social or political goods according to government quotas requires the threat of physical force or the use of it, and this requirement violates the moral principles and legal rights at the core of ordered liberty. Such attempts also violate the laws of economics: forced redistribution of wealth drastically alters supply and demand dynamics, reduces work incentives, distorts resource allocation, and short-circuits production and consumption signals provided by free market prices. Material shortages, not the promised prosperity for all, are the inevitable result. History validates the economic fact that prosperity for all citizens can develop only in free markets under strictly enforced property rights. As already noted, however, violations of rights and the laws of economics are not the only evils of redistribution. Use of the state's power for that purpose sets people against each other in a war over who gets what and how much from whom. To seek distributive or social justice is to invite an authoritarian government that abolishes economic freedom and creates social conflict.

Social Equality

Radical liberalism promises equality of social status in the general population, a goal just as absurd as the promise of economic equality. One's social status is affected by reputation, gossip, family status, social manners, personal conduct, media reports, membership in admired professions and any number of other factors, not to mention the observer's personal preferences. Because government has little control over how individuals are perceived or treated, its efforts to equalize social status by any means, including forced membership in otherwise exclusive groups, always violate rights of free association. Inevitably, some people will be viewed as the social superiors of others and will be treated accordingly. Attempts to override these natural social ranking processes result in more government perpetrated injustices.

In addition, the facts of human development make it possible to rate the *competence* of human beings by measuring the extent to which they have achieved certain developmental milestones. By these measures the population shows wide variation, i.e., *inequality,* in occupational and social skill, self-reliance, cooperation, moral integrity, relevant knowledge, coping ability and an infinite variety of other traits in addition to the ability to acquire wealth. In terms of these traits, some human beings are clearly the superiors, not the equals, of others. But inequalities of this type are simply inevitable variations that characterize the human condition, not injustices to be remedied by the state. Indeed, the only inequalities that *should be* outlawed by government are political and legal inequalities; they are the only ones incompatible with ordered liberty. Legal equality means that no one is above the law, exempt from its rules, or entitled to special favors from the law. Political equality means that the one-citizen-one-vote rule holds for all citizens and that no one is *lawfully* entitled to more political influence than his fellows. The liberal agenda actually *causes* political and legal inequality with its entitlements to unearned wealth, prohibitions against membership exclusion and affirmative action programs, among others.

Pluralism

In their commitment to pluralism, modern liberals claim an ideal of inclusiveness: social policy should accommodate varied races, ethnic groups and cultures, and accept their alternative moralities, lifestyles and political visions. The history of American immigrant assimilation is cited in support of this ideal, and any opposition to it is promptly condemned as bigotry. In fact, however, serious problems arise with the liberal version of inclusiveness whenever its tolerance for diversity ends up excusing would-be citizens from the obligations of liberty. America's success in integrating diverse races, cultures and religions into its social fabric is due precisely to its insistence on the new citizen's respect for the principles of civilized freedom. *America has assimilated immigrants of all stripes only because they are willing and able to commit to the morality, rights, laws and traditions that lie at the heart of its freedoms. All of the earth's races and nearly all of its extant cultures, ethnic groups and traditions have been welcomed in America's borders, but only on the condition that these new pluralisms are added to, and not substituted for, the fundamental principles of liberty.*

Most critical to this process are the liberty rights that protect people, property and promises, but the virtues of self-reliance, mutual consent and moral integrity are implied by those rights and equally important. By insisting on these and other principles basic to ordered liberty, a *rational* pluralism demands that all immigrants to America commit to the rights and duties essential to civilized freedom. By contrast, modern liberalism's *irrational* pluralism passively ignores or actively rejects these principles. In their misguided zeal to respect all lifestyles and anyone's rules for living, radical liberals deny that the ideals on which liberty is based are indeed foundational. As a result, radical liberalism endorses principles that are incompatible with liberty and rejects principles that are essential to it.

This fault is especially apparent in two critical arenas, academia and religion. Despite their claims to openness toward varied ideas, modern liberal intellectuals have proved to be strikingly intolerant in the debate between individualism and collectivism. Faculty members in most colleges and universities, for example, are openly hostile to students who oppose socialist ideals and may even ban them from the academy. In a similar vein, liberal historians have rewritten standard textbooks to extol principles of modern liberalism to the neglect of conflicting views. Matters are no better in the religious arena. A few radical liberals immerse themselves in quasi-religious doctrines of cosmic unity, but most radical liberals are dedicated secularists, if not atheists, who are openly hostile to religion and its contribution to social order. Echoing Marx, modern liberals assert that religion is the opiate of the masses. Not surprisingly, however, this antagonism also makes them hostile to America's origins. It is no accident that the greatest political system in human history was founded by devout Christians on the assumption that its citizens would live by Judeo-

Christian ideals. The ideal of service to one's fellows, for example, is critical not only for its reinforcement of traditional moral commandments but also for its altruistic character. The Christian call to service is the innate human disposition to good will and good purpose made manifest in good works for the benefit of others. In fact, a strong communitarian spirit has always complimented the American spirit of individual liberty, thus reflecting, as any good social policy must, the bipolar nature of man: the ideal of liberty honors individual autonomy while the ideal of service honors the virtue of cooperation.

Universal Love and Compassion

Closely related to modern liberalism's principle of inclusiveness are its ideals of universal love, compassion, peace and brotherhood. Preaching an ethic of acceptance, tolerance, altruism and empathy for all human beings, modern liberalism envisions an international family of citizens united in brotherly affection under a one-world government. Under this vision the universal state will guarantee peace and prosperity for everyone and fuse all previously disparate nations into a global union. Central to this ideal is the assumption that human beings are naturally benevolent and commit evil deeds only when pernicious economic, social and political factors such as poverty, discrimination, ignorance, political oppression and economic exploitation force them to do so. Abolition of these factors by a one-world government will create a world-wide family of benevolent siblings, all of whom take care of each other.

The reality behind this vision of love, compassion, peace and brotherhood is strikingly different. Despite its immersion in sympathy for the disadvantaged, modern liberalism's paradigm of villains and victims teaches the world to whine and complain, promotes envy and blame, encourages anger and outrage, and expends great effort to make designated evildoers feel guilty and ashamed. The radical liberal's vicious rhetoric against villains, its incitement of class warfare, and its use of power to enforce its collectivist policies are anything but loving, compassionate or peaceful, and its use of coercion to achieve its ends contradicts the very definition of altruism.

The liberal attitude is also not empathetic, despite its claims. As noted earlier, the pseudo-empathy of modern liberalism is actually a perversion of the deep and wide ranging insight that defines authentic empathy. Most of what the liberal mind calls empathy is a maudlin pity that is wholly inappropriate to distressed adults precisely because it discourages initiative, invites regression and fosters helplessness. Authentic empathy, by contrast, comprehends not only the suffering of the other but also the particular developmental deficits that handicap him, the actions he must take to overcome his plight, and the growth he must achieve to reach competence. Liberalism's pseudo-empathy is, in fact, a passive substitute for active caretaking; one can easily watch from a distance while government bureaucrats make indiscriminant transfers to recipients. In this and many other effects, collectivism is the opiate of modern liberals.

Anti-war and Anti-violent Attitudes

In its declared commitment to love, peace, compassion, and brotherhood, and in its belief that all problems can ultimately be solved by understanding, acceptance, tolerance and empathy, radical liberalism denies the need for defensive violence and hence the need for war. It is an unfortunate fact of human nature, however, that in all historical times and places, a substantial number of individuals in nearly all populations are driven by intensely criminal motives.[1] These motives give rise to rapists, murderers, thieves, child molesters, terrorists, dictators and other perpetrators of atrocities. Whether they act singly or jointly, it is impossible to defend against such persons without the use of force, including military force when and where it is necessary. Radical liberalism denies this reality for various reasons, the most important of which is denial of its own propensity for hatred and violence. The liberal mind is an angry mind determined to force people into its stereotyped categories but unable to acknowledge that its own political coercion is a form of criminal violence.

A similar mechanism operates in the liberal mind to deny the extent and nature of evil. The criminal motives just mentioned are a subcategory of human destructiveness and are proof in themselves, if any is needed, of the widespread existence of evil. In fact, both science and common sense confirm the fact that the potential for evil is not only pervasive but innate in human biology. [2] Additional observations prove that evil is not caused by social factors. Children who are given enough affection, empathy, love and moral training in their early years can acquire good will and benevolent purpose even under conditions of widespread poverty, ignorance, social turmoil, political oppression and racial and ethnic discrimination. Conversely, children subjected to early emotional neglect, deprivation and abuse are likely to become destructive in the most evil ways no matter how favorable the economic, social and political circumstances in which they are reared.

Thus the standard liberal theory of the social origins of evil is simply wrong and contrary to the evidence. In fact, the most important variable in the control of human evil is the presence of positive relationships at critical periods in the child's life. Even with early developmental trauma and brutal societal turmoil, some children are still able to become benign and even benevolent adults who respect the rights and sovereignty of others. These individuals typically report having benefited at some time in their childhoods from the love, affection, guidance and protection of a relative, friend, teacher or minister. A relationship of this type can provide nurturing and role modeling from which a previously neglected, deprived or abused child can neutralize pathological aggression and internalize healthy images of adult competence, self-reliance and mutuality. These fortunate outcomes may overcome the strongly negative effects of early trauma. In some cases, religion can also play a critical role in rescuing young souls from an antisocial life, and it can play an equally critical role in the emotional salvation of severely traumatized adults. The incorporation of Judeo-Christian or other benevolent religious ideals at any age, along with a passionate identification with and allegiance to a benevolent deity—but not to a coercive government—can transform an otherwise derailed development into a morally competent citizen with good will toward others. In any case, it is a simple empirical fact that economic, social and political conditions can aggravate evil but will not produce it directly without the effects of early emotional trauma.

A striking example of this process is evident in the hatred and violence of radical liberals toward America. As children the vast majority of these people have been raised under favorable economic, social and political conditions, those of middle and upper class American affluence. But they are, by late adolescence, notorious for their venomous speech, intentional damage to property and even criminal battery of innocent citizens. Their rages against alleged capitalist oppression, U.S. imperialism, racial discrimination, economic exploitation and other liberal rants are used to justify their transference hatred of early caretakers, now directed at contemporary political symbols. Neither America's historic liberations of countries dominated by dictators nor its respect for the sovereignty of countries it has defeated in battle has any effect on modern liberal propaganda about imperialism and exploitation. In the radical liberal mind, the victim/villain paradigm is omnipotent against reality.

Environmentalism

Because of our ultimate dependency on the earth's ecosystems for survival, the only rational attitude for human beings toward the environment is a combination of love and respect. These sentiments ought to be similar to those which a child develops toward his mother during his formative years. When her care of him goes well enough, his growing recognition of her personal sovereignty forbids him from callous disregard of her and from any efforts to exploit her. A comparable respect for mother earth and the nurturing she provides would seem to be imperative on self-interest grounds alone; preserving the biosphere on which we depend for survival is clearly in everyone's long-term rational interest. Hence, radical liberalism is appropriately committed to preserving the earth's physical environment. The liberal agenda strongly advocates against any activities that would seriously pollute, damage or destroy its vital systems. But that observation is not the only one that matters.

The liberal agenda's environmental policies become troublesome, not from its goals, but from its efforts to solve pollution problems by relying on government bureaucracies. A few observations are worth making in this regard. First, a substantial part of environmental protection properly depends on the legal enforcement of ordinary property rights. If Smith's factory dumps waste onto land owned by Jones or emits pollutants that contaminate the air breathed by Jones, then Jones' right to use and enjoy his property is violated. Legal remedies attached to that right entitle Jones to use civil or criminal laws to stop Smith's polluting. Similarly, if Smith's factory dumps waste into a river, then riparian rights entitle common owners to stop Smith from polluting the water. If Smith's factory spews pollutants into air that blows over properties owned by other citizens or over publicly held property, then again the government may proceed against Smith to stop him from polluting. Thus, a significant amount of protection against environmental injury can be achieved by the application of property rights, including those that protect publicly held property. In principle and in practice, these protections do not require massive government agencies. Instead, they require strict enforcement of certain rights in relevant federal, state and local jurisdictions.

Based on these considerations, some libertarians argue that for environmental as well as economic reasons, all or nearly all property should be held only privately and not by any government. They assert that the private owner is likely to protect the earth he mines, farms, builds on or lives on because it is in his long-term personal and economic interest to do so. The rational businessman, it is argued, will preserve the environment, first because he also lives in it, and second because exhausting its resources will quickly end his profits. Liberals, by contrast, stand this argument on its head. They argue that callous self-interest and short-term economic interest not only may not preserve the environment but may, and often do, ravage it. They assert that capitalists ruthlessly or carelessly exploit, damage or destroy the environment in their greed for money and power. For that reason, liberals believe that much if not most property should be government owned, because only governments will protect it for the common good.

Problems arise from both sides of this debate because ruthless government officials, not just ruthless capitalists, may and often do, exploit, damage or destroy the environment. There is no question that the private business world has a substantial population of personality and character disorders, especially narcissists and sociopaths, who are callously indifferent to the environment or frankly exploitative in their relations with it, just as they are in their relations with other persons. The worst members in this subset are essentially criminal characters who exploit, despoil and mutilate precious ecosystems in the same manner as those who exploit, despoil and mutilate other persons: they defile people and things for the satisfaction of being destructive. The man who savagely beats his wife and children to injury or death has counterparts in businessmen who ravage the earth to satisfy hateful impulses and to taste the exhilaration of power over physical systems. Unfortunately, matters are no better in governments. In fact, modern liberalism's appeal to governments for environmental protection is a little like asking the lion to guard the lamb. Government officials seeking power and money are not motivated to protect the earth that sustains them. In fact, the lure of government office tends to select out of the general population those persons who are most intrigued by the exercise of power and most adept at manipulating it for their own benefit. The fact that government policies are decided primarily by the self-interest of such officials should raise doubts about how well they will protect the earth's ecosystems. *In fact, history reveals that governments are the planet's worst environmental polluters and destroyers. It is governments, not private parties, that contaminate the environment directly with discarded military weapons and the waste that develops in their manufacture. It is government officials bribed by business interests who look the other way when private industry violates property and environment laws that should be invoked to protect the nation's private and common property.* For their own gains in money and power, government officials have long been complicit in the spoiling of the environment. Moreover, rational environmental policies are heavily dependent upon environmental science, which can be readily manipulated for political purposes.

Thus, the libertarian's overestimation of the long-term economic reasonableness of the private property owner and the modern liberal's overestimation of the benign nature of government have something in common: narcissists, sociopaths and other character disorders, whether in the public or private sectors, will use and abuse the power of private ownership or the power of government to exploit and even destroy the environment. Note that in both cases the ultimate problem is the failure of law enforcement and government officials to enforce laws designed to protect all kinds of property.

A final observation on environmental policy relates to a more general characteristic of modern liberalism, especially its radical variant. In its childlike demands, the liberal mind seeks a world of cost-free benefits. The radical liberal denies the fact that to choose one alternative in the real world is to forgo another, that tradeoffs attend all real world decisions. The world of environmental policy choice is no different. Radical liberals oppose on-shore and off-shore domestic drilling but object to fuel prices resulting from dependence on foreign oil. They oppose new oil refineries but want higher quantities of cleaner burning fuel mixtures. They want to eliminate petroleum based fuels but oppose nuclear energy. They favor wind-powered electricity but oppose the aesthetic impact of wind-farms on the landscape. They want cheaper and cleaner energy but oppose the environmental effects of geothermal drilling. These examples illustrate the immaturity of the liberal mind. They echo its immaturity in others areas: its self-indulgence, moral permissiveness, search for easy gratification, protest against responsibility and accountability, and belief that The Modern Parental State can and should provide whatever is needed, including ample energy, without significant costs or tradeoffs. Ultimately, provision of sufficient energy in the modern world will involve some compromise with the environment regardless of who produces it. Hopefully those chosen will not jeopardize the long term integrity of its ecosystems.

Education

In keeping with The Modern Parental State's role as caretaker-in-chief, America's public schools are the primary channel through which children are to be prepared for life in contemporary society. Modern liberalism's underlying collectivist philosophy is evident in the content of its school social studies; in the thrust of its sex-education, values assessment and counseling programs; and in the dominance of its teachers unions in hiring, firing and wage negotiations. The enormous amount of taxpayer money used to fund public schools is touted as a measure of education's importance to the nation and the costs of effective teaching, but these claims are not reflected in real world results. Put bluntly, and with rare exceptions, American public education is simply mediocre, and so is the teaching behind it. Not only does public education not prepare a large portion of its students for life in the broader sense, it does not even teach the minimal skills needed to make a living or seek higher learning. Local and national testing at primary and secondary levels reflects the ignorance of public school students and the incompetence of their teachers. The schools themselves are poorly disciplined and often dangerous. Unqualified teachers are removed only with great difficulty. Salary levels are unrelated to job performance, as is tenure. The cost of public education is either unrelated to or inversely proportional to results and always vastly exceeds the costs of comparable or superior private schools. In fact, the most basic function of public schools, to teach the foundations of knowledge and how to learn it, is subordinated to other goals. Instead of dedicating themselves to the student's intellectual growth, for example, liberal teachers now emphasize the protection of self-esteem. In some schools under this policy, marking a student's mistakes with red pencil has been deemed too harsh; using a different color is mandatory in order to make him feel less criticized. Here the modern liberal's neurosis is projected onto the ordinary student and implemented in absurd social policy.

Abortion

Based on a claimed right to privacy, or right to choose, the radical liberal defends the right to abort a fetus at any stage of its intrauterine development, including near-term and full-term gestation. A right to abort can also be argued on the right of dominion over one's own body. On these arguments a pregnant woman has a right to put her own desires concerning her body and its wellbeing before any other competing interests, including any interests or rights alleged on behalf of the fetus. In a rare congruence with liberals, some libertarians view the fetus as a foreign body or parasite in the maternal womb, not as a human being, or proto-human being, toward which protective liberty rights might apply and protective sentiments might be felt. On this view the fetus can be viewed as an intrusion that ought to be removed from a woman's body. (Rothbard 1998) The position that a fetus is a foreign body to be eliminated instead of a developing person to be preserved is clearly easier to take in the early weeks of pregnancy. It is not so easy to take when imaging techniques reveal an increasingly strong resemblance of the fetus to a newborn baby.

A few observations are in order here. First, it is clear that pregnancy and delivery are momentous events from a biological perspective. After sexual intercourse, conception, and full term pregnancy, delivery of a viable baby is the next critical step in fulfilling biology's most important function, that of reproducing the species. This fact makes the birth of a baby one of biology's "default positions." After all, human beings are physically and psychologically constructed to have and raise babies; if they don't have them and raise them, then human life ceases to exist. A second observation recalls that morality is ultimately grounded in the value of human life and the conditions that preserve and promote good lives. Given the fact that birth is the necessary beginning of any good life, most adults believe that doing everything possible to bring a pregnancy to term is a moral imperative, and to abort it without urgent cause is immoral. This is especially true for late-term and full-term abortions. To the vast majority of adults, and especially to those who are competent, the very thought of a late-term or full-term abortion, also known as partial-birth abortion, is horrifying and the moral equivalent of murder. This reaction arises out of the innate human disposition to nurture and protect, but it also recognizes the fetus as a person, or potential person, deserving of certain rights that apply to all other citizens.

These capacities for nurturing, protection and recognition are integral to human reproductive instincts. They are fundamental and powerful when normally developed. But in the radical liberal who adamantly demands full-term abortion, these basic capacities are not normally developed. In his mind the fetus is an impersonal object, a piece of waste or perhaps a parasite to be eliminated from the body and discarded into the sewer or thrown out in the garbage. The absence of nurturing sentiments in such persons, especially the intensely protective sentiments of maternal or parental tenderness, is striking and appalling to the competent mind.

That said, however, the question then arises as to when, if ever, deliberate termination of a pregnancy at one stage or another is morally justified. No general answer can be given to this question. As just noted, the general proposition that *all* abortions are acceptable is contradicted by the understandable abhorrence with which most persons view even mid-term abortion, let alone full-term abortion. The contrary proposition that *no* abortions are acceptable is not tenable either: in the event that a mother's pregnancy seriously threatens her life, for example, there are no grounds on which to claim that the fetus's right to live overrides hers. Based on comparable real life dilemmas it is easy to construct additional exceptions to either generalization: that all abortions are acceptable, or no abortions are acceptable. Accordingly, radical liberalism's demands for unqualified abortion rights are simply irrational.

Feminism

With origins in the Enlightenment and evolution over the past two hundred years, the original feminist movement has sought to extend to women the same blessings of liberty typically enjoyed by free men. Put simply, its stated goal has been to end male dominance and achieve equal freedoms for women in economic, social, sexual, educational, legal and political arenas. By the end of the twentieth century, and with few exceptions, these goals have been realized in America and elsewhere in the western world. In the political realm, a woman's right to vote is now universal in western democracies, and many high political offices are occupied by women. In social arenas, numerous women have become prominent, esteemed and highly influential on their merits. In the workplace, women enjoy greatly expanded opportunities for hiring, wage increases and promotions. In virtually every occupation, women are now successful, sought after and welcomed by male peers. In the educational arena, women are prominent at all levels as respected administrators, able students and tenured faculty members. In recent decades, laws against gender discrimination and sexual harassment in work environments have reduced the vulnerability of women to unfair exclusion and unwanted attention from men. All of these advances reflect an increased recognition of the dignity and sovereignty of women.

The notable exceptions to this positive picture involve primarily the direct physical abuse of women. In domestic relationships, especially, widespread violence by men against women, often with tragic outcomes, continues to defy law enforcement and court ordered protections. The fight against rape in both domestic and non-domestic settings has been a major focus of feminist efforts, but *any* non-defensive use of violence against women, sexual or otherwise, deserves unqualified censure by all citizens. In this respect, the sentiments of mainstream feminists and their allies are identical to those of all persons committed to freedom and respectful of the most basic of rights, the right against violence to one's own person.

In fact, in contemporary American life, essentially all of the abuses of which women justifiably complain arise from society's failure to enforce ordinary criminal laws protecting person and property. This failure is attributable in part to inherent limitations in the ability of any law enforcement system to prevent crimes, especially those committed in private places. But some of this failure derives from our culture's deficits in recognizing the sovereignty of women. Ironically, this deficit is common among women themselves: women, as often as men, fail to assert the dominion they rightfully have over their own persons and lives; they fail to demand the freedom from violence and intimidation to which they are entitled by law and the most basic standard of morality. The personality traits associated with this deficit include submissiveness, self-effacement, excessive dependency and overestimation of men, to mention a few. Among the worst male chauvinists, in fact, are shame-based women who have been raised to believe that their self worth, and indeed their very identities, depend upon "having a man," and that putting up with humiliation, poverty, abuse and even injury at the hands of men is the price they must pay for intimacy. An additional irony finds that these women have often acquired beliefs of this kind from their mothers, not just from their fathers or other males, and not from adverse social conditions as alleged by liberal pundits.

Radical Feminism

If classical feminists have been committed to the expansion of women's essential liberty rights, a very different dynamic has characterized the late twentieth century's radical feminists. In the minds of these women, the feminist goal is not to achieve equality with men in matters critical to liberty. The movement is dedicated instead to a vicious propaganda attack on everything that defines men along with an aggressive political attack on much that defines liberty. This strikingly hateful, essentially paranoid posture blames men for all of the world's evils in general and all of the woes of women in particular. It angrily denies the ideal of an enduring bond in which the complimentary qualities of a man and woman allow for a harmonious division of life's labors between them. The primitive defense mechanism behind this posture projects onto maleness all that is bad in human nature, then splits the world into villainous males and victimized females. In this view, all of women's problems are attributable to the wickedness of men. Any idea that a woman might bear some responsibility for her own problems is angrily scorned. In fact, anger is at least as central to radical feminism as it is to radical liberalism. The imagined remedies for the world's problems are similar as well: essentially collectivist in their political values, radical feminists advocate a nearly totalitarian reconstruction of society through big government intervention. Marriage, family, religion, liberty rights, free markets and capitalism, among other allegedly male dominated institutions, must be abolished by the Radical Feminist State because they inflict intolerable agony on women. Reality is irrelevant in this argument: radical feminists routinely ignore the fact that large numbers of women with varied racial, ethnic, social, cultural and economic backgrounds are able to make their own choices, realize their own dreams, and lead fulfilling lives in allegedly male-dominated America. This fact might suggest that women who are unhappy suffer not because males oppress them but because certain personal limitations of their own hold them back: limitations due to emotional conflicts as well as deficits in initiative, industry, ability and motivation, for example, can easily prevent the making of a good life even under ideal circumstances. But this kind of analysis, depending as it does on "male logic," is unacceptable to the radical feminist.

Ostensibly, radical feminism advocates every woman's growth to robust independence, especially from men. But what it actually promotes is dependence upon a villain/victim paradigm that portrays half the population as devils and the other half as slaves. Authentic independence cannot be based on a conviction that women are puppets dominated by male puppet masters. Self-reliance and self-responsibility are not achievable when blaming men is the essential worldview. Adult competence will not emerge in a subculture devoid of noble goals but united in hateful delusions of persecution. Radical feminism celebrates a woman whose basic sentiments toward men center around fear, rage, belligerence, self-pity, demandingness, vulgarity and contempt. The default position for women vis-à-vis men is helplessness. The radical cure for this state is domination over men or even elimination of them. Despite its purported celebration of female personhood, radical feminism succeeds in dehumanizing women by portraying them as helpless puppets controlled by male institutions. In this image, women lack the powers of choice, agency, initiative and autonomy that enable them to run their own lives. Of interest in this regard is the suggestion that a major dynamic driving the radical feminist is a deep seated fear of freedom. In the real western world, a woman now has both the authority and obligation to run her own life as decisively as a man does. In contemporary America, in particular, women have unprecedented opportunities to choose their education and careers, to decide how and with whom they live and have sex, to decide whether and whom they marry, and to choose whether or not to have children.

Especially curious is the fact that radical feminism, with its contemptuous rejection of men as the proper objects of a woman's love, has evolved as women have become more obsessed with their sexual attractiveness to men. While radical feminism condemns all sex with men as rape, radical liberalism, by contrast, declares that the seduction of men is the route to self-esteem and that enjoying a man's lust is what life is all about. These conflicting values are only part of the story, however: from the combined influences of modern liberalism, radical feminism and mainstream conservatism, women now get mixed messages about every aspect of their lives: sexuality and sexual expression, the importance or unimportance of men, the virtues and evils of men, the importance or unimportance of a career, the joy and agony of marriage, and the glory and burdens of children. But all of these messages testify to the enormous *freedom* with which women can now live their lives. Despite the protests of radical feminists, the choices confronting all women have never been more numerous or attractive.

The negative effects of radical feminism extend beyond the domain of personal choices, however. The movement's rejection of motherhood as an acceptable female role threatens the quality of society's child rearing, and its rejection of marriage, family and religion threatens institutions critical to the socializing and civilizing of children and to stabilizing community relationships. Indeed, clinical observation suggests that early deficits in maternal nurturing of children along with the decline of the culture's respect for modesty has contributed to an increasing prevalence of narcissistic personality pathology in both sexes, a trend observed by Kohut more than thirty years ago. (Kohut 1971). The rise of female narcissism as an element of the "Me Generation" has paralleled a decline in the nurturing functions of the family. In fact, radical feminists appear to be in conflict with themselves over the issue of nurturing. On the one hand, feminists believe that traditional female/welfare values of nurturing, caring, sympathy, inclusion, connection, compassion and community should be central to *public policy* and should inform the state's collectivist programs. But these same values are seen as oppressive and demeaning when embodied in a conventional marriage and child rearing, a curious prejudice given the historic association between these values and femaleness.

[1]   *In some highly religious and relatively small populations criminal activity is rare.*

[2]   *On evil: systematic observations by primate anthropologists have confirmed that chimpanzees engage in brutal individual and gang violence against other chimpanzees and other primate species in the wild. These observations are striking evidence of the biological disposition to violence in higher primates, but they are only a portion of the evidence of innate biological evil in human beings.*

48

Integrity and Treatment

Where there is id, there shall ego be.
Sigmund Freud

The patient who thus transfers his conflict in all its desperate immediacy becomes at the same time resistive to all attempts at making him see the situation in a detached way, at formulating its meaning.
Erik Erikson

Integrity and the Lifecycle

In Erikson's scheme, the onset of old age heralds the eighth and final phase of the human life cycle.[1] The developmental challenge in this era is the achievement of a sense of *psychological integrity* and the avoidance of despair and disgust as dominant sentiments. While he offered no precise definition of integrity, he did describe a number of its features. In his view, the achievement of integrity confers upon an older person certain capacities for *acceptance:*

- Acceptance of himself as the person he is and has been, not the idealized person of his dreams
- Acceptance of his actual history of successes, failures and losses, not a fictional history of successes only
- Acceptance of the people and relationships that actually became important to him

- Acceptance of his parents as the persons they were
- Acceptance of responsibility for the choices he made that shaped his life
- Acceptance of old age decline and the inevitability of death
- Acceptance of the one and only life he can live.

These ideas extend the concept of integrity well beyond its common sense usage. Integrity usually means wholeness, completeness, soundness or lack of impairment, and Erikson clearly applies these meanings to his ideas about life's last phase. Integrity can also have more specialized meanings. A person with moral integrity, for example, adheres to high standards of virtue in his personal conduct. In intellectual inquiry, integrity seeks truth based on verifiable facts and sound logic. Conceptual integrity requires an idea to be internally consistent, not self-contradictory. An individual displays integrity when he represents himself honestly, acts in good conscience and honors just obligations. A family displays integrity when, through shared ideals and bonds, its members validate the parental marriage, rear children to adult competence, establish a refuge of love and caretaking for each other, and discharge the economic, social and political functions appropriate to families. An economic, social, political or legal institution exhibits integrity when it rewards adult competence and reinforces the rights, laws and duties that maximize freedom within the constraints needed for social order. Society itself demonstrates integrity when its members, families, institutions and traditions recognize the nature of man and coordinate it with the ideals of civilized freedom. These observations imply the need for integrity at all levels of a coherent social system: in the individual, in the family, and in the institutions that sustain the overarching structure of society. In analogy to a living organism whose survival and function depend upon its constituent organs, a society may be seen as a dynamic entity whose overall integrity depends upon the integrity of each of its interacting parts. To achieve a *systemic* integrity—to avoid a literal disintegration of the whole—a society must permit the free but orderly incorporation of man's biological, psychological and social nature into its economic, social and political fabric.

True to his theory of man embedded in social process, Erikson believed that the individual's *identity* in all phases of the life cycle, including the era of old age, is determined by multiple influences: the inherited traits that give the individual his biological uniqueness; the impact of early caretaking and family dynamics; the myriad racial, ethnic, cultural, economic, social and political factors that shape human lives; and the personal choices that give one's life its unique direction. These influences operate over the entire lifespan. The major question here is whether the adult identity that emerges from this complex process is integrated or not: that is, whether it is stable and coherent within itself, or in conflict with itself, and whether it is in harmony or in conflict with other persons and the social institutions with which it constantly interacts. It is the thesis of the present book that the bipolar nature of man, with its essential dispositions to autonomy and mutuality, is dependent for its full realization on a society structured for ordered liberty, and *vice versa*. Because of their bipolar nature, human beings cannot thrive without ordered liberty; conversely, a society conceived in ordered liberty will disintegrate into disordered tyranny if its citizens and institutions fail to support autonomy and mutuality.

The Threat of Despair

The final phase of the lifecycle takes on a special task: to avoid the chronic demoralization, disgust and bitterness that arise from the actualities of old age—the decline of one's physical and mental powers, the accumulated losses, the disabilities of illness, and the increasing nearness of death. Erikson used the word despair to label this depressive syndrome. He understood its enduring presence in late life as a failure of lifecycle integration marked by, among other things, a feeling that one is finished, passed by, no longer viable. Particularly painful in one's later years is the realization that life has become too short to embark on a new path to integrity; there is no time left to construct a new identity, no time to relive a life that has not been lived well enough. Hopelessness is a constant threat in this phase, one likely to recall the basic mistrust of infancy along with the shame, doubt, guilt and inferiority of subsequent developmental failures.

With the achievement of integrity, on the other hand, and with good enough physical health, late life is more likely to be an era of contentment, an occasion for philosophical reflection in those so inclined, and an opportunity for what Erikson called grand-generativity, a continuing sense of self-fulfillment through contributing to the common good. A late-life integration that harmonizes the elderly self with past roles, past endeavors and past relationships; with the historical and cultural influences of a lifetime; and with reassuring connections to the present, bodes well for an old age of pleasant relatedness and even serenity, instead of isolation, despair and helplessness.

The Integrity of Self and Society

Thus the achievement of psychological integrity in old age is a special case of the lifelong process of integration. As is true in all phases, the integrative process in the last phase attempts to keep the elderly individual connected to his personal history and to the community in which he lives. The success or failure of this process depends in part on the nature and coherence of society's institutions. Integrity in late life is more likely to be achieved when what is being integrated in the elderly person compliments, and is complimented by, the economic, social and political institutions of a well-integrated society. This idea was visited in earlier chapters in a discussion of competence. The growth of the individual to integrity in old age, like his growth to competence in his youth, involves the coordination of his capacities for autonomy and mutuality with the culture that surrounds him. This growth does not occur in a vacuum. Like other virtues, autonomy and mutuality are best validated in a culture that respects their defining roles in ordered liberty. They will not be validated in a society organized around the enveloping intimidation of liberal government.

Evaluation and Diagnosis in Modern Liberalism

Like the concept of competence, the concept of integrity offers a standard by which to evaluate the pathology of modern liberalism. As in any evaluation, a careful inquiry into the presenting signs and symptoms of the disorder is essential to adequate diagnosis. To that end the following paragraphs review again the manifestations of the liberal neurosis, its destructive effects on social process, and the manner in which it undermines the integrity of the individual's relationship to society at all levels. These effects can then be understood as the symptoms of a *societal* neurosis, one affecting the structure and functions of ordered liberty, not just the liberal mind itself. Insight based on these observations provides the basis for an educational campaign designed to neutralize the neurosis of liberalism at both individual and societal levels before it destroys ordered liberty beyond repair.

Recent chapters have set out in great detail the misconceptions of modern liberalism, its irrational prescriptions for social policy, its disastrous economic, social and political consequences, and its destructive effects on the development of adult competence. Special emphasis has been placed on liberalism's conflicts with the defining characteristics of human nature and the conditions of human existence. Throughout this exposition the madness of its agenda has become most obvious in its violations of the ideals and values essential to civilized freedom. A summary list of these ideals and values is paired below with the destructive effects of modern liberalism. In the competent society, the competent individual is able to:

- Acknowledge the value of individual lives. *[Modern liberalism devalues individual lives by violating individual rights and by treating citizens as fungible elements of economic, social or political classes.]*

- Honor the sovereignty, agency, autonomy and freedom of human beings. *[Modern liberalism curtails individual freedom of choice and action, substitutes regulation and dependency for autonomy and freedom, and overrides personal sovereignty.]*

- Honor the freedom to consent and not consent that defines social cooperation. *[Modern liberalism devalues voluntary cooperation in favor of government coercion and invalidates freely made contractual agreements.]*

- Recognize the right to be let alone as a foundation right to individual liberty. *[By invading every aspect of his life, modern liberalism's endless taxes and regulations violate the right of the citizen to be let alone.]*

- Earn a living through self-reliance and voluntary exchange with others. *[Modern liberalism's philosophy of dependency coupled with business regulations, licensure requirements, wage laws and union rules discourage and even preclude self-reliance and voluntary exchange.]*

- Honor the liberty rights and obligations that protect people, property and promises. *[Modern liberalism's policies invalidate promises, violate property rights, indenture the citizen's labor, and overrule contracts in accordance with the state's latest pronouncements on social justice.]*

- Relate with honesty and integrity to other persons who can act similarly. *[Modern liberalism's social justice programs institutionalize theft and invite manipulation. Its ideals of indulgence and permissiveness undermine the moral integrity of the people.]*

- Treat others with decency, courtesy, civility and thoughtfulness. *[Modern liberalism promotes hostility, vulgarity, rudeness and defiance as justified rebellion against imaginary oppression, discrimination and exploitation.]*

- Take care of children, the elderly and the chronically ill or disadvantaged. *[Modern liberalism undermines the family, the institution best able to rear children and care for the elderly. Its welfare programs preempt charitable activities and community altruism through government welfare programs.]*

- Aspire to the western ideal of individuated man: the self-reliant, self-directing and freely-choosing but ethical, moral and charitable individual who cooperates with others by mutual consent in a society ruled by law. *[Modern liberalism promotes the collectivized man: the self-effacing, government-dependent and government-supervised man. It seeks a government administered welfare state regulated by ruling elites and supported by indentured workers. Morality in this utopia is adjusted to the appetites of the moment. Gratification of need, not the rule of law, is the controlling ideal.]*

- Act effectively and legitimately under the rule of law, act freely because coercion is prohibited, act cooperatively because consent is voluntary, and act mutually by respecting the rights of others. *[The policies of modern liberalism render individual action less effective because it is disempowered by the state, illegitimate because it is condemned by the state, unfree because it is oppressed by the state, less cooperative because it is coerced by the state, and less mutual because it is depersonalized by the state.]*

- Accommodate the realities of human nature and the human condition; the moralities of obligation and aspiration; the negative rights that define liberty and justice; and the reciprocal interactions of the competent individual, competent family and competent society. *[Modern liberalism ignores the realities of human nature and the human condition; degrades the moralities of obligation and aspiration; undermines the competence of the individual, family and society; and invites childlike subservience to the state.]*

The liberal agenda is the liberal neurosis made manifest. It is not a rational program for the organization of human action. It is instead an irrational conglomeration of neurotic defenses which the modern liberal uses for his mental and emotional equilibrium. By attacking the sovereignty of the individual and the institutions essential to ordered liberty, the agenda attacks the very foundations of a free society. In fact, modern liberalism does not seek authentic freedom, despite its historical association with that ideal, nor does it foster the individual's growth to competence. It does *not* promote the virtues of individual liberty: not self-reliance, responsibility, dependability or accountability; not cooperation by consent or initiative or industry; not high moral standards or caring or altruism. It does not seek a society of sovereign citizens, but fosters instead a society of allegedly victimized dependents under the custodial care of the state. In keeping with its origins in early childhood, the liberal agenda endorses self-indulgence through short-term hedonism and primitive impulse gratification. In keeping with its ethic of injustice collecting, the agenda seeks ever increasing government regulation to defeat alleged villains, and ever increasing levels of unearned compensation, reparation and restitution to compensate alleged victims. In keeping with its secular tradition, modern liberalism attacks the legitimacy of formal religion, dismisses its historical importance and denies its critical role in maintaining the nation's moral integrity .

The entire agenda is a product of wishful thinking: it attempts to transform the real world of adult relationships into a fantasy world whose fictions will sooth the liberal's neurotic misery. It is a utopian world imagined by childlike adults longing for universal benevolence, brotherhood, generosity and love, but in its rhetorical proclamations and real world operations the agenda is viciously hostile. The liberal ideal of inclusion promises that no one will be deprived of what he needs, but the plan by which all of the earth's citizens will adopt each other in a universal welfare state is never explained. In the liberal's fantasies, the world will be notably peaceful, but not because of respect for the law nor because the threat of retaliation deters aggression. The liberal's idealized world will be at peace because empathy, sympathy, understanding, identification, negotiation, charity and appeasement will dissolve any adversary's destructive motives. Unfortunately, however, history records the futility of this wishful thinking. Liberalism's past attempts to realize these fantasies have brought catastrophic damage on millions by empowering governments with the means to dominate their citizens. For all of the reasons noted, the liberal agenda, whether benign or radical, is completely incompatible with rational social order.

Symptoms of Neurotic Liberalism

Arising from early developmental trauma acting on inherited temperament, the neurosis of the liberal mind is an enduring maladaptive and harmful pattern of thinking, emoting, behaving and relating, and thus strongly resembles a personality disorder. The signs and symptoms of the disorder result from the combined effects of deprivation, neglect and abuse, and the defense mechanisms erected against mental and emotional pain. The neurosis manifests itself in various beliefs, emotions, behaviors and modes of relating that are acted out in, or focused on, the political arena. Typical transference psychodynamics include at least some of the following:

- Mistrust of mutually consenting relationships
- Fear of helplessness
- False perceptions of helplessness in others
- False perceptions of exploitation, injustice and abuse by others

- Excessive fear of separation or abandonment
- An excessive need for nurturance and support
- An excessive urgency to seek caretaking from others
- A need for others to assume responsibility
- A sense of entitlement to the services of others
- Unjustified suspicion that others intend harm
- Excessive hostility and blame toward others
- Exaggerated self-importance
- An attitude of superiority without proportionate achievement
- A belief that one is special or belongs to an elite class
- Overestimation of one's talents, abilities or appeal
- An excessive need for admiration
- Prominent arrogance
- Preoccupation with envy
- Insistence on exemption from ordinary obligations, duties and responsibilities

In addition to these dynamics, the liberal neurosis predisposes to anxiety, insecurity, hopelessness, depression, despair, cynicism, shame, disgust, spite, anger, rage, bitterness, jealousy, hatefulness, guilt, blaming, grudge holding, excessive competitiveness, feelings of inadequacy, and doubt about one's lovability. The use of primitive defense mechanisms of externalization, projection, splitting, denial and projective identification is prominent; so is the use of manipulation and coercion. The radical liberal's neurosis distorts the realities of human relating by transferring the experiential traumas of his formative years into the contemporary arenas of economic, social and political process. The liberal's mind's neurotic transferences strongly determine how he thinks, feels, behaves and relates in these realms.

Spontaneous Remission
Like other conditions arising from early developmental trauma the liberal neurosis tends to persist over time. It endures for many reasons already noted: it defends powerfully against psychic pain, gratifies primitive needs for hope and attachment, promises to satisfy dependency longings, endorses self-centeredness and self-indulgence, wards off shame, discharges aggression, avenges envy, mitigates feelings of inferiority, and provides identity, affiliation and self-esteem, to name a few benefits. Nevertheless,

some liberals, even those of a radical bent, are able eventually to renounce the madness of liberalism and become competent adults. What usually triggers these conversions are the recurrent collisions of the liberal agenda with the realities of adult life, especially those that expose the agenda's irrational nature and destructive consequences. In these cases, the facts of life overcome the dogma of illusion: a combination of painful experience with liberal social policy, coupled with healthy growth that mitigates early trauma, allows the reflective liberal to reject the fallacies of liberalism for the truths of ordered liberty. In these fortunate cases, the individual is able to disconnect his neurosis from its projections into the political world. The result is that both types of madness, neurotic and political, are seen for what they are.

The Treatment of Modern Liberalism

Once the liberal neurosis is no longer disguised as a rational political philosophy, it can be analyzed and treated in whatever manner is necessary to overcome symptomatic distress and functional impairment. Treatment of the underlying personality and character disturbances through a combination of psychoanalytic, cognitive-behavioral and educative techniques stands the best chance of resolving the primitive dynamics that drive the neurosis. The condition's major defects in autonomy and mutuality must be addressed. Prominent among them are a basic mistrust of cooperation; false perceptions of victimization; intense envy and underlying shame; a need to vilify and blame others; deficits in self-reliance and self-direction; a marked fear and avoidance of responsibility; infantile demandingness; an intense and often paranoid hostility; a need to manipulate, control and depend on others; a lack of courage, resilience and frustration tolerance; and various defects in ego ideals, conscience and impulse control. Therapy must also address the liberal's self-pathology, especially his immaturity, self-centeredness and grandiosity; his lack of empathy for and recognition of others; his marked sense of entitlement; and his impaired self-esteem and identity. Educational programs to cure the liberal's ignorance of free-market economics, libertarian political process, constitutional democracy, and the psychology of cooperation rank high among therapeutic priorities. Theory and techniques for treatment of this type are described in detail in standard psychiatric texts; additional discussion of these topics is beyond the scope of this book.

Treatment of a *society* stricken with neurotic liberalism depends upon the insight of its citizens into the agenda's destructive effects on human relating and the irrational beliefs and values at its core. Only widespread knowledge of the nature and causes of the disorder will allow a society to recover from its liberal madness and restore itself to economic, social and political health. This knowledge must be grounded in a comprehensive understanding of human nature, the human condition and the individual's reciprocal relationship to his society. Large-scale public discussions of the biological, psychological and social nature of man, especially his essential dispositions to autonomy and mutuality and his embeddedness in economic, social and political processes, are the starting point for a program to counteract the unreason of modern liberalism. A clear understanding of ordered liberty and the indispensable rights and obligations that structure it is a critical part of the discussion. The rational citizen must realize that the nature of man, his relatedness to others, the ideal of ordered liberty, and the conditions necessary for that order are not mere hypotheses; they are not simply optional alternatives to equally valid competing theories of how a viable society may be organized. The realities of human nature generate certain verifiable and non-negotiable rules for the governance of human affairs. Widespread education of the citizenry on these principles is imperative. The future of civilized freedom depends upon it.

[1] *See Erikson & Erikson 1997 for a discussion of a ninth phase of the life cycle.*

Bibliography

Barnett, Randy E., 1998, *The Structure of Liberty: Justice and the Rule of Law.* Oxford: Oxford University Press.

Balint, Michael, 1979, *The Basic Fault: Therapeutic Aspects of Regression.* Evanston, IL: Northwestern University Press.

Barzun, Jacques, 2000, *From Dawn to Decadence: 1500 to the Present: 500 Years of Western Cultural Life*, New York: Harper Collins.

Benjamin, Jessica, 1995, *Like Subjects, Love Objects: Essays on Recognition and Sexual Difference*, New Haven: Yale University.

Berkowitz, Peter, ed., 2004, *Varieties of Conservatism in America*, Stanford, CA: Hoover Institution Press.

Berkowitz, Peter, ed., 2004, *Varieties of Progressivism in America.* Stanford, CA: Hoover Institution Press.

Black, Jim Nelson, 1994, *When Nations Die: America on the Brink: Ten Warning Signs of a Culture in Crisis.* Wheaton, IL: Tyndale House Publishers.

Blankenhorn, David, 1995, *Fatherless America: Confronting Our Most Urgent Social Problem,* New York: Basic Books.

Blos, Peter, 1967, "The Second Individuation Process of Adolescence," *The Psychoanalytic Study of the Child,* New York: International Universities Press.

Branden, Nathaniel, 1997, *Taking Responsibility: Self-Reliance and the Accountable Life,* New York: Fireside.

Bullock, Alan and Trombley, Stephen, 1999, The Norton Dictionary of Modern Thought, New York: W. W. Norton & Company.

Burnham, James, 1975, *Suicide of the West*, New Rochelle, NY: Arlington House.

Butler, Eamonn, 1985, *Hayek: His Contribution to the Political and Economic Thought of Our Time,* New York: Universe Books.

Cloninger, Robert C., and Svrakic, Dragen M., 2000, "Personality Disorders," in *The Comprehensive Textbook of Psychiatry*, 7th Ed., Saddock, Benjamin J., and Saddock, Virginia A., eds., Philadelphia: Lippincott, Williams & Wilkins.

Colarusso, Calvin A. 2000, "Adulthood," in *The Comprehensive Textbook of Psychiatry*, 7th Ed., Saddock, Benjamin J., and Saddock, Virginia A., eds., Philadelphia: Lippincott, Williams & Wilkins.

Coles, Robert, 2000, *The Erik Erikson Reader*, New York: W.W. Norton & Company.

Cook, James R. (a), July, 1995, "Behavioral Genocide" in Gloom and Doom Reports, Minneapolis: Investment Rarities, Inc.

Cook, James R. (b), September, 1995, "Age of Excess" in Gloom and Doom Reports, Minneapolis: Investment Rarities, Inc.

Cotton, Nancy S., 2000, "Normal Adolescence" in *The Comprehensive Textbook of Psychiatry*, 7th Ed., Saddock, Benjamin J., and Saddock, Virginia A., eds., Philadelphia: Lippincott, Williams & Wilkins.

Diagnostic and Statistical Manual of Mental Disorders, 1994, 4th Ed., Washington, D.C.: American Psychiatric Association.

Epstein, Richard, 1995, *Simple Rules for a Complex World*, Cambridge, MA: Harvard University Press.

Epstein, Richard, 1998, *Principles for a Free Society; Reconciling Individual Liberty with the Common Good,* Reading, MA: Perseus Books.

Epstein, Richard, 2003, *Skepticism and Freedom; A Modern Case for Classical Liberalism,* Chicago, IL: University of Chicago Press.

Erikson, Erik H., 1950, 2nd Ed. 1963, *Childhood and Society,* New York: W. W. Norton & Company.

Erikson, Erik H., 1959, "Identity and the Life Cycle," *Psychological Issues,* 1:1, pp. 18-164.

Erikson, Erik H., 1964, *Insight and Responsibility,* New York: W. W. Norton & Company.

Erikson, Erik H., 1968, *Identity, Youth, and Crisis,* New York: W. W. Norton & Company.

Erikson, Erik H., and Erikson, Joan M., 1997 (extended version), *The Life Cycle Completed,* New York: W. W. Norton & Company.

Finnis, John, 1980, *Natural Law and Natural Rights,* Oxford: Clarendon Press.

Fraiberg, Selma H., 1959, *The Magic Years: Understanding and Handling the Problems of Early Childhood,* New York: Charles Scribner's Sons.

Fuller, Lon L., 1969, *The Morality of Law,* New Haven: Yale University Press.

Gabbard, Glen G., 2000, "Theories of Personality and Psychopathology," in *The Comprehensive Textbook of Psychiatry,* 7th Ed., Saddock, Benjamin J., and Saddock, Virginia A., eds., Philadelphia: Lippincott, Williams & Wilkins.

Greenspan, Stanley I., 1997, *The Growth of the Mind: The Endangered Origins of Intelligence,* Reading, MA: Addison-Wesley.

Hart, H. L. A., 1994, *The Concept of Law*, New York: Oxford University Press.

Hazlitt, Henry, 1969, *Man Versus the Welfare State*, New Rochelle, NY: Arlington House.

Hazlitt, Henry, 1988, *The Foundations of Morality*, Lanham, MD: University Press of America.

Hughes, Robert, 1993, *Culture of Complaint: The Fraying of America*, New York: Oxford University Press.

Huizinga, Johan, 1955, *Homo Ludens: A Study of the Play Element in Culture*, Boston: Beacon Press.

Johnson, Allan G., 1995, *The Blackwell Dictionary of Sociology: A User's Guide to Sociological Language*, Blackwell, Malden, Massachusetts.

Kekes, John, 1995, *Moral Wisdom and Good Lives*, Ithaca, NY: Cornell University Press.

Kekes, John, 1998, *A Case of Conservitism*, Ithaca, NY: Cornell University Press.

Kekes, John, 1997, *Against Liberalism*, Ithaca, NY: Cornell University Press.

Kelley, David, 1998, *A Life of One's Own: Individual Rights and the Welfare State*, Washington, D.C.: Cato Institute.

Keyes, Alan L., 1995, Masters of the Dream: The Strength and Betrayal of Black America. New York: William Morrow & Company.

Kiplinger Letter, June 2, 1995, Washington D.C. The Kiplinger Washington Editors.

Kohut, Heinz, 1971, *The Analysis of the Self: A Systematic Approach to the Treatment of Narcissistic Personality Disorders.* New York: International Universities Press.

Lakoff, George, and Johnson, Mark, 1999, *Philosophy in the Flesh: The Embodied Mind and its Challenge to Western Thought*, New York: Basic Books.

Lidz, Theodore, 1968, *The Person: His Development Throughout the Life Cycle*, New York: Basic Books.

Loevinger, Jane, 1976, *Ego Development*, San Francisco: Jossey-Bass.

Maultsby, Maxie C. Jr., 1984, *Rational Behavior Therapy*, Englewood Cliffs, NJ: Prentice-Hall.

Moynihan, Daniel P., 1965, *The Negro Family: The Case for National Action.* Washington, D.C.: Department of Labor.

Murray, Charles, 1984, *Losing Ground: American Social Policy 1950-1980,* New York: Basic Books.

Nozick, Robert, 1974, *Anarchy, State, and Utopia*, New York: Basic Books.

Pearce, Jane, and Newton, Saul, 1969, *The Conditions of Human Growth*, New York: The Citadel Press.

Pfeffer, Cynthia R., 2000, "Psychiatric Treatment of Adolescents" in *The Comprehensive Textbook of Psychiatry*, 7th ed., Saddock, Benjamin J., and Saddock, Virginia A., eds., Philadelphia: Lippincott, Williams & Wilkins.

Pruett, Kyle, 2002, "Family Development and the Roles of Mothers and Fathers in Child Rearing," in Lewis, Melvin (ed.) *Child and Adolescent Psychiatry,* 3rd Ed., Lippincott Williams & Wilkins, Philadelphia.

Roazen, Paul , 1997, Erik H. Erikson: *The Power and Limits of a Vision*, Northvale, NJ: Jason Aronson.

Rothbard, Murray N., 1998, *The Ethics of Liberty*, New York: New York University Press.

Sowell, Thomas, 1980, *Knowledge and Decisions*, New York: Basic Books.

Sowell, Thomas, 1987, *A Conflict of Visions: Ideological Origins of Political Struggles*, New York: William Morrow & Company.

Sowell, Thomas, 1995, *The Vision of the Anointed: Self-Congratulation as a Basis for Social Policy*, New York: Basic Books.

Sowell, Thomas, 1999, *The Quest for Cosmic Justice,* New York: Simon & Schuster.

Stolorow, Robert D., Atwood, George E., and Brandchaft, Bernard, 1994, *The Intersubjective Perspective,* Northvale, NJ: Jason Aronson.

Suttie, Ian D., 1988, *The Origins of Love and Hate*, London: Free Association Books.

Sykes, Charles J., 1992, *A Nation of Victims: The Decay of the American Character*, New York: St. Martin's Press.

Theodorson, George A., and Theodorson, Achilles G., 1969, *A Modern Dictionary of Sociology*, New York: Thomas Y. Crowell.

Wallerstein, Robert S., and Goldberger, Leo, 1998, *Ideas and Identities: The Life and Work of Erik Erikson*, Madison, CT: International Universities Press.

Wiggins, Osborne P., and Schwartz, Michael A., 1999, "The Crisis of Present-Day Psychiatry: Regaining the Personal." *Psychiatric Times*, Parts I & II, August and September, Irvine, CA, CME Inc.

Wilson, James Q., 2002, Marriage Woes: How Our Culture Has Weakened Families. New York, HarperCollins.

Yates, Timothy, 2000, "Theories of Cognitive Development" in Lewis, Melvin ed.) *Child and Adolescent Psychiatry,* 3rd Ed., Lippincott Williams & Wilkins, Philadelphia.

Index

G

Generativity 21, 104, 108, 115, 227, 261, 313, 399
Golden Rule 15, 151, 192, 244

H

Hart, H. L. A. 280, 284, 296, 303, 305
Hazlitt, Henry 5
Hope viii, 29, 123, 141, 174, 180, 189, 217, 257, 265, 274, 292, 320, 339, 345, 365, 404
Hypothetical Imperative 296, 299, 327

I

Ideals 6, 12, 21, 43, 47, 54, 56, 62, 82, 85, 86, 120, 121, 152, 170, 182, 219, 234, 255, 265, 278, 301, 317, 328, 346, 380, 397, 400
Identity 36, 51, 66, 88, 103, 115, 132, 150, 175, 193, 206, 218, 220, 235, 251, 258, 261, 274, 275, 281, 305, 328, 351, 360, 373, 398, 404
Imperative 49, 58, 163, 179, 216, 235, 287, 296, 327, 386, 406
Individualism 6, 28, 37, 44, 64, 85, 136, 140, 150, 169, 218, 235, 256, 268, 275, 302, 311, 355, 367, 382
Individuation 37, 129, 140, 149, 171, 176, 196, 211, 218, 238, 256, 274, 341
Industry 32, 79, 103, 185, 205, 212, 221, 227, 239, 250, 265, 271, 287, 304, 328, 338, 349, 361, 370, 388, 394, 402
Infancy 116
Inferiority 31, 87, 104, 111, 214, 258, 316, 342, 379, 398, 404
Initiative 104, 141, 180, 190, 258, 271, 349, 358
Injustice 99, 165, 265, 318, 321, 329, 333, 346, 373, 377, 402
Integrity 25, 31, 63, 76, 88, 104, 125, 136, 148, 165, 182, 208, 227, 244, 255, 271, 292, 306, 323, 347, 360, 368, 375, 389, 399, 403
Intersubjective 17, 20, 34, 131, 146
Intimacy 102, 175, 183, 215, 227, 254, 265, 287, 393
Isolation 10, 13, 104, 111, 137, 149, 260, 272, 337, 369, 399

J

Judiciousness 159, 162
Just social order 323
Just state 322-3
Justice vii, 121, 129, 165, 208, 219, 241, 247, 265, 277, 292, 303, 320, 321, 331, 334, 347, 367, 380, 401
Juvenile 193, 207, 218, 305, 313, 350, 361, 365

K

Kekes, John 285

W

ABOUT THE AUTHOR

Lyle H. Rossiter, Jr. received his medical and psychiatric training at the University of Chicago and served for two years as a psychiatrist in the U.S. Army. He is board certified in both general and forensic psychiatry. For more than forty years he has diagnosed and treated mental disorders, with a special interest in personality pathology and its developmental origins. He has been retained by numerous public offices, courts and private attorneys as a forensic psychiatrist and has consulted in more than 2,700 civil and criminal cases in both state and federal jurisdictions. He has lectured to various groups on subjects ranging from psychotherapy to the prevention of suicide.

Quick Order Form

For credit card orders, please visit our website at:
www.LibertyMind.com

To order by mail, you may use this form. Please make your check or money order payable to: *Free World Books LLC*.

Name: _____

Address: _____

City: _____ **State:** _____ **Zip:** _____

Telephone: _____

Email address: _____

Item	Price	Quantity	Totals
Book: The Liberal Mind	**$19.95**		
Sales Tax 7.5% (Illinois Residents)			
Shipping and handling in the U.S.: $4.00 for first book and $2.00 for each additional book.			
S&H International: $9.00 for first book; $5.00 for each additional.			
		Total	

Please send your order to : Free World Books, LLC
41 Aintree Road
St. Charles, Illinois 60174
630-587-5710

I understand that I may return the book(s) within 30 days for a full refund.